Young People and Learning Processes in School and Everyday Life

Volume 5

This book series provides analyses of contemporary issues and questions related to being young and becoming an adult in a global educational landscape. It examines education pathways in relation to characteristics of transitional processes that are part of this transformational and developmental process, as well as sociocultural aspects. It investigates areas such as education, everyday life, leisure time, family, subcultural affiliations, medialization, work and intimacy.

The series highlights the following areas:

- Contemporary challenges in education and the educational system.
- Young people's experiences and varying living conditions and its influence on academic performance.
- New emerging social and existential identities in relation to education.
- Challenges for education – Inclusion and exclusion in terms of risk behaviours, psychological distress and social unrest.
- Theoretical renewal and a conceptual adaption to education, and the societal and cultural challenges of contemporary school systems.
- Digitalisation, technology and media in modern education. Educational pathways for specific groups.
- Contextual challenges for educational ambitions, such as poverty, politics, war and exclusion of groups.

The series introduces ground-breaking interdisciplinary works in the area of education, challenging the orthodoxies in this field of research, and publishes works on the globalization of education. Furthermore, it introduces research on youth, thus advancing current knowledge on education in relation to the young person's everyday life, nationalities, socio-economic backgrounds and living conditions. In addition, it presents new methodological and theoretical approaches to this research field.

Please contact Astrid Noordermeer at Astrid.Noordermeer@springer.com if you wish to discuss a book proposal.

More information about this series at http://www.springer.com/series/15702

Joan DeJaeghere • Erin Murphy-Graham

Editors

Life Skills Education for Youth

Critical Perspectives

 Springer

Editors
Joan DeJaeghere 🆔
University of Minnesota
Minneapolis, MN, USA

Erin Murphy-Graham 🆔
University of California, Berkeley
Berkeley, CA, USA

This book is an open access publication. This title is freely available in an open access edition with generous support from the Library of the University of California, Berkeley.

ISSN 2522-5642   ISSN 2522-5650   (electronic)
ISBN 978-3-030-85216-0   ISBN 978-3-030-85214-6   (eBook)
https://doi.org/10.1007/978-3-030-85214-6

This Springer imprint is published by the registered company Springer Nature Switzerland AG
The registered company address is: Gewerbestrasse 11, 6330 Cham, Switzerland

Acknowledgments

We would like to thank Echidna Giving for sponsoring a workshop on life skills education at the University of California, Berkeley that generated the idea for this volume.

Contents

Contributors

Aditi Arur Christ (Deemed to be) University, Bengaluru, Karnataka, India

Rebecca Bailey Harvard Graduate School of Education, Cambridge, MA, USA

Katharine E. Brush Harvard Graduate School of Education, Cambridge, MA, USA

Nancy Chervin Education Development Center, Waltham, MA, USA

Alison K. Cohen Epidemiology & Biostatistics, School of Medicine, University of California, Berkeley, USA

Laura Cordisco Tsai Carr Center for Human Rights Policy, Harvard Kennedy School, Cambridge, MA, USA

Joan DeJaeghere University of Minnesota, Minneapolis, MN, USA

Catherine Honeyman World Learning, Washington, DC, USA

Stephanie M. Jones Harvard Graduate School of Education, Cambridge, MA, USA

Christina Ting Kwauk The Brooking Institution, Washington, DC, USA

Margaret Meagher Be the Change Inc, Duluth, MN, USA

Emily Meland Harvard Graduate School of Education, Cambridge, MA, USA

Erin Murphy-Graham University of California, Berkeley, Berkeley, CA, USA

Bryan Nelson Harvard Graduate School of Education, Cambridge, MA, USA

Diana Pacheco-Montoya University of California, Berkeley, Berkeley, CA, USA

Natasha Raisch Harvard Graduate School of Education, Cambridge, MA, USA

Urvashi Sahni Study Hall Education Foundation, Lucknow, Uttar Pradesh, India

Melanie Sany Education Development Center, Waltham, MA, USA

Dana Schmidt Echidna Giving, San Francisco, CA, USA

Mansi Sharma KU Leuven, Leuven, Belgium

Lucy Strickland Refugee Education Consultant, Melbourne, Australia

Janice Ubaldo 10ThousandWindows, Knoxville, TN, USA

Yohannes Wogasso Ministry of Education, School Improvement Directorate, Addis Ababa, Ethiopia

Sileshi Yitbarek Kotebe Metropolitan University (KMU), Addis Ababa, Ethiopia

Abbreviations

10KW	10ThousandWindows
ABE	Alternative Basic Education
ACMHE	Addressing Child Marriage through Holistic Education
CASEL	Collaborative for Academic, Social, and Emotional Learning
DHS	Demographic Health Surveys
DBR	Design-Based Research
EDC	Education Development Center
EFA	Education for All
ESD	Education for Sustainable Development
ESDP	Education Sector Development Plan
EU NESET	European Union's Network of Experts working on the Social dimension of Education and Training
FDRE	Federal Democratic Republic of Ethiopia
GECFDD	General Education Curriculum Framework Development Department
HEY	Holistic Education for Youth
ICT	Information and Communication Technologies
IRC	International Rescue Committee
J-PAL	Abdul Latif Jameel Poverty Action Lab
LSE	Life Skills Education
MDGs	Millennium Development Goals
MELQO MODEL	Measurement of Early Learning Quality and Outcomes Measurement of Development and Early Learning
MEPI	US Middle East Partnership Initiative
MESH	Mindsets, Essential Skills, and Habits
MI	Motivational Interviewing
MIFOTRA	Rwandan Ministry of Public Service and Labour
MOE/MoE	Ministry of Education
NER	Net Enrollment Rate
NPES	National Pastoralist Education Strategy

NEET	Not in Education, Employment, or Training
NGOs	Nongovernmental Organizations
OECD	Organisation for Economic Co-operation and Development
PTA	Parent Teacher Association
QESSP	Quality Education Strategic Support Program
REB	Regional Education Bureau
SAT	*Sistema de Aprendizaje Tutorial* (Tutorial Learning System)
SC	Scheduled Castes
SD	Sustainable Development
SDGs	Sustainable Development Goals
SEL	Social and Emotional Learning
SFD	Sport for Development
SRH	Sexual and Reproductive Health
ST	Scheduled Tribes
STEP	Soft Skills Training and Empowerment Program
TI	Teach India
TVET	Technical and Vocational Education and Training
UNESCO	United Nations Educational, Scientific and Cultural Organization
UNICEF	United Nations Children's Fund
USAID	United States Agency for International Development
WDA	Rwandan Workforce Development Agency
WHO	World Health Organization
WEO	Woreda Education Office
WRN	Work Ready Now

List of Figures

List of Tables

Chapter 1
Introduction

Joan DeJaeghere and Erin Murphy-Graham

Abstract This chapter provides an overview of how life skills are conceptualized and taken up in curriculum, teaching, and measurement in different educational settings around the world, as discussed in the chapters in this book. We focus on life skills programming in low- and middle-income countries because bilateral and multilateral aid organizations have significantly shaped discourse and programming in life skills education. We intentionally included studies utilizing a variety of research methodologies, which allow for a deep understanding of both the micro level (curriculum, pedagogy, and youth engagement and outcomes) and macro level (organizational processes and assumptions) in life skills programming and policy. Chapters in the book highlight a disconnect between the dominant individualistic behavioral approach used by many organizations and programs and the life skills that youth and local communities emphasize as important to change social and economic problems. To respond to this disconnect, this chapter provides an overview of a capabilities approach to life skills, with the purpose of focusing on wellbeing. We suggest that life skills education should develop the capabilities that societies and individuals have reason to value.

Keywords Life skills · Low and middle-income countries · Capabilities approach · Wellbeing

Acronyms

NGOs   Nongovernmental organizations
SDGs   Sustainable Development Goals
USAID   United States Agency for International Development
UNICEF   United Nations Children's Fund

J. DeJaeghere (✉)
University of Minnesota, Minneapolis, MN, USA
e-mail: deja0003@umn.edu

E. Murphy-Graham
University of California, Berkeley, Berkeley, CA, USA
e-mail: emurphy@berkeley.edu

© The Author(s) 2022   1
J. DeJaeghere, E. Murphy-Graham (eds.), *Life Skills Education for Youth*, Young
People and Learning Processes in School and Everyday Life 5,
https://doi.org/10.1007/978-3-030-85214-6_1

Rahul, a youth from India, learned that gender roles were not fixed—and that he wanted "an environment at home where no one is getting oppressed, or beaten and abused, everyone is equal and happy." Ramona, a young woman from Honduras, learned "how to work in a disciplined way with respect, responsibility and to be more responsible and work as a team." A youth named Hamadou, a member of the Afar nomadic population of Ethiopia, described the importance of the cultural practice of sharing: "if someone has extra money or resources like food, you share it with your neighbors." These three youth from different geographic regions of the world have the common experience of participating in educational processes that were intended to build "life skills," but their disparate commentaries illustrate that "life skills" can encompass diverse values, cultural practices, habits and behaviors, attitudes, and aspirations. Life skills education stems from the idea that youth need more than traditional academic skills to thrive; they need skills to be able to live life well.

While life skills education has a global reach, there is much conceptual confusion about these categories in the field of education. What life skills are important to teach? And to whom? And why? In the United States, where life skills education took root decades ago, the media has picked up on this confusion and has tried to help clarify. National Public Radio covered the issue in 2017: "more and more people in education agree on the importance of learning stuff other than academics. But no one agrees what to call that 'stuff'" (Kamenetz, 2015). Seven categories of "stuff" were identified, including character, noncognitive traits and habits, soft skills, grit, social and emotional skills, growth mindset, and twenty-first Century skills. The confusion that the media was responding to is not new, and it is not limited to the United States. For example, in Australia, public and academic debate focused on youth and skills for the labor market throughout the 1990s (Taylor, 2005). There have been efforts to halt this semantic debate by introducing phrases such as "skills for success" which is meant to encompass the habits, mindsets, and non-technical skills that are integral to academic, personal and professional success (Tooley & Bornfreund, 2014). Even so, "skills" has become a catch-all phrase, lacking precision and conceptual clarity.

Perhaps because of or in spite of this lack of clarity, life skills education has gained considerable attention in the past decade among education policymakers, researchers, and educators around the globe as being the sine qua non for later achievements in life. It is easy to refer to life skills as important, but there is greater disagreement around which ones are important and why. Global and national education policies, including the Sustainable Development Goals (SDGs), and international development education initiatives, such as USAID's workforce development programs, emphasize the teaching of life skills as essential for a diverse set of purposes: reducing poverty, achieving gender equality, promoting employment and economic growth, addressing climate change, fostering peace and global citizenship, and creating sustainable and healthy communities. Teaching academic knowledge as well as life skills to support these goals is a broad and hefty task for educators. Yet, many education systems and non-formal programs are engaged in this work.

The aim of the book and each chapter is to examine how life skills have been conceptualized and implemented, particularly in contexts where youth are marginalized—out-of-school, not employed, living in low-income or violent settings, and/or experiencing multiple forms of inequality (e.g., gender, caste, racial, socio-economic). While we assume that life skills are important for all children and youth to learn, youth in these contexts and conditions have been particularly targeted by life skills education initiatives. Yet, teaching marginalized youth in these different contexts requires an examination of some of the core assumptions of life skills education: How can these skills enhance their employability, health outcomes, and social outcomes, and how should educators teach them to achieve such outcomes?

This book arose out of a workshop hosted at the University of California, Berkeley in May 2018, where a group of experts gathered to examine how research on life skills reveals some of the assumptions of programs and to consider how to refocus educational efforts for greater effectiveness—that is, in helping youth to do life well. The workshop emerged from the recognition that youth organizations working in low-income countries increasingly see that youth need more than just traditional academic skills to succeed in school and beyond, and therefore they support life skills development. For some of these organizations, the term refers to building resilience, shaping aspirations, increasing self-confidence, and developing critical thinking skills. For others, it means teaching specific content such as financial literacy and/or sexual and reproductive health. During the workshop, we considered the contributions of scholars and practitioners in the fields of psychology, cognitive science, economics, and education, among others, who have collectively built a body of knowledge that defines the skills and mindsets that support youth wellbeing. Several early versions of chapters in this volume were part of our workshop deliberations.

The authors in this volume critically review a diverse body of scholarship and practice that informs the conceptualization, curriculum, teaching, and measurement of life skills in education settings around the world. We selected chapters from a wide range of geographic locations to capture how life skills programming has been implemented in different contexts. The following questions guided authors' analysis of life skills education and the organization of chapters in the volume:

What are life skills? How is the teaching of life skills enacted by various actors in the fields of international development and education?

Which life skills are most important, who needs to learn them, and how should they be measured in each context?

What are the synergies and differences between life skills education and initiatives to promote social and emotional learning, vocational/employment education, health and sexuality education and other related skills? How might learning be shared across these different types of initiatives and fields?

How might life skills be better incorporated into basic and secondary education, as part of the formal curriculum, given that many life skills interventions are taught through non-formal programs (and by NGOs)?

How do or can life skills education, both conceptually and pedagogically, address structures and relations of power to help youth achieve desired future outcomes, and the goals set out in the SDGs?

How do life skills connect with the sustainable development goals and notions of
quality education advanced in international policy agendas?

How can these bodies of practice and research evidence among thought leaders and
donors converge to inform and reshape life skills programming?

Life Skills in Low- and Middle-Income Countries

We focus on life skills programming in low- and middle-income countries because
bilateral and multilateral aid organizations, such as USAID and UNICEF, have significantly shaped discourse and programming in life skills education. Several chapters in this volume, including those by Honeyman et al. and Murphy-Graham, are
based on research and programming funded by USAID. Other chapters present
research that stems from private or family philanthropic funding, as well as corporate foundations (Pacheco & Murphy-Graham, Chap. 10, this volume; Sahni, Chap.
9, this volume). The scale of donor funding and involvement in this field is related
to the growing recognition that national education systems are not adequately preparing youth with quality education that will improve their lives, particularly at the
secondary level.

Over the last several decades, low- and middle-income countries made considerable progress in ensuring that all children have access to primary education (typically ending at grade 6). More recently, priorities have expanded to include universal
access through 9th grade (see SDG 4). The expansion of schooling opportunities for
youth is a step in the right direction. But secondary education traditionally served an
elite, university-bound segment of the population and the curriculum is often geared
towards preparation for tertiary (university) entrance. Many youth still drop out of
secondary school due to high fees, the disconnect between the curriculum and their
lives, and the need to work to support their families. So one aim of life skills programs, both those created by international organizations and governments, has been
to provide skills that these youth need to be successful in life beyond those needed
and learned in the formal education system. This includes life skills programs oriented toward preparing youth for different work options. In this area, USAID has a
particularly strong presence in shaping life skills for employability (see Honeyman
et al., Chap. 6, this volume).

International organizations and governments also target youth in low- and
middle-income countries who are out-of-school and not employed in the formal
sector because they need life skills to be healthy and safe in their communities.
These programs address concerns around engaging in risky behaviors that lead to
unhealthy lives, including sexually transmitted diseases, early pregnancies, and
drugs or other illicit activities. Life skills play a critical role in preparing youth to
live life well within these challenging contexts of poor or inaccessible education,
limited formal employment opportunities, and social challenges. The program in
the Philippines for trafficked youth in Honeyman et al.'s chapter and the sports programs reviewed by Kwauk are examples of life skills programs oriented toward

these aims. In analyzing these life skills programs, we reveal their implicit assumptions about youth's lives and how they can live life well, as well as the ways that these programs are recontextualized to address the skills that matter for youth in these contexts.

We critically analyze life skills programs by elevating the voices of participants through the use of qualitative and participatory research. We intentionally included studies utilizing a variety of research methodologies including design-based research, action research, case study, systematic reviews, and mixed methods. The methodological diversity allows for a deep understanding of both the micro level (curriculum, pedagogy, and youth engagement and outcomes) and macro level (organizational processes and assumptions) in life skills programming and policy. Through such analyses, chapters highlight a disconnect between the dominant individualistic behavioral approach used by many organizations and programs that teaches young people to manage their lives within social and economic constraints (as discussed by DeJaeghere, Chap. 4, this volume) and the life skills that youth and local community emphasize as important to change social and economic problems (see Arur & Sharma, Chap. 8, this volume; Yitbarek et al., Chap. 11, this volume). Collectively, the chapters of this volume clarify that assumptions about life skills have to be adapted to address local cultural values, needs and contexts.

The Purpose of Life Skills: To Live Life Well

The book makes critical contributions to the current debates about the purposes and practices of education more broadly, and considers how life skills education contributes to these issues: How can education foster sustainable economies and communities? What and how do we effectively teach children during a pandemic and during other crises, when learning inequalities are being further exacerbated, and which can have longer term effects on children's wellbeing? How can education address growing inequalities? Life skills education is not a panacea for addressing inequalities and future wellbeing outcomes, but life skills, when effectively contextualized and oriented toward valued outcomes, are critical to learning and living life well, particularly in precarious times.

We consider life skills, broadly defined, as the ability to live life well (see Murphy-Graham & Cohen, Chap. 2, this volume). This implies the need for a clear conception of well-being, and theory of the role of education in fostering such well-being. The capability approach is one theoretical framework that we find particularly useful in conceptualizing well-being. It attends to the freedoms, or real opportunities, to achieve well-being, and the public values about what constitutes well-being for individuals within societies (Robeyns, 2017). The capability approach does not measure economic wealth as a sole indicator of well-being, but rather it focuses on multiple dimensions of well-being: of what people are able to be and do. While it focuses on the assessment of individual level freedoms and achievements, it also demands an understanding of the social and institutional arrangements, including past injustices and current policies, that affect one's freedoms to achieve wellbeing (Robeyns, 2017).

The capability approach has been used extensively in educational research to examine how different forms and processes of education support the expansion of freedoms–or real opportunities–so that inequalities can be redressed and well-being achieved (DeJaeghere & Walker, 2021). Writing from this perspective, Tikly and Barrett (2011) define good quality education as:

> Education that provides all learners with the capabilities they require to become economically productive, develop sustainable livelihoods, contribute to peaceful and democratic societies and enhance individual well-being. The learning outcomes that are required vary according to context but at the end of the basic education cycle must include at least threshold levels of literacy and numeracy as well as **life skills…** (p. 9, emphasis ours).

Beyond the threshold of skills, they argue that quality education that fosters wellbeing must also be relevant, inclusive, and support economic productivity, democratic participation, and sustainability.

From a capability approach, the purpose of education is to enhance well-being in many domains of life which include physical, mental, and emotional health, economic productivity, democratic participation, and having close relationships and social ties. This framing of the purpose of education allows for a more comprehensive and multi-faceted concept of what life skills are and why they matter. As discussed in Chap. 2, two discourse communities that have a longer history of working with life skills education (life skills for labor market outcomes and life skills for prevention) have a narrower focus on specific domains of well-being (e.g., employment and prevention of disease/harmful behavior, respectively). In education, life skills capture a broader purpose of promoting various dimensions of well-being, including social and emotional outcomes and civic participation.

One distinguishing feature of the capability approach that may prove useful to the thinking about life skills education is the recognition of the ultimate worth of education in its own right (Nussbaum, 2000; Tikly & Barrett, 2011). The literature on life skills often conceptualizes them as a means to other ends, including improving employment, reducing pregnancy and marriage, and even keeping youth engaged in school. While there is indeed emerging evidence to support the fostering of life skills as a means to these outcomes, life skills may have "ultimate value" in learning and doing them even if they do not have strong causal linkages with typically-measured development outcomes, such as delayed fertility, earnings, or total years of schooling (Robeyns, 2017, p. 54).

From a capability perspective, life skills education should develop the capabilities that societies and individuals have reason to value, as well as examine whether or not an individual is "being put in the conditions in which she can pursue her ultimate ends" (Robeyns, 2017, p. 49). While not all chapters in this book utilize a capability approach to analyzing life skills education, it does offer a broader framework for the book in thinking about what it means to live life well, and to education for the real opportunities to achieve well-being in different contexts.

Contributions of the Volume and Chapter Summaries

The chapters in this volume make two critical contributions to our understanding of life skills education. First, authors pay particular attention to defining the specific life skills within the particular programs and contexts they analyze. They do not assume that life skills programs, which are designed for some particular set of desired outcomes, contexts, and youth, are relevant in other settings. They address how life skills are linked with the particular economic, political, and social aims of that program or context. Some chapters illustrate how international and national goals for such education may be in conflict with local community values and participants' experiences. These analyses suggest that in order for life skills education to contribute to addressing inequalities, creating more sustainable futures, and achieving well-being, they must identify both the valued outcomes and the constraints to achieving these outcomes.

Second, authors reflect on ways that specific life skills and programs can be reframed and adapted so that they not only focus on cultivating individually possessed behaviors and attitudes in young people, but they also address contextual constraints that inhibit young people from using their skills. In this way, the analyses presented in this volume do not offer a simple set of technical guides to developing a life skills education curriculum, nor how these programs can be adapted and expanded to improve outcomes for more youth. Rather, they assert that life skills education can and needs to transform certain values and practices that currently curtail young people's ability to live life well. Authors call for careful consideration of the values, knowledge, and behaviors that are important for young people to achieve well-being in these challenging contexts, so that policymakers and educators can more effectively design, implement, and evaluate life skills education programs according to valued outcomes.

To set up the book and the analyses in subsequent chapters, Murphy-Graham and Cohen undertake a review of theoretical, programmatic, and empirical research on life skills from different disciplinary perspectives. This chapter first broadly identifies life skills as those skills necessary to do life well. This is a broader conceptualization than the outcomes desired in the three discourse communities they identify: prevention and protection, labor market outcomes, and quality education. Through a thorough analysis of theoretical and empirical literature, they identify core life skills that overlap among these discourse communities: critical ways of thinking, development of social and emotional competencies, and mastery of certain tasks and information. These skills are a "least common denominator" of what is necessary to teach young people in order to live life well. They call for the need to contextualize these life skills within programs to examine what living well or wellbeing means for youth in across different contexts.

Social and emotional learning (SEL), a key component of most life skills programs, is examined in-depth in Chap. 3 by Brush et al. The authors explain that SEL is referred to by many names, often overlapping with life skills education and other initiatives to improve learning, health, and developmental outcomes for children and youth. The chapter provides an overview of SEL and its relationship to life skills education, and identify where clarity and cohesion do or do not exist within the field of SEL by exploring how it is conceptualized, measured, and promoted in different settings around the world. The authors present work from the Harvard Graduate School of Education's Taxonomy Project, drawing on data collected over a series of research projects. By applying a common coding system to SEL frameworks, programs, and measurement/assessment tools, the authors identify areas of overlap and divergence between them. The chapter summarizes key findings from these projects while highlighting the need for both deeper contextualization and localized research and development, and concludes by discussing implications for research and practice.

In Chap. 4, DeJaeghere examines how life skills education programs often emphasize teaching behaviors to young people to overcome their problems, such as youth unemployment and teen pregnancy. Her analysis, which is informed by two studies conducted on life skills—one as part of a youth livelihood program in East Africa, and the other a life skills program for lower caste and lower class girls in India—suggests that programs have an underlying individualist, psycho-social, and behavioralist approach. She points out that teen pregnancy and youth unemployment, among other issues, are social problems that an individualistic approach will not be able to fully address: "such an approach does little to address the systemic social and economic conditions that create injustices and inequalities" (p. 77). To think differently about how to use life skills to foster a "good life" that is just, equitable, and sustainable, the chapter offers a transformative framing based on a critical and relational approach that includes values and perspectives that youth desire and need within their challenging contexts. So, for example, rather than focus on "responsibility," life skills could be framed as emphasizing "reciprocity." Positive attitude can be reframed as "hope" and "empathy" reframed as "solidarity." In specifying how to reconceptualize life skills, the chapter offers an alternative for how we can teach young people to live in changing social, economic, and environmental contexts that are marked by greater precarity and inequality.

A transformative approach to life skills education programs is also the focus of Kwauk's chapter, which analyzes sports programs designed to empower girls. Through an analysis of 10 life skills approaches guiding sport for development (SFD) programs, Kwauk examines how organizations often take an "unintentional and uncritical approach to education through sport—or in this case a normative approach to life skills education— … to teach skills like teamwork, communication, and goal orientation" (p. 95). In contrast, she asks if they can "take a more transformative approach aimed at altering the conditions of inequality that have marginalized populations in the first place" (p. 95). She identifies the life skills and desired outcomes of each of these programs, which often place a heavy emphasis on pro-social and interpersonal skills. In order to be more transformative, she suggests that programs should pay more attention to the intrapersonal skills of values, identity, and perspectives, so as to change the way that young people think about their world and interact in it. She calls for re-thinking skills, such as teaching how to engage differences, to foster reciprocity and solidarity, and to develop partnerships and coalitions such that the onus for changes toward greater empowerment is not solely on the girl.

Honeyman et al.'s chapter illustrates how different organizations, working within a framework set out by USAID's life skills programs, engaged in a community of practice to learn from each other to develop and adapt their institutional approach. Their collective work in three different countries, Rwanda, Algeria, and the Philippines, highlights the importance of contextualizing programs, determining and training effective pedagogical approaches, and sustaining and scaling up these initiatives. Each institutional program engaged with different participants, including connecting out-of-school youth with vocational/entrepreneurial opportunities (Rwanda), working to integrate school completers into formal employment (Algeria), and reintegrating survivors of human trafficking into a safe workforce (Philippines). Each program adapted life skills frameworks from USAID within their organizations to navigate the diverse set of power relations among actors in order to implement a locally relevant program. They also illustrate the challenges that funded programs have in developing relevant curricula and pedagogy, including a lack of support for the training of educators/facilitators in teaching life skills, which is different from teaching content knowledge. Finally, they argue life skills programs could be more fully integrated into educational systems as a cross-cutting focus of instruction, or even through a wholehearted overhaul of general teacher pedagogy, in order to sustain and scale such programs.

In another example of programs aimed at employment, Murphy-Graham's chapter about a sports-based, life skills job-training program in Honduras and Guatemala shows the value of learning life skills as conditions for other capabilities, and as an outcome itself. Using a capability approach to analyze pre-conditions, capabilities, and wellbeing outcomes, she shows how certain life skills foster particular values that serve as pre-conditions for youth to act on their capabilities, or sets of opportunities that arise from the program. These include beliefs and attitudes about themselves, such as no longer feeling stuck, having self-confidence, and developing a sense of discipline and work ethic. Furthermore, she illustrates how certain life skills serve as both means and ends, particularly those that build relationships and social ties. Developing relationships with their peers and learning teamwork were critical to fostering a sense of affiliation, something most the program participants did not have because they were out-of-school, not employed, and disconnected from positive social networks. These life skills further enabled them to make new friends, a desirable outcome itself. This analysis points out that according to many of the participating youth, these kinds of life skills—as values that serve as pre-conditions to other capabilities, and as means and ends in themselves—were as important as getting a job, which was a desired outcome of the program, but which was further constrained by the socio-economic environment in which they lived. Murphy-Graham calls for life skills education programs to take into consideration the values that are desired for youth's wellbeing as well as the conditions in their environment that might constrain them from realizing what they value from these programs.

Arur and Sharma's chapter examines a different set of life skills—informational literacies—that are critical for preparing young Indian boys for future employment in precarious conditions. While informational literacy may be regarded as a set of technical, or cognitive, skills, Arur and Sharma use a sociocultural and transformational approach to show how it is also imbued with social and political values about who one can become through their future work. In this way, literacy skills are connected with the identity domain discussed in Chap. 3 by Brush et al., in terms of understanding one's goals and preferences within a specific social-cultural context. By placing career information and skills within a framework of education for sustainable development, Arur and Sharma also show that such life skills for young boys go beyond gaining knowledge and information about getting employed, and toward skills for assessing/ identifying more equitable and sustainable livelihoods. These "skills" include understanding the gendered and casted nature of the labor market; identifying alternative, local and "green" employability options; and identifying one's emotional responses and needs in relation to work, and the uncertainties of it. Finally, like Pacheco-Montoya and Murphy-Graham, the authors also illustrate the pedagogical tools they used to enhance these skills, including videos taken by boys of relevant social issues in their community in which they want to engage.

Sahni's chapter examines how the Prerna School in Uttar Pradesh, India focuses not on life skills as such, but on a broader concept of "life knowledge"—in other words, the type of knowledge and education that allow youth to navigate the difficult terrain of their lives. Sahni, an Indian feminist whose work on at the Prerna School for girls is renowned around the world and is recounted in her book, *Reaching for the Sky* (Sahni, 2017), describes the action research project she is currently engaged in with young men in the recently created Prerna Boys School. Realizing that "if we want a better world for our girls, then their fathers, brothers, and future husbands need to be part of the solution" (p. 200), the chapter explains the rationale and process through which the school was created. A key life skill that the school focuses on is developing a feminist consciousness in boys, utilizing critical dialogues on a wide range of topics including masculinity, violence against women at home and on the street, gender, and marriage. The chapter includes several excerpts of critical dialogues with male youth that illustrate, for example, how boys are able to discuss what they have learned about the differential treatment of boys and girls and whether they think it is fair. The chapter argues that life skills should not be considered an "add on" in an afterschool or extracurricular program, but rather fully integrated into the official curriculum, thereby "redefining the scope of education, deepening and widening it to make it more relevant in the lives of its students and the societies that they live in and can change in the future" (p. 214).

In another examination of how to shift gender inequalities through life skills education, Pacheco-Montoya and Murphy-Graham's chapter delves deeply into critical thinking, an oft-included but not well understood life skill. Their study illustrates how critical thinking is taught and used by young women and men in Honduras in an effort to prevent early marriage, and to alter gendered attitudes and relations more broadly. As a design-based study, they walk the reader through the development of a specific set of curricular and pedagogical tools, including using peer educators that acted as critical mirrors in examining gendered assumptions, and scenarios based on real experiences of youth that provoked discussions of alternatives to hegemonic gender beliefs. Through the use of these tools, they show how youth grappled with the cognitive dissonance that is produced between commonly held beliefs and alternative perspectives. Finally, they illustrate how these new perspectives and knowledge informed young people's decisions in their daily lives. This chapter provides educators and development practitioners helpful examples of curricula and pedagogy that can foster these important life skills for transforming gender inequalities in this specific context.

In an examination of how education can support economically and socially sustainable pastoral communities, Yitbarek et al.'s chapter offers another contextually grounded and rich case study of the life skills that are valued by pastoralist communities in Ethiopia, and analyze whether and how they are taught in their school curricula. Through data gathered from a range of pastoralist community members, they show that the forms of education and life skills they value should be connected to their livelihoods in agriculture, while also preparing young people for a changing socio-economic future caused by economic challenges and climate change. Learning about livestock husbandry as well as construction of homes are central to pastoralists' ways of life, but they are not well integrated into the formal or non-formal education systems. In particular, they draw attention to the indigenous forms of knowledge that need to be taught and learned, which are also relevant for their specific environmental and social conditions. Community members also stressed the importance of learning about their culturally specific forms of community governance, conflict resolution, and values of sharing and reciprocity. Through an analysis of the current, official curriculum, they show that these forms of knowledge and skills are insufficiently included in the curriculum, which focuses more broadly on national values and skills to live together. They also call for specific pedagogical approaches used within pastoralist communities for effectively teaching such life skills, including experiential learning, mentorship and apprenticeship, and observation and listening—pedagogical practices that are also mentioned as relevant for young people's life skills for employment by Honeyman et al.

Our concluding chapter, authored by Dana Schmidt, identifies some of the cross-cutting themes of this book. She poignantly argues that:

> Youth of today are part of a generation that will grapple with rising levels of inequality, the economic and health fall out of a global pandemic, the near and present danger of climate change, and more challenges which we cannot yet imagine. They need and deserve these skills to have a fighting chance of living life well. We owe it to them to continue working to define and teach these skills, and to do it at scale (p. 277).

Schmidt identifies three important contributions of the volume regarding how to engage life skills education from a critical perspective. First, life skills are especially important for marginalized adolescents, but should not be used as an excuse to put the onus of creating a life well lived entirely upon the individual, particularly not on an individual already marginalized within his or her socioeconomic context. Second, there are some common denominators with respect to which skills are important: clusters of social and emotional skills and cognitive abilities, such as critical thinking stand out. Critical thinking skills related to who holds power in society, and why, emerges as a key requirement to sparking social change. Finally, how life skills are taught may be as important, if not more important, than prescribing a very specific set of skills to teach. Given this, the ways in which teachers are prepared to teach life skills and the skills they themselves embody is crucial.

Conclusions

This book brings together a rich body of literature on life skills education that, we hope going forward, can help policymakers, educators, and practitioners in formal and non-formal education spaces. The analyses in this volume highlight ways to frame, contextualize, and teach life skills for purposes of ensuring that youth can live life better in conditions of precarity, inequality, and injustice. Drawing on critical perspectives and analysis, the authors in this book illustrate that life skills education is shaped by divergent purposes and contexts, not always aligned with what youth and their communities need nor value. By aligning life skills education, its content, and its pedagogies with what is valued for living life well, such education can go a long way toward achieving the goals that the SDGs, governments, organizations, and young people aspire to achieve.

References

DeJaeghere, J., & Walker, M. (2021). The capabilities approach in comparative and international education: A justice-enhancing framework. In T. Jules, R. Shields, & M. Thomas (Eds.), *The Bloomsbury handbook of theory in comparative and international education*, Chap. 27.

Kamenetz, A. (2015, May 28). Nonacademic skills are key to success. But what should we call them? *NPR*. http://www.npr.org/sections/ed/2015/05/28/404684712/non-academic-skills-are-key-to-success-but-what-should-we-call-them

Nussbaum, M. (2000). Women's capabilities and social justice. *Journal of Human Development, 1*(2), 219–247.

Robeyns, I. (2017). *Wellbeing, freedom and social justice: The capability approach re-examined.* Open Book Publishing.

Sahni, U. (2017). *Reaching for the sky: Empowering girls through education.* Brookings Institution Press.

Taylor, A. (2005). What employers look for: The skills debate and the fit with youth perceptions. *Journal of Work and Education, 18*(2), 201–218.

Tikly, L., & Barrett, A. (2011). Social justice capabilities and quality of education in low income countries. *International Journal of Educational Development, 31*(1), 3–15.

Tooley, M., & Bornfreund, L. (2014, November 21). Skills for success: Supporting and assessing key habits, mindsets, and skills in PreK-12. *New America*. https://www.newamerica.org/education-policy/policy-papers/skills-for-success/

Chapter 2
Life Skills Education for Youth in Developing Countries: What Are They and Why Do They Matter?

Erin Murphy-Graham and Alison K. Cohen

Abstract Drawing from a review of theoretical, methodological, and empirical literature on life skills from the fields of education, public health, psychology, economics, and international development, this paper attempts to clarify basic definitional and conceptual issues that relate to life skills education. It addresses the questions: (1) What are life skills, and how has the term emerged in academic and donor agency literature? And (2) What bodies of practice and research evidence converge in the rise of 'life skills' programming and increased interest in 'life skills' among thought leaders and donors in the field of international education? The paper identifies implications from this analysis to be considered in research and interventions that focus on life skills for adolescents, particularly in light of global efforts to improve the quality of education.

Keywords Life skills · Adolescents · International education · Quality education · Low-income countries

Introduction: Clarifying the Muddy Waters of Life Skills Education

'Life skills' is a popular concept in the field of education. One review of the literature on 'life skills' education found that there were as many definitions of life skills as there were global education actors and thought leaders (Dupuy & Halvorsen, 2016). Non-governmental organizations and international aid agencies such as the UK Department for International Development (DFID), the United States Agency

E. Murphy-Graham (✉)
University of California, Berkeley, Berkeley, CA, USA
e-mail: emurphy@berkeley.edu

A. K. Cohen
Epidemiology & Biostatistics, School of Medicine, University of California, Berkeley, USA

© The Author(s) 2022
J. DeJaeghere, E. Murphy-Graham (eds.), *Life Skills Education for Youth*, Young People and Learning Processes in School and Everyday Life 5,
https://doi.org/10.1007/978-3-030-85214-6_2

13

for International Development (USAID), the World Bank, and UNICEF embrace the idea that education should prepare individuals both academically and with 'skills,' also referred to as 'life skills,' 'non-cognitive skills,' 'character skills' and/ or 'socio-emotional skills.'[1] Acquiring 'skills' is commonly mentioned as a characteristic of quality education (e.g., Sayed & Ahmed, 2015; Sustainable Development Goal Target 4.4; Tikly & Barrett, 2011). The meanings and terminologies associated with the concept of life skills vary, and methods for systematically measuring and tracking changes in life skills are not well defined. While life skills might be a catchy phrase, specification of the cognitive, socio-emotional and behavioral learning outcomes is needed, particularly for researchers interested in examining how and if interventions can lead to improvements in people's lives.

Drawing from a review of theoretical, methodological, and empirical literature on life skills from the fields of education, public health, psychology, economics, and international development, this chapter attempts to clarify basic definitional and conceptual issues that relate to life skills education. It addresses the questions:

- What are life skills, and how has the term emerged and changed over time in academic and donor agency literature?
- What bodies of practice and research evidence converge in the rise of life skills programming and increased interest in life skills education for youth?

Based on our review of existing research and program/institutional documents, we identify distinct but overlapping discourse communities that use the term 'life skills' that have converged in the field of education. A discourse community is a group of people who share a set of basic values, assumptions, and goals, and use communication to achieve these goals (Swales, 1990).[1] While there is some overlap in how these discourse communities conceptualize life skills, the goals of each of these are somewhat distinct, and therefore the *ways in which they invoke 'life skills' varies*. These discourse communities include the education community in which we situate ourselves and our concern with the quality of education, particularly in developing country contexts. Two more longstanding discourse communities, which indeed spill into the quality education community, include: (a) scholars and practitioners of public health and social work who are concerned with skills for 'prevention and protection;' and (b) economists, who have focused on 'labor market outcomes' and draw upon work in the field of psychology. We describe each of these discourse communities in greater detail, as well as the areas of overlap in how they use the term 'life skills' in their interventions and publications. After discussing the findings from our examination of 'life skills' in the academic and donor agency literature, we conclude by explaining how the capabilities approach to education, which explicitly links education with a social justice perspective and provides a wider set of outcomes from life skills education than offered by any single

---

[1] We use the term "discourse community" rather than "field" or "discipline" because it also allows to capture the various actors working in educational settings, including non-governmental organizations, local education stakeholders, and the youth, facilitators, and community members that are engaged in life skills education programming around the world.

discourse community, can help inform future work on education and life skills for youth (Robeyns, 2017; Tikly & Barrett, 2011; Walker, 2012).

Skill as the Ability to Do Something Well

Before proceeding, we explain what we mean by 'skill' and 'life skills,' although there is a great deal of variability in how these concepts are defined in the studies we review below. The terms 'skill' and 'competency' are commonly collapsed, but in the past the word 'skill' referred to the ability to undertake a task in the context of work and the skilled worker was trained (Taylor, 2005, pp. 201–18). Skill often focused on manual skills that involved both physical psychomotor abilities and mental cognitive abilities (Winterton et al., 2006). Very briefly defined, 'skill' refers to the ability, coming from one's knowledge, practice, and aptitude, to do something well.

The term 'cognitive skills' has traditionally been used to refer to processes that occur in the brain to learn to do something well. Cognitive skills are associated with activities such as problem solving, reasoning, thinking, assessing, concluding and include the mental processes of analysis, synthesis and evaluation (Westera, 2011, p. 77). More recent research has introduced the idea of 'embodied cognition' – that the brain is actually part of a broader system that involves perception and action as well (Shapiro, 2007). Performing tasks therefore requires a complex synergy between cognitive and bodily functions. Driving is an example that helps explain this synergy:

> In skills training, substantial repetition, which allows learners to gradually improve their performance levels in terms of speed, precision and fluency, is usually involved. As a consequence, skills performance becomes more and more automated: experienced drivers, for example, are hardly aware of the complex cognitive tasks they perform, while their inexperienced counterparts must consciously think about almost any operation they carry out (Westera, 2011, p. 77).

Skills are connected with the accomplishment of specific tasks (driving, solving problems) and repetition is often required to improve performance. A combination of perceptual, cognitive and motor skills is involved in the demonstration of skilled performance. Training programs can provide opportunities to gain the knowledge and practice in specific domains that lead to skill mastery.

If we take the idea that a skill is the ability to do something well, then 'life skills,' in its broadest and most simplistic definition is **to be able to do life well**. But more commonly, it refers to skills that help a person through everyday tasks and to be active and engaged members of a community.

Review and Analysis of Life Skills Education

To better understand how various actors in the field of international development education are engaging with the term 'life skills,' in other words to clarify the "muddy waters," we conducted a review to become acquainted with the organizations and scholars that are doing work related to life skills education. The process used for this analysis included the following core elements.

First, we engaged in a search and analysis of actors and stakeholders working in the field of international development education that are engaged in life skills education. This involved:

- Systematic online searches using key words (life skills, non-cognitive skills, skills, adolescent girls) to identify key stakeholders and initiatives in the field at global, regional, and national levels;
- A detailed desk review of key global initiatives using websites and other available resources, particularly policy or project documents;
- Interviews with key actors in life skills education including researchers, donors, and multi-lateral agencies who convened for a workshop on Life Skills education held at UC Berkeley in May, 2018. Additionally, we have attended panel sessions at international conferences to gain insights into work that has not yet been published or posted on agency websites.
- A comprehensive review of published studies to examine the evidence base regarding the impact of life skills education (Murphy-Graham & Cohen, 2019, included in Table 2.4).

This analysis of actors and stakeholders, as well as the empirical literature, allowed us to identify emerging categories that we subsequently labelled "discourse communities."

Findings: What Are Skills and Why Do They Matter for Education?

Our review and analysis suggest three converging bodies of research and practice that have resulted in the rise of life skills education programming. The first includes work among scholars and practitioners in the field of prevention science, which broadly sees life skills as important for preventing drug and alcohol use, as well as preventing sexually transmitted diseases (particularly HIV), early pregnancy, and other risky behaviors. The second is the discourse community that has been influenced by the work of Nobel-prize winning economist James Heckman, who with co-authors, has argued that the predictive power of skills rivals that of cognitive skills, and so interventions should focus on fostering such skills. Life skills are *instrumental* to 'promoting lifetime success' particularly in the labor market (Kautz et al., 2014). Heckman and co-authors have drawn upon the Big Five Personality theory in the field of Psychology, a framework for understanding personality traits with five factors: openness, contentiousness, extraversion, agreeableness, and neuroticism. Finally, a third community focuses on life skills because they see getting youth into school as an insufficient step in transforming lives and communities. Rather, they focus on broadening what is taught in school to ensure education can be useful for life broadly (not just for health or work). Table 2.1 below summarizes these three discourse communities, and each are described in greater detail in the sections that follow.

Table 2.1 Summary of three discourse communities that emphasize life skills

Discourse community & related disciplines	Goals	Life skills emphasized as…	Examples of organizations/ interventions aligned with this discourse community
Prevention and protection (Public Health/ Social Work)	Life skills for healthy choices Protection from risky behavior (e.g. drug use, unprotected sex, gang involvement)	Decision-making Communication Resist peer pressure Self-knowledge and care	Life Skills Training program 10 programs reviewed in 'Sexuality Education: a ten country review of school curricula in East and Southern Africa' (Population Council, 2012)
Labor market outcomes (Economics)	Life skills for labor market outcomes including employment, productivity, job quality, entrepreneurship, earnings.	'Big five' personality domains (conscientiousness, openness, extraversion, agreeableness, neuroticism/emotional stability) Teamwork Communication Problem-solving	A Ganar Program (Sports-based life skills training program for youth in 21 countries) *Juventud y Empleo* (Youth and Employment program in the Dominican Republic) Programs reviewed in 'Skills Training Programs' (J-PAL, 2017)
Quality education (Education)	Life skills for range of well-being outcomes & meeting day to day challenges and making informed decisions	Leadership Communication Critical thinking Social and emotional competencies Twenty-first century skills	CAMFED (Campaign for Female Education for girls in five African countries) Room to Read Brookings Institution (see Kwauk & Braga, 2017; Winthrop & McGivney, 2016)

Table 2.2 Core ideas and areas of overlap in the three discourse communities

Areas of overlap:	Prevention and protection	Labor market outcomes	Quality education
Mastery of certain tasks/knowledge/information	HIV/STD prevention knowledge and proper use of birth control methods Drug/alcohol harm reduction and knowledge Legal information (e.g., legal drinking age)	Specific information or performance tasks related to jobs or entrepreneurship (e.g., carpentry, computer technician, social outreach, sales and marketing)	Range of academic subjects Identification of life goals Ability to identify power structures in society Familiarity with the concepts of gender norms, equality vs. equity
Social and emotional competencies	Self-control Communication Assertiveness/refusal Empathy Negotiation Self-Confidence/esteem	Regulating emotions Communication Teamwork Perseverance/grit Personal awareness & management	Negotiation Self-confidence Relationships (mentors) Perseverance Empathy Self-reliance Communication (facilitation, presentation skills, 'voice')
Critical thinking/ways of thinking	Critical examination of power structures in society related to gender and social class	Problem solving Decision making Critical creative thinking	Critical thinking and problem solving Need to analyze context and power Goal-orientation Decision making

The three discourse communities have different areas of emphasis for their work in life skills, though there is some overlap. While these three discourse communities conceptualize and have different outcome targets, there is also convergence around the idea that adolescents need to: (1) **master certain tasks, knowledge and/or information, (2) develop a group of social and emotional competencies that will lead to valuable behaviors, and; (3) have ways of thinking that we consider to fall within the category of critical thinking**. Table 2.2 summarizes these areas of convergence, and each of these discourse communities is described in greater detail in the sections that follow.

At a general level, this common ground across the three discourse communities (mastery of certain tasks/knowledge/information; group of social and emotional competencies; critical thinking/ways of thinking), might help to create a better starting place for identifying common programmatic pedagogies, goals, and assessments. Furthermore, a brief understanding of the historical development and evolution of these discourse communities helps clarify why there is so much variability in the outcomes programs currently emphasize. Understanding this history is a critical step towards improving future work in life skills education.

Life Skills for Prevention

In 'prevention' education programs (drugs, tobacco, alcohol, violence, teenage sex, pregnancy, other risky behavior), life skills have a long history of prominent placement. One of the leading life skills programs in this field, called Life Skills Training (LST), began in the 1970s under the leadership of Dr. Gilbert Botvin. Botvin was trained as a clinical and developmental psychologist at Columbia University, and his first job was with the American Health Foundation, which was at the cutting edge of the field that eventually became known as preventative medicine. He became interested in risk reduction and behavioral interventions that might modify or enrich the development or risk factors. Convinced that major social and psychological factors promote the initiation of substance use and other risky behaviors, he developed a program he eventually called 'life skills' that had to do with promoting overall competency and more effective adolescent development, a more comprehensive approach targeting individual risk factors. LST is perhaps the best-known drug prevention program, and has been used with youth in all 50 states and all the territories of the USA, and it has been used in 39 countries across all six habited continents. LST has also demonstrated beneficial outcomes in over 35 rigorous evaluation studies (see Botvin LifeSkills Training, n.d.).

The LST program consists of three major components that "cover the critical domains found to promote drug use... Research has shown that students who develop skills in these three domains are far less likely to engage in a wide range of high-risk behaviors" (See: https://www.lifeskillstraining.com/lst-overview/). The three components are drug resistance skills, personal self-management skills, and general social skills. Given the goals of this program, the empirical work on LST emphasizes outcomes of drinking, cigarette, and drug use, rather than measuring life skills as outcome variables. Different variations of the curriculum have been tested (the standard curriculum lasts 15 weeks and is implemented in schools).

Prevention programs that targeted the HIV/AIDS epidemic followed this model, often linking life skills training with content knowledge about how to prevent disease transmission (similar to linking content knowledge about tobacco, alcohol, and drugs in LST). As Boler and Aggleton (2005) explain, in the early 1990s, "when it became apparent that many young people (and adults) were not going to change their sexual behavior merely because they were told that they should, the international development community – particularly UNICEF— rallied around the idea of teaching life skills as part of HIV/AIDS education" (p. 1). The idea had its roots in the same body of scholarship from North America and European psychology, but not necessarily referencing prevention. Rather, it focused on the qualities of successful leadership. Over time, and in an attempt to make the skills more appealing to governments and communities, the term 'life skills' began to encompass an

ever-increasing level of generic skills, including communicating, listening carefully, empathy-building, and income-generation. In 2005, Boler and Aggleton
argued that claims regarding the role of these life skills in preventing HIV were
made largely with no evidence (particularly with regards to sexual behavior).

A review of the effects and effectiveness of Life Skills Education for HIV prevention in young people (Yankah & Aggleton, 2008) found that most interventions
to prevent HIV included a life skills component, and that programs worked best to
positively influence knowledge, attitudes, intentions, skills, and abilities. However,
life skills programs rarely produced consistent effects on sexual behavior or biological outcomes (the contraction of STDs). (This finding appears to remain true for
more recent studies, such as Dunbar et al., 2010.) Similar to the LST studies, these
evaluations focus on behavioral outcomes and so we can learn little about the ways
in which the programs impact life skills (as outcomes in and of themselves) and if
changes in life skills are associated with any beneficial long-term outcomes (such as
egalitarian intimate relationships) over time.

Despite a lack of documented impact of life skills training programs to prevent
HIV, a "regional curriculum scan" conducted in 2011 (commissioned by UNESCO
and UNFPA and authored by the Population Council, 2012) found that some form
of "skills" was included in the HIV/prevention curricula of 10 African countries.
However, the content was often deemed 'weak', particularly in terms of fostering
critical thinking skills and advocacy skills. A subsequent review (Haberland, 2015)
of rigorous evaluations of sexuality and HIV education programs found that most of
the programs that met the review criteria had "skills" (not precisely defined) as a
component of their curricula. However, what the review found was that the programs that addressed gender and power were five times more likely to be effective
than those that did not. This points to the idea that the skill of 'critical thinking about
gender and power' might be among the most important life skills for the prevention
of HIV and changing sexual behavior.

We identified 43 empirical studies focusing on life skills for youth in developing
country contexts published after 2005 – of these, we classified 35 in the prevention
discourse community. As detailed in Table 2.4, many of these studies are from India
(N = 21). Other countries include Iran, Nigeria, Kenya, South Africa, Indonesia,
Mexico, Pakistan, Thailand, Zambia and Zimbabwe. Many outcome variables are
studied: health risk behavior; condom use; HIV knowledge; smoking; and a range
of psychosocial outcomes ("positive emotions," resisting peer pressure, self-
knowledge). The rigor of these studies is quite variable, and the totality of evidence
is not compelling due in part to the time frame (with research conducted immediately upon program completion) and the lack of specificity regarding measures used
and research procedures (see Table 2.4).

Skills for Labor Market Productivity

In a recently published paper "Does Education Strengthen the Life Skills of Adolescents?" the "elevator pitch" is that "life skills, sometimes referred to as non-cognitive skills or personality traits (e.g., conscientiousness or locus of control – the belief to influence events and their outcomes), affect labor market productivity" (Schurer, 2017, p. 1). This paper is consistent with the discourse community of economists, who, drawing upon the work of personality psychologists, explore the relationship between "skills" and later life outcomes (including health and labor market). They also seek to understand which traits are malleable through educational interventions.

The work of James Heckman, Nobel Laureate in economics and Professor at the University of Chicago, and his co-authors on skills has allowed the concept to gain heft but unfortunately has not helped provide conceptual clarity. This is in part because Heckman's own use of the term has evolved over time. In earlier publications, Heckman referred to "non-cognitive" skills (Heckman et al., 2006, pp. 411–82). In a much-cited paper published by the National Bureau of Economics Research, Heckman and his co-author Tim Kautz use the term "character skills" (2013). In an OECD report that draws upon this 2013 paper, the authors revert to the term "non-cognitive" (Kautz et al., 2014). In his 2016 paper published in the journal *Human Development and Capabilities,* Heckman and his co-author Chase Corbin use the term "skills" without a modifier (Heckman & Corbin, 2016). While the specific wording of his argument has evolved, the crux of Heckman's message is that the notion of "skill" is a useful one because "skill suggests that these attributes can be learned...*all attributes can be shaped*" (Heckman & Kautz, 2013, p. 10; emphasis added). Heckman has also been consistent in his message regarding the inadequacy of outdated modes of measuring what might predict long-term life outcomes, namely IQ and other achievement tests.[3] Interventions must also target "character skills" valued in the labor market, in school, and other domains (Heckman & Kautz, 2013).

Given the widespread popularity and diffusion of these ideas, a closer examination of how Heckman and his co-authors conceptualize "skills" is warranted. Table 2.3 below lists ways in which Heckman and co-authors have explained and written about skills.

Heckman and his co-authors use the term "skill" as the broadest possible category – essentially to capture anything important for personal and social well-being (even referring to "health" as a skill). In Heckman and Kautz (2013), greater attention is given to the field of psychology and its "relatively well-accepted" taxonomy of descriptors or temperament attributes of personality. These are the "Big Five" domains, including conscientiousness, openness to new experience, extraversion, agreeableness, and neuroticism/emotional stability.[4] From these traits, Heckman and Kautz (drawing upon a table adapted from psychologists John and Srivastava) list a number of facets, related skills, and "analogous childhood temperament skills" (2013, p. 12). However, they are careful not to use the label "traits" as they believe

Table 2.3 Heckman and co-authors' conceptualizations of skills

	Skills are:
Heckman and Kautz (2013)	Character skills are universally valued across all cultures and societies (p. 4) Skills enable people. They are capacities to function. Greater levels of skill foster social inclusion and create social well-being. Skills give agency to people to shape their lives in the present and to create future skills (p. 5). Character skills include perseverance ("grit"), self-control, trust, attentiveness, self-esteem and self-efficacy, resilience to adversity, openness to new experience, empathy, humility, tolerance of diverse opinions and the ability to engage productively in society (p. 6).
Heckman and Corbin (2016)	Skills – broadly defined – are major sources of well-being and flourishing in society (p. 344). The current literature on the economics of human development recognizes the multiplicity of skills that characterize human diversity and contribute to creating flourishing lives (p. 343). Personality skills – that is, "soft skills" such as trust, altruism, reciprocity, perseverance, attention, motivation, self-confidence, and personal health – are also important (p. 345). Health and mental health are essential skills (p. 345).

that this term signifies a sense of "permanence and possibly also of heritability" (Heckman & Kautz, 2013, p. 10).

Heckman and Kautz explain that they use the term skills rather than traits because "skills suggests that these attributes can be learned, both cognitive and character skills can change and *be changed* over the course of the lifecycle" (2013, p. 10; emphasis added). While research in psychology does indicate that personality traits change throughout the lifecycle,[5] the claim Heckman and Kautz make regarding how traits can "be changed" (through interventions) is debatable. How and why personality traits change and the degree to which they can change through interventions over time is an active research area in the field of psychology.

Heckman's work is cited by a number of donor agencies that work in the life skills area – including the World Bank, who published the brief "Life Skills: What Are They, Why do They Matter, and How Are They Taught?' in 2013. In this brief, they draw heavily from Heckman's work as well as other economists who write from a human capital perspective. In short, in this perspective, life skills matter because they have positive implications for health, education, and labor market outcomes.

The empirical evidence base regarding the effectiveness of labor market training programs that focus on life skills suggests mixed results, with some studies showing that training has little effect and others finding a positive long run effect (J-PAL, 2017). Some of this research has focused on the pedagogy and educational strategies used to deliver training programs, and some encouraging results from randomized evaluations of programs that combine an emphasis on "cognitive" and "noncognitive" skills training improve educational trajectories and graduation rates, and they have positive effects on labor market outcomes (J-PAL, 2017). One example of this is the randomized evaluation of the A Ganar program, a sports-based job training program that emphasizes technical skills as well as "life and employability" skills featured in Murphy-Graham (Chap. 7, this volume). While the program did not have any significant effect on the employment rate, or number of jobs or hours worked by participating youth, there was a positive impact on job "quality" as measured by wages, benefits, and job satisfaction (Duthie et al., 2018).

A recent review of interventions to strengthen the life skills of adolescents found that there is a small evidence base regarding labor market outcomes, and so general conclusions are not possible. Measurement of life skills has also proven very difficult, which raises concerns regarding the validity of the findings (Schurer, 2017). Despite these findings, there is some consensus that adolescence offers a window of opportunity to teach life skills through training programs. However, compared with early-childhood programs, the evidence on adolescent programs is less abundant (Heckman & Kautz, 2013). Furthermore, "there remains a feeling that [skills] training must be a key component of labor market integration given the large gap between the very low skill level of young people and the needs of firms, especially in developing countries" (J-PAL, 2017, p. 1). Table 2.4 includes two additional studies that focus on labor market outcomes, both of which had mixed results.

Life Skills for Quality Education

"*A poor quality education is almost like no education. Great progress has been achieved in enrolling children in school around the world. But it is not enough to get children in school. We also need to ensure they learn to read, count and acquire the necessary life skills.*" This message, which appears on the front page of the Global Partnership for Education website,[2] exemplifies how life skills are a key component of the "bottom line" message about educational quality that currently circulates among key policy actors in the field of international development education. In addition to basic literacy and numeracy, life skills are a key component of education quality. In short, there is consensus that improving the quality of education is a key international goal, but there are many different notions of what constitutes quality education. Among these different conceptualizations of quality education, there is consensus that students should develop life skills (Barrett et al., 2006; DeJaeghere et al., 2016; Nikel & Lowe, 2010; Tikly & Barrett, 2011; UNICEF, 2010; World Bank, 2018).

This third discourse community, which we call "quality education," has emphasized life skills education in part due to growing recognition that children and adolescents in developing countries do not always benefit from extended years of schooling in terms of what they are learning. Referred to as the "learning crisis", the critique is that the curriculum is highly academic and that it is disconnected from what adolescents need to learn to do everyday tasks and engage in community life. Furthermore, what the curriculum does emphasize, namely basic literacy and

---

[2] See https://www.globalpartnership.org/education

Table 2.4 Summary of life skills interventions for adolescents identified in empirical review

Paper	Intervention	Delivery	Impact	Country	Discourse community	Life skills area of impact
Adebiyi (2015)	Curriculum focusing on moral reasoning, social adjustment, and study skills	6 weeks teaching of positive life skills	Decrease in truancy	Nigeria	Prevention	Social and emotional competency, Knowledge
Anand et al. (2013)	Life skills training thru PowerPoints, focusing on nutrition	2 sessions of 1 h each	+knowledge, +attitude, +practices relating to dietary behavior	India	Prevention, Quality education	Knowledge
Arpana and D'Souza (2012)	Individual life skills training and group life skills training with focus on assertiveness training	8 sessions for 60 days	−cognitive/affective, −physiological, −action oriented, −total shyness	India	Prevention	Social and emotional competency
Ayodele et al. (2016)	Life skills training to influence individual participants' sexual behavior, or to influence their perception of sexual behavior in relation to others	9 weeks of life skills training	Sexual behavior improved (behave in healthy ways)	Nigeria	Prevention	Social and emotional competency
Chaudhary and Mehta (2012)	Activity based and participatory life skill education	20 sessions	+self-image, +self-understanding	India	Labor market outcomes, Prevention	Knowledge, Psychosocial competency
Choudhary et al. (2016)	Curriculum focused on child survival and safe motherhood	Information, education, communication, behavior change	+ knowledge about nutrition and pregnancy, 0 knowledge of delivery and early childhood	India	Prevention	Knowledge

Dindigal (2007)	Life skills education	10 vignettes over 3 months, with information imparted in story form	increases in: problem solving, decision making, critical thinking, creative thinking, empathy, self-awareness, coping w emotions, coping w stress, interpersonal relation skills, effective communication, overall psychosocial competence	Iran	Prevention	Psychosocial competency
Drishti et al. (2014)	Life skills education program with focus on keeping SAFE (sequential, active, focused, explicit) practices in mind	4 weekly sessions of 120 min each	0violent behavior, +protective behavior (+life appreciation, 0social support)	India	Prevention	Psychosocial competency
Dunbar et al. (2010)	SHAZ!: life-skills-based HIV education, training and supports for entrepreneurship	10 interactive sessions on life skills, 9 days on business training	+HIV knowledge and income and savings and power in nonsexual relationship, 0 currently sexually active and power in sexual relationship and condom use and future plans	Zimbabwe	Labor market	Psychosocial competencies
Ghadiri Bahramabadi et al. (2015)	Life skills training focusing on self-assertion	5 sessions	+psychological well-being, +satisfaction with school	Iran	Prevention	Psychosocial competency, Critical thinking

(continued)

Table 2.4 (continued)

Paper	Intervention	Delivery	Impact	Country	Discourse community	Life skills area of impact
Ghasemian and Kumar (2017a, b, c)[a]	Psychological distress emphasis; topics included decision-making, problem-solving, creative thinking, critical thinking, emotion regulation, stress management, self-awareness, empathy, communication skills, interpersonal relationships	8 sessions	−psychological stress	India	Prevention	Psychosocial competencies
Ghasemian and Kumar (2017a, b, c)[a]	Emotional empathy emphasis; topics included decision making, problem solving, creative thinking, critical thinking, emotion regulation, stress management, self-awareness, empathy, communication skills, interpersonal relationships	8 sessions	+emotional empathy	India	Prevention	Psychosocial competency
Ghasemian and Kumar (2017a, b, c)[a]	Emphasis on autonomy; topics included decision making, problem solving, creative thinking, critical thinking, emotion regulation, stress management, self-awareness, empathy, communication skills, interpersonal relationships	8 sessions	Increases in emotional autonomy, functional autonomy, attitudinal autonomy, total autonomy	India	Prevention	Psychosocial competency

					Prevention	Knowledge
Givaudan et al. (2007)	"A Team Against AIDS" program paired with the Mexican life-skills program Planeando tu vida; HIV focused, school-based educational program	15 weekly 2 h sessions over one school year	Increases in all: personal variables (self-knowledge, self-efficacy regarding condom use, and decision making), intervening variables (subjective norms about, knowledge about HIV/AIDS, and attitudes toward condoms), and outcome variables (communication on sexuality and intentions to use condoms)	Mexico		Knowledge
Haider and Burfat (2018)	Life Skills Based Education, with topics including friendship and relationships, human rights, gender and sex, puberty and body changes, and infectious diseases	Teaching of Life Skills Based Education curriculum in class	− aggression, − smoking, +confidence, +self-awareness, +assertiveness, +resistance to peer pressure, +sharing problems, +knowledge improvement	Pakistan	Quality education	Psychosocial competency, Knowledge
Hewett et al. (2017)	Adolescent Girls Empowerment Program curriculum; topics included intrapersonal and interpersonal skills, reproductive health, STIs (including HIV/AIDS), life skills (including healthy relationships and sex), gender and gender-based violence, leadership, human rights	38 sessions	Evaluation in progress	Zambia	Quality education	Psychosocial competencies

(continued)

Table 2.4 (continued)

Paper	Intervention	Delivery	Impact	Country	Discourse community	Life skills area of impact
Hita (2018)	Life skills education and training on six of the ten core life skills (as outlined by the WHO) with emphasis on promoting skills concept, skill acquisition, maintenance and generalization of skills	10 sessions of 120 min each, occurring twice a week; included group discussions, oral presentations, skill-based activities, tasks to sensitize participants to key issues, video viewings, individual and group work, and homework assignments	+social competency for both genders	India	Prevention	Psychosocial competency
Hita and Kumar (2017)	emotional distress focus; topics included problem-solving, decision-making, communication, interpersonal skills, stress management, emotion regulation	10 2-h sessions	+positive emotions, – negative emotions	India	Prevention	Psychosocial competencies
Joseph and Thomas (2017)	life skills education focused on personal, interpersonal, and society skills	10 sessions ranging from 60–105 min each; 5 sessions per day over 2 days	All outcomes significant: decision making, problem solving, empathy, self-awareness, communication, interpersonal, coping with emotions, coping with stress, creative thinking, critical thinking	India	Protection	Knowledge, Psychosocial competency

Kaligis et al. (2017)	Life skills education program developed by the WHO; topics include communication, decision-making, critical thinking, assertive actions, coping with emotions, development of self-esteem, dealing with peer pressure, and social interaction	3 week-long modules occurring 2–3 h a day.	−low self-esteem, −negative self-perception, 0self consciousness, 0instability, − total difficulties, 0emotional symptoms, 0conduct problems, 0hyperactivite, 0peer problems, − prosocial	Indonesia	Prevention	Psychosocial competency
Kaur (2011)	Life skills training focusing on emotional intelligence skills. Topics include self-esteem, empathy, social skills, interpersonal relationships, self-regulation, self-motivation, and self-awareness	120-min sessions twice a week over 3 months	+emotional intelligence skills	India	Prevention	Psychosocial competency
Lokoyi (2016)	life skills training focusing on interpersonal skills, problem solving skills, and environmental health education	1-h sessions, twice a week for 8 weeks	− violence, − health risk behavior	Nigeria	Prevention	Psychosocial competency, Critical thinking
Mirdrikvand et al. (2016)	Weekly curriculum	10-session curriculum	+ psychological capital and adaptability	Iran	Quality education	Psychosocial competencies
Mohammadi and Poursaberi (2018)	stress coping strategies and life skill trainings, including lecture, group discussion, videos, pamphlets, and leaflets	13 daily sessions of 45 min each	all significantly increased: somatic symptoms, anxiety/ insomnia, depression, social dysfunction, GPA	Iran	Prevention	Psychosocial competency

(continued)

Table 2.4 (continued)

Paper	Intervention	Delivery	Impact	Country	Discourse community	Life skills area of impact
Monkong et al. (2009)	cognitive experiential self-theory and life skill technique development program: training on concept of thinking, strategies to resolve problems and control emotions	5 days of training with a booster every fortnight for 9 months	+attitude, +knowledge and practice on coping with stress by problem solving and emotional management, − stress	Thailand	Prevention	Critical thinking
Motepe (2005)	life skills programme for early adolescent AIDS orphans, developed by researcher	10 sessions	+ a good sense of identity and self-esteem; + communication skills; + assertiveness skills; + self-awareness; + coping and stress management; + decision making skills; + problem solving skills; + conflict management skills; 0 critical and creative thinking skills; + maintaining a healthy lifestyle	South Africa	Prevention	Knowledge, Critical thinking, Psychosocial competency
Mutiso et al. (2018)	Life Skills Education and psychoeducation with goals of: promote awareness, inform on available treatment modalities, coping strategies and appropriate behavior/attitude change	7 two hour sessions	− externalizing problems (aggressive behavior, delinquent behavior), 0 internalizing problems (withdrawn, somatic complaints, anxiety/ depression), − total problems (after 9 months)	Kenya	Prevention	Psychosocial competency

Naseri and Babakhani (2014)	life skills training with topics including rage control, decision making, problem solving, self-knowledge, stress strategies, connection skills	14 sessions of 90 min over 3 months	− physical aggression, − verbal aggression	Iran	Prevention	Psychosocial competency
Paghale et al. (2014)	Weekly curriculum	12 sessions of 1.5 h each	+ social adjustment and academic performance	Iran	Prevention	Psychosocial competencies
Parvathy and Pillai (2015)	Life skills education module prepared by the researchers	Not specified	0self awareness, increase in: knowledge of the 10 life skills, critical thinking, creative thinking skill, decision making, problem solving, effective communication, interpersonal skills, coping with emotions, coping with stress	India	Quality education	Psychosocial competency, Critical thinking
Pathania and Chopra (2017)	Life skill education in the form of flashcards/handouts/puppets and small activities	Module consisting of small activities based on day-to-day life situations	0 decision making, +interpersonal relationship, 0communication skills, 0self-esteem, +critical thinking, 0creative thinking, +problem solving, 0empathy, 0stress management	India	Prevention	Critical thinking, Psychosocial competency
Prasad (2009)[b]	Life-skills based health education, focusing on substance use awareness.	Not Available	0attitude towards substance use, +awareness of various substances	India	Prevention	Knowledge
Refahi (2008)[b]	Training for coping skills, problem solving and decision-making skills, communication skills and self-awareness	16 sessions	−suicide tendency, −negative self-concept, 0runaway thinking	Iran	Prevention	Psychosocial competency

(continued)

Table 2.4 (continued)

Paper	Intervention	Delivery	Impact	Country	Discourse community	Life skills area of impact
Sahebalzamani et al. (2013)	Life skills education. Topics included managing emotions, problem solving, assertiveness, self-awareness, resiliency, anger control, critical thinking, decision making, effective communication, and stress management	8 sessions, 90 min each, over 2 months	− stress, − anxiety, − depression	Iran	Prevention	Psychosocial competency
Shaiju and Rages (2018)	"Edutainment" – entertainment education; brainstorming sessions, games, screening of Hindi movies on rights of children, and group discussions	Watching the Hindi movie "Siddhart" and having time to discuss and clarify doubts	+ critical thinking, + creative thinking	India	Quality education	Critical thinking
Sreehari et al. (2018)	Life skills program working on enhancing psychosocial competency and imposing a positive effect on mental health	2 sessions a week for 7 weeks	− fear of negative evaluation; + self-image	India	Prevention	Psychosocial competency
Srikala and Kishore (2010)	Life skills education integrated into the school mental health program; focusing on developmental issues	Once a week for an hour over 12–20 sessions during the school year	+coping, +self-esteem, +adjustment, 0psychopathology	India	Quality education	Critical thinking, Psychosocial competency

				Prevention	Psychosocial competency
Subasree (2012)	life skills training program through discussions, activities, feedback, lectures, and role play; objectives included teaching the students to know their self-value; to understand their strengths, weaknesses and opportunities; and to teach them the 10 core Life Skills as defined by the WHO	3 days	+self-awareness, +self-management, +internality, 0motivation, +empathy, +social skills	India	Prevention	Psychosocial competency
Vishwas and Hussain (2014)	Reproductive health curriculum based on Life Skills Training (LST) that participants helped adapt to make relevant for them	5-8 sessions; 1 h focused on empowerment for health	+knowledge about menstruation, family planning, STIs and HIV	India	Prevention	Knowledge
Waithima (2017)	Life skills enhancement, focusing on self-awareness, decision making, problem solving, coping skills, and drug refusal skills	Weekly sessions for 6 months	Substance use reduced significantly	Kenya	Prevention	Psychosocial competency
Yankey and Biswas (2012)	Life skills training module introducing the 10 life skills defined by the WHO, along with sub-skills; techniques included brainstorming, role playing, and group discussion	30 basic sessions and 15 additional sessions for students who were not able to comprehend life skills in one session	– school stress, – future stress, 0peer stress, 0home stress. –leisure stress, 0opposite sex stress, –self stress	India (focusing on Tibetan refugees)	Prevention	Psychosocial competency, Critical thinking

We categorize these studies by the discourse communities and the domains of overlap identified in Table 2.2

aThese papers report different outcomes from the same study

bWe report results here only from paper abstracts – we were unable to access full copies of these studies despite search of databases at the University of California and McGill University numeracy, also has abysmal outcomes. This recognition and its perceived importance spurred the publication of the World Bank World Development Report "Learning to Realize Education's Promise", which begins with an overview of the dimensions of the learning crisis (World Bank, 2018).

Policy statements and documents from the World Bank, blogs by Washington think tanks such as the Brookings Institution, and commissioned research programs such as DFID's EdQual or the Raising Learning Outcomes in Education Systems (RLO) attempt to grapple with how to improve teaching and learning in formal schools. Against this backdrop, international education actors including philanthropic foundations, bilateral and multilateral donors, and local and international non-governmental organizations have launched what is likely to be thousands of non-formal education programs that focus on life skills (a review of programs in just three countries identified 103 programs for adolescent girls) (Dupuy et al., 2018). These programs are intended to fill the void that is left by poor quality schools by serving children and adolescents who are enrolled in school with afterschool or summer programs. Additionally, they serve children and adolescents who never attended or have dropped out of school (potentially, at least in part, due to low quality).

Life skills education for adolescent girls has particularly gained prominence in the last decade. Advocates for girls' education have increasingly come to realize that the "get them into school and all will be well" was a faulty assumption (Sahni, 2017, and also in her discussion of the Prerna school, this volume). For many years, scholars and international organizations such as CARE and Plan International focused not on "life skills" per se, but rather on girls' and women's empowerment through education. Getting girls into school, through expanded access that often involved scholarships and cash transfers was just the first step of the empowerment process. The hope was, and continues to be, that education can be a site to challenge the gender norms that have caused under-representation of girls in the system. However, empowering educational experiences for girls within the formal system are rare (see Murphy-Graham & Lloyd, 2016 for a review of empowering education for adolescent girls).

Some organizations that emphasize life skills education for girls often simultaneously emphasize girls' empowerment. However, a discursive shift seems to have taken place whereby life skills has recently become the focal point for organizations working with girls. These include organizations such as Advancing Girls' Education, BRAC, CAMFED, CARE, Plan International, Room to Read, and Save the Children. It is possible that "life skills" is a more palatable term for interventions because they do not explicitly include the word "power" and may therefore seem less radical or politically motivated. Engaging the term "life skills" may allow these organizations to more effectively engage ministries of education, who may be familiar and supportive of life skills programming because it is already a part of their HIV/AIDS prevention or technical and vocational training curriculum (mentioned in our discussion of the first and second discourse communities). Likewise, using the term "life skills" for girls rather than empowerment may enable NGOs to better forge allegiances with stakeholders familiar with labor market training programs (such as the business community).

An earlier review of programs to empower adolescent girls identified four competencies for empowerment that appeared across interventions. These included developing critical ways of thinking and learning, personal competencies, social competencies, and productive competencies (Murphy-Graham & Lloyd, 2016). These same categories are often included in conceptualizations of life skills for adolescent girls. In addition to our Table 2.1 above, Kwauk and Braga (2017) and Dupuy et al. (2018) list organizations and their life skills definitions – common are an emphasis on critical thinking (sometimes called cognitive skills), personal skills, and interpersonal skills (including community living). However, as Kwauk and Braga (2017) point out, at the level of life skills education programming for girls, practitioners have often limited their scope to quite specific outcomes, such as sexual and reproductive health, gender-based violence, or labor market outcomes (and our identification of these as distinct discourse communities clarifies why this is the case). As such, life skills programming and its focus on communication, negotiation, self-efficacy, and self-esteem focuses on imparting technical knowledge and does not enable girls to act differently in her everyday life in her home and community (Kwauk & Braga, 2017):

> A narrow focus on skills, together with conflating knowledge as skills, can lead to problems in program, curriculum, and policy design, implementation, and assessment. In particular: misaligned interventions and outcomes; misidentified target skills; overlooked building blocks and/or strategic knowledge; ineffective pedagogy or program delivery; problems with measurement; and overstated claims about an intervention or the importance of specific skills (p. 6).

Kwauk and Braga further point out that life skills programs focus on impacts including risk for substance abuse, reduced risky sexual behavior, and mindset change, there is too little attention to whether or not life skills education leads to *"transformative* change between the individual girl and her social, political, and economic environment. It also does not address whether or how such change for a girl might combine into broader collective action that transforms existing social norms, behaviors, and power relations that have systematically placed girls and women at a disadvantage" (Kwauk & Braga, 2017, p. 7). They propose a reconceptualization of life skills as competencies that are a mix of interpersonal, intrapersonal, and cognitive skills. Coupled with knowledge, and attitudes, these constitute a set of competencies (life skills) that enable youth to function, thrive, and adapt in their everyday lives (Kwauk & Braga, 2017, p. 5). Their proposal is to more explicitly link or to "translate" girls' life skills education to social change. This feature – linking life skills competencies to social change – is not commonly present in most work on life skills, particularly from the other two discourse communities. An explicit focus on social change – and the life skills needed to foster change processes – is a more recent feature of scholarship that is consistent with earlier work on education for youth empowerment (see DeJaeghere et al., 2016; Murphy-Graham, 2012).

In part due to the recency of work in this discourse community, there is quite a slim evidence base regarding the effectiveness of interventions that attempt to improve the quality of education for youth (see Table 2.4). We found that, overall, there is little evidence to date that interventions have positive effects on life skills conceptualized as a combination of interpersonal, intrapersonal and cognitive skills. An earlier review of life skills education programs found that, while there are a very small number of rigorous evaluations of life skills programs benefitting adolescents, they "generally positively influence psycho-social and attitudinal outcomes, health and relationships. They can help to prevent early marriage and they help to develop important economic and cognitive skills" (Dupuy et al., 2018).

A narrative systematic review of life skills education (Nasheeda et al., 2018) reviews twenty-five studies (that met their inclusion criteria) in both developed and developing countries. This review concludes that the totality of quantitative evidence for the studies reviewed delivers encouraging prospects for improving life skills education programs. At the same time, their conclusions also echo Kwauk and Braga's (2017) finding that studies tend to focus on "life skills components" as opposed to "understanding what knowledge, skills and attitudes adolescents require in order for positive behavior change to occur" (Nasheeda et al., 2018, p. 13). There are two additional impact evaluations of life skills programming in progress: The Adolescent Girls Empowerment Program (Hewett et al., 2017) evaluation includes a number of validated scales/measures of self-efficacy, gender-normative beliefs, financial literacy, knowledge of sexual and reproductive health, as well as other outcomes of interest (including behavioral and biological outcomes). In addition to this study, the findings from a randomized control trial of the girls' education and life skills program implemented by Room to Read in India includes a life skills assessment tool that includes self-reported scales and activity-based tasks. While these two studies are informed by a notion of life skills that is broader in nature – consistent with the educationist discourse community studies –they will, unfortunately, still not be able to capture the extent to which life skills programming can foster "transformative change between girls and her social, political and economic environment" (Kwauk & Braga, 2017, p. 7).

Conclusion

The aim of this chapter has been to gain a clearer understanding of how life skills education has been conceptualized, given its popularity in the field of education. We identified three distinct discourse communities that are concerned with life skills education. To recap, these are: (1) 'prevention and protection' which includes practitioners and scholars in public health and social work, (2) 'labor market outcomes' which draws from the work of economists, and (3) 'quality education' which draws on the work of educationists. We identify three areas of synergy among these distinct communities which include mastering specific tasks/information and knowledge; development of a set of social and emotional competencies; and fostering critical ways of thinking.

The identification of these synergies should not be considered a new framework or conceptualization of life skills – it is really intended to provide a least common denominator of sorts across these discourse communities. Focusing only on what is common across these discourse communities may be overly reductive. At the same time, a common framework or shared way of thinking about life skills that is multi-dimensional will be necessary to advance research and practice in the field. The identification of these three distinct discourse communities explains why actors in the field focus on differential program goals. Highlighting the core life skills elements across the discourse communities – critical ways of thinking, development of social and emotional competencies, and mastery of certain tasks and information – allows for a common set of *broadly shared* goals for life skills programming.

This chapter, explaining how three discourse communities conceptualize life skills, and the areas of overlap between them, can help provide conceptual clarity and will hopefully advance research and knowledge in developing, implementing, and evaluating high-quality interventions that are adapted to local contexts to best support youth to live life well.

Acknowledgments We would like to thank Lana Downs, Neha Zahid, and Fernanda Chacon for research assistance, Cynthia Lloyd for comments, and Echidna Giving for financial support.

References

Adebiyi, O. O. (2015). *Effects of three positive life skills on in-school adolescents' delinquent behavior of truancy in public secondary schools in Ibadan Metropolis, Nigeria* [Unpublished master's thesis]. University of Ibadan. http://ir.library.ui.edu.ng/handle/123456789/719

Anand, T., Ingle, G. K., Meena, G. S., Kishore, J., & Yadav, S. (2013). Effect of life skills training on dietary behavior of school adolescents in Delhi: A nonrandomized interventional study. *Asia Pacific Journal of Public Health, 27*(2), 1616–1626. https://doi.org/10.1177/1010539513486922

Arpana, S., & D'Souza, L. (2012). Effectiveness of individual and group life skills training on shyness among adolescents. *Journal of Psychosocial Research, 7*(2), 249–255. Retrieved from https://search.proquest.com/docview/1346900673?accountid=12339

Ayodele, K., Olanipekun, O., & Akinlana, T. (2016). Fostering positive sexual attitude among Nigerian adolescents through life skills training. *Babcock University Journal of Education, 1*(1), 32–38. https://www.babcock.edu.ng/oer/journals/bujed_september_2015.pdf#page=32

Barrett, A. M., Chawla-Duggan, R., Lowe, J., Nikel, J., & Ukpo, E. (2006). *The concept of quality in education: A review of the 'international' literature on the concept of quality in education* (EdQual working paper no. 3). University of Bristol.

Boler, T., & Aggleton, P. (2005). *Life skills-based education for HIV prevention: A critical analysis* (No. 3). Save the Children and ActionAid International.

Botvin LifeSkills Training. (n.d.). *LST Overview.* https://www.lifeskillstraining.com/lst-overview/

Chaudhary, S., & Mehta, B. (2012). Life skill education for the economically backward adolescent boys and girls: An intervention programme. *International Journal of Social Sciences & Interdisciplinary Research, 1*(5), 63–72.

Choudhary, A. K., Saxena, D. M., & Kaushal, R. (2016). A study to assess empowerment of adolescent girls in terms of knowledge-based life skills education about child survival and safe motherhood practices. *The Journal of Obstetrics and Gynecology of India, 66*(6), 480–484. https://doi.org/10.1007/s13224-015-0733-6

DeJaeghere, J., Pellowski Wiger, N., & Wangsness Willemsen, L. (2016). Broadening educational outcomes: Social relations, skills development, and employability for youth. *Comparative Education Review, 60*(3), 457–479.

Dindigal, A. (2007). *Impact of life skills education on psychosocial competence of adolescents* [Unpublished master's thesis]. Karnatak University. http://hdl.handle.net/10603/96188

Drishti, S., Kishore, J., Sharma, N., & Shukla, A. (2014). Pilot study for process evaluation of school-based life-skills education program for prevention of violence in adolescents. *Indian Journal of Youth and Adolescent Health, 1*(2), 12–26.

Dunbar, M. S., Maternowska, M. C., Kang, M.-S. J., Laver, S. M., Mudekunye-Mahaka, I., & Padian, N. S. (2010). Findings from SHAZ!: A feasibility study of a microcredit and life-skills HIV prevention intervention to reduce risk among adolescent female orphans in Zimbabwe. *Journal of Prevention & Intervention in the Community, 38*(2), 147–161. https://doi.org/10.1080/10852351003640849

Dupuy, K., & Halvorsen, S. (2016). *Life skills, girls, and non-formal contexts in developing countries: A global literature review* [Unpublished draft manuscript]. Chr. Michelsen Institute.

Dupuy, K., Bezu, S., Knudsen, A., Halvorsen, S., Kwauk, C., Braga, A., & Kim, H. (2018). *Life skills in non-formal contexts for adolescent girls in developing countries* (CMI report no. 5). CMI & Brookings Institution.

Duthie, M., Pucilowski, M., Anzoategui, L., Agpoon, B., & Murphy-Graham, E. (2018). *A Ganar alliance impact evaluation synthesis report Guatemala and Honduras*. Social Impact. Washington, D.C. Available online https://pdf.usaid.gov/pdf_docs/PA00T78T.pdf.

Ghadiri Bahramabadi, F., Michaeli Manee, F., & Issazadegan, A. (2015). The effect of life skills training on psychological well-being and satisfaction among female adolescents. *Journal of Research and Health, 5*, 347–357. http://jrh.gmu.ac.ir/files/site1/pages/ghadir10694i.pdf

Ghasemian, A., & Kumar, G. V. (2017a). Effect of life skills training on psychological distress among male and female adolescent students. *Indian Journal of Health and Wellbeing, 8*(4), 279–282.

Ghasemian, A., & Kumar, G. V. (2017b). Enhancement of emotional empathy through life skills training among adolescents students–A comparative study. *Journal of Psychosocial Research, 12*(1), 177–185.

Ghasemian, A., & Kumar, G. V. (2017c). Evaluate the effectiveness of life skills training on development of autonomy in adolescent students: A comparative study. *Indian Journal of Positive Psychology, 8*(1), 68–72.

Givaudan, M., Van de Vijver, F. J., Poortinga, Y. H., Leenen, I., & Pick, S. (2007). Effects of a school-based life skills and HIV-prevention program for adolescents in Mexican high schools. *Journal of Applied Social Psychology, 37*, 1141–1162. https://onlinelibrary.wiley.com/doi/abs/10.1111/j.1559-1816.2007.00206.x

Haberland, N. A. (2015). The case for addressing gender and power in sexuality and HIV education: A comprehensive review of evaluation studies. *International Perspectives on Sexual and Reproductive Health, 41*(1), 31. https://doi.org/10.1363/4103115

Haider, S. I., & Burfat, F. M. (2018). Improving self-esteem, assertiveness and communication skills of adolescents through life skills based education. *Journal of Social Sciences and Humanities, 26*(2), 157–175.

Heckman, J. J., & Corbin, C. O. (2016). *Capabilities and skills* (Working paper no. 22339). National Bureau of Economic Research. https://doi.org/10.3386/w22339

Heckman, J. J., & Kautz, T. (2013). *Fostering and measuring skills: Interventions that improve character and cognition* (Working paper no. 19656). National Bureau of Economic Research.

Heckman, J. J., Stixrud, J., & Urzua, S. (2006). The effects of cognitive and noncognitive abilities on labor market outcomes and social behavior. *Journal of Labor Economics, 24*(3), 411–482.

Hewett, P. C., Austrian, K., Soler-Hampejsek, E., Behrman, J. R., Bozzani, F., & Jackson-Hachonda, N. A. (2017). Cluster randomized evaluation of Adolescent Girls Empowerment Programme (AGEP): Study protocol. *BMC Public Health, 17*(1). https://doi.org/10.1186/s12889-017-4280-1

Hita, C. R. (2018). Life skills for enhancing social competence during adolescence. *International Journal of Basic and Applied Research, 8*(6), 526–535. http://www.pragatipublication.com/assets/uploads/doc/87b20-526-535.13314.pdf

Hita, C. R., & Kumar, G. V. (2017). Effect of life skills training on emotional distress: A comparative study between adolescent boys and girls. *The International Journal of Indian Psychology, 5*(1), 145–155. https://doi.org/10.25215/0501.018

Joseph, D., & Thomas, B. (2017). Life skills development training for adolescent girls at risk-rescued Devadasi girls in Karnataka. *Artha – Journal of Social Sciences, 16*(1), 1. https://doi.org/10.12724/ajss.40.1

J-PAL. (2017). *J-PAL skills for youth program review paper* (Review Paper). Abdul Latif Jameel Poverty Action Lab.

Kaligis, F., Diatri, H., & Dharmono, S. (2017). Life skills program for improving adolescent mental health in the aftermath Mount Merapi eruption, Yogyakarta-Indonesia. *ASEAN Journal of Community Engagement, 1*(1), 59–71.

Kaur, T. D. (2011). A study of impact of life skills intervention training on emotional intelligence of college adolescents. *Indian Journal of Psychological Science, 2*(2), 112–125. http://www.napsindia.org/wp-content/uploads/2017/05/112-125.pdf

Kautz, T., Heckman, J. J., Diris, R., ter Weel, B., & Borghans, L. (2014). *Fostering and measuring skills: Improving cognitive and non-cognitive skills to promote lifetime success* (Working Paper No. 20749). National Bureau of Economic Research. https://doi.org/10.3386/w20749

Kwauk, C., & Braga, A. (2017). *Translating competencies to empowered action: A framework for linking girls' life skills education to social change.* Center for Universal Education at Brookings.

Lokoyi, O. O. (2016). *Effects of school-based life skills training on violence and health risk behaviours among in-school adolescents in delta state* [Unpublished master's thesis]. University of Ibadan. http://ir.library.ui.edu.ng/handle/123456789/4044.

Mirdrikvand, F., Ghadampour, E., & Kavarizadeh, M. (2016). The effect of life skills training on psychological capital and adaptability of adolescent girls with irresponsible parents. *Quarterly Journal of Social Work, 5*(3), 23–30.

Mohammadi, M., & Poursaberi, R. (2018). The effects of stress-coping strategies and life skills trainings on the mental health and academic progress of adolescent cancer patients: A quasi-experimental study. *Nursing and Midwifery Studies, 7*(1), 12–17.

Monkong, L., Pongpanich, S., Viwatwongkasem, C., Chantavanich, S., Wongpiromsarn, Y., & Katz, L. (2009). The effectiveness of program developed from cognitive–experiential self- theory and life skills technique on adolescent coping with stress. *Nepal Medical College Journal, 11*(4), 225–228.

Motepe, M. M. (2005). *A life skills programme for early adolescent aids orphans* [Unpublished doctoral dissertation]. University of Pretoria. https://repository.up.ac.za/handle/2263/29211

Murphy-Graham, E. (2012). *Opening minds, improving lives: Education and women's empowerment in Honduras.* Vanderbilt University Press.

Murphy-Graham, E., & Cohen, A. (2019, April 14–18). *Life skills education for adolescents: A landscape analysis and empirical review* [Conference paper]. Comparative and International Education Society Conference, San Francisco, CA.

Murphy-Graham, E., & Lloyd, C. (2016). Empowering adolescent girls in developing countries: The potential role of education. *Policy Futures in Education, 14*(5), 556–577. https://doi.org/10.1177/1478210315610257

Mutiso, V., Tele, A., Musyimi, C., Gitonga, I., Musau, A., & Ndetei, D. (2018). Effectiveness of life skills education and psychoeducation on emotional and behavioral problems among adolescents in institutional care in Kenya: A longitudinal study. *Child and Adolescent Mental Health, 23*, 351–358. https://doi.org/10.1111/camh.12232

Naseri, A., & Babakhani, N. (2014). The effect of life skills training on physical and verbal aggression male delinquent adolescents marginalized in Karaj. *Procedia - Social and Behavioral Sciences, 116*, 4875–4879. https://doi.org/10.1016/j.sbspro.2014.01.1041

Nasheeda, A., Abdullah, H. B., Krauss, S. E., & Ahmed, N. B. (2018). A narrative systematic review of life skills education: Effectiveness, research gaps and priorities. *International Journal of Adolescence and Youth, 24*(3), 1–18. https://doi.org/10.1080/02673843.2018.1479278

Nikel, J., & Lowe, J. (2010). Talking of fabric: A multi-dimensional model of quality in education. *Compare: A Journal of Comparative and International Education, 40*(5), 589–605. https://doi.org/10.1080/03057920902909477

Paghale, Z., Paghale, S., Jadidi Feighan, M., & Nazary, M. (2014). The effect of life skills training on social adjustment and academic performance of adolescent female students. *Knowledge & Research in Applied Psychology, 15*(4), 121–129.

Parvathy, V., & Pillai, R. R. (2015). Impact of life skills education on adolescents in rural school. *International Journal of Advanced Research, 3*(2), 788–794.

Pathania, R., & Chopra, G. (2017). Enhancement in life skills of adolescent girls through intervention. *Studies on Home and Community Science, 11*(1), 29–31. https://doi.org/10.1080/0973718 9.2017.1351073

Population Council. (2012). Sexuality education: A ten-country review of school curricula in East and Southern Africa. Regional Report. UNESCO & UNFPA.

Prasad, D. S. (2009). *Effect of life skills-based health education on adolescent students' awareness of and attitude toward substance use* [Unpublished master's thesis]. Indian Institute of Technology. http://eprint.iitd.ac.in/bitstream/handle/12345678/5812/TH-3930.pdf?sequence=2

Refahi, Z. (2008). Life skills training as a prevention strategy for adolescent social psychopaths. *Journal of New Approach in Educational Administration, 1*(2), 135–151. https://www.sid.ir/en/journal/ViewPaper.aspx?ID=184654

Robeyns, I. (2017). *Wellbeing, freedom and social justice: The capability approach re-examined.* Open Book Publishers. https://doi.org/10.11647/OBP.0130

Sahebalzamani, M., Moraveji, M., Farahani, M., & Feizi, F. (2013). Investigation the effect of life skills training on students' emotional reactions. *Journal of Applied Environment and Biological Sciences, 3*(9), 134–137.

Sahni, U. (2017, September 13). *Reframing girls' education in India.* Education plus development, Brookings. https://www.brookings.edu/blog/education-plus-development/2017/09/13/reframing-girls-education-in-india/

Sayed, Y., & Ahmed, R. (2015). Education quality, and teaching and learning in the post-2015 education agenda. *International Journal of Educational Development, 40*, 330–338. https://doi.org/10.1016/j.ijedudev.2014.11.005

Schurer, S. (2017). Does education strengthen the life skills of adolescents? *IZA World of Labor.* https://doi.org/10.15185/izawol.366

Shaiju, P., & Rages, J. (2018). Impact of edutainment programme in developing life skills with specific reference to critical and creative thinking among adolescent students of Chattisgarh State. *Artha-Journal of Social Sciences, 17*(1), 9–22. https://doi.org/10.12724/ajss.44.2

Shapiro, L. (2007). The embodied cognition research programme. *Philosophy Compass, 2*(2), 338–346.

Sreehari, R., Varghese, J., & Thomas, J. R. (2018). Effect of life skills training on fear of negative evaluation and self-image among school adolescents. *Indian Journal of Positive Psychology, 9*(1), 193–195. https://doi.org/10.15614/ijpp.v9i01.11771

Srikala, B., & Kishore, K. K. (2010). Empowering adolescents with life skills education in schools – School mental health program: Does it work? *Indian Journal of Psychiatry, 52*(4), 344–349. https://doi.org/10.4103/0019-5545.74310

Subasree, R. (2012). Promoting personal profile of adolescents through life skills training programme. *Indian Journal of Positive Psychology, 3*(3), 224–228.

Swales, J. (1990). *Genre analysis: English in academic and research settings* (1st ed.). Cambridge University Press.

Taylor, A. (2005). What employers look for: The skills debate and the fit with youth perceptions. *Journal of Education and Work, 18*(2), 201–218. https://doi.org/10.1080/13639080500085984

Tikly, L., & Barrett, A. M. (2011). Social justice, capabilities and the quality of education in low income countries. *International Journal of Educational Development, 31*(1), 3–14. https://doi.org/10.1016/j.ijedudev.2010.06.001

UNICEF. (2010). *Basic education and gender equality: Quality of education.* https://www.unicef.org/education/index_quality.html

Vishwas, M., & Hussain, M. (2014). Empowerment of adolescent girls for reproductive health base. *Human Rights International Research Journal, 2*(1), 84–88.

Waithima, C. W. (2017). Life skills enhancement for psychoactive substance use reduction among school going adolescents in Kenya. *PEOPLE: International Journal of Social Sciences, 3*(2), 2000–2014. https://doi.org/10.20319/pijss.2017.32.20002014

Walker, M. (2012). A capital or capabilities education narrative in a world of staggering inequalities? *International Journal of Educational Development, 32*(3), 384–393. https://doi.org/10.1016/j.ijedudev.2011.09.003

Westera, W. (2011). On the changing nature of learning context: Anticipating the virtual extensions of the world. *Educational Technology & Society, 14*(2), 201–212.

Winterton, J., Delamare, F., & Stringfellow, E. (2006). *Typology of knowledge, skills and competences: Clarification of the concept and prototype.* Office for Official Publications of the European Communities.

Winthrop, R., & McGivney, E. (2016). *Skills for a changing world: Advancing quality learning for vibrant societies.* Center for Universal Education at Brookings.

World Bank. (2018). *Learning to realize education's promise.* World Development Report.

Yankah, E., & Aggleton, P. (2008). Effects and effectiveness of life skills education for HIV prevention in young people. *AIDS Education and Prevention, 20*(6), 465–485. https://doi.org/10.1521/aeap.2008.20.6.465

Yankey, T., & Biswas, U. N. (2012). Life skills training as an effective intervention strategy to reduce stress among Tibetan refugee adolescents. *Journal of Refugee Studies, 25*(4), 514–536. https://doi.org/10.1093/jrs/fer056

Chapter 3
Social and Emotional Learning: From Conceptualization to Practical Application in a Global Context

Katharine E. Brush, Stephanie M. Jones, Rebecca Bailey, Bryan Nelson, Natasha Raisch, and Emily Meland

Abstract Social and emotional learning (SEL) is an effective way to promote positive learning, health, and wellbeing outcomes among children and youth, but the field lacks consensus about which skills and competencies are most important, what they should be called, and how they should be promoted and measured across diverse global contexts. SEL is also referred to by many names, often overlapping with life skills education (LSE) and other initiatives to improve learning, health, and developmental outcomes for children and youth. This chapter begins by describing SEL and its relationship to LSE and the United Nation's Sustainable Development Goals. It then showcases where clarity and cohesion do or do not exist within the field of SEL by exploring how SEL is conceptualized, measured, and promoted in different settings around the world. We draw on data collected over a series of research projects in which we applied a common coding system to SEL frameworks, programs, and measurement/assessment tools in order to identify areas of overlap and divergence between them. The chapter summarizes key findings from these projects while highlighting the need for deeper contextualization and localized research and development and concludes by discussing implications for research and practice.

Keywords Social and emotional learning · Culture and context · Interventions · Measurement/assessment tools · Frameworks

K. E. Brush (✉) · S. M. Jones · R. Bailey · B. Nelson · N. Raisch · E. Meland
Harvard Graduate School of Education, Cambridge, MA, USA
e-mail: katharine_brush@gse.harvard.edu; stephanie_m_jones@gse.harvard.edu; rebecca_bailey@gse.harvard.edu; nraisch@gse.harvard.edu; bryan_nelson@mail.harvard.edu; emily_meland@gse.harvard.edu

J. DeJaeghere, E. Murphy-Graham (eds.), *Life Skills Education for Youth*, Young People and Learning Processes in School and Everyday Life 5,
https://doi.org/10.1007/978-3-030-85214-6_3

Acronyms

CASEL	Collaborative for Academic, Social, and Emotional Learning
EU NESET	European Union's Network of Experts working on the Social dimension of Education and Training
IRC	International Rescue Committee
LSE	Life skills education
MELQO MODEL	Measurement of Early Learning Quality and Outcomes Measurement of Development and Early Learning
MESH	Mindsets, Essential Skills, and Habits
NGO	Non-governmental organization
OECD	Organisation for Economic Co-operation and Development
SEL	Social and emotional learning
United Nations SDGs	Sustainable Development Goals
UNESCO	United Nations Educational, Scientific and Cultural Organization
UNICEF	United Nations Children's Fund
USAID	United States Agency for International Development

Introduction

Children and youth require more than just academic and vocational skills to succeed in school, work, and life. Numerous studies have shown that social, emotional, behavioral, and character skills, knowledge, attitudes, and competencies – often collectively referred to as nonacademic skills and competencies – matter for many areas of development, including learning, health, and general wellbeing (e.g., Jones et al., 2015; Jones & Kahn, 2017; Merrell & Gueldner, 2010; Moffit et al., 2011). Moreover, these skills and competencies are essential to achieving international education and development goals, including developing responsible citizens, addressing poverty and conflict, ensuring quality and equitable education, and achieving global sustainability. However, while there is agreement about the importance of nonacademic skills, there remains a lack of consensus about which skills are most important, what they should be called, and how they should be promoted and measured – which has led many in the field to express concern about the lack of precision with which we discuss and measure them (Care et al., 2017; Engber, 2016; Gehlbach, 2015; Reeves & Venator, 2014; Sánchez Puerta et al., 2016; Whitehurst, 2016; Zernike, 2016).

It is within this broad and somewhat contentious nonacademic domain that the fields of life skills education (LSE) and social and emotional learning (SEL) are situated. LSE has long been a common approach to promoting and reinforcing nonacademic skills and competencies in the international education and development sector.

More recently, there has also been growing international interest in the separate but related field of SEL, with many governmental bodies, multilateral organizations, and international non-governmental organizations (NGOS) beginning to incorporate SEL concepts and programming into their work, either in coordination with or in parallel to LSE efforts. Reflecting the broader nonacademic field, SEL lacks clarity around how skills and competencies are conceptualized, defined, taught, and measured across diverse approaches. SEL is often treated as monolithic, but the frameworks used to guide SEL policy and practice, as well as the programs and measurement tools designed to promote and measure SEL skills, do not all include or target the same set of skills, nor do they use the same language to describe them, making it difficult to ensure alignment between SEL research, programming, and assessment.

This chapter addresses three major topics: (a) describing SEL and distinguishing it from LSE, (b) showcasing where clarity and cohesion do or do not exist within the field of SEL, and (c) discussing the implications for research and practice. To do so, the chapter first defines SEL, highlights its relevance to the field of international education and development and its role in supporting the United Nation's Sustainable Development Goals (SDGs), and distinguishes it conceptually from the field of LSE. Second, it lays out a major challenge facing SEL, describing how a lack of clarity and transparency in the field makes it difficult to accurately translate research into practice. This section introduces a coding system designed to respond to this challenge by acting as a "Rosetta Stone" for the field, identifying points of alignment and divergence across distinct yet related SEL frameworks, programs, and measures. It also explores issues related to the relevance and fit of SEL in settings outside of the United States. Finally, the third section of the chapter analyzes data from three projects that applied the coding system to SEL frameworks, programs, and measurement/assessment tools in order to better understand where alignment does or does not exist between the theoretical conceptualization and practical application of SEL. The chapter concludes by sharing the implications of these challenges for research and practice.

What Is Social and Emotional Learning?

Broadly speaking, social and emotional learning, or SEL, refers to the process through which individuals learn and apply a set of social, emotional, and related nonacademic skills, attitudes, behaviors, and values that help direct their thoughts, feelings, and actions in ways that enable them to succeed in school, work, and life (Jones et al., 2017). As we describe in this chapter, there are many ways of thinking about and categorizing specific SEL skills and competencies,[1] but in general SEL

---

[1] There are many different terms used to describe the different constructs and components that fall under SEL, LSE, and other related fields (e.g., skills, competencies, behaviors, attitudes, beliefs, values, knowledge, etc.). For the purposes of this chapter, we use the two terms "skills and competencies." Both a skill and a competency refer to what one is able to do: Skills are abilities acquired

tends to encompass some combination of cognitive, social, and emotional skills and competencies (Aspen Commission, 2019). For example, cognitive skills and competencies enable children to manage their thoughts, feelings, and behavior toward the attainment of a goal; emotional skills and competencies enable children to identify, understand, and manage their own feelings as well as relate to the emotions of others through empathy and perspective-taking; and social skills and competencies enable children to build and maintain healthy relationships, resolve conflicts, and work and play well with others (Jones & Bouffard, 2012). Importantly, but oftentimes overlooked in the field of SEL, these skills and competencies are also accompanied by a *belief ecology*: a set of beliefs, values, and attitudes – ways of viewing and understanding ourselves and the world around us – that are based on our unique combination of knowledge, skills, and dispositions and which serve as an internal guide for driving and directing our behavior (Aspen Commission, 2019). This belief ecology not only influences the development of the skills and competencies included in the cognitive, social, and emotional domains, but also the ultimate purpose and end to which one puts those skills to use (e.g., whether we use strong perspective-taking skills to empathize vs. harm).

Research demonstrates that social and emotional skills and competencies are malleable and teachable (Jones & Kahn, 2017) and can be successfully developed and promoted through high-quality SEL programming (Durlak et al., 2011; Sklad et al., 2012; Taylor et al., 2017; Wiglesworth et al., 2016), particularly in educational settings, both formal and informal. Research also suggests that SEL may be particularly relevant for children and youth who face poverty, violence, and discrimination around the world (Inter-Agency Network for Education in Emergencies (INEE), 2016; Alexander et al., 2010), as children's social-emotional development is particularly sensitive to the negative effects of stress and trauma (Evans & Kim, 2013; Noble et al., 2005; Raver et al., 2013). Importantly, SEL programs also tend to have the greatest impact on students who face the greatest number of risks, including those with lower socio-economic status and those who enter school behind their peers either academically or behaviorally (Bailey et al., 2019; Jones et al., 2011).

But it is important to highlight that high-quality SEL programming and assessment is about more than just targeting, teaching, and measuring skills and competencies. Social-emotional development does not occur in a vacuum; instead, it is deeply influenced by a variety of developmental and contextual factors including experiences, environments, and relationships, as well as the sociocultural norms and the political and economic realities of the settings in which people learn, play, and grow (Jones et al., 2017). The most effective SEL efforts are therefore sensitive to how skills and competencies are being developed and deployed across home, school, and community settings, and seek to provide safe and supportive learning

---

through training and practice and competencies are the application of those skills to specific tasks in ways informed by one's knowledge, beliefs, and values. For example, perspective-taking is a skill and the ability to use perspective-taking to navigate social situations effectively is a competency.

environments, build teacher skills and capacity, and involve families and communities in decision-making and learning (Jones et al., 2018).

Relevance of Social and Emotional Learning to International Education and Development Goals

In the international education and development sector, social and emotional skills and competencies are important for both individual and national self-reliance, prosperity, and harmony (United States Agency for International Development (USAID), 2019). First, skills like responsible decision-making, problem-solving, goal-setting, peaceful conflict resolution, and empathy enable individuals to make the most of the resources and opportunities available to them, advocate for positive social and political change, and decrease prejudice and conflict. Second, SEL has an important role to play in achieving the United Nation's SDGs, particularly SDG 4: "ensure inclusive and equitable education and promote lifelong learning opportunities for all," by providing students with the skills, competencies, and learning environments they need to be effective and engaged learners. Decades of research in human development suggest that social, emotional, and cognitive development are integral to mastering academic content and developing learning behaviors that support students to reach academic benchmarks (Jones & Zigler, 2002; Immordino-Yang & Damasio, 2007; Immordino-Yang, 2011). SEL efforts have also been linked to safer, better-functioning schools and classrooms characterized by positive relationships and a supportive culture and climate (Jones & Bouffard, 2012; Merritt et al., 2012; Okonofua et al., 2016a, b; Schonert-Reichl, 2017).

As highlighted in a recent policy brief by USAID (2019), SEL and other "soft skills" efforts can support educational access and quality in international settings by improving academic outcomes, promoting safety and inclusivity, mitigating the negative impact of trauma on learning and development, and building teachers' capacity to effectively support all students – including even the most marginalized learners, such as girls, children with disabilities, and children from racial/ethnic minority groups. For example, a recent impact evaluation in the Democratic Republic of Congo found that teacher professional development paired with an SEL curriculum improved student perceptions of their school as safe and supportive and led to improvements in their literacy and numeracy skills (Torrente et al., 2019). The same USAID brief also suggests that education programs that intentionally incorporate SEL may have the potential to help foster inclusivity at school by removing institutional barriers like inequitable discipline, school management, and instructional practices that prevent marginalized learners from accessing or participating fully in learning opportunities.

Distinguishing Social and Emotional Learning from Life Skills Education

SEL and LSE are at times conflated or used interchangeably as umbrella terms that refer to the same broad and general set of nonacademic skills and competencies, erasing important differences in how they are conceptualized and operationalized across the two fields. Other terms and disciplines often blended or conflated with SEL and LSE include twenty-first century learning, character and citizenship education, psychosocial supports, conflict resolution and peace education, employability skills, and youth development, to name just a few. In other instances, SEL is seen as a sub-group of LSE. This is a tempting assessment to make, as LSE does incorporate a focus on social and emotional skills and competencies; however, SEL as a field is its own entity, with its own research tradition, focus, goals, terminology, and desired outcomes that do not necessarily always align with those of LSE.

We conceptualize the relationship between LSE and SEL in the following way: The nonacademic domain represents a broad area of research and practice that encompasses an array of separate but related fields, including SEL and LSE, among many others. Importantly, LSE and SEL are rooted in different disciplines – or sets of knowledge and research traditions – that influence which skills and competencies they deem important and for whom, how they think about and organize those skills and competencies, and even what they call them. The field of SEL, for example, is grounded in developmental psychology and prevention science and traditionally focuses on elementary and primary school-age children, primarily in schools or other educational settings, although its use in secondary school and out-of-school-time settings is growing. Accordingly, SEL efforts typically seek to target some combination of social, emotional, and self-regulation skills and competencies shown to impact school readiness, academic achievement, and classroom culture/climate in ways that predict a variety of longer-term positive outcomes related to school, employment, health, and wellbeing. And importantly, most of the literature on which SEL is based comes from the United States, with only small – albeit growing – number of rigorous SEL studies conducted outside of Western contexts.

LSE, on the other hand, is in some ways a conglomeration of multiple disciplines and research traditions. While LSE has its origins in health-related prevention and education contexts with a focus on providing adolescents and young adults with the knowledge and skills required to make healthy choices related to drugs and alcohol, violence, and sexual/reproductive health, over the years that focus has expanded to incorporate additional concentration on the technical and vocational skills required for employment, as well as the empowerment of women and girls. Consequently, LSE tends to target skills/competencies and use terminology more appropriate for adolescent development, and frequently builds social and emotional skills and competencies alongside or in the context of health, parenting, vocational, and other related programming. Therefore, while the fields of SEL and LSE target similar nonacademic skills and competencies and overlap in many ways, they are not the same, and caution should be exercised when using the terms interchangeably or trying to fit one field under the other.

While the fields are conceptually separate, there remain many opportunities to learn and share best practices across them. Many organizations currently focus on either SEL or LSE, or silo their efforts in each area with separate initiatives for each, but it is true that both fields have a strong focus on social-emotional development and outcomes and there may be value in intentionally coordinated or combined approaches to SEL and LSE that are mutually reinforcing rather than separate or redundant. For example, coordinated SEL and LSE efforts can provide opportunities for social-emotional development across the age span, beginning with SEL in the early years and transitioning or broadening to LSE as students age. Just as SEL programs looking to expand into secondary school could learn from LSE, organizations engaged in life skills programming could benefit from a solid foundation in SEL, which would enable them to build foundational social and emotional skills and competencies with younger children, setting them up for later success as programming expands into other areas of LSE that are more developmentally appropriate for older youth, such as labor market skills and more complex nonacademic skills and competencies related to identity, agency, and empowerment.

Complexity in the Field of Social and Emotional Learning

A Lack of Consensus, Clarity, and Precision

Despite the growing popularity and promise of SEL, there remains a lack of consensus about which social, emotional, and related skills and competencies are most important, what they should be called, and whether and how they relate to each other. Underlying this challenge, and in some ways compounding it, is the fact that major SEL stakeholders have put forth competing frameworks. Frameworks are designed to describe and organize skills/competencies in order to guide research, policy, and practice, but often differ from one another in a number of key ways. For example, they might (a) prioritize different skills, (b) organize them into different groups and hierarchies, or (c) use different or even conflicting terminology to describe similar sets of skills (Jones et al., 2019a). This diversity of focus and approach is not inherently a problem; frameworks are highly aligned with their specific purposes and objectives, making for a rich and vibrant field that offers a variety of options and approaches from which to choose based on the unique needs of a population or setting. However, when this type of complexity results in differing or conflicting terminology as it has for SEL, LSE, and related fields, it becomes difficult to communicate clearly about what is important and make decisions about the right strategies and approaches to use in practice.

In order to effectively translate research for practice, there must be a clear link between what research says about how the outcome of interest is related to a particular skill (the evidence, often distilled into frameworks), how that skill can be developed in children and youth (the program/strategy), and how to measure it to determine if the program or intervention efforts were successful (the evaluation). When there is terminological messiness, it can be difficult to see at face-value where SEL frameworks, values, programs and practices, and measures align. For example, SEL currently suffers from a problem known as the "jingle and jangle" effect: frameworks, programs, and measures often refer to the same skill or competency by different names, or alternatively, use the same name to refer to two conceptually distinct skills (Jones et al., 2016b; Reeves & Venator, 2014), making it difficult to identify whether frameworks and terms are referring to similar or distinct concepts.

When working in diverse global contexts, it is also important to consider how various SEL skills and competencies are understood and valued among different cultures and communities. The way in which SEL skills and competencies are conceptualized, prioritized, defined, and displayed are highly tied to culture, or the shared norms, beliefs, customs, values, and behavioral standards of a society that shape the way people understand, interpret, and make meaning of their experiences (Gay, 2018). Culture plays an integral role in defining and guiding beliefs about which social and emotional skills and competencies are considered important or deemed acceptable, and for which individuals or groups. Moreover, behavioral expression of those skills and competencies – for instance, outward expressions of emotion and empathy – may also differ across contexts.

In general, there is limited research on SEL in diverse global contexts (Castro-Olivo & Merrell, 2012; Garner et al., 2014). Much of the research comes out of the United States or other high-income, Western countries, and as a result, many frameworks – even those developed for use outside of the U.S. – are based on literature from Western contexts and therefore reflect Western, Eurocentric values, beliefs, and terminology (Jones et al., 2019d; Jukes et al., 2018). The SEL concepts and terms used in Western frameworks and literature do not always align with the values and interests of different contexts and cultures (Jukes et al., 2018) and sometimes do not translate easily – or even exist at all – in other languages (Jones et al., 2019d). This has important implications for both programming and assessment in that not only must frameworks, interventions, and assessment tools be aligned to each other but they must also reflect culturally relevant competencies and be designed to describe, teach, and measure those competencies in ways that are appropriate and accurate for the context (Jones et al., 2020).

Without greater clarity and a mechanism for making connections between diverse perspectives and terminology, stakeholders may end up cherry-picking programs or measures that may or may not be aligned with each other, with the outcomes being targeted, or with the cultural context – and therefore risk missing, misunderstanding, or simply not achieving the intended effects. Jones et al. (2019c) have suggested that this type of misalignment may help explain some of the mixed findings that have plagued SEL program evaluations over the years. They point, for example, to a large-scale study conducted by the Social and Character Development (SACD) Research Consortium (2010) that revealed no overall differences in social-emotional outcomes for schools randomized to a variety of social and character development interventions versus those in the no-intervention condition. The study, however, used a general measurement battery to look at a mix of different program approaches rather than using measures aligned to the specific skills being targeted by each program. Several of the individual randomized control trials included in the broader SACD study did find positive outcomes, which Jones and colleagues suggest may be the result of using measurement tools more closely tied to those programs' theories of change.

Responding to the Challenge: Explore SEL Website and Coding System

Over the past 5 years, we have developed a coding system and set of online tools (Explore SEL) that serve as a "Rosetta Stone" for the broad nonacademic domain (Jones et al., 2019a). Much like how the Rosetta Stone enabled historians to discover connections between ancient alphabets, Explore SEL is designed to enable users to make sense of and navigate between different frameworks, programs, and measures in the nonacademic domain, regardless of differences in terminology. The basis of Explore SEL is a coding system that, when applied to frameworks, programs, and measures, can be used to identify related areas of focus across them, thus enabling comparisons based on how the terms, strategies, and items are defined and described, rather than what they are called or labeled. The coding system captures whether/when the various competencies described within each framework, program, and measurement tool align with 550+ common nonacademic skills and competencies (e.g., "identifies emotions in others") across 6 broad domains and 23 sub-domains, as presented in Table 3.1.[2] Each domain represents a conceptual category of focus in the broader nonacademic domain and they are representative of the kinds of skill/competency areas seen across many different fields. Within each domain is a set of more specific sub-domains, and within those sub-domains are a list of yet more specific skills, competencies, behaviors, and beliefs related to that conceptual category of focus. It is important to note that this coding system is not intended to serve as its own framework or to fit all nonacademic fields into its structure; it is merely meant to serve as method of cutting through surface-level terminological differences to see where frameworks, programs, and measures in the nonacademic domain are focusing on similar skills and competencies.

---

[2] The coding system used for Explore SEL was derived from a comprehensive review of the literature on social, emotional, and related nonacademic skills and competencies that are linked to an array of positive outcomes. It has been updated and refined over the course of multiple projects to incorporate skills and competencies from across the broad nonacademic domain, including the fields of SEL, LSE, positive youth development, character education, virtues/values, twenty-first century skills, employability skills, citizenship education, personality, and more. The complete coding system can be found online at https://exploresel.gse.harvard.edu

Table 3.1 Six broad domains of SEL

Domain	Description	Related sub-domains
Cognitive	Skills required to successfully and efficiently direct behavior toward the attainment of a goal. Skills in this domain are involved in tasks that require you to concentrate and focus, remember instructions, prioritize tasks, control impulses, set and achieve goals, interpret and use information to make decisions, and more.	Attention Control, Working Memory and Planning Skills, Inhibitory Control, Cognitive Flexibility, Critical Thinking
Emotion	Skills that help you recognize, express, and control your emotions as well as understand and empathize with others. Skills in this domain are important not only for managing your own feelings and behavior, but also for interacting with and responding to others in prosocial ways.	Emotional knowledge and expression, Emotional and behavioral regulation Empathy/ perspective-taking
Social	Skills that help you accurately interpret other people's behavior, effectively navigate social situations, and interact positively with others. Skills in this domain are required to work collaboratively, solve social problems, build positive relationships, and coexist peacefully with others.	Understanding Social Cues, Conflict Resolution/Social Problem Solving, Prosocial/ Cooperative Behavior
Values	Skills, character traits/virtues, and habits that support you to be a prosocial and productive member of a particular community. This includes values like understanding, caring about, and acting upon core ethical values; the desire to perform to one's highest potential; an eager and thoughtful approach to knowledge and learning; and the habits required to live and work together with others as a friend, family member, and citizen.	Ethical Values, Performance Values, Civic Values, Intellectual Values
Perspectives	A person's perspective is how they view and approach the world. It impacts how they see themselves, others, and their own circumstances and influences how they interpret and approach challenges in their daily life. A positive perspective can help children and youth protect against and manage negative feelings to successfully accomplish tasks and get along with others.	Gratitude, Optimism, Openness, Enthusiasm/zest
Identity	Identity encompasses how people understand and perceive themselves and their abilities. It includes knowledge and beliefs about themselves, including their ability to learn and grow. When a person feels good about themselves; sure of their place in the world; and confident in their ability to learn, grow, and overcome obstacles, it becomes easier to cope with challenges and build positive relationships.	Self-Knowledge, Purpose, Self-Efficacy/ Growth Mindset, Self-Esteem

Since the start of our work developing Explore SEL, we have applied the coding system to 40 frameworks, 25 programs, and 34 measures.[3] The resulting database of coded frameworks, programs, and measurement/assessment tools can be used to make comparisons within and across these areas of SEL and related fields, highlighting areas of alignment or divergence. For example, some programs or measurement tools focus exclusively on conflict resolution, while others focus on empathy, mindfulness or executive function, and still others focus on character values like integrity or honesty. By identifying the focus or composition of specific programs, measurement tools, and frameworks, stakeholders can better understand the skills being targeted in each effort, can select appropriate measures for evaluation or monitoring, and can understand and contribute to the growing body of research in accurate ways. In this chapter, we use the data generated from these projects to explore how SEL is conceptualized in frameworks and operationalized in practice through programs and measurement/assessment tools.

Comparing Frameworks, Programs, and Measures for Social and Emotional Learning

One way to learn more about how skills and competencies are conceptualized and defined across the field of SEL is to look carefully at the frameworks that different organizations, programs, and funders use to guide policy and practice in these areas. Frameworks carry a great deal of weight and influence because they are used to distill ways of thinking and prioritizing in order to tell stakeholders what to aim for, or in other words, what outcomes we can or should expect from any program, strategy, or practice. In the case of SEL, this means the kinds of knowledge, skills, and attitudes we should look for in children and youth, and when we should expect to see them across development (Jones et al., 2019a). As one of the most common ways of communicating about and organizing SEL skills, frameworks are frequently used to guide an organization, program, or funder's approach to the domain. Consequently, they often drive which skills and outcomes are prioritized, addressed, and measured.

But how do frameworks actually get translated into practice across the field? An analysis of frameworks illustrates how social, emotional, and related nonacademic skills and competencies are defined and conceptualized in the field of SEL. Yet frameworks are aspirational – they merely represent a blueprint for the skills we *can* or *should* target in order to move the needle on desired outcomes. One way to better understand how SEL skills and competencies are operationalized in the field is to look more closely at SEL programs and measurement tools. Programs, curricula,

---

[3] The coding occurred as part of three separately funded research projects: The Explore SEL website (http://exploresel.gse.harvard.edu; Jones et al., 2020), the Navigating SEL Guide (Jones et al., 2017), and the Interagency Network for Education in Emergencies Quality and Equitable Learning Outcomes SEL Mapping Project (Jones et al., 2020)

and measurement/assessment tools dictate which nonacademic skill/competency areas, or domains, are emphasized in practice, and whether they align with those outlined by guiding frameworks.

It is important to clearly understand the skill/competency areas, or domains, on which frameworks, programs, and measures focus, and to understand which programs and measures align best with specific frameworks – because as NGOs, schools, governments, and intergovernmental organizations around the world increasingly seek to integrate SEL into the fabric of learning environments, stakeholders need to know what has been shown to be effective in addressing important outcomes. Since SEL is often treated as an all-encompassing umbrella term, it is possible to assume that all SEL programs will target every skill outlined in SEL frameworks, that those skills will be the same across all frameworks and programs, and that all SEL measurement tools will be able to capture the impact and effectiveness of any SEL program. In reality, however, SEL programs and measures target a wide gamut of skills and competencies and vary in scope from a narrow or specific focus on one or a few domains to a broad emphasis on many different ones.

The ability to select programs and measures that align to specific needs or outcomes is critical for the field of SEL to be successful over time. By applying the Explore SEL coding system to SEL frameworks, programs, and measurement/assessment tools, it is possible to identify which skill areas are typically targeted or emphasized in practice and identify the existing links or gaps between frameworks, programs, and measures.

A Closer Look at SEL Frameworks

Out of the current Explore SEL database of 40 coded frameworks, 10 have been designed specifically for the field of SEL and/or have a strong foundation in SEL research and intentionally incorporate skills and competencies identified in the literature on SEL, and it is these we have included in our analysis below. It should be noted that this is a relatively small sample of frameworks and therefore should not be considered a definitive representation of the SEL field, particularly given the growing number and variety of organizations that study and implement SEL programming around the world. However, this sample includes frameworks that represent the perspectives of many important and influential actors in the fields of SEL and international education and development, including the Collaborative for Academic, Social, and Emotional Learning (CASEL); the Organisation for Economic Cooperation and Development (OECD); the European Union (EU); International Rescue Committee (IRC); as well as the United Nations Children's Fund (UNICEF); the United Nations Educational, Scientific and Cultural Organization (UNESCO), the World Bank, and the Center for Universal of Education at Brookings Institution (as part of the Measuring Early Learning Quality and Outcomes, or MELQO, initiative).

Of the 10 frameworks included in the sample, four were developed for use across multiple countries: OECD's social and emotional learning competencies, IRC's social and emotional competencies, the MELQO Measure of Development and Early Learning (MODEL) framework, and the EU's Network of Experts working on the Social dimension of Education and Training (NESET) framework. And while designed primarily with U.S. contexts in mind, the CASEL framework is also frequently cited as an influential guide and resource by organizations that develop social, emotional, and related nonacademic skills and competencies in countries around the world (Jones et al., 2019d). Another five frameworks were designed for use in specific country or local contexts: The Anchorage and Connecticut standards; Mindsets, Essential Skills, and Habits (MESH) framework; and the Transforming Education framework were developed for use in U.S. contexts and the Vision of the Haitian Child framework was designed to guide SEL work in Haiti. More information about each of these frameworks can be found online at the Explore SEL website (http://www.exploresel.gse.harvard.edu), which houses more detailed framework profiles and a set of visual tools for making direct comparisons between all 40 frameworks in the database.

On Which Skills Do SEL Frameworks Focus?

Table 3.2 shows each framework's general focus by making it clear which domains receive the most attention in that framework. The percentages in the table indicate how much emphasis each framework places on the six domains of our coding system based on how many codes from each (i.e., cognitive, emotion, social, values, perspectives, and identity; see Table 3.1 for detailed descriptions) were applied to the terms included in that framework. Please see the Explore SEL website for a more detailed description of how frameworks were coded.

Table 3.2 Percent breakdown of domain focus across SEL frameworks

Framework	Cognitive	Emotion	Social	Values	Persp.	Identity
Anchorage K-12 SEL Standards	8%	25%	31%	22%	4%	10%
CASEL Framework for Systemic SEL	20%	23%	28%	20%	3%	8%
Connecticut K-3 SEL Standards	33%	21%	28%	10%	4%	4%
EU NESET Framework for Social and Emotional Education	24%	13%	20%	28%	2%	13%
IRC Social and Emotional Learning Competencies	28%	39%	17%	11%	6%	0%
MELQO MODEL Module	38%	31%	27%	4%	0%	0%
MESH	28%	6%	6%	39%	0%	22%
OECD SEL Framework	21%	14%	21%	33%	7%	2%
Preparing Youth to Thrive	20%	27%	7%	47%	0%	0%
Vision of the Haitian Child in Society: SEL Framework	17%	17%	21%	25%	6%	15%
Average across all frameworks	24%	22%	21%	24%	3%	7%

As indicated by Table 3.2, there is considerable variability in the relative emphasis SEL frameworks place on each skill domain; however, all SEL frameworks include at least some focus on the cognitive, social, emotion, and values domains. When averaging across the entire sample, there tends to be a relatively balanced focus on the cognitive, social, emotion, and values domains (24%, 21%, 22%, and 24% respectively). This emphasis on the cognitive, social, and emotional domains aligns well with the literature on SEL, which tends to focus on the skills young children require to achieve academic success and function successfully in classroom and school environments: the need to be able to pay attention to the teacher and remember important instructions and rules, to regulate their emotions and behaviors, and to work and get along well with others. Interestingly, the MESH framework stands out as an outlier for including little focus on both the social and emotion domains (both 6%), perhaps because it places a greater emphasis on intrapersonal competencies related to motivation, such as self-control and believing in one's ability to improve and succeed.

Interestingly, while values are often less explicitly discussed as being part of SEL work, some SEL frameworks get coded as having a strong emphasis on values. This may be because, to a certain extent, what is deemed a useful skill or appropriate behavior is tied to the social norms and values of a community. It may be difficult to define and describe their purpose without alluding to values in some way. For example, CASEL's definition of "social awareness" acknowledges the importance of understanding social *and ethical* norms for behavior and the OECD's framework includes a willingness to forgive as an important part of the "trust" required to collaborate or work well with others. However, SEL frameworks also show considerable variation in how much emphasis they place on the values domain (SD = 13.53). The MELQO MODEL framework, for example, includes very little focus on values, perhaps because it is designed to guide measurement and therefore describes skills in ways that more closely resemble their empirical definitions without much additional elaboration.

SEL frameworks also rarely focus on the identity and perspectives domains. One reason for a general lack of focus on identity may be that skills and competencies that fall under the identity domain like self-efficacy, confidence, purpose, and agency are often areas that receive more attention in work with older children and youth as they explore who they are and what they want to do in the world. This may in fact be more the within the purview of the life skills field, which is often targeted more toward adolescents and young adults in health and vocational training programs, for whom these areas may be more developmentally and contextually appropriate. And even more so than identity, SEL frameworks include little to no emphasis on the perspectives domain: of the seven SEL frameworks in which it appears, it never makes up more than 7% of the codes applied. Attitudes and perspectives like gratitude, optimism, openness, and enthusiasm/zest rarely appear in the literature on SEL; those seeking to study, develop, and measure those particular constructs might see more emphasis on them in other corners of the nonacademic domain, in frameworks and literature that focus on personality traits, character education, virtues and values, mental health/psychosocial supports, or even mindfulness, which often incorporates aspects associated with openness into mindfulness practice (e.g., remaining open and receptive to the present moment).

A Closer Look at SEL Programs

Recent meta-analyses have demonstrated that high-quality, evidence-based SEL programs produce positive outcomes for students, including improved behavior, attitudes, and academic performance (Durlak et al., 2011). There are many types of SEL programming available, including school-based prevention and intervention programs, schoolwide behavior management systems, and teacher-focused instructional and pedagogical practices. The most common approach involves comprehensive, scripted curricula that provide explicit SEL skill instruction through sequenced lessons (Jones et al., 2019b). But as mentioned earlier in this chapter, high-quality SEL is about more than just building skills; children's social-emotional development is highly influenced by their surroundings, from the immediate environments of their classrooms, homes, and communities to the larger socio-political forces operating around them. SEL programming is therefore most successful when it creates safe and supportive learning environments, supports the social-emotional competence of adults, engages caregivers and builds strong family-school-community partnerships, and provides opportunities to practice and apply SEL skills outside of regular classroom and school settings such as on the playground and at home (Jones et al., 2017). When implemented with fidelity, high-quality SEL programming has been shown to produce benefits for all children and youth, regardless of geographical setting (e.g., urban, suburban, rural) or socio-demographic background (Bridgeland et al., 2013; DePaoli et al., 2015; Durlak et al., 2011; Taylor et al., 2017).

At the same time, we know very little about what is "inside" SEL programs – the specific skills, strategies, and programmatic features that drive these positive outcomes. There are a great number of SEL programs available for schools and other educational organizations to choose from, and those programs vary widely in skill focus, teaching strategies, implementation supports, and general approach toward SEL. Some SEL programs primarily target emotion regulation and prosocial behavior, while others focus on executive function, growth mindset, character traits, or other skills. Some programs rely heavily on discussion as the primary teaching strategy, while others incorporate other instructional methods such as read-alouds, games, roleplays, music, and more. Programs also vary substantially in regard to their emphasis and material support for adult skill-building, community engagement, and other components beyond child-focused activities or curriculum.

Which Skills and Competencies Do SEL Programs Build?

This section focuses on a set of 15 coded programs.[4] All self-identify as SEL programs and are designed to target a range of social, emotional, and nonacademic skills. Most of these programs are designed for use in formal elementary

---

[4] These 15 programs were selected for this analysis from the 25 nonacademic programs included in the Explore SEL database because they met the following criteria: (a) a self-reported focus on SEL (versus, for example, other fields like character education or positive youth development), and (b) at least one RCT showing positive impacts on social-emotional outcomes for students.

school settings (approximately grades K-5 or ages 5–11) in the United States, but many have also been used in or provide adaptations for informal and out-of-school-time settings such as afterschool programs, summer camps, mentoring organizations, sports programs, and more. As previously mentioned, while there are emerging efforts to develop and design SEL programs for other countries, cultures, and contexts around the world, most of these SEL programs originate from U.S. contexts, and in many cases SEL efforts abroad consist of adapting programs developed in the U.S. for use in other countries and settings (Jones et al., 2019d).

Table 3.3 displays the percentage of activities within a given program that target each domain in the Explore SEL coding system. Because a single program activity may target more than one domain, percentages across a single program may total more than 100%. There is quite a bit of variation in the skills that SEL programs build. For example, RULER and Conscious Discipline have a strong focus on the emotion domain, while the Good Behavior Game does not include any activities that build emotion skills. Often when you examine programs more closely, reasons for these distinctions become clear. For example, RULER's main objective is to promote emotional literacy; Conscious Discipline's Feeling Buddies curriculum is focused on emotion regulation and teaching children to recognize, label, accept, and manage emotions; and the Good Behavior Game is designed to teach children to choose positive over disruptive classroom behaviors and therefore does not ever specifically delve into emotion-related skills or competencies. Yet, despite these clear differences, there is a tendency to think of all SEL programs as the same.

Similar to SEL frameworks, almost all programs include at least some activities that target the cognitive, emotion, social, and values domains while perspectives/identity are not included at all in many programs. On average, SEL programs focus most on the emotion and social domains, followed by the cognitive domain. Interestingly, while SEL frameworks tend to place a strong emphasis on the values domain, all but three SEL programs include fewer than 15% of activities that focus on values-related content. The three programs (Lions Quest, Too Good for Violence, and Positive Action) include character and/or health education components that are not as present in other SEL programs, which may in part account for their higher focus on skills and competencies in the values domain, like responsible and ethical decision-making. The overall greater emphasis on emotion and social skills within SEL programs may suggest that these skills are easier to observe, target, and promote in concrete ways, in contrast to values and perspectives, which tend to be slightly more ambiguous, personal, and perhaps in some cases even personality- or trait-based, which brings into question their malleability and responsiveness to intervention, as well as what it means to value certain ways of being over others.

Table 3.3 Percentage of program activities that target each domain

Program	Cognitive	Emotion	Social	Values	Persp./Identity
The 4Rs Program	12%	27%	43%	14%	0%
Caring School Community	8%	33%	78%	13%	0%
Conscious Discipline	14%	75%	54%	4%	7%
Competent Kids, Caring Communities	30%	28%	23%	10%	23%
Good Behavior Game	33%	0%	100%	0%	0%
I Can Problem Solve	65%	65%	55%	3%	0%
Lions Quest	18%	23%	60%	19%	7%
MindUP	44%	28%	18%	4%	19%
PATHS	30%	75%	59%	12%	2%
Positive Action	10%	57%	33%	32%	43%
Responsive Classroom	34%	2%	26%	1%	0%
RULER	10%	94%	51%	3%	0%
Second Step	40%	52%	49%	7%	1%
Too Good for Violence	12%	53%	67%	42%	5%
WINGS	16%	41%	36%	9%	3%
Average across all programs	25%	44%	50%	12%	7%

Note. Programs were coded before frameworks and measures using an earlier version of the coding system, which included only five domains instead of the current six: Cognitive, Emotion, Social, Character/Values, and Mindset. The Mindset domain in the original coding system roughly corresponds to a combination of the Perspectives and Identity domains in the current coding system, and it is therefore described that way in Table 3.3 for ease of comparison with the framework and measure data

A Closer Look at Measures of Social-Emotional Development

Measurement is currently one of the most challenging and contentious topics in the field of SEL (Duckworth & Yeager, 2015). Being able to effectively measure SEL skills and evaluate SEL and LSE efforts is important for a variety of reasons, including progress tracking, course correction, and effective program evaluation that ultimately provides the field with valuable information about what is or is not working (Jones & Barnes, 2018). But as with SEL programs, there are a wide variety of measurement/assessment tools available to choose from that target a range of different skills. For example, some tools have a narrow focus on a very specific skill or set of skills such as emotion knowledge, while others cast a wider or more general net across a variety of different skills. Due to the terminological complexity in the field, it is not always easy to determine where these differences exist in order to select a tool or combination of tools that target the skills one cares about (Jones et al., 2016a, b; Sánchez Puerta et al., 2016). These challenges are also of relevance to those working in the field of LSE; life skills programs with a strong emphasis on social-emotional outcomes seeking to identify appropriate measurement tools that target their desired outcomes can benefit from greater clarity and transparency. The goal is to find measures of social-emotional skills and competencies that are well-aligned with the skills and competencies targeted in program activities and articulated in their theory of change or guiding framework.

Moreover, SEL measures need to capture more than just individual skills and competencies. There is a tendency among existing measurement efforts to focus on assessing individual achievement; however, a relational approach to measurement – one that takes into account the dynamic interaction between individuals and their environments – may be a better approach. To begin with, focusing solely on children's skills and competencies incorrectly implies that the goal of SEL is to "improve" or "fix" children (Jones & Barnes, 2018). Secondly, decades of research make clear the important role environment and context play in children's social-emotional development (e.g., Bronfenbrenner & Morris, 1998; Jones & Molano, 2016; Milkie & Warner, 2011; Osher et al., 2018; Sameroff, 2000). Without examining features of the setting that may be contributing to or hindering children's social-emotional development, we risk merely capturing children's responses to characteristics of the environment rather than anything meaningful about their overall social-emotional development. For example, students might display certain social-emotional skills in one setting but not in another because of differences in the resources – either emotional, relational, or material – available to them in any given moment. Considering context and features of the environment in assessment efforts is important for ensuring a more accurate picture of a child's functioning and development rather than just a snapshot of their response to the other children they are with, their relationship with their teacher, or the resources and materials available to them (Jones & Barnes, 2018; Jones et al., 2016b).

Which Skills and Competencies Do Measures of Social-Emotional Development Assess?

The sample used in our analysis includes 35 measures selected in part for their focus on nonacademic constructs, appropriateness for children ages 0–18, and use in diverse international contexts, including Africa, South Asia, Latin America, the Pacific Islands, Eastern Europe, Central Asia, and the Middle East. While not all of the 35 measures are designed specifically for use in the field of SEL, all assess social-emotional development in some capacity and were cited by stakeholders from around the world as tools commonly used to measure social and emotional skills and evaluate SEL programming. (Please see Jones et al., 2020 for more detailed selection criteria and additional background information for each measurement tool.)

As with SEL frameworks and programs, there is a great deal of variation in the emphasis different SEL measurement/assessment tools place on each domain, and as shown in Table 3.4, only nine tools capture skills across all six domains. For

Table 3.4 Percent breakdown of domain focus across SEL measurement/assessment tools[a]

Measurement tool	Cognitive	Emotion	Social	Values	Persp.	Identity
Amal Alliance Local facilitator assessment (Amal-Facilitator)	0%	36%	16%	40%	0%	8%
Amal Alliance parent assessment (Amal-Parent)	8%	25%	25%	29%	4%	8%
Amal Alliance student assessment (Amal-Student)	13%	17%	17%	17%	13%	22%
Child Behavior Questionnaire (CBQ)	29%	14%	14%	7%	14%	21%
The Children's Hope Scale	25%	0%	0%	25%	25%	25%
Caregiver Reported Early Childhood Development Instruments long form (CREDI-Long)	46%	23%	23%	8%	0%	0%
Caregiver Reported Early Childhood Development Instruments short form (CREDI-Short)	43%	29%	14%	14%	0%	0%
Child and Youth Resilience Measure (CYRM-28)	0%	11%	22%	33%	0%	33%
Devereux Student Strengths Assessment long form (DESSA-Long)	15%	10%	23%	36%	10%	5%
Devereux Student Strengths Assessment short form (DESSA-mini)	33%	0%	17%	33%	17%	0%
EPOCH Measure of Adolescent Wellbeing (EPOCH)	10%	10%	10%	30%	30%	10%
Emotion Regulation Questionnaire (ERQ)	0%	100%	0%	0%	0%	0%
Short Grit Scale (Grit-S)	50%	0%	0%	50%	0%	0%
General Self-Efficacy Scale (GSE)	33%	17%	0%	17%	17%	17%
Holistic Assessment of Learning and Development Outcomes (HALDO)	44%	22%	11%	0%	0%	22%
International Civic and Citizenship Study – Introduction to School (ICCS School)	11%	0%	33%	44%	0%	11%
International Civic and Citizenship Study – Introduction to Student (ICCS Student)	0%	0%	26%	66%	3%	6%
International Development and Early Learning Assessment (IDELA)	32%	26%	16%	16%	0%	11%
International Social and Emotional Learning Assessment (ISELA)	0%	29%	38%	10%	5%	19%
KIDCOPE	18%	24%	35%	0%	12%	12%
Malawi Development Assessment Tool (MDAT)	14%	29%	29%	29%	0%	0%
MELQO Measurement of Development and Early Learning direct assessment (MELQO MODEL-DA)	75%	25%	0%	0%	0%	0%

(continued)

Table 3.4 (continued)

Measurement tool	Cognitive	Emotion	Social	Values	Persp.	Identity
MELQO Measurement of Development and Early Learning parent/caregiver report (MELQO MODEL-P)	33%	25%	8%	33%	0%	0%
MELQO Measurement of Development and Early Learning teacher report (MELQO MODEL-T)	33%	25%	8%	33%	0%	0%
Programme for International Student Assessment for Development student questionnaire (PISA-D)	0%	22%	22%	11%	17%	28%
Preschool Self-Regulation Assessment assessor report (PSRA-AR)	34%	25%	19%	16%	3%	3%
Preschool Self-Regulation Assessment direct assessment (PSRA-DA)	71%	0%	29%	0%	0%	0%
RTI International's Confidence and Curiosity measure (RTI Tanzania-CC)	0%	0%	17%	50%	0%	33%
RTI International's Pilot Parent Questionnaire for SEL Quantitative Study in Tanzania (RTI Tanzania-P)	23%	8%	21%	41%	5%	3%
RTI International's Pilot Teacher Questionnaire for SEL Qualitative Study in Tanzania (RTI Tanzania-T)	23%	10%	19%	48%	0%	0%
Strengths and Difficulties Questionnaire (SDQ)	19%	15%	35%	23%	4%	4%
Social Emotional Health Survey-Secondary (SEHS-S)	13%	19%	0%	13%	19%	38%
Social Provisions Scale (SPS)	0%	20%	20%	20%	20%	20%
YouthPower Action's Soft Skills Program Staff Tool (YouthPower-S)	21%	16%	26%	26%	0%	11%
YouthPower Action's Softskills Youth Tool (YouthPower-Y)	15%	21%	21%	24%	3%	18%
Average across all tools	22%	19%	18%	24%	6%	11%

[a]Please see profiles in Jones et al. (2020) for more detailed information about each measurement tool

example, the Children's Behavior Questionnaire (CBQ; a survey that captures various aspects of temperament in children ages 3–7), focuses to varying degrees on all six domains, the Social Provisions Scale (SPS; an interview tool that captures the availability of social support that has been used with participants ages 9–20+) provides a balanced focus on five domains, and other tools like the Emotion Regulation Questionnaire (ERQ; an interview tool that measures a respondent's tendency to regulate their emotions through cognitive reappraisal and expressive suppression) and the Grit Scale Survey (GRIT-S; a self-report tool that captures perseverance and passion for long-term goals in youth ages 14+) have a narrow focus on only one or two domains. This suggests that organizations or programs seeking to assess child progress or evaluate programming may need to use a combination of tools to capture the full range of skills and competencies they care about.

That said, four tools in the sample that are designed specifically to capture social-emotional competence and SEL skills each include items that focus on at least five domains: the Devereaux Student Strengths Assessment (DESSA-long and DESSA-mini; for grades K-8), the International Development and Early Learning Assessment (IDELA; for ages 3.5–6) and its version for older children International Social and Emotional Learning Assessment (ISELA; for ages 6–12), and the Holistic Assessment of Learning and Development Outcomes (HALDO; for ages 4–12 in conflict and crisis-affected contexts). While only a small sample, this may indicate that tools intentionally designed to assess general SEL competence may tend to have a broader scope than tools that focus on assessing more narrow constructs like grit or emotion regulation. Despite this variation, the tools in our sample tend to focus most on the cognitive and values domains, followed by the social and emotional domains. Similar to SEL frameworks and programs, the measurement/assessment tools in our sample focus least on the perspectives domain.

How Do SEL Measures Take Context into Consideration?

As noted above, SEL is about more than just child-focused competencies. To that end, we also analyzed the extent to which SEL measurement/assessment tools capture aspects of a child's environment that may hinder or promote the development and expression of SEL skills across five contextual factors: ecology, equity, health, safety, and adult support (see Table 3.5 for more detailed descriptions). This list of factors was decided upon based on a combination of: (a) desk research to determine contextual factors commonly considered by researchers in their analysis of measurement/assessment tools, and (b) factors that came up in the measurement/assessment tools in our sample during the coding process.

Findings from our coding for contextual factors confirm that most measurement tools focus on individual skills and competencies. Some measures like the International Civic and Citizenship Study (ICCS) and the Programme for International Student Assessment for Development (PISA) capture substantial information about features of the home/learning/community environment and aspects of a child's identity that impact their experiences (i.e. ecology, and to a lesser extent, equity), but a majority of tools capture little to no information about any of the contextual factors, suggesting there is an opportunity to expand SEL measurement efforts to capture richer information about children's relationship to their surroundings to paint a more complete picture of their social and emotional functioning.

Table 3.5 Contextual factor descriptions

Factor	Description	Example items[a]
Ecology	The social networks, relationships, beliefs and resources present in different areas of a child's life (e.g., at home, in school, with friends, in the broader community, etc.) that shape their daily experiences.	Have you seen someone reading at home? Can you tell me the names of your good friends? Teachers have a positive attitude towards school Are there adults in your community who care about your health and safety?
Equity	Dimensions of a child's identity, background, and experiences that may give them an advantage or disadvantage in society (e.g., gender, race, socio-economic status, immigration status, disability status, language, etc.).	What language(s) do you speak at home? What language do you learn at school? What is the highest level of schooling completed by your mother? Do you have any concerns about [child]'s development?
Health	Aspects of a children's physical and mental health as well as public health conditions (e.g., access to water, sanitation, etc.).	How often did you miss school because you were sick? I cry for no reason. Are you currently using any method to delay pregnancy? Does your home have running water?
Safety	A child's actual or perceived physical and psychosocial safety (e.g., bullying, sexual and gender-based violence, etc.).	I feel unsafe walking to and from school. Teacher reported that [child] was bullied by other students.
Adult support	Support offered to adults (e.g., teachers, caregivers, program staff, etc.) related to their own psychosocial or social-emotional wellbeing or to supporting children's psychosocial and social-emotional wellbeing.	Teachers receive support in positive classroom management. Teachers are trained to detect cases of abuse or trauma among their students.

[a]Please see Context Factor codebook in Jones et al. (2020) for detailed context factor descriptions and examples

Discussion of Alignment Between SEL Frameworks, Programs, and Measures

There are some notable points of consistency across SEL frameworks, programs, and measures. Every framework, measure, or program targeted social skills, although the extent to which they did so varied (Table 3.6). All three groups also

Table 3.6 Average domain focus across frameworks, programs, and measures

SEL resource	Cognitive	Emotion	Social	Values	Persp.	Identity
Frameworks	24%	22%	21%	24%	3%	7%
Programs	25%	44%	50%	12%	7%[a]	–
Measures	22%	19%	18%	24%	6%	11%

[a]Represents a combination of Perspectives and Identity domains

Note. Program percentages represent something slightly different than the framework and measurement/assessment tool percentages. The program percentages are simply the total percentage of activities in a program that received a code in a particular domain (e.g., all program activities that received a cognitive code ÷ all program activities), whereas the framework and measure percentages represent how much emphasis is placed on that domain relative to the other domains (e.g., all cognitive codes applied to framework or measure ÷ all codes from any domain applied to framework or measure). For this reason, we should be careful when making direct comparisons between these data; that said, we can use the data to see trends in skill emphasis and focus across frameworks, programs, and measurement/assessment tools and use that information to make general comparisons

rarely focused on the perspectives domain, indicating that fostering attitudes like optimism, enthusiasm, openness, and gratitude is not a priority in the field of SEL. However, while most frameworks and programs tended to include at least some focus on all six domains, only a quarter of measurement/assessment tools a focused on all six domains, and five (~15%) had a particularly narrow focus on only one, two, or three domains. This may indicate that many SEL measurement/assessment tools may be more targeted to a particular skill area than the typical SEL framework or program, and therefore cannot be used on their own to capture all relevant outcomes associated with a framework or program that targets a broader array of skills. Care must therefore be taken to carefully align measurement/assessment tools with framework definitions and program content, and in some cases multiple measures might be required to capture the full gamut of skills. Indeed, appropriate and psychometrically valid and reliable measures might not yet exist for all the key areas we need to capture, and therefore effort to build, contextualize, and test measures is important as well.

There are also notable differences in which domains received the greatest emphasis. SEL programs tended to place a greater emphasis on emotion skills than either frameworks or measures. Similarly, SEL frameworks and measures tended to emphasize values, but even while many programs targeted skills in that domain to some extent, they tended to do so sparingly. Programs also tended to focus on cognitive skills less frequently than do frameworks or measures. While it is certainly not necessary for every SEL program to target every domain, this may indicate there is an opportunity in the field to more intentionally address cognitive skills and values like executive function, compassion, and ethical decision-making that enable children to successfully marshal and direct those emotion and social skills more commonly targeted in programs toward academic and prosocial goals. While stakeholders and organizations may have different ideas and priorities about which skills are important to build, they should take care to select a program that includes the full array of skills they hope to promote as outlined in their framework or plan, whether that is a narrow focus on a particular set of skills and competencies, or a broader focus on a range of skills and competencies.

Conclusion

It is clear that SEL has a critical role to play in the success and wellbeing of young people around the world; however, there remain issues related to clarity, precision, and alignment, as well as cultural relevance and fit, that must be resolved in order to effectively deliver and assess social, emotional, and related skills and to achieve meaningful impacts for children and youth at scale. The wide array of skills and competencies included in, and the many fields that contribute to, the nonacademic domain can make it difficult to sort through and compare all of the research and guidance available in order to carefully align frameworks, programs, and measures in ways that cohesively promote and assess social-emotional development. As this chapter shows, there are many ways of thinking about what skills are important and which should be prioritized within the field of SEL, and there remain many unanswered questions about the relevance and fit of predominantly Western SEL frameworks, programming, and measures for diverse global contexts.

Careful alignment between frameworks, programs, and measures is therefore imperative so as not to overlook or misinterpret results in ways that give detractors reason to call into question the value of the nonacademic field as a whole (Dupuy et al., 2018; Jones et al., 2019c; Kwauk et al., 2018), and it is also becoming increasingly clear that contextualization – ideally in partnership with diverse local stakeholders (Jones et al., 2019d; Jukes et al., 2018) – is a critical step in developing or adapting nonacademic frameworks, programs, and measures to local contexts in order to effectively promote and measure skills in settings outside of the US and other Western countries.

While SEL and LSE are two distinct areas of study and we must be clear about where they overlap or diverge in order to coordinate approaches and select programming and measures that align with the needs, goals, and desired outcomes of a particular initiative, there exist opportunities for increased coordination and collaboration between them. The analyses in this chapter help clarify how SEL is being understood, taught, and measured by various SEL stakeholders in ways that support those working in the adjacent field of LSE to identify potential throughlines between the fields of SEL and LSE and identify trends in programming and measurement that can inform their own efforts to support the social-emotional development of youth. Progress in the field will occur when we begin to more intentionally develop and link frameworks to strategies, programs, and measures, and in ways that are sensitive and responsive to the local culture and context. Moving forward, the Explore SEL coding system and similar efforts to (a) increase clarity and precision in the field and (b) support careful and effective coordination and communication across nonacademic fields and organizations, will help ensure effective and precise translation of research into practice, and ultimately achieve greater results for children and youth around the world.

Funders & Collaborators

Bill & Melinda Gates Foundation
Echidna Giving
Einhorn Family Charitable Trust
Funders Collaborative for Innovative Measurement (FCIM)
Inter-agency Network for Education in Emergencies (INEE)
Porticus
Overdeck Family Foundation
Raikes Foundation
Wallace Foundation
William and Flora Hewlett Foundation

References

Alexander, J., Boothby, N., & Wessells, M. (2010). Education and protection of children and youth affected by armed conflict: An essential link. In *Protecting education from attack: A state of the art review* (pp. 55–67).

Aspen Commission. (2019). *From a Nation at Risk, to a Nation at Hope: Recommendations from the National Commission on Social, Emotional, and Academic Development.* The Aspen Institute. http://nationathope.org/wp-content/uploads/2018_aspen_final_report_full_web-version.pdf

Bailey, R., Stickle, L., Brion-Meisels, G., & Jones, S. M. (2019). Re-imagining social-emotional learning: Findings from a strategy-based approach. *Phi Delta Kappan, 100*(5), 53–58.

Bridgeland, J., Bruce, M., & Hariharan, A. (2013). *The missing piece: A national teacher survey on how social and emotional learning can empower children and transform schools.* Collaborative for Academic, Social, and Emotional Learning. https://casel.org/wp-content/uploads/2016/01/the-missing-piece.pdf

Bronfenbrenner, U., & Morris, P. A. (1998). The ecology of developmental processes. In W. Damon & R. M. Lerner (Eds.), *Handbook of child psychology: Theoretical models of human development* (pp. 993–1028). Wiley.

Care, E., Kim, H., Anderson, K., & Gustafsson-Wright, E. (2017). *Skills for a changing world: National perspectives and the global movement.* Center for Universal Education at the Brookings Institution. https://youtheconomicopportunities.org/sites/default/files/ uploads/resource/skills-for-a-changing-world.pdf

Castro-Olivo, S. M., & Merrell, K. W. (2012). Validating cultural adaptations of a school-based social-emotional learning programme for use with Latino immigrant adolescents. *Advances in School Mental Health Promotion, 5*(2), 78–92.

DePaoli, J. L., Fox, J. H., Ingram, E. S., Maushard, M., Bridgeland, J. M., & Balfanz, R. (2015). *Building a Grad Nation: Progress and challenge in ending the high school dropout epidemic: Annual update 2015.* https://files.eric.ed.gov/fulltext/ ED556759.pdf

Duckworth, A. L., & Yeager, D. S. (2015). Measurement matters: Assessing personal qualities other than cognitive ability for educational purposes. *Educational Researcher, 44*(4), 237–251.

Dupuy, K., Bezu, S., Knudsen, A., Halvorsen, S., Kwauk, C., Braga, A., & Kim, H. (2018). *Life skills in non-formal contexts for adolescent girls in developing countries.* CMI Report

Number 5. Center for Universal Education at the Brookings Institution. https://www.cmi.no/publications/6495-life-skills-in-non-formal-contexts-for-adolescent

Durlak, J. A., Weissberg, R. P., Dymnicki, A. B., Taylor, R. D., & Schellinger, K. B. (2011). The impact of enhancing students' social and emotional learning: A meta-analysis of school-based universal interventions. *Child Development, 82*(1), 405–432.

Engber, D. (2016, May 8). Is grit really the key to success? *Slate*. http://www.slate.com/articles/health_and_science/cover_story/2016/05/angela_duckworth_says_grit_is_the_key_to_success_in_work_and_life_is_this.html

Evans, G. W., & Kim, P. (2013). Childhood poverty, chronic stress, self-regulation, and coping. *Child Development Perspectives, 7*(1), 43–48.

Explore SEL. http://exploresel.gse.harvard.edu/

Garner, P. W., Mahatmya, D., Brown, E. L., & Vesely, C. K. (2014). Promoting desirable outcomes among culturally and ethnically diverse children in social emotional learning programs: A multilevel heuristic model. *Educational Psychology Review, 26*(1), 165–189.

Gay, G. (2018). *Culturally responsive teaching: Theory, research, and practice*. Teachers College Press.

Gehlbach, H. (2015, April 15). Name that baby: Why 'non-cognitive' factors need a new name. *Education Week*. http://blogs.edweek.org/edweek/rick_hess_straight_up/2015/04/noncognitive_factors_need_new_name.html

Immordino-Yang, M. H. (2011). Implications of affective and social neuroscience for educational theory. *Educational Philosophy and Theory, 43*(1), 98–103.

Immordino-Yang, M. H., & Damasio, A. (2007). We feel, therefore we learn: The relevance of affective and social neuroscience to education. *Mind, Brain, and Education, 1*(1), 3–10.

Inter-Agency Network for Education in Emergencies (INEE). (2016). *INEE background paper on psychosocial support and social and emotional learning for children and youth in emergency settings*. Alves. https://inee.org/system/files/resources/INEE_PSS-SEL_Background_Paper_ENG_v5.3.pdf

Jones, S. M., & Barnes, S. P. (2018). *What's missing in SEL measurement and assessment? Context*. https://measuringsel.casel.org/whats-missing-in-sel-measurement-and-assessment-context/

Jones, S. M., & Bouffard, S. M. (2012). Social and emotional learning in schools: From programs to strategies and commentaries. *Social Policy Report, 26*(4), 1–33.

Jones, S. M., & Kahn, J. (2017). *The evidence base for how we learn: Supporting students' social, emotional, and academic development*. Aspen Institute. https://www.aspeninstitute.org/publications/evidence-base-learn/

Jones, S. M., & Molano, A. (2016). Seasonal and compositional effects of classroom aggression: A test of developmental-contextual models. *Journal of Cognitive Education and Psychology, 15*(2), 225–247.

Jones, S. M., & Zigler, E. (2002). The mozart effect: Not learning from history. *Journal of Applied Developmental Psychology, 23*(3), 355–372.

Jones, S. M., Brown, J. L., & Aber, J. L. (2011). Two-year impacts of a universal school-based social-emotional and literacy intervention: An experiment in translational developmental research. *Child Development, 82*(2), 533–554.

Jones, D. E., Greenberg, M., & Crowley, M. (2015). Early social-emotional functioning and public health: The relationship between kindergarten social competence and future wellness. *American Journal of Public Health, 105*(11), 2283–2290.

Jones, S. M., Bailey, R., Barnes, S. P., & Partee, A. (2016a). *Executive Function Mapping Project: Untangling the terms and skills related to executive function and self-Regulation in early childhood*. OPRE Report #2016–88, Washington, DC: Office of Planning, Research and Evaluation, Administration for Children and Families, U.S. Department of Health and Human Services. https://www.acf.hhs.gov/sites/default/files/opre/efmapping_report_101416_final_508.pdf

Jones, S. M., Zaslow, M., Darling-Churchill, K. E., & Halle, T. G. (2016b). Assessing early childhood social and emotional development: Key conceptual and measurement issues. *Journal of Applied Developmental Psychology, 45*, 42–48.

Jones, S. M., Brush, K. E., Bailey, R., Brion-Meisels, G., McIntyre, J., Kahn, J., Nelson, B., & Stickle, L. (2017). *Navigating SEL from the inside out: Looking inside & across 25 leading SEL programs: A practical resource for schools and OST providers (elementary school focus).* Wallace Foundation. https://www.wallacefoundation.org/knowledge-center/Documents/Navigating-Social-and-Emotional-Learning-from-the-Inside-Out.pdf

Jones, S. M., Bailey, R., Brush, K. E., & Kahn, J. (2018). *Preparing for effective SEL implementation.* https://www.wallacefoundation.org/knowledge-center/Documents/Preparing-for-Effective-SEL-Implementation.pdf

Jones, S. M., Bailey, R., Brush, K. E., & Nelson, B. (2019a). *Introduction to the Taxonomy Project: Tools for selecting & aligning SEL frameworks.* https://measuringsel.casel.org/wp-content/uploads/2019/02/Frameworks-C.1.pdf

Jones, S., Bailey, R., & Kahn, J. (2019b). The science and practice of social and emotional learning: Implications for state policymaking. *State Education Standard, 19*(1), 18–24.

Jones, S. M., Bailey, R., Kahn, J. & Barnes, S. P. (2019c). Social-emotional learning: What it is, what it isn't, and what we know. *Education Next.* https://www.educationnext.org/social-emotional-learning-isnt-know/

Jones, S. M., Bailey, R., Meland, E., Brush, K. E., & Nelson, B. (2019d). *Integrating international frameworks into the taxonomy project: A report for Echidna Giving.* Echidna Giving.

Jones, S. M., Bailey, R., Temko, S., Donaher, M., Raisch, N., & Ramirez, T. (2020). *SEL and PSS measurement and assessment tools in education in emergencies: Identifying, analyzing, and mapping tools to global guidance documents.* Inter-Agency Network for Education in Emergencies (INEE).

Jukes, M., Gabrieli, P., Mgonda, N. L., Nsolezi, F., Jeremiah, G., Tibenda, J., & Bub, K. L. (2018). "Respect is an investment": Community perceptions of social and emotional competencies in early childhood from Mtwara, Tanzania. *Global Education Review, 5*(2), 160–188.

Kwauk, C., Braga, A., Kim, H., Dupuy, K., Bezu, S., & Knudsen, A. (2018). *Non-formal girls' life skills programming: Implications for policy and practice.* Chr. Michelsen Institute. https://files.eric.ed.gov/fulltext/ED586317.pdf

Merrell, K. W., & Gueldner, B. A. (2010). *Social and emotional learning in the classroom: Promoting mental health and academic success.* The Guilford Press.

Merritt, E. G., Wanless, S. B., Rimm-Kaufman, S. E., Cameron, C., & Peugh, J. L. (2012). The contribution of teachers' emotional support to children's social behaviors and self-regulatory skills in first grade. *School Psychology Review, 41*(2), 141.

Milkie, M. A., & Warner, C. H. (2011). Classroom learning environments and the mental health of first grade children. *Journal of Health and Social Behavior, 52*(1), 4–22.

Moffitt, T. E., Arseneault, L., Belsky, D., Dickson, N., Hancox, R. J., Harrington, H., Houts, R., Poulton, R., Roberts, B. W., Ross, S., Sears, M. R., Thomson, W. M., & Caspi, A. (2011). A gradient of childhood self-control predicts health, wealth, and public safety. *Proceedings of the National Academy of Sciences, 108*(7), 2693–2698.

Noble, K. G., Norman, M. F., & Farah, M. J. (2005). Neurocognitive correlates of socioeconomic status in kindergarten children. *Developmental Science, 8*(1), 74–87.

Okonofua, J. A., Paunesku, D., & Walton, G. M. (2016a). Brief intervention to encourage empathic discipline cuts suspension rates in half among adolescents. *Proceedings of the National Academy of Sciences, 113*(19), 5221–5226.

Okonofua, J. A., Walton, G. M., & Eberhardt, J. L. (2016b). A vicious cycle: A social–psychological account of extreme racial disparities in school discipline. *Perspectives on Psychological Science, 11*(3), 381–398.

Osher, D., Cantor, P., Berg, J., Steyer, L., & Rose, T. (2018). Drivers of human development: How relationships and context shape learning and development. *Applied Developmental Science,* 1–31.

Raver, C. C., Blair, C., & Willoughby, M. (2013). Poverty as a predictor of 4-year-olds' executive function: New perspectives on models of differential susceptibility. *Developmental Psychology, 49*(2), 292–304.

Reeves, R. V., & Venator, J. (2014, December 19). *Jingle-jangle fallacies for non-cognitive factors.* Brookings Institution. http://www.brookings.edu/blogs/social-mobilitymemos/posts/2014/12/19-jingle-jangle-fallacies-noncognitive-factors-reeves

Sameroff, A. J. (2000). Developmental systems and psychopathology. *Development and Psychopathology, 12*(3), 297–312.

Sánchez Puerta, M. L., Valerio, A., & Bernal, M. G. (2016). *Taking stock of programs to develop socioemotional skills: A systematic review of program evidence* (English). Directions in development paper. World Bank Group. http://documents.worldbank.org/curated/en/249661470373828160/Taking-stock-of-programs-to-develop-socioemotional-skills-a-systematic-review-of-program-evidence

Schonert-Reichl, K. A. (2017). Social and emotional learning and teachers. *The Future of Children, 27*(1), 137–155.

Sklad, M., Diekstra, R., De Ritter, M., Ben, J., & Gravesteijn, C. (2012). Effectiveness of school-based universal social, emotional, and behavioral programs. Do they enhance students' development in the area of skill, behavior, and adjustment? *Psychology in the Schools, 49*, 892–909.

Social and Character Development (SACD) Research Consortium. (2010). *Efficacy of school-wide programs to promote social and character development and reduce problem behavior in elementary school children* (NCER 2011–2001). National Center for Education Research, Institute of Education Sciences, U.S. Department of Education.

Taylor, R., Oberle, E., Durlak, J. A., & Weissberg, R. P. (2017). Promoting positive youth development through school-based social and emotional learning interventions: A meta-analysis of follow-up effects. *Child Development, 88*, 1156–1171.

Torrente, C., Aber, J. L., Starkey, L., Johnston, B., Shivshanker, A., Weisenhorn, N., Annan, J., Seidman, E., Wolf, S., & Tubbs Dolan, C. (2019). Improving primary education in the Democratic Republic of the Congo: End-line results of a cluster-randomized wait-list controlled trial of Learning in a Healing Classroom. *Journal of Research on Educational Effectiveness, 12*(3), 1–34.

Whitehurst, G. J. (2016). *Hard thinking on soft skills.* Brookings Institution. http://www.brookings.edu/research/reports/2016/03/24-hard-thinking-soft-skills-whitehurst

Wiglesworth, M., Lendrum, A., Oldfield, J., Scott, A., ten Bokkel, I., Tate, K., & Emery, C. (2016). The impact of trial stage, developer involvement and international transferability on universal social and emotional learning programme outcomes: A meta-analysis. *Cambridge Journal of Education, 46*, 347–376.

Zernike, K. (2016, February 29). *Testing for joy and grit? Schools nationwide push to measure students' emotional skills.* The New York Times. http://www.nytimes.com/2016/03/01/us/testing-for-joy-and-grit-schools-nationwide-push-tomeasure-students-emotional-skills.html?version=meter+at+2&module=meterLinks&pgtype=article&contentId=&mediaId=&referrer=&priority=true&action=click&contentCollecti on=

Chapter 4
Reframing Life Skills: From an Individualistic to a Relational Transformative Approach

Joan DeJaeghere

Abstract This chapter examines how life skills education draws on a dominant individualistic behavioral approach that aims to teach skills to young people so they can overcome various social and economic problems. Life skills are taught to girls so that they can be empowered to overcome health issues, such as HIV/AIDs or early pregnancy. They are also targeted at boys who are deemed 'at risk' of engaging in asocial behaviors in efforts to reduce violence and to contribute to the economy. Yet many of these societal problems are linked to changing social, economic and environmental relations. To think differently about how to use life skills to foster a good life that is just, equitable, and sustainable, the chapter offers a transformative framing based in a critical and relational approach. Such an approach requires a reframing of skills to consider the values and perspectives that are often implicitly taught, such as individual responsibility and self-promotion, and to reorient these skills around values that youth desire and need within their challenging contexts. It concludes with a discussion of some common life skills and how they can be reframed to achieve transformation in society so youth can live life well – oriented toward greater justice, equality and peace.

Keywords Youth · Life skills · Transformative social learning · Relational

Acronyms

J-PAL	Abdul Latif Jameel Poverty Action Lab
MDGs	Millennium Development Goals
SDGs	Sustainable Development Goals
UNICEF	United Nations Children's Fund
USAID	The United States Agency for International Development
WHO	World Health Organization

J. DeJaeghere (✉)
University of Minnesota, Minneapolis, MN, USA
e-mail: deja0003@umn.edu

© The Author(s) 2022
J. DeJaeghere, E. Murphy-Graham (eds.), *Life Skills Education for Youth*, Young People and Learning Processes in School and Everyday Life 5,
https://doi.org/10.1007/978-3-030-85214-6_4

Introduction

In a non-formal livelihoods program in Tanzania and Uganda for youth who had not completed their secondary education, life skills were taught to young women and men to set goals, to be responsible and conscientious, and to develop confidence so that they could have a livelihood through formal or informal work (DeJaeghere, 2017). Development organizations and program staff assumed that youth who didn't have these life skills, as well as other technical ones, were constrained from working. In another life skills program, young girls in India were learning how to set goals, make decisions, solve problems, and develop their self-esteem so that they would continue in school and not get married early (Arur & DeJaeghere, 2019). Similar to the livelihoods program, donors and staff again assumed that if girls possessed these life skills, they would succeed in school. These programs were teaching life skills to empower young people, to help them achieve at school and in their work. But both of these programs did not necessarily achieve these outcomes for many young people because other conditions also influenced whether youth worked or continued through schooling. These programs shared some common life skills that are deemed important for all youth, but they did not adequately account for the values and perspectives of these young people and their families/communities, nor for the economic and social conditions that affected their ability to live life well, as Murphy-Graham and Cohen (Chap. 2, this volume) describe as a goal for life skills education..

These education programs are based in a dominant narrative that if we teach children and youth life skills, they will be able to solve problems they face, and they will not be a risk to society by being unemployed, married early or involved in illicit activities. Yet many concerns facing young people, including a lack of jobs, social or political conflict, and discrimination and harassment based on sex, race, or other social inequalities, cannot be addressed solely through an individual's ability to set goals, communicate, and make decisions. These skills may be important for everyone to live as a particular kind of educated person (Levinson et al., 1996), but they are insufficient to achieving a broader set of goals for living life well, which includes addressing the social and economic inequalities that many young people face around the world.

There is now a considerable body of literature on life skills education examining its purposes and effects on various outcomes for different groups of youth (see Murphy-Graham & Cohen, Chap. 2, this volume; Brush et al., Chap. 3, this volume). The dominant body of literature frames life skills as individually learned and a psycho-social phenomenon, drawing on psychology, child and youth development, prevention science/health, and economics, as indicated in Murphy-Graham and Cohen's chapter (Chap. 2, this volume). Programs from this perspective teach life skills to decrease risky behaviors as measured by health outcomes, and to increase youth's productivity in society as measured by school and work outcomes. This individual and productive oriented approach does not necessarily question the underlying purpose of these life skills, or the values they purport to represent. In stark contrast, literature from sociological, anthropological, and critical (feminist) perspectives, including new childhood studies and youth studies, focus on the broader ecology and systems that affect child and youth life outcomes. This socio-cultural and critical perspective emphasizes that educators and policymakers need to consider the larger societal values and systems, including constraints and possibilities within which young people develop and enact life skills. From this perspective, scholars have argued that life skills are not skills per se, but rather they are a set of values, attitudes and beliefs. In most life skills education programs, the values and beliefs are implicit, and they are influenced by dominant discourses and perspectives on what young people are to do and be: healthy and productive youth (Butterwick & Benjamin, 2006). But life skills education can also be informed by alternative frameworks that consider broader values and approaches to what it means to live life well.

The introduction chapter to this book (DeJaeghere & Murphy-Graham, Chap. 1, this volume) lays out the critical role that life skills play in achieving the Sustainable Development Goals (SDGs) that guide education policy and practice. But many questions remain as to how teaching the dominant framing of life skills can achieve broad social outcomes of peace, sustainability and gender equality. This chapter takes up these questions by examining the assumptions and values that underlie life skills education and how these skills can be reframed to address goals of greater justice, equality and peace.

This chapter has two aims. First, it discusses problems related to the dominant conceptualization of life skills and the values therein. I show how different groups of young people are targeted for purposes of achieving individualistic behavioral outcomes, such as teaching "poor" girls life skills to empower them to delay marrying or having children, or teaching out-of-school youth skills to earn a livelihood in a precarious economy, when these life skills tend to responsibilize young people to take control of and improve their own lives. The purpose of learning these skills is to ensure that youth do not become social or economic risks for others, including the state. Such an orientation does little to address the systemic social and economic conditions that create injustices and inequalities. A second aim of this chapter is to offer an alternative framing of life skills based in a critical and relational approach. It explains how a relational worldview and values shift how we think about life skills and how they could be taught and learned. This approach accounts for and aims to transform social relations that create inequalities, violence and injustices that many young people face today. It also requires us to rethink the values needed to live life well.

In the next section, I examine literature that has influenced how life skills are conceptualized and taught in order to illustrate the underlying orientation of an individualistic behavioral approach. By this, I mean that the life skills most commonly identified are those that are individually held values and perspectives that, when acted upon through a person's behaviors, can achieve desired outcomes such as being healthy, employed, and satisfied with one's life. My analysis is informed by two studies I have conducted on life skills: one on youth livelihoods programs in East Africa, and the other a life skills program for mostly Dalit (those placed in lower castes) girls in India, aimed at reducing early marriage[1]. While these studies have been written about elsewhere, the findings from these studies informed a critical and relational conceptualization that I describe in the second section (Arur & DeJaeghere, 2019; DeJaeghere, 2019a, b; DeJaeghere et al., 2019). By relational, I mean that these values, perspectives, and skills are situated within relationships with others and within societal structures, and therefore youths' power to enact these skills requires changing unequal relationships to other people and structures. In that section, I also draw on critical sociology, anthropology and youth studies literature to consider how this alternative framing can be used to transform young people's lives and livelihoods. The chapter concludes with a discussion of some common life skills and how they can be reframed to be transformative toward the goals of gender equality, sustainability, and peace.

Life Skills as Individualistic Behaviors for Social and Economic Success

The dominant conceptualization of life skills for over two decades has drawn from an individualistic behavioral orientation that positions young people as being able to learn these skills and use them to achieve desired outcomes – namely, being productive workers through employment, and having appropriate social behaviors that contribute to healthy and peaceful families and communities. This orientation regards young people as lacking these necessary skills, and if they do not accomplish these outcomes, they have not been successful. This has been referred to as a deficit approach to education. For instance, life skills education programs have particularly targeted girls, as well as youth living in poor conditions, in order to achieve greater productivity (through employment) and reduce factors that affect such productivity, including early marriage, pregnancy, and school dropout. Boys have also been recipients of such programs, particularly when they are deemed to be involved in "unproductive" or asocial behaviors. Many of the skills identified two decades ago continue to be taught to achieve similar outcomes, yet the social and economic environments in which youth live are precarious in different ways, and the values they hold for a good life are also shifting.

In the 1990s, the World Health Organization (1999) identified life skills as important for personal and social development, defining them as "psychosocial skills that are required to deal effectively with the demands and challenges of everyday life" (p. 3). They categorized various skills along the domains of cognitive, personal, affective, and social and interpersonal abilities. Years later, UNICEF (2012), in its review of life skills programs, used a similar categorization of skills: cognitive, personal and interpersonal (p. 9), and included 10 specific skills that

---

[1] These studies were approved by the ethics review board of the University of Minnesota, and they followed ethical guidelines for research with young people in these specific contexts.

young people should learn. Interpersonal skills (and sometimes referred to as social skills, see Gates et al., 2016) refer to collaboration, negotiation, and communication, while intrapersonal, or socio-emotional skills, include confidence, motivation, coping with emotions/stress, and persistence. Cognitive skills consist of decision-making and problem-solving, as well as critical and creative thinking. While the current literature reviewing life skills programs states that there is still contestation over which skills are important for, and effective toward, achieving different outcomes, there is considerable agreement on these broad categories and these specific skills (see Gates et al., 2016).

The teaching of certain life skills, such as motivation or communication, is widely regarded as necessarily positive in fostering the ability to live life well. Rarely considered, however, are value orientations and social relations of power that might be implicated in the use of these skills in different settings. For instance, learning to communicate with others who have perpetrated violence of which one was a victim is different than communicating with others to be hired for a new job. Research and educational programs also tend to focus on the more easily, and individually, taught skills that can be seen through individually observable behaviors rather than socially enacted and value-laden skills for achieving complex social outcomes, such as communicating to reduce violence (Gates et al., 2016; Heckman, et al., 2006; Kautz, et al., 2014).

Both the WHO's and UNICEF's reviews of life skills noted that they are universally relevant and are important to promote broader social outcomes, including gender equality, good citizenship, and peace – all elements taken up in the SDGs. They also state that life skills are necessary for young people in order to prevent or address violence, conflict and environmental issues (WHO, 1999, p. 4) or "to deal with specific risks … [such as] sexual and reproductive health and … disaster risk reduction" (UNICEF, 2012, p. viii). But teaching these skills carries a set of assumptions that youth can use them to avoid, change, or be resilient against these economic, social, or environmental risks. In order to achieve these desired outcomes, life skills education has tended to focus on two different groups with slightly different assumptions about the desired outcomes. First are programs that assume life skills can empower girls by teaching them skills of communication, negotiation, self-esteem and decision-making that will delay marriage and child-birth and improve their chances of becoming educated and employed. Another set of programs focuses on boys, teaching them socio-emotional skills, confidence, and coping with stress, in efforts to improve their employment, reduce poverty and conflict, and foster peace.

Life Skills Education for Girls

As discussed in Murphy-Graham and Cohen's, Pacheco Montoya and Murphy-Graham's, Sahni's, and Kwauk's chapters in this book, girls have often been recipients of life skills education to achieve the goals of gender empowerment and eliminating gender inequalities. But these larger goals are to be achieved through short-term objectives, such as reducing early marriage, fostering sexual health (and reducing early pregnancy), and improving employment. In a recent report on non-formal education programs of life skills for adolescent girls, Dupuy et al. (2018) identified five areas of positive outcomes for girls: (1) psycho-social and attitudinal outcomes, (2) health and relationships, (3) early marriage, (4) economic skills, and (5) cognitive skills. Teaching skills for these outcomes often focus on behaviors as immediate outcomes, such as setting goals for future work, but the link between an individual girl's behavior and being successful in her life and livelihoods, as the report indicates, is less clear. For example, girls may acquire economic skills, but whether they are able to use them toward employment and earning in different contexts requires attention to social and economic values and structures that inhibit or provide these opportunities.

A common approach to teaching life skills is to focus on individual behaviors that can be learned and changed. This point is further exemplified in how life skills are defined, and then conceptualized and enacted through programs. Dupuy et al.'s (2018) review of life skills programs for girls further illustrates the individualistic behavioral orientation:

> [they are] tools for achieving positive change. For instance, decision-making and problem-solving skills enable *individuals to assess options* for courses of action, as well as the effects of these different options, and to deal constructively with problems. Creative and critical thinking skills *empower individuals to analyze* information, explore alternatives, and respond adaptively to situations. Through communication and interpersonal skills, *individuals can positively express themselves* verbally and non-verbally. Self-awareness and empathy entail recognition and understanding of the self and others, while *coping skills allow individuals to manage* negative emotions and stress (pp. 10–11, my emphasis).

The report recognizes that girls are particularly challenged by poverty and gender discrimination, but with these life skills they are expected to "overcome these challenges" (Dupuy et al., 2018, p. 1). This means that girls are expected to create opportunities within, or even change, the same social and economic environments that produce the challenges and inequalities they face.

While formal schooling for girls, and life skills education specifically, can foster higher academic outcomes, lower marriage and birth rates, enable future employment, and support a healthy family (e.g., Herz & Sperling, 2004; Mirdrikvand et al., 2016; Paghale et al., 2014; Schultz, 2002), these outcomes are not synonymous with achieving gender equality, sustainable livelihoods, or a non-violent society (see Chisamya et al., 2012; Kwauk & Braga, 2017; Moeller, 2014). The onus to address these societal issues is placed on girls and their skills to change society themselves (Vavrus, 2002). Considerable literature on girls' education and gender inequalities has raised the concern that educating girls alone cannot create transformative change, yet the renewed focus on life skills for girls is another iteration of seeking educational solutions to do so (Kabeer, 1999; Stromquist, 2015). Kwauk and Braga (2017), writing about a framework of girls' life skills for social change, state that life skills literature and programs do "not address whether or how such change for a girl might combine into broader collective action that transforms existing social norms, behaviors, and power relations that have systematically placed girls and women at a disadvantage" (p. 7). Despite raising these concerns, the dominant approaches to life skills do not conceptually or in practice create much engagement with unequal power structures and relations that disadvantage girls (see also Kwauk, Chap. 5, this volume).

Life Skills Education for Boys

Life skills education also targets boys and young men for the purposes of changing asocial behaviors that will, in turn, reduce violence (see Blattman, et al., 2015; Herrenkohl et al., 2012), and engage them in productive work (see programs discussed by Honeyman et al., Chap. 6, this volume). Programs that focus on "at risk" and asocial behaviors teach young boys and men to learn emotion management, such as coping with stress, as well as conflict management. The aim is to reduce asocial behaviors in society, and in turn, foster peaceful and sustainable livelihoods. Here again, the dominant approach comes from literature in psychology, prevention science, and youth development, which identifies specific attitudes and behaviors associated with engaging in or preventing youth from these risks (e.g., Blattman et al., 2015; Herrenkohl et al., 2012). While many programs have multiple components to address attitudes and behaviors linked with engaging in violence, such as gangs and terrorism, teaching life skills is a critical one.

A review by J-PAL (2017) of what they call non-cognitive (or life) skills training programs showed mixed results in affecting asocial behaviors in the short and long-term. For example, one program in Liberia offered cognitive behavioral therapy and/or cash to men who were involved in crime, violence, or drugs, in order to see if and how each intervention reduced these asocial behaviors. Both interventions targeted individual behaviors by teaching men to think and respond to situations that put them "at risk" (through cognitive behavioral therapy) and by fostering individual choices about spending money for their livelihoods. They did not find consistent reduction in asocial behaviors, though the therapy seemed promising if followed by cash, but not alone (Blattman et al., 2015). A different study used similar approaches of teaching conflict and emotion management and goal setting to young men in Chicago who were unemployed and participating in crime. It did not find an effect of the therapy program, though other aspects of the program (employment) seemed to have an effect on reducing arrests for violent crimes (Heller, 2014). These examples illustrate the complexity of changing attitudes and behaviors to effect social change, such as to reduce violence. Furthermore, programs often do not take a structural or ecological approach to addressing social concerns of violence or unsustainable livelihoods. Rather, these programs assumed that if young men learned how to control their emotions or to manage conflict, violence will be reduced. This approach did not attend to the complex nature of structural violence (including poverty, racism, and shame) that constrains the possibilities for a peaceful community and sustainable livelihood.

In another recent review of strategies for preventing and countering violent extremism, Kelly (2019) found that some programs working with youth in conflict settings, such as Somalia or West Africa, may reduce the "risk factors", or types of behaviors related to conflict, by providing counseling and teaching peaceful attitudes and behaviors, but the long-term impacts are not discernible. The review noted that some programs concentrated on the individual level factors for engaging in extremism but neglected the structural causes, including state-induced conflict, disenfranchisement, unemployment, and other violations of rights.

Finally, a key goal for life skills programs targeting youth (both boys and girls, but often boys) living in poor conditions or who are socially and economically marginalized is to promote employment and reduce poverty. For example, a key aim of the USAID YouthPower Initiative is to develop life skills for employment (Gates et al., 2016; Honeyman et al., Chap. 6, this volume; Lippman et al., 2015). This use of life skills education has been particularly supported by economics research that has shown positive effects of some life skills, such as communication and self-control, on securing employment or increasing income (e.g., Heckman et al., 2006). But increasing employment and earnings, particularly in precarious economies characterized by growing non-formal sector employment, necessity entrepreneurship, and little expansion in the formal labor market and social sector, is not the same as a sustainable livelihood. The ILO defines decent work as that which is productive and delivers a fair income, security in the workplace and social protection for families, better prospects for personal development and social integration, freedom for people to express their concerns, organize, and participate in the decisions that affect their lives, and equality of opportunity and treatment for all women and men (International Labour Organization, 2015). Life skills programs tend to focus on helping youth to attain employment, rather than how employers, workplaces and the government can provide for decent work and wellbeing through such employment.

Youth employability and employment programs that include life skills also show mixed results, even on the short-term measures of increasing employment or income (Olenik and Fawcett, 2013). Furthermore, there is little evidence of how life skills specifically affect workforce outcomes (Gates et al., 2016). Most programs assume that intrapersonal skills, such as self-confidence or persistence, are helpful to finding and retaining work, but the link between these skills and outcomes is tenuous. For instance, Alcid (2014) and DeJaeghere et al. (2019) show how having these skills and then securing employment do not ensure that young people are able to continue working long-term, or be paid fair wages. Decent work or sustainable livelihoods for youth living in contexts of poverty are affected by many other factors, including a lack of education/training certification, discrimination, as well as unpredictable labor markets and few social supports (See Lefebvre, et al., 2018). Therefore, this individualistic behavioral orientation to life skills for employment misses many other factors that affect sustainable livelihoods (DeJaeghere, et al., 2019).

Much of the literature on life skills education concludes with a call for more research on identifying necessary skills and how they are taught to different groups of young people to attain the outcomes of employment/poverty reduction, gender equality, and a reduction in violence. This approach is primarily technocratic, instrumentalist, and individualistic, often assuming a neutral orientation to these skills. Programs assume that these individually-focused life skills are the right skills for marginalized youth to achieve particular outcomes that help build a more stable and productive society. While seemingly neutral, this approach is embedded in values that deem these particular skills and goals as important for living life well. But living well for many marginalized youth is more than having work, not getting pregnant, or not engaging in crime; it is about having a sustainable livelihood, being in a relationship characterized by gender equality, or living securely and in peace.

Within the dominant approach's definitions and application of life skills, there is insufficient consideration of how youth, equipped with these skills, can transform complex social problems. This requires another orientation, one that is imbued with the value that teaching life skills is for the purpose of creating a more just and equitable society, if young people are to live life well. The next section offers a transformative perspective on how to define and teach life skills to achieve these broader social aims.

Life Skills as Relational and Transformative

Outside life skills education, there is a growing body of scholarship and educational practice focused on how economic and social relations affect young people's livelihoods and wellbeing amidst economic, social, and ecological adversity. This literature comes from a variety of perspectives, including new childhood studies (or the new sociology of childhood) (e.g., Maithreyi, 2019); youth studies, and particularly critical perspectives and youth activism (e.g., DeJaeghere et al., 2019; Taft, 2010); and anthropological studies of education and youth (e.g., Mains, 2012). This body of literature offers a social-cultural explanation of the knowledge and skills youth learn and use within their communities, and therefore it shows what is valued and why for living within the community. It is skeptical of labeling youth as "at risk", recognizing that this tends to characterize the individual in a deficit way, while overlooking the societal factors that shape how young people can live a good life (Maithreyi, 2017, 2019). Finally, these studies are concerned with relational aspects of young people's lives – how the social, economic, and environmental relations, both local and global, have influence on youth's ability to attain a sustainable livelihood and to live life well. These studies suggest that education – and life skills – should be oriented toward transforming connections, including unequal power relations, among humans as well as between humans and their environment, so that young people can achieve a good life – one that is characterized by collective wellbeing and solidarity.

What is a relational approach to education, and specifically to life skills? And how can it be transformative to address social and economic inequalities that constrain youth from living life well? A relational approach assumes that humans live and learn always in relation to others and their environment. This approach does not refer to the kinds of relations we have with others, such as good or trusting relationships, though these are important to learn from a life skills perspective. Rather, it is used analytically to consider how our lives interconnect with others, as well as the material and social world around us, and to examine how power is used to either oppress or transform these relations (Mohanty, 2003; Spivak, 1988; see also DeJaeghere, 2019a). Analyzing these relationships allows us to see dependencies, both equal and unequal, that can result (Ferguson, 2013). A relational approach is present in worldviews among African and Indigenous peoples. For instance, Le Grange (2012, p. 61) refers to *ubuntu* – a worldview embedded in many communities in Africa that means "humanity is ideally expressed in relationship with others" – as a relational way of living and being in the world. He argues that it is a value that can be taught through education to restore the suffering not only of the self, but also of society and nature. In this way, these relations are not only human, but also with non-human aspects of our societies, including the economy and the environment. While this chapter does not allow for a deeper discussion of a relational approach to education, its aim is to rethink life skills education and how it can consider the different relations (human and non-human) that can foster a good life.

This relational perspective was also evident in the youth's lives in the studies in East Africa and India that I led (Arur & DeJaeghere, 2019; DeJaeghere, 2019b). For instance, these life skills programs taught young women to be self-confident in their skills so that they could be employed or earn a livelihood. They could use this confidence to influence how others saw them and their abilities to work. But community members and the material environment around them also affected whether they were confident or how they used their skills. For example, if an employer pays a young woman less than others, her material environment and these social relations do not value her in the same way as they value others. Therefore, her confidence is dependent on the social or material environment in which she enacts it. In this example, teaching confidence as a life skill requires examining the social relations and material structures that affect a young woman's understanding of and realization of her particular goals. This may mean that life skills programs should not only teach young girls, but they must also consider and work with others in their environment to create change so that young women can have more just and equitable livelihoods.

This framing and teaching of life skills as relational is concerned not only with how people's lives are dependent on others in order to live life well; it also attends to the kind of changes needed in their environments in order to live life well. Dupuy et al. (2018) note that life skills should create positive change, but they do not specify whether this is individual or social change, nor the type of change. In contrast, Kwauk and Braga (2017) call for conceptualizing life skills so that they can achieve transformative change between the individual girl and her social, political, and economic environment, and particularly through collective action that might transform inequalities that girls face. This means that life skills education needs to consider the relations that inhibit young people from achieving a good life. Life skills educators also need to understand what it means to live life well from youth's perspective rather than assuming it means being employed or delaying marriage, or some other desired outcome.

Redefining Life Skills Toward Achieving Justice

If the goals of education, and life skills as a component of it, include fostering well-being, justice and sustainable livelihoods as the SDGs suggest (Walker, 2012), then we need to think more expansively about life skills – how they are learned and enacted, for whom and for what kind of social changes (see also DeJaeghere, et al., 2016). Transformative social learning offers one way to reframe life skills, and how and for what purposes they are taught (Lotz-Sisitka et al., 2015; Reed et al., 2010). Social learning draws on a relational approach because it regards learning as constitutive of the social life and environments in which we live. Furthermore, it recognizes that education can either work to reproduce or change social structures and norms that create inequalities. The transformative component of social learning is oriented toward creating equitable and just ways for all to live a good life (e.g., Murphy-Graham, 2012). This use of transformative social learning calls attention to how we think about and teach life skills relationally as well as the outcomes desired from learning them.

Reframing life skills relationally and transformatively requires changing what we call these skills and how we assume they are learned, and in turn, reimagining ways to teach these skills through social processes. In Table 4.1 below, I suggest ways to relabel and reframe several life skills found throughout the literature through a relational approach. These relational skills are not ideal forms; they are found in empirical examples of young people's lives as they navigate and negotiate their precarious and uncertain worlds (Correa & Murphy-Graham, 2019; DeJaeghere, 2017). For example, Correa and Murphy-Graham (2019) illustrate how a program that aims to improve processes of community life, meaning those aspects of community life that are valued to live a good life, teaches young people transformative agency. Here, transformative agency is not only about individual skills and actions, but acting within and upon their own environments to improve them. This example

Table 4.1 Redefining a set of transformative life skills

Common life skills	Transformative life skills
Self-concept and self-esteem	Dignity (through recognition of value) of species (persons, non-humans)
Self-motivation (and goal orientation)	Collective aspirations
Responsibility	Reciprocity – mutual dependence
Positive attitude; optimism	Hope
Empathy	Solidarity – mutual support and care

suggests that transformative social learning of life skills requires a form of agency that is collective and oriented toward community wellbeing.

What might these transformative life skills be? How can we redefine and teach common skills such, as self-esteem, self-motivation, and responsibility, among others, through a transformative social learning process? Self-esteem is regarded in many life skills education programs as necessary for achieving life outcomes, particularly for out-of-school and other marginalized youth. Brush et al. (Chap. 3, this volume) refer to self-esteem as a domain of identity – as shaping how young people view themselves. Expanding on this, Dupuy et al. (2018) suggest this concept is linked to how young people process information they receive from others about themselves and the forms of status that others attribute to them. Both of these points suggest that 'self'-esteem or 'self'-concept is not individually developed; it is fostered in relations with others and the environment. If one's self-esteem is linked to how status is attributed, then it can also be negatively affected in an environment of racism, gender inequalities, or marginalization.

A transformative life skill approach might focus on how other people in the community regard young people as having dignity and value, or as having esteem, which shifts the focus from the individual to society. Seeing young people as valued may, in turn, allow them access to social and economic opportunities from which they had been excluded. Fostering dignity requires a different engagement with and response from people and institutions who do not value youth and regard them as "Others" – as poor, at risk, and delinquent. This means that life skills programs and pedagogy need to understand why some youth are "Othered". For example, youth who had not completed their secondary school in Tanzania were regarded as idle and not able to contribute to their community. Developing dignity for these youth meant helping them identify how they could contribute and what gave them a sense of dignity, as well as what conditions in their environment gave them a sense of indignity. Then the program fostered connections with others in the community, and worked to developed trusting relationship with them. As community members learned more about the youth, they saw them in new ways and valued them and their contributions. In sum, they regarded the youth as a person with value and esteem (DeJaeghere, 2019a, 2019b).

Another life skill that is particularly linked with workforce development is to teaching young people self-motivation: to develop goals so that they can achieve their education and be employed. Goal-setting and the steps to achieve goals are often taught in life skills programs (see examples in Honeyman, et al., Chap. 6, this volume; and Kwauk, Chap. 5, this volume). But when goals are not achieved, young people are either blamed for not being motivated enough, or they adjust their goals to something that is achievable, often regarded as more realistic but not what they aspired to. Self-motivation is an important attribute, but it may not be sufficient to obtain work in a precarious economy or to have a fair and just working environment.

A transformative approach to self-motivation might include identifying collective aspirations that are shared with and supported by others, and which are oriented toward achieving more just and sustainable livelihoods. Such aspirations take into account, as Appadurai (2004) has argued, that notions of the future are situated within the interactive and contested spaces of culture, or what young people can be and do with their family, peers, and community. Critical to the process of identifying collective aspirations is to develop a sense of them being shared, and if they are not shared, then there needs to be the space for debate about how to address the obstacles to achieving them. While not all collective aspirations are achieved, the process of identifying and working together on goals allows youth to support each other emotionally, socially, and even financially. Tzenis' (2019) study of Somali youth in the US offers pedagogical practices for how aspirations can be identified and discussed in relation to collective concerns of families, communities, and young people. She used an identity wheel to help youth discern what was important to them, and how these different identities related to their future aspirations. In this case, a youth's goal to pursue further education and become a doctor was informed by the needs and the history of her family and of Somali refugees; these goals did not come solely from within. While becoming a doctor may or may not be eventually achieved, her goals were supported by her family and other youth who shared similar aspirations for how they would use their education to help others.

Responsibility is another core skill included in life skills education programs to achieve various outcomes, including employment/livelihoods, peace, and sustainable development. Honeyman et al. (Chap. 6, this volume) note it as one of the key skills identified in the USAID study on youth workforce success. Teaching responsibility includes attending to related skills like self-control (over one's behaviors), as well as values that support youth to engage in pro-social, or socially acceptable and responsible behavior (see Brush et al., Chap. 3, this volume, on these related values). But teaching responsibility to young people who face injustices and precarity is based upon the assumption that certain kinds of pro-social behaviors – such as the skill to take care of oneself – will fix the failures of the economic, social and political systems that have left some youth marginalized.

A transformative life skill would be responsible solidarity, or reciprocity among people living and working together, which contrasts with an individualized notion of responsibility (Miller & Rose, 2008). Reframing this skill as reciprocity orients one toward caring for others, and in turn, one is also cared for (see more below on solidarity, which is a related life skill). This notion of reciprocity is also grounded in the ethos of *ubuntu,* discussed above, as a way to reframe life skills as relational. As such, reciprocity requires a different value orientation to how youth think about themselves and others, and how they can achieve a good life. Much education, and particularly life skills education for employability and entrepreneurship, teaches a young person to take responsibility for their own employment, to care for themselves, and to ensure their own wellbeing. Reciprocity requires thinking about and engaging with others to improve a collective wellbeing, including generating and sharing wealth together. Yet, as both Brush et al. (Chap. 3, this volume) and Kwauk (Chap. 5, this volume) find in their review of life skills programs, many do not attend to values that are needed to address today's societal problems. Or certain values, such as competition and individual advancement, are implicitly fostered through such skills training when developing responsibility. Furthermore, from our studies in East Africa and India, the value of reciprocity is already part of daily life, but it needs to be strengthened among youth who are marginalized. Kwauk (Chap. 5, this volume) also proposes the related skill of giving back, or of sharing knowledge and skills to contribute to the community, which was promoted in some sports life skills programs.

Positive attitude is another desired characteristic for youth that enables their participation in society as good citizens. Brush et al. (Chap. 3, this volume) and Kwauk (Chap. 5, this volume) refer to this as a perspective of optimism, and how we view and approach the world. An individualized approach, however, places the onus on young people to create a positive attitude, or to feel optimistic, even when life is filled with violence, discrimination, and uncertainty. And yet whether a youth has a positive attitude is certainly influenced by the possibilities and opportunities, or lack therefore, available to them. A transformational approach to this skill is fostering hope. Hope is future-oriented, based in a shared sense of a better world. Hope is not only an internal perspective or feeling; it is cultivated through relationships. Mains' (2012) study of young Ethiopian men illustrates that hope for their future is embedded in a complex network of relationships in which they are regarded as dignified through social and economic relationships with others. Through these relationships, they can maintain hope for their future. Without these relationships that shape who they are and can be, they are deemed hopeless, future-less, and without dignity. Mains (2012) also shows how an orientation that fosters hope through social relationships contrasts with the current economic and social order that glorifies individualized self-esteem and privately-owned wealth, thereby producing inequalities. Hope, like dignity, collective aspirations, and reciprocity, needs to be cultivated through life skills education by discussing values and fostering relationships that are important for a good life. Kwauk's chapter adds some important perspectives that need to be cultivated that may also foster hope, including resourcefulness to navigate barriers and map out opportunities, and understanding and using power effectively. These skills offer a way to negotiate challenges toward living life well.

Empathy is included in most life skills programs as a component of emotional skills. Brush et al. (Chap. 3, this volume) include it in their mapping of life skills programs as managing emotions in relation to others and responding to others in pro-social ways. Empathy, therefore, has both an affective and cognitive component for understanding how someone else is feeling (Lippman et al., 2015). But in their review of studies on the relationship of empathy with violence, Lippman et al. (2013) find that the affective element is more important than the cognitive understanding of another person's life. The focus on empathy in life skills programs is often directed at others, and yet for marginalized youth, they may be the victims of such violence. For instance, Honeyman et al. (Chap. 6, this volume) note that a program for victims of violence had to shift their focus so that the young people not only learned how to adapt to others, but also how to prioritize their own health and safety.

A transformational approach to empathy considers the relations that inhibit a young person from living life well. This can be fostered through the value and behaviors of solidarity. Solidarity means that one's life and wellbeing is intimately connected with others' wellbeing. It is more than the ability to understand another's feelings; it requires seeing how another's experiences are connected with one's own and then taking actions of care to challenge injustices. For example, youth in East Africa who participated in a life skills program to foster livelihoods/entrepreneurship exemplified this value. When they were able to earn from their work, they often spoke about using their earnings to help others who couldn't earn at that time. They felt empathy – an understanding of another's situation – but they also valued and acted upon the idea of solidarity, or the sense that if they care for someone now, they will also be cared for in the future and everyone will have a better life. To cultivate this value and behaviors, educational pedagogies and activities can focus on care and solidarity to show how our lives are intertwined with and affected by one another. Zembylas et al. (2014) show how such care can be fostered through critical pedagogies; they argue that care links concepts of power, emotion, and responsibility to change social and economic structures that inhibit living a good life.

In sum, reconceptualizing these life skills is an attempt to reconsider the underlying values and assumptions of self-esteem, responsibility, and self-motivation, among others, which place an onus on youth's individual behaviors and efforts to achieve living life well. These individualistic life skills may be important in some contexts and for achieving certain outcomes, but they are not sufficient to transform the social, economic, and environmental precarity and inequalities that affect so many youth's lives. This orientation is also not incompatible with many of the life skills programs discussed in this book. These chapters have illustrated the important need to contextualize life skills within the broader social and cultural values of a society, as well as with regard to the specific inequalities that affect youth.

If life skills education programs are to achieve the SDG goals set out in target 4.7 that reference knowledge and skills for sustainable development, including sustainable livelihoods, gender equality, and peace, then we need to think about and enact transformative social learning, as Lotz-Sisitka et al. (2015) have called for. This requires more than individually learning knowledge, skills, and attitudes; it requires shifting our ways of thinking about education as it interfaces with society, and the specific pedagogies and practices we use. Finally, teaching life skills from this relational perspective means they are applicable to all children and youth to live life well, not only those who are marginalized in an effort to catch them up or get them out of poverty. If living life well includes how we relate to others in our communities, including the material and ecological environment, then developing collective aspirations, hope, solidarity, and dignity are important life skills for all of us.

Acknowledgements I would like to thank Dr. Aditi Arur for her valuable insights and contributions to a study of life skills for girls in India, and Drs. David Chapman, Nancy Pellowski Wiger, and Acacia Nikoi for their contributions and ideas related to a study of youth livelihoods in East Africa. My thanks also go to the many colleagues who contributed to these studies. Finally, much appreciation to colleagues at the UC Berkeley workshop on girls' life skills; the University of Free State, South Africa's symposium on a capability approach; and Bristol University's workshop on Transforming Educational Systems for Sustainable Development workshop, where ideas for this chapter have been shared.

References

Alcid, A. (2014). *A randomized control trial of Akazi Kanoze youth in rural Rwanda*. Education Development Center. https://www.edc.org/randomized-controlled-trial-akazi-kanoze-youth-rural-rwanda

Appadurai, A. (2004). The capacity to aspire: Culture and the terms of recognition. In V. Rao & M. Walton (Eds.), *Culture and public action* (pp. 59–84). Stanford University Press.

Arur, A., & DeJaeghere, J. (2019). Decolonizing a girls' education program in Brahminical India: A Dalit Bahujan perspective. *Gender and Education, 31*(4), 490–507. https://doi.org/10.1080/09540253.2019.1594707

Blattman, C., Jamison, J. C., & Sheridan, M. (2015). *Reducing crime and violence: Experimental evidence on adult noncognitive investments in Liberia*. National Bureau of Economic Research.

Butterwick, S., & Benjamin, A. (2006). The road to employability through personal development: A critical analysis of the silences and ambiguities of the British Columbia (Canada) life skills curriculum. *International Journal of Lifelong Education, 25*(1), 75–86.

Chisamya, G., DeJaeghere, J., Kendall, N., & Khan, M. A. (2012). Gender and education for all: Progress and problems in achieving gender equity. *International Journal of Educational Development, 32*(6), 743–755.

Correa, B., & Murphy-Graham, E. (2019). Everything has a beginning and an end and we are on our way: Transformative agency in the Colombian preparation for social action program. In R. Aman & T. Ireland (Eds.), *Educational Alternatives in Latin America* (pp. 89–112). Palgrave Macmillan.

DeJaeghere, J. (2017). *Educating entrepreneurial citizens: Neoliberalism and youth livelihoods in Tanzania*. Routledge.

DeJaeghere, J. (2019a). Reconceptualizing educational capabilities: A relational capability theory for redressing inequalities. *Journal of Human Development and Capabilities, 21*(1), 17–35. https://doi.org/10.1080/19452829.2019.1677576

DeJaeghere, J. (2019b). A capability pedagogy for excluded youth: Fostering recognition and imagining alternative futures. *Education, Citizenship and Social Justice*. https://doi.org/10.1177/1746197919886859

DeJaeghere, J., Pellowski Wiger, N., & Willemsen, L. W. (2016). Broadening educational outcomes: Social relations, skills development, and employability for youth. *Comparative Education Review, 60*(3), 457–479.

DeJaeghere, J., Morris, E., & Bamattre, R. (2019). Moving beyond employment and earnings: Reframing how youth livelihoods and wellbeing are evaluated in East Africa. *Journal of Youth Studies, 23*(5), 667–685. https://doi.org/10.1080/13676261.2019.1636013

Dupuy, K., Bezu, S., Knudsen, A., Halvorsen, S., Kwauk, C., Braga, A., & Kim, H. (2018*). Life skills in non-formal contexts for adolescent girls in developing countries*. CMI & Brookings Institution. https://www.brookings.edu/wp-content/uploads/2018/04/life-skills-in-non-formal-contexts-for-adolescent.pdf

Ferguson, J. (2013). Declarations of dependence: Labour, personhood, and welfare in southern Africa. *Journal of the Royal Anthropological Institute, 19*(2), 223–242.

Gates, S.,Lippman, L., Shadowen, N., Burke, H., Diener, O., & Malkin, M. (2016). *Youthpower action: Key soft skills for cross-sectoral youth outcomes*. USAID. https://www.fhi360.org/sites/default/files/media/documents/resource-soft-skills-report.pdf

Heckman, J. J., Stixrud, J., & Urzua, S. (2006). The effects of cognitive and noncognitive abilities on labor market outcomes and social behavior. *Journal of Labor economics, 24*(3), 411–482.

Heller, S. (2014). Summer jobs reduce violence among disadvantaged youth. *Science, 346*(6214), 1219–1223.

Herrenkohl, T. I., Lee, J., & Hawkins, J. D. (2012). Risk versus direct protective factors and youth violence: Seattle social development project. *American Journal of Preventive Medicine, 43*(2), 41–56.

Herz, B., & Sperling, G. B. (2004). *What works in girls' education: Evidence and policies from the developing world*. Council on Foreign Relations.

International Labour Organization. (2015). *Advancing social justice, promoting decent work*. https://www.ilo.org/global/topics/decent-work/lang%2D%2Den/index.htm

J-PAL. (2017). *Skills for youth program review paper*. Abdul Latif Jameel Poverty Action Lab. https://www.povertyactionlab.org/sites/default/files/documents/Youth%20Initiative%20 Review%20Paper%20Executive%20Summary.pdf

Kabeer, N. (1999). Resources, agency, achievements: Reflections on the measurement of women's empowerment. *Development and Change, 30*, 435–464.

Kautz, T., Heckman, J. J., Diris, R., ter Weel, B., & Borghans, L. (2014). *Fostering and measuring skills: Improving cognitive and non-cognitive skills to promote lifetime success* (National Bureau of Economic Research Working Paper No. 20749). https://www.nber.org/papers/w20749

Kelly, L. (2019). *Preventing and countering violent extremism*. K4D. https://assets.publishing.service.gov.uk/media/5db80ed1e5274a4aa423ea2d/668_lessons_from_CVE.pdf

Kwauk, C., & Braga, A. (2017). *Translating competencies to empowered action: A framework for linking girls' life skills education to social change*. Center for Universal Education at Brookings Institution. https://www.brookings.edu/research/translating-competencies-to-empowered-action/

Le Grange, L. (2012). Ubuntu, ukama and the healing of nature, self and society. *Educational Philosophy and Theory, 44*(2), 56–67.

Lefebvre, E., Nikoi, A., Bamattre, R., Jafaar, A., Morris, E., Chapman, D., & DeJaeghere, J. (2018). *Getting ahead and getting by in youth livelihoods and employment.*. The Mastercard Foundation. https://mastercardfdn.org/research/getting-ahead-and-getting-by-exploring-outcomes-of-youth-livelihoods-programs/

Levinson, B., Foley, D., & Holland, D. (1996). *The cultural production of the educated person: Critical ethnographies of schooling and local practice*. State University of New York.

Lippman, L. H., Ryberg, R., Terzian, M., Moore, K. A., Humble, J., & McIntosh, H. (2013). Positive and protective factors in adolescent well-being. In B. Asher, F. Casas, I. Frones, & J. E. Korbin (Eds.), *The handbook of child well-being: Theories, methods, and policies in global perspective* (pp. 2823–2866). Springer.

Lippman, L. H., Ryberg, R., Carney, R., & Moore, K. A. (2015). *Key "soft skills" that foster youth workforce success: Toward a consensus across fields*. Child Trends. https://www.childtrends.org/wp-content/uploads/2015/06/2015-24WFCSoftSkills1.pdf

Lotz-Sisitka, H., Wals, A. E., Kronlid, D., & McGarry, D. (2015). Transformative, transgressive social learning: Rethinking higher education pedagogy in times of systemic global dysfunction. *Current Opinion in Environmental Sustainability, 16*, 73–80. https://doi.org/10.1016/j.cosust.2015.07.018

Mains, D. (2012). *Hope is cut: Youth, unemployment, and the future in urban Ethiopia*. Temple University Press.

Maithreyi, R. (2017). Childhood as 'risky' and life as 'skills'. In T. S. Saraswathi, S. Menon, & A. Madan (Eds.), *Childhoods in India: Traditions, trends and transformations* (pp. 252–274). Taylor & Francis.

Maithreyi, R. (2019). Children's reconstruction of psychological knowledge: An ethnographic study of life skills education programmes in India. *Childhood, 26*(1), 68–82.

Miller, P., & Rose, N. (2008). *Governing the present: Administering economic, social and personal life*. Polity.

Mirdrikvand, F., Ghadampour, E., & Kavarizadeh, M. (2016). The effect of life skills training on psychological capital and adaptability of adolescent girls with irresponsible parents. *Quarterly Journal of Social Work, 5*(3), 23–30.

Moeller, K. (2014). Searching for adolescent girls in Brazil: The transnational politics of poverty in "The girl effect". *Feminist Studies, 40*(3), 575–601.

Mohanty, C. T. (2003). *Feminism without borders: Decolonizing theory, practicing solidarity.* Duke University Press.

Murphy-Graham, E. (2012). *Opening minds, improving lives: Education and women's empowerment in Honduras.* Vanderbilt University Press.

National Research Council. (2012). *Education for life and work: Developing transferable knowledge and skills in the 21st century.* The National Academies Press. https://doi.org/10.17226/13398

Olenik, C., & Fawcett, C. (2013). *State of the field report: Examining the evidence in youth workforce development.* USAID. https://www.usaid.gov/sites/default/files/documents/1865/USAID%20state%20of%20the%20field%20youth%20workforce%20development%20final%202_11.pdf

Paghale, Z., Paghale, S., Jadidi Feighan, M., & Nazary, M. (2014). The effect of life skills training on social adjustment and academic performance of adolescent female students. *Knowledge and Research in Applied Psychology, 15*(4), 121–129.

Reed, M., Evely, A., Cundill, G., Fazey, I., Glass, J., Laing, A., Newig, J., Parrish, B., Prell, C., Raymond, C., & Stringer, L. (2010). What is social learning? *Ecology and Society, 15*(4), r1. http://www.ecologyandsociety.org/vol15/iss4/resp1/

Schultz, T. P. (2002). Why governments should invest more to educate girls. *World Development, 30*(2), 207–225.

Spivak, G. C. (1988). Can the subaltern speak? In C. Nelson & L. Grossberg (Eds.), *Marxism and the interpretation of culture* (pp. 272–313). University of Illinois Press.

Stromquist, N. P. (2015). Women's empowerment and education: Linking knowledge to transformative action. *European Journal of Education, 50*(3), 307–324.

Taft, J. K. (2010). *Rebel girls: Youth activism and social change across the Americas.* NYU Press.

Tzenis, J. A. (2019). Understanding youths' educational aspirations in the Somali diaspora. *Journal of Youth Development, 14*(2), 10–24.

UNICEF. (2012). *Global evaluation of life skills education programmes.* United Nations Children's Fund.

Vavrus, F. (2002). Constructing consensus: The feminist modern and the reconstruction of gender. *Current Issues in Comparative Education, 5*(1), 51–63.

Walker, M. (2012). A capital or capabilities education narrative in a world of staggering inequalities? *International Journal of Educational Development, 32*(3), 384–393. https://doi.org/10.1016/j.ijedudev.2011.09.003

World Health Organization. (1999). *Partners in life skills education: Conclusions from a United Nations inter-agency meeting.* WHO. https://www.who.int/mental_health/media/en/30.pdf

Zembylas, M., Bozalek, V., & Shefer, T. (2014). Tronto's notion of privileged irresponsibility and the reconceptualisation of care: Implications for critical pedagogies of emotion in higher education. *Gender and Education, 26*(3), 200–214.

Chapter 5
Empowering Girls Through Sport: A Gender Transformative Approach to Life Skills?

Christina Ting Kwauk

Abstract From the Pacific Islands to Sub-Saharan Africa, development organizations have positioned sport as an ideal tool for building important life skills that can be transferred from the playing field to day-to-day realities. Sport has also been positioned as a key space for girls' empowerment, especially in contexts where gender norms limit girls' mobility and/or their opportunities to engage in activities stereotyped as being for boys. But an approach that solely focuses on empowering girls through sport by depositing in her useful life skills ignores the structural conditions that have disempowered her in the first place. This chapter examines the gender transformative potential of sport-based life skills programs by exploring the skills that are being targeted, especially for girls' empowerment, by the sport for development (SFD) community. The chapter then examines the implications for our understanding of life skills approaches to gender transformative social change, particularly as it pertains to addressing the conditions that have held girls back.

Keywords Life skills · Sport · Gender · Education · Empowerment · Transformation

Acronyms

SFD   Sport for development
SEL   Social and emotional learning
KSA   Knowledge, skills and attitudes

C. T. Kwauk (✉)
The Brookings Institution, Washington, DC, USA

© The Author(s) 2022   91
J. DeJaeghere, E. Murphy-Graham (eds.), *Life Skills Education for Youth*, Young People and Learning Processes in School and Everyday Life 5,
https://doi.org/10.1007/978-3-030-85214-6_5

Introduction

Within the last two decades, there has been a proliferation of sport for development (SFD) programs in the Global South.[1] In 2013 there were less than 500 registered organizations on the International Platform on Sport and Development; today there are over 1000 (Kwauk, 2014). The growth of SFD has been grounded on two assumptions: (1) that sport is a 'powerful' tool for building important life skills that youth need to participate successfully in social, economic, and political life, and (2) that the skills learned on the playing field can transfer to non-sport contexts like school, home, or the workplace. Indeed, life skills development is often the core education component of any SFD program. However, whether SFD programs are accurately targeting the skills that youth need to achieve improved life outcomes remains to be determined.

Part of the problem faced by SFD organizations and their approaches to life skills is the perennial problem of definition. Much like life skills for other purposes, as indicated by Chaps. 2 and 3 of this volume, the literature on life skills development and sport is centered around studies in the Global North interrogating *how life skills are developed* through participation in sport (see for example, Holt et al., 2009; Jones & Lavallee, 2009; Pierce et al., 2016; Theoka et al., 2008). Few studies have actually investigated which life skills are targeted and developed in the context of sport, especially in the context of SFD programs targeting vulnerable populations in the Global South. Indeed, many of the critiques surrounding SFD approaches to life skills development are bolstered by the fact that SFD programs vaguely define what they mean by life skills and are often uncritical in their adoption of the term (Darnell, 2012; Forde, 2014; Hayhurst, 2014). As a result, SFD programs often end up perpetuating the status quo by equipping youth with the skills to successfully navigate a predetermined world around them, rather than to reciprocate by influencing or radically transforming the world around them (Hartmann & Kwauk, 2011).

This chapter aims to better understand this normative-transformative gap by exploring how SFD programs conceptualize life skills, especially when girls' empowerment is a core desired outcome. Considering nearly half of SFD programs target girls and women (Hancock et al., 2013), it is incumbent upon the field to tackle the question of definition and scope to ensure that programs for girls' empowerment through life skills development are working in a way that is transformative rather than placing the onus of change on the shoulders of girls (Moeller, 2018). This chapter examines a selection of SFD programs that have a strong girls' empowerment focus to understand the possibilities as well as the limitations of current sport-based approaches to girls' life skills development.

---

[1] UNICEF, an early adopter of sport-based approaches to life skills development, defines sport for development as "the use of sport, or any form of physical activity, to provide both children and adults with the opportunity to achieve their full potential through initiatives that promote personal and social development" (UNICEF, 2019, p. 7).

Theoretical Framework

SFD organizations can be categorized in two ways when it comes to their approaches to education and development: normative and transformative (Hartmann & Kwauk, 2011). One way includes organizations that take an unintentional and uncritical approach to education through sport—or in this case a normative approach to life skills education through sport—where the theory of change rests on normative assumptions and stereotypes about "the power of sport" to teach skills like teamwork, communication, and goal orientation. Such a dominant approach functions to reproduce neoliberal logics in which the individual, especially those from "at-risk" and "marginalized" populations who may need support on their journey to becoming "model citizens," is expected to bear the brunt of modern government by pulling themselves up by the bootstraps through an instrumentalist, individualistic regimen of self-discipline, self-development, and self-management (Harvey, 2005; Ferguson, 1994; see also DeJaeghere, Chap. 4, this volume). Although the end goal may be to achieve transformation (e.g., the achievement of gender equality, the elimination of gender-based violence, girls' empowerment), a dominant approach operates through the recalibration—or the re-skilling—of the individual, having little do at the end of the day with changing the conditions that put the individual at risk or in marginal positions in society.

Another approach is when organizations take a more transformative approach aimed at altering the conditions of inequality that have marginalized populations in the first place. The theory of change here rests on the notion that sporting contexts create the necessary and sufficient conditions for social change. That is, through a purposeful and critical design, youth must have the opportunity to understand the broader structures of power and privilege in which they are embedded. They must learn to decode the dominant culture with the aim to transform not only their own experiences in the world, but also the world itself. The development of life skills, then, is a process of critical reflection and action that enables individual and collective meaning-making and resistance against hegemonic structures, including especially the recognition of structures and relations of power and how these inform youth experiences and opportunities in life. Such a "radical interventionist" approach does not assume that life skills passively or automatically materialize through participation in sport, however. Rather, it requires that an approach to life skills education entails proactively recognizing, challenging, and transforming structures of inequality, oppression, and exploitation.

Girls' empowerment and gender equality have been popular targets for many SFD organizations since sport for development and peace emerged as a "new" social movement during the Millennium Development Goals era (Kidd, 2008). In earlier work (Hartmann & Kwauk, 2011), we did not take into consideration how attention to girls' empowerment could at once engender a transformative approach aimed at destabilizing harmful gender stereotypes and relations of power, yet still be firmly rooted in the dominant logics of neoliberalism (Chawansky & Hayhurst, 2015). That is, SFD programs may promise to liberate women from patriarchal oppression only to position them squarely in another, less visible social and economic system of oppression (Forde & Frisby, 2015; Hayhurst, 2014). Such a confluence of transformation and reproduction remind us that the development project can easily bend a radical agenda toward a neoliberal one.

The conceptual framework that informs this chapter builds upon this earlier work to identify the gap between life skills programs that result in neoliberal outcomes of self-improvement and those that achieve more radical, transformative social change (Kwauk & Braga, 2017). A starting assumption is that life skills are understood as a combination of knowledge (K, what one knows), skills (S, what one has), and attitudes (A, what one believes and values). Together, these form a set of competencies (what one can do) that the individual should be able to activate in any given situation (represented by the image of KSA networks in the brain in Fig. 5.1). If the development of life skills is intended to lead to empowered, liberatory action, the approach must take into consideration the individual's relationship to the sociopolitical contexts and cultural structures in which she is embedded historically, in the present, and in the possible future (represented by the figure of the girl on the right). This relationship comes to bear during the process of translating competencies into action (represented by the long arrow) as her ability to apply life skills in a manner that improves her outcomes is mediated by what we call opportunity structures (represented by the second image in the series) in her environment, like policies, institutions, and social networks. Such opportunity structures, in combination with her sense of agency (represented by the third image in the series) and whether her agency is recognized by others (represented by the back and forth arrow), act as opposing or supporting forces that could inhibit or enable her ability to translate competencies into action.

With this understanding in mind, a dominant approach to girls' life skills education, as also discussed in DeJaeghere's chapter (Chap. 4, this volume), would be characterized as one that focuses solely on depositing (and measuring) knowledge and skills within the individual girl in an effort to put her at a more equal starting point as her more privileged peers within an existing system. In contrast, a transformative approach would attend to the metacognitive elements of equipping girls with the tools to read, decode, and act upon the opportunity structures around her, as well as the sociological elements of building collective resistance against conditions of

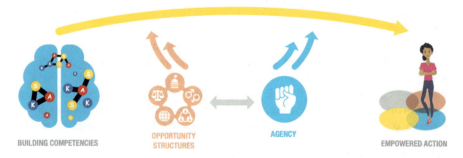

Fig. 5.1 Mediating the translation of competencies to empowered action

inequality. Drawing upon frameworks discussed in Hartmann and Kwauk (2011) and Kwauk and Braga (2017), this chapter aims to understand whether SFD programs focused on girls' empowerment are contributing to the reproduction or to the transformation of the conditions holding girls back from achieving their full potential.

Methodology

This paper draws on an analysis of 10 life skills approaches[2] guiding SFD programs delivered by 7 globally recognized SFD organizations[3]: ChildFund's Pass It Back, Futuremakers by Standard Chartered, Grassroots Soccer, Moving the Goalposts, Right To Play, Soccer Without Borders, and Women Win. Each SFD organization's life skills approach was analyzed in two steps.

First, to understand the breadth of skills being targeted and to compare different constructions of skills across different programs, skills were given one or more codes from the Explore SEL coding scheme.[4] For this particular analysis, the 177 "benchmarks" for each of the six domains (cognitive, emotion, social, values, perspectives, and identity) identified in the Explore SEL tools were used to code skills mentioned explicitly in the SFD programs' life skills documents.[5] In the event that the organization did not have an actual life skills framework, program curricula and/or monitoring and evaluation tools were used instead. When coding the latter, only explicitly stated learning objectives, learning outcomes, or behavioral descriptors were coded; lesson overviews and activity descriptions were excluded due to time limitations. A focus on stated objectives or outcomes—where a life skills framework was absent—helped to ensure parameters were in place to conservatively interpret organizational intent with regard to targeted skills.

In the first analysis, some skills were not codable using the Taxonomy's coding scheme. This was a limitation that fortuitously provided an opportunity for a secondary inductive analysis of the remaining life skills. Specifically, the "leftover,"

---

[2] For simplicity, the term life skills approach will be used herein to refer to the programmatic documents included in this study, including life skills frameworks, program curricula, program descriptions, theories of change or logic models, and monitoring and evaluation tools, depending on what was made available by the organization.

[3] For the purposes of this analysis, I will use the term SFD organization when referencing the seven organizations and programs included in this study, whether or not the organization formally identifies this way.

[4] See Chap. 3 (Brush et al., this volume) for an overview of the Explore SEL project.

[5] See http://exploresel.gse.harvard.edu/compare-terms/ for the Taxonomy Project's benchmarks used to code life skills in this analysis. For ease of analysis, this paper adopts the Taxonomy Project's conceptualization of life skills as being defined by domains of socioemotional learning and codable by observable behavioral benchmarks. As such, this may miss other domains of life skills, including knowledge, skills, and attitudes important for catalyzing social change, which we discuss in Kwauk and Braga (2017).

un-codable skills were analyzed to generate new sub-domain categories of skills that are conceptualized more towards gender transformative outcomes for girls.

Second, to understand the normative and transformative elements of the life skills approaches, a more in-depth analysis was conducted of all the targeted skills identified in the first analysis. Targeted skills were coded as being normative, transformative, or context-dependent based on the description of the skill given by the life skills document. Skills were coded as normative if the outcome associated with it could be characterized as putting the girl at a more equal starting point as her male peers in a pre-existing system or enabling a girl to function more successfully within existing social structures. An example of a normative skill would be "listening to what others have to say without interrupting them." Such skills could be interpreted as coming from a dominant approach to girls' life skills education where even a girls' empowerment approach could be instrumentalized toward achieving a more individualistic, neoliberal agenda of self-improvement rather than serve as a mechanism for transforming relations of power.

In contrast, skills were coded as transformative if the outcome associated with it could be characterized as equipping girls with the tools to read, decode, and act upon the opportunity structures or existing social structures around her in ways that enable her to fulfill her own desired outcome(s) rather than what is expected of her because of her gender. For example, "identify how society's definition of girlhood leads to oppression of women and girls" or "navigating power and gender relationships" are skills that could be interpreted as coming from a more transformative approach, attending more to the metacognitive elements of "reading" one's world to be better positioned to transform it.

Some descriptions of skills were less clear in terms of their normative or transformative intention. For instance, "having a support system of people who model positive behavior and support you" could be interpreted as building a network of peers that help you ascribe to socially acceptable norms of good behavior (a normative outcome) or as building allies to engage in collective resistance against conditions of inequality. Such ambiguous skills were coded as "context-dependent."

Table 5.1 provides a brief overview of the life skills programs included in this analysis, all of which use either a sport-based or play-based curriculum to deliver life skills education. Programs were selected for inclusion based on convenience of access to both program materials (e.g. has a substantive online presence) and program staff, as well as purposefully to ensure geographic diversity and diversity of targeted outcome (e.g. economic empowerment, gender equality, and improved sexual and reproductive health, education, or employment opportunities) (see Table 5.2 for an overview of program targeted outcomes). Curricular or program documents were collected by the author from either the organization's website or through personal communication with program staff.

All programs either target girls specifically, place a special emphasis on the participation of marginalized, vulnerable, or disadvantaged girls, or take special measures to ensure girls are recruited to participate in equal numbers as boys and that programs are delivered in gender-sensitive and inclusive ways. Right To Play extends its focus on gender beyond girls, looking to also promote "positive

Table 5.1 Overview of SFD life skills programs included in this study

Organization	Life skills program	Program start year	Age range targeted	Targets girls only?	Type of girl targeted	Program setting	Dosage	Delivery mechanism	Country
Futuremakers by Standard Chartered	GOAL (Employability and Entrepreneurship)	2006	12–18 years	Yes; a few markets include boys	Girls in underserved communities	Through sport-based NGO partners	Weekly, over 10 months	Play-based curriculum	23+ countries
Grassroots Soccer	SKILLZ (Peace Corps SKILLZ and SKILLZ Girls Zambia)	2010; 2013	Peace Corps SKILLS: 9–19 years; SKILLZ Girls Zambia: 14–19 years	Peace Corps SKILLZ: No, but includes a special emphasis on girls SKILLZ Girls Zambia: Yes	SKILLZ Girls Zambia: At-risk adolescent girls from historically disadvantaged and economically marginalized communities	After-school at school facilities	12 90-min sessions	Soccer-based curriculum	Global; Zambia
Moving the Goalposts	MTG Leadership Curriculum	2002	9–25 years	Yes	Vulnerable girls and young women (school-based and out of school) in rural and urban areas	Public spaces (e.g. soccer pitch)	N/A	Soccer-based curriculum	Kenya

(continued)

Table 5.1 (continued)

Organization	Life skills program	Program start year	Age range targeted	Targets girls only?	Type of girl targeted	Program setting	Dosage	Delivery mechanism	Country
ChildFund, World Rugby, Asia Rugby	Pass It Back	2015	11–16 years	No, but includes a special emphasis on girls	N/A	Out of school	32 sessions over 6–8 months	Rugby-based curriculum	Cambodia, Laos, Philippines, Timor Leste, Vietnam
Right To Play	Holistic Child Development Framework	2000	2 to 18+ years	No, but includes a special emphasis on girls	N/A	In schools and after school	Weekly	Play-based curriculum with 2 modalities of explicit and implicit skill building	15 countries across Africa, Asia, the Middle East, and North America
Soccer Without Borders	Soccer Without Borders	2007	5–23 years	No, but includes a special emphasis on girls	Nicaragua program targets only girls	N/A	N/A	Soccer clubs	Nicaragua, Uganda, United States
Women Win	Leadership competencies and Transferable skills from the Leadership and Economic Empowerment Pathway (LEEP) Framework	2011	10–18, with a special emphasis on 10–14 years	Yes	Most marginalized adolescent girls	Through sport-based NGO partners	N/A	Targeted sport of the implementing NGO	100+ countries across Africa, Asia, the Middle East, and North and South America

Table 5.2 Targeted outcomes of sport-based life skills education programs

Life skills program	Targeted outcome areas
Standard Chartered's GOAL Program (Employability and Entrepreneurship)	Health (hygiene, sexual and reproductive health, and menstrual hygiene management) Self-confidence (communications and valuing what it means to "be a girl") Empowerment (rights, freedom from violence, access to resources/institutions and social networks in the community) Economic empowerment (financial literacy, employment, and entrepreneurship)
Grassroots Soccer (Peace Corps SKILLZ and Girls SKILLZ Zambia)	Assets (increased health knowledge and the confidence to use it) Access (increased uptake of high-quality health services) Adherence (adherence to medical treatment, therapy, and healthy behaviors)
Moving the Goalposts Leadership Curriculum	Education (scholarships) Sexual and reproductive health and rights Livelihoods (skills for financial independence)
Child Fund Pass It Back	Rugby knowledge and sport skills Leadership development (voice, confidence, vision, ability to drive change, resilience) Safety (healthy and positive relationships, awareness and prevention of violence, taking action and providing support) Planning for the future (planning and setting goals, risks and positive behaviors, understanding community resources) Understanding gender (gender roles, rights, violence, peer pressure)
Right To Play's Holistic Child Development Framework	Quality education Gender equality Child protection Peaceful communities Health and well-being
Soccer Without Borders	Growth (skills that break barriers, build girls' confidence and voice as leaders) Inclusion (build teams that feel like family) Personal success (help young women reach their goals; access a community of supportive peers and mentors)
Women Win (Leadership Framework and LEEP Transferable Skills Framework)	Decreased gender-based violence Improved sexual and reproductive health and rights (including service access) Increased girls' economic empowerment (education and entrepreneurial or career development)

masculinities by building boys' life skills around communication, expressing emotions and resolving conflicts peacefully" (Right To Play [RTP], 2018, p. 2). In contrast, Moving the Goalposts, while not explicitly involving boys, does recognize the need to engage boys in equal partnerships and participation with girls through friendly co-ed matches. Their approach, however, views such engagement as opportunities for girls to learn to negotiate public spaces that boys and men often dominate. Engaging boys, then, is less about intentionally shifting boys' gender attitudes and more about providing girls safe spaces to practice "claiming what is theirs" (Moving the Goalpost [MTG], 2019, p. 7). As such, girls' empowerment was either an explicitly stated goal or component of the program (e.g. Standard Chartered's GOAL Program includes a module on girls' empowerment), or an implicit goal as described by the organization's mission and objectives (e.g. Right To Play's website, righttoplay.com, states that "Play saves lives […] It gives girls the power to say no to unwanted sex, and make healthy decisions about their bodies and their futures.").

Findings: From Normative to Transformative Approaches

How have SFD programs approached girls' empowerment through life skills? To answer this, this section provides an overview of the breadth of skills targeted by sport-based life skills programs and suggests these programs may not differ much from non-sport programs that have leaned heavily toward a prosocial, self-improvement paradigm. If we look strictly at how SFD programs describe their targeted skills, the dominant normative approach of "fix the girl, not the system" is quite pervasive. Nevertheless, there is transformative potential as well in some of these constructions, of which programs should be made aware in order to help pivot the remainder of their targeted life skills toward more gender transformative outcomes.

Normative Constructions of Life Skills

Other studies have demonstrated that (non-sport) life skills programs place a heavy emphasis on social and interpersonal skills as well as on the acquisition of knowledge (c.f. Dupuy et al., 2018). This analysis confirms this trend, finding a heavy emphasis on skills within the Social and Emotion domains (constituting together approximately 43% of codable targeted skills), as well as a heavy emphasis on skills that fell under the Cognitive domain (approximately 26% of codable skills) (see Fig. 5.2). The cognitive emphasis can be partly explained by the conflation of knowledge with "life skills." This is not surprising, as many non-sport-based life skills programs define and target life skills according to the sector of the organization from which the program originates (Dupuy et al., 2018). As a result, learning

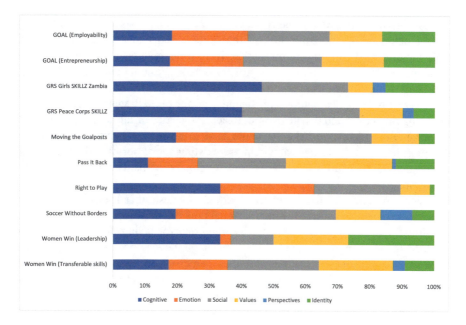

Fig. 5.2 Relative values of SFD programs' targeted life skills, by domain

objectives are heavily tied to content areas (or subject knowledge) core to the organization's mission rather than to the acquisition of skills. To illustrate, the GOAL
programs were spearheaded by Standard Chartered and have a strong focus on
financial literacy; their approach toward life skills tends to focus on acquiring
knowledge of banking services and effective business practices, and the development of cognitive skills like goal setting and problem solving. The SKILLZ programs reflects Grassroots Soccer's focus on adolescent sexual and reproductive
health; their approach toward life skills tends to focus on gaining knowledge about
HIV/AIDS and other sexually transmitted diseases and building cognitive skills like
planning and consequential thinking.

When it comes to interpersonal skills under the Social and Emotion domains,
sport-based life skills programs may be missing an important opportunity to orient
their programs toward more transformative ends. For instance, programs rarely target skills that could help increase girls' understanding of social cues. In fact, Social
skills that fall under "understanding social cues" constitute only 9% of coded skills
and dealt primarily with being able to interpret others' body language and tone of
voice in order to recognize hostile motivations or friendly intentions and to be able
to respond appropriately. Such an approach to understanding social cues is more
closely associated with emotional intelligence rather than with strengthening girls'
abilities to read her context (e.g. power cues or social opportunities) as a means of
determining how to translate, transfer, and apply life skills to different life situations
(Kwauk & Braga, 2017).

Instead, SFD life skills frameworks place a heavy emphasis on prosocial, cooperative behavior—comprising 88% of the skills coded under the Social domain. This includes skills to engage more effectively in teamwork, in building positive relationships, and to demonstrate respect for others. Without coupling such prosocial skills with, for instance, attention towards non-violent "anti-social" skills of a more civil disobedience nature (e.g. standing up for oneself against peer pressure, engaging in conflict and debate in order to achieve justice or fairness), such a heavy emphasis on cooperative behavior could lead to normative behavioral outcomes where girls are taught to behave within pre-existing social norms and expectations rather than to question social structures that may perpetuate oppressive gender norms.

Indeed, research on transformative learning suggests that life skills programs should pay more attention to the intrapersonal domains of Values, Perspectives, and Identity. Such domains may be critically important for laying the foundations for the kind of "epistemic learning" needed to change the way people think about and exist in the world and, therefore, how they perceive and interact with the world (O'Brien, 2018; Sterling, 2010). This would include actively deconstructing assumptions, beliefs, and values held about gender and gender roles, and the consequent gendered practices and structures that shape girls' and boys' experiences and influence their beliefs and interactions with each other.

However, in the analysis of codable skills (those targeted skills that could be coded using the Explore SEL coding scheme), it appears as though SFD programs are not paying attention to these domains. To illustrate, on average, only 2% of targeted life skills were coded under the Perspectives domain (e.g. openness to new ideas and new experiences). While the Values and Identity domains fared a little better (17% and 12% on average, respectively), the discrepancy in attention across domains (see Figure 5.2) suggest that there is not a clear consensus—or awareness—around the importance of these domains for life skills development. Consequently, the high attention to the Cognitive, Emotion, and Social domains and the scant attention paid to the Values, Perspectives, and Identities domains means that sport-based life skills programs are giving girls ample opportunity to develop skills to think and feel better and to be better with others, while giving girls little opportunity to critically reflect upon, make new meaning of, and resist social structures and social practices that may be stacking the cards against them.

Context-Dependent Constructions of Life Skills

Figure 5.3 provides a clearer illustration of the extent to which SFD programs approach life skills in a normative versus transformative way. Of all the targeted skills (N = 359) identified for this analysis, 74% were constructed in a normative manner—that is, intended to improve girls' self-development, self-management, and/or ability to function successfully in society. In stark contrast, only 4% of targeted skills were constructed in a transformative way—that is, aimed at enabling

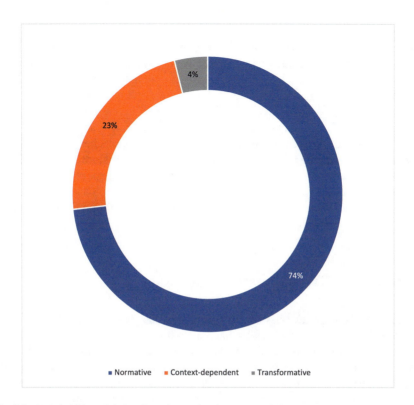

Fig. 5.3 Coded skills and their orientation to development and change

girls to alter the conditions of inequality and discrimination created on the basis of her gender.

Such a lopsided distribution suggests that individualistic, neoliberal logics about life skills dominate SFD programs. However, nearly a quarter of targeted skills were constructed in ways that were difficult to determine whether they were wholly normative or wholly transformative. Rather, these skills could be classified as context-dependent, depending on how programs contextualize and operationalize these targeted skills through program activities. More importantly, the outcomes of these skills are highly dependent on whether program staff emphasize their application as a means to become immune and resilient to sexist and patriarchal structures, or to challenge and resist them.

To illustrate, one type of skill or outcome area that SFD life skills frameworks targeted was the ability to access community services—in a sense, to embolden and empower girls to avail themselves of their right to services that can improve their health and well-being. In short, leveraging opportunity structures. Such a degree of awareness and resourcefulness could be normative—that is, seeking to put girls on equal footing as others in society. However, if combined with an emphasis on challenging discriminatory policies or exclusionary practices, this skill could be interpreted to be transformative. Another example is "seeing the possibility for change." Depending on how facilitators help girls to define change and the intended outcomes from that change, such a perspective could either help to norm girls and their aspirations to a socially defined "good life," or to help girls materialize a future of their own choosing.

While some programs' targeted skills contained more context-dependent skills than others—and some programs contained more normative approaches to skills than others—the span of normative to transformative approaches to life skills is a reminder that SFD programs are not monolithic. While the majority of their targeted life skills are aimed at equipping girls to better fit and successfully navigate their world, there is cause for optimism in the nuance that programs can be more radical. Specifically, there is room for programs to pivot toward enabling girls to see, challenge, and transform their world.

Toward More Transformative Possibilities

Based on a thematic analysis of the "uncodable" targeted life skills, this section proposes new sub-domains of skills that help to illustrate how life skills can be contextualized within a more transformative, feminist agenda (see Table 5.3). As mentioned earlier, the terms used for the new sub-domains and the descriptions of the observable skills were developed through an inductive analysis of the uncodable skills and learning objectives described in the curricular and framework documents.

For starters, under the Social domain, new sub-domains like "engaging difference" could work to counter the more normative skills that promote the socialization of marginalized groups into the dominant culture. "Reciprocity and solidarity," which captures the spirit of "giving back" that several programs emphasized, could ensure that skills are targeted that help to amplify or cascade individual empowerment to the collective level, building on the notion that structural change does not happen alone but rather through collective social change. Similarly, "partnerships and coalitions" could help distribute the onus of change from the individual girl to the collective. This new sub-domain emerges out of SFD programs' heavy emphasis on developing role models and peer mentors.

To address the need for more attention to intrapersonal skills that are foundational to transformative learning, this analysis generated five new sub-domains under the Perspectives and Identity domains that are not only targeted at reading the world but also actively engaging it. Two of these sub-domains (resistance and power) were particularly prominent in the list of uncodable life skills. This includes things like being aware of how gender norms can be oppressive, understanding ways to help others break free of gender stereotypes, increasing understanding about how power manifests in relationships, and how to make joint decisions about things that affect more than oneself. Such attention to issues of gender and power have been demonstrated in the literature to be important for improving girls' reproductive health outcomes (Haberland, 2015). Integrating such skills into our

Table 5.3 New sub-domains for a more gender transformative life skills taxonomy

Domain of SEL	New sub-domain	Observable skill
Social	Engaging difference	Communicates and engages effectively with others from different backgrounds (e.g., gender, sexual orientation, religion, caste, race, etc.) Recognizes one's own value and experiences, and the unique contributions that one can make in a group as a result of one's difference, and vice versa (e.g., that others are unique and have valuable contributions to make as a result)
	Reciprocity and solidarity	Understands the importance of "passing it back" to the community (e.g., shares new knowledge and skills with others) Shows solidarity with those who have given them support or invested in their growth and development
	Partnerships and coalitions	Can recognize good qualities (e.g., leadership, positive influence) in others Can recognize how a relationship (e.g., between mentee and mentor) could be helpful and/or strategic Can build social assets and social networks that can be beneficial in their life
Perspectives	Resourcefulness	Aware of barriers to access to key resources, services, and institutions in the community and can identify strategies for overcoming such barriers Can map out opportunities, both present and in the future
	Resistance	Understand social expectations and their sources (e.g., family, friends, media, etc.) Aware of how dominant, hegemonic scripts (e.g., traditional gender norms, patriarchy) can limit people from achieving their full potential Can identify ways to push back against hegemony and write new, liberating and empowering social scripts
	Power	Understands and can map power dynamics within social units (e.g., intimate partnerships, the household, community) Can effectively, strategically, and safely negotiate unequal power dynamics with others, especially those with more "power over" or "power to" Shares decision making power with an intimate partner and/or with others
Identity	Self-awareness	Recognizes how others may be perceiving their communication, expression of emotions, or body language Can identify and articulate one's skills, strengths, and talents, as well as weaknesses and areas for development to others
	Self-advocacy	Aware of their rights, beliefs, needs, and accomplishments, and are willing and motivated to speak up and to speak out in defense of or in promotion of these

understanding of life skills would help to ensure that more programs actively think about these competencies in their design.

To address the absence of "anti-social" skills of a civil disobedience nature, this analysis generated several sub-domains focused on resisting and challenging social structures. This includes a self-advocacy sub-domain under the Identity domain to ensure that girls develop the ability to speak up and speak out on behalf of themselves, their rights, their needs, their beliefs, and their accomplishments and successes. While the Taxonomy Project includes attention to whether the individual stands up for him or herself (and others) in the face of peer pressure or bullying, this focus does not get at the underlying intention of many SFD programs to combat negative self-image and to give girls voice by granting them permission to own up to their achievements, beliefs, and rights in contexts where they are taught early on that they are not of value or worth because of their gender. In a way, these new sub-domains capture what could be described as "empowerment skills," at least in terms of the behaviors that one could expect of an "empowered" (read: outspoken) girl.

While these 8 new sub-domains synthesize what was left uncoded after the initial analysis of SFD life skills frameworks, existing skills within the remaining domains of Cognitive, Emotion, and Values could also be made more gender transformative. For example, one could argue that the Cognitive domain's critical thinking sub-domain could include new benchmarks that capture skills like the ability to understand and recognize unequal power relations or to hear what is "unspoken," as well as to include additional sub-domains like strategic thinking. The Values domain could include attention toward ethical uses of power that do not violate the rights of others, or a focus on understanding and taking action toward challenging harmful (gender, racial, class, religious, ability) stereotypes, or even more foundational beliefs in the importance of solidarity, social justice, gender equality, and the equal value of all human beings. The possibilities are endless. What this analysis of SFD approaches to life skills education for girls demonstrates is how contextualizing life skills within a critical feminist agenda could help shift dominant understandings of life skills toward more transformative ends.

Limitations and Opportunities for Further Insight

There were three limitations inherent to this analysis. The first limitation was technical: the analysis was limited by the scope of the documents that could be included. Because not every organization included in this study has a life skills framework guiding their life skills program, other documents like coaching guides, program curriculum, and monitoring and evaluation tools were included instead. Generalizations about program intent and targeted skills should thus be understood with this caveat. In addition, whether program implementation is aligned with these documents or whether targeted skills are actually developed are matters beyond the focus of this analysis on the conceptualization of life skills by program documents.

The second limitation was one of interpretation. Because documents other than life skills frameworks were included, I had to take the liberty of interpreting targeted skills based on an analysis of learning objectives, which were oftentimes couched in the language of knowledge areas rather than skills, abilities, or competencies. Programs that vaguely define life skills also frequently misidentify targeted skills in program design and measurement outcomes (see Kwauk & Braga, 2017). Due to the terminology challenge around life skills, which Murphy-Graham and Cohen (Chap. 2, this volume) explore, I used the Explore SEL as a way to arrive at a common understanding of the life skills targeted by different SFD programs. As such, my interpretation of the life skills identified or described in the SFD programs' documents may not be what the program designers would have interpreted.[6]

The third, and more interesting limitation, was conceptual: the analysis was at once enabled yet constrained by the Explore SEL coding scheme, pointing to how life skills frameworks have not yet dealt with issues of normativity and transformativity when it comes to the orientation of life skills towards development and social change. While the coding scheme allowed disparate approaches to life skills development to be compared based on how skills, behaviors, and desired outcomes were described, it was in examining the uncodable skills that the lack of attention to life skills for social transformation came into stark relief. Such a gap highlights the tendency for life skills to be conceptualized at the individual (self-improvement) level, rather than in relation to the social structures and social relationships that have marginalized certain communities in the first place.

This gap reveals several issues worth investigating further. The most immediate opportunity is to investigate how a critical feminist lens may generate new (sub) domains of skills, and/or lead existing definitions and descriptions of skills to be revised toward a more social and gender transformative vision. For example, the prosocial, cooperative behavior of "Follows classroom/institution/society rules and expectations (norms, directions) and exhibits appropriate behavior for context" could be read as promoting the reproduction of normative behaviors deemed socially acceptable by the dominant culture, putting marginalized groups into further positions of disadvantage. Furthermore, such a targeted behavior ignores whether obedience of rules by marginalized groups (who are often the target of life skills education)

---

[6] This was particularly the case for "skills" coded across the Cognitive domain that were described in terms of knowledge areas by the program document. For example, the document used to analyze Grassroots Soccer's Girls SKILLZ Zambia life skills framework included a learning objective like "Identify how society's definition of girlhood leads to oppression of women and girls," which was coded as "Identifies and understands the existence and nature of problems," a critical thinking skill under the Cognitive domain. The learning objective "Describe contraceptive use as joint decision between both partners" was coded as "Recognizes multiple sides of an issue and/or understands multiple perspectives" (a critical thinking skill under the Cognitive domain). And, the objective "Describe positive self-talk and how it can be used to build your confidence" was double coded as "Shifts attention from one task, aspect, or perspective to another" (a cognitive flexibility skill under the Cognitive domain) and "Expresses confidence in oneself and one's ability to improve or succeed" (a self-efficacy/growth mindset skill under the Identity domain).

for the sake of coexisting peacefully with others (often the dominant culture) creates the necessary and sufficient conditions for the empowerment of the former.

Another issue is how to balance attention across knowledge areas and targeted skills if we are to conceptualize life skills as a combination of what one knows (knowledge), has (skills), and believes and values (attitudes). The analysis illuminates how programs have conceptualized—or at least how they have described in their documents—life skills education as the acquisition of content-specific knowledge like financial literacy, sexual and reproductive health, or how to find (or create) a job. While some programs take a feminist approach and target knowledge areas especially important for gender empowerment (e.g. recognizing how gender roles create a "man box" or "woman box" of gender stereotyped behavior), SFD programs are missing an important opportunity to target competencies that can transform knowledge of saving and borrowing money, knowledge of modern contraceptives, or knowledge of business resource acquisition and allocation, for example, into double-edged swords that help girls fundamentally alter financial, health, and corporate systems of oppression.

A final area that needs more investigation is the relationship between life skills development and agency—a key component mediating the translation of life skills into empowered action (Kwauk & Braga, 2017). Although the SFD programs analyzed here all have an eye toward empowering the girl to be a more autonomous, agentic self, such framing follows an individualistic conceptualization of agency as a skill to be developed in itself, a capacity that one can possess, and a sense of possibility and self-worth that can be deposited into a girl in a safe and nurturing setting. However, as explained elsewhere (ibid.), agency is both individual and relational, iterative and dialogical. A girl's sense of agency depends as much on whether others recognize her as an autonomous individual—what DeJaeghere (Chap. 4, this volume) extends to a discussion of dignity—as on whether she has had the opportunity to successfully exercise her agency in the past. However, conceptualizations of agency by sport-based life skills programs tend to ignore the relational achievement of agency, missing an important opportunity to address the achievement of agency in a more transformative way.

Conclusion

According to this analysis of 10 sport-based life skills approaches, SFD programs do not appear to be wholly neoliberal nor wholly transformative. Rather, their approach to girls' empowerment through life skills development is a complicated patchwork. Some aspects of their approaches frame life skills development from a normative paradigm, especially when it comes to framing issues of health for "at risk" youth (e.g. sexual and reproductive health, HIV/AIDS). Other aspects position SFD programs as coming from a transformative approach, especially when it comes to issues of gender and identity (e.g. pushing against gender stereotypes, exercising one's voice), or taking into account mediating factors (e.g. community services, boys and men). It is in the midst of this patchwork, however, where critical, postcolonial, and transnational feminist critiques of life skills should be brought to bear in order to help ensure that radical interventions around gender transformative social change do not get cloaked in individualism or co-opted by the unintentional reproduction of dominant neoliberal logics.

Overall, SFD programs appear to be no different than non-sport-based life skills programs in terms of the heavy attention to knowledge areas and socioemotional skills—although this analysis also found a heavy emphasis on cognitive skills as well. More interesting, however, are the insights gained by looking at the skills targeted by SFD programs that could not be coded according to the Explore SEL current coding scheme. In short, the coding scheme—like dominant frameworks of life skills—is gender blind, missing an important opportunity to serve as a tool to help program designers and implementers conceptualize life skills in a more transformative way. Concepts like self-advocacy, power negotiation, power mapping, resistance against hegemony, and recognizing social assets and strategic relationships would not only help to give the Explore SEL tools a gender lens, but also help push the field of life skills education beyond its neoliberal underpinnings toward a more radical interventionist approach that equips youth with the tools to both read the world and to act on that world.

SFD programs are a unique platform for life skills development. However, programs must be designed more intentionally in order to leverage the necessary and sufficient conditions created by sport: they need to pay greater attention to gender transformative skills, pivot context-dependent skills toward more transformative ends, and re-examine the neoliberal logics undergirding presently normative skills. Similar to Hartmann and Kwauk (2011), this chapter concludes that it is vital to recognize the contributions of SFD programs' sporting *and* non-sporting components to open opportunities for girls to engage in critical reflexive practice around gender transformative mindsets and behaviors. Only then can SFD programs begin to disrupt social structures of oppression and inequality that have held girls back from realizing their full potential in the first place.

Acknowledgements   The author would like to thank Natalie Starr Wyss for her invaluable research support, as well as Grassroots Soccer, Moving the Goalposts, Naz Foundation, Pass It Back, Right to Play, Soccer Without Borders, Standard Chartered, and Women Win for sharing their life skills curricula, frameworks, theories of change, as well as their programmatic insights for this analysis. An additional thanks goes to Women Win for facilitating introductions to a number of organizations included in this analysis.

References

Chawansky, M., & Hayhurst, L. M. C. (2015). Girls, international development and the politics of sport: Introduction. *Sport in Society, 18*(8), 877–881. https://doi.org/10.1080/1743043 7.2014.997587

Darnell, S. (2012). *Sport for development and peace: A critical sociology*. Bloomsbury Academic.

Dupuy, K., Bezu, S., Knudsen, A., Halvorsen, S., Kwauk, C., Braga, A., & Kim, H. (2018). Life skills in non-formal contexts for adolescent girls in developing countries. *CMI Report*, 5. Chr. Michelson Institute.

Ferguson, J. (1994). *The anti-politics machine: 'Development', depoliticization, and bureaucratic power in Lesotho*. University of Minnesota Press.

Forde, S. D. (2014). Look after yourself, or look after one another? An analysis of life skills in sport for development and peace HIV prevention curriculum. *Sociology of Sport Journal, 31*, 287–303. https://doi.org/10.1123/ssj.2013-0103

Forde, S. D., & Frisby, W. (2015). Just be empowered: How girls are represented in a sport for development and peace HIV/AIDS prevention manual. *Sport in Society, 18*(8), 882–894. https://doi.org/10.1080/17430437.2014.997579

Haberland, N. (2015). The case for addressing gender and power in sexuality and HIV education: A comprehensive review of evaluation studies. *International Perspectives on Sexual and Reproductive Health, 41*(1), 31–42. https://doi.org/10.1363/4103115

Hancock, M. G., Lyras, A., & Ha, J. (2013). Sport for development programmes for girls and women: A global assessment. *Journal of Sport for Development, 1*(1), 15–24.

Hartmann, D., & Kwauk, C. (2011). Sport and development: An overview, critique, and reconstruction. *Journal of Sport and Social Issues, 35*(3), 284–305. https://doi.org/10.1177/0193723511416986

Harvey, D. (2005). *A brief history of neoliberalism*. Oxford University Press.

Hayhurst, L. M. C. (2014). The 'Girl Effect' and martial arts: Social entrepreneurship and sport, gender and development in Uganda. *Gender, Place and Culture, 21*(3), 297–315. https://doi.org/10.1080/0966369X.2013.802674

Holt, N. L., Tamminen, K. A., Tink, L. N., & Black, D. E. (2009). An interpretive analysis of life skills associated with sport participation. *Qualitative Research in Sport and Exercise, 1*(2), 160–175. https://doi.org/10.1080/19398440902909017

Jones, M. I., & Lavallee, D. (2009). Exploring perceived life skills development and participation in sport. *Qualitative Research in Sport and Exercise, 1*(1), 36–50. https://doi.org/10.1080/19398440802567931

Kidd, B. (2008). A new social movement: Sport for development and peace. *Sport in Society, 11*, 370–380. https://doi.org/10.1080/17430430802019268

Kwauk, C. (2014). *Playing for the future: Sport and the production of healthy bodies in policy and practice*. Doctoral dissertation, University of Minnesota. University of Minnesota Digital Conservancy. http://hdl.handle.net/11299/181761

Kwauk, C., & Braga, A. (2017). *Translating competencies to empowered action: A framework for linking girls' life skills education to social change*. Brookings Institution.

Moeller, K. (2018). *The gender effect: Capitalism, feminism, and the corporate politics of development*. University of California Press.

Moving the Goalposts. (2019). *MTG model – Step by step*. https://mtgk.org/

O'Brien, K. (2018). Is the 1.5C target possible? Exploring the three spheres of transformation. *Current Opinion in Environmental Sustainability, 31*, 153–160. https://doi.org/10.1016/j.cosust.2018.04.010

Pierce, S., Gould, D., & Camiré, M. (2016). Definition and model of life skills transfer. *International Review of Sport and Exercise Psychology, 10*(1), 186–211. https://doi.org/10.1080/1750984X.2016.1199727

Right to Play. (2018). *Gender equality policy*. https://righttoplaydiag107.blob.core.windows.net/rtp-media/documents/Gender_Equality_Policy_RTP_2018.pdf

Soccer Without Borders. (n.d.). Organization website. http://soccerwithoutborders.org

Sterling, S. (2010). Transformative learning and sustainability: Sketching the conceptual ground. *Learning and Teaching in Higher Education, 5*, 17–33.

Theoka, C., Danish, S., Hodge, K., Heke, I., & Forneris, T. (2008). Enhancing life skills through sport for children and youth. In N. L. Holt (Ed.), *Positive youth development through sport* (pp. 71–81). Routledge.

UNICEF. (2019). *Getting into the game: Understanding the evidence for child-focused sport for development*. UNICEF Office of Research - Innocenti.

Chapter 6
Workforce Skills Curriculum Development in Context: Case Studies in Rwanda, Algeria, and the Philippines

Catherine Honeyman, Laura Cordisco Tsai, Nancy Chervin, Melanie Sany, and Janice Ubaldo

Abstract Life skills programming in the field of international workforce development operates within a professional community of practice that is shaped by dynamics of power, influence, and resources, as well as by specific local contexts and actors. This chapter gives detailed insight into three case studies of youth workforce life skills programming developed by the organizations World Learning, Education Development Center, and 10ThousandWindows in different national settings and with distinct youth populations, highlighting how these organizations have interacted with the larger field and learned from one another to address issues of contextualization, pedagogy, sustainability, and scale. Through descriptions of programming in Rwanda, Algeria, and the Philippines, the chapter offers insight into the complexities of life skills curriculum development and contextualization processes and highlights issues that remain difficult to resolve, as well as new frontiers for programming in rapidly changing economies.

Keywords Youth employment · Workforce development · Soft skills · Life skills · Rwanda · Algeria · Philippines

C. Honeyman (✉)
World Learning, Washington, DC, USA
e-mail: catherine.honeyman@worldlearning.org

L. Cordisco Tsai
Carr Center for Human Rights Policy, Harvard Kennedy School, Cambridge, MA, USA
e-mail: laura_cordisco_tsai@hks.harvard.edu

N. Chervin · M. Sany
Education Development Center, Waltham, MA, USA
e-mail: nchervin@edc.org; MSany@edc.org

J. Ubaldo
10ThousandWindows, Knoxville, TN, USA
e-mail: jubaldo@pticebu.org

J. DeJaeghere, E. Murphy-Graham (eds.), *Life Skills Education for Youth*, Young People and Learning Processes in School and Everyday Life 5,
https://doi.org/10.1007/978-3-030-85214-6_6

Acronyms

10KW	10ThousandWindows
EDC	Education Development Center
MIFOTRA	Rwandan Ministry of Public Service and Labour
MEPI	US Middle East Partnership Initiative
MI	Motivational Interviewing
MOE	Ministry of Education
NEET	Not in Education, Employment, or Training
STEP	Soft Skills Training and Empowerment Program
TVET	Technical and Vocational Education and Training
USAID	United States Agency for International Development
WDA	Rwandan Workforce Development Agency
WRN	Work Ready Now

Introduction

One major domain of life skills programming falls within the workforce development field, which broadly focuses on preparing people for employment or self-employment in particular social and economic contexts (related to what Murphy-Graham & Cohen, Chap. 2, [this volume] categorize as labor market outcomes). Workforce development programming may focus on different age groups and on a range of workforce concerns; this chapter's focus is on life skills for youth workforce programming in the international development arena.

Diverse youth workforce development actors have their own institutional perspectives on life skills—whether referred to as transferable skills, social emotional skills, soft skills, or under other names. There is growing consensus, however, that these skills play a crucial role in youth employment, entrepreneurship, and earning outcomes and should be a focus of investment in addition to the more traditional emphasis on academic, technical, and vocational skills. At the national level, workforce development actors involved in life skills education include government agencies, technical and vocational education and training (TVET) agencies, higher education institutions, non-governmental organizations (NGOs), and private sector representatives. Multilateral organizations, bilateral donors and philanthropy funders, and international nonprofit and for-profit organizations are also involved in workforce development programs in various contexts.

Approaches to life skills in these circles are shaped by a variety of factors, including funders and their priorities, exchanges among implementing organizations, research, and local concerns. This chapter focuses on how three organizations involved in youth workforce development have interacted with these different forms of influence on life skills programming, confronting questions of contextualization, pedagogy, sustainability, and scale in three very different contexts—Rwanda, Algeria, and the Philippines. In particular, we focus on donor and developed country institutions as powerful actors in an international field of influence that shapes programming, and the discourse of an ad hoc professional community of practice that shares ways of thinking and doing around life skills—while also showing that this international influence is tempered by efforts to adapt life skills programming for particular contexts and populations.

Influences of an International Community of Practice

The three organizations whose cases are featured in this chapter, World Learning, Education Development Center (EDC), and 10ThousandWindows (10KW), are all nonprofit organizations active in the youth workforce development field. While World Learning and EDC are both based in Washington, DC and operate various types of educational programming in multiple countries around the world, 10KW focuses its work specifically on survivors of human trafficking and violence in the Philippines. As organizations, we have come into contact in a variety of spaces focusing on international workforce development and life skills programming for employability—including in conferences, webinars, workshops, and email listservs. These spaces have created, both intentionally and organically, a large professional community of practice characterized by a shared interest in teaching employability skills internationally. By "community of practice" we mean the social relationships that naturally develop among people and institutions engaging in related activities, who over time develop shared ways of thinking and doing through situated learning, as described in the ethnographic work of Jean Lave and Etienne Wenger (1991). This particular ad hoc community of practice also includes many other members from the international development community.

The situated learning around employability life skills programming that takes place within this community of practice is influenced by factors of power, positionality, and command of resources (Bourdieu, 1972, 1990), as well as by research, context, and learning from experience. Major developed-country education systems and large private corporations have significant influence in this international community of practice, as life skills curricular frameworks such as Equipped for the Future, SCANS, P21, and ATC21S, reflecting the input of companies such as Apple, Microsoft, CISCO, and Intel, have been taken up as references for developing country contexts (See Stites, 2011 for more on the history of corporate frameworks and influences). Other organizations and funders, including the OECD (Kautz et al., 2014), the World Bank (2019), the World Economic Forum (2018), and the MasterCard Foundation (2017), also publish influential resources on life skills and their relationship to improving employment outcomes, carrying significant weight with practitioners due to these organizations' economic, cultural, and social capital (Bourdieu, 1986).

For many organizations implementing international youth workforce programs, the United States Agency for International Development (USAID) also plays a prime, influential role as one of the largest funders of international workforce development programming. USAID-funded workforce development projects, each typically 3–5 years in length, operate in some 30 countries around the world. Recent figures suggest they reach approximately 200,000 youth per year (Honeyman & Fletcher, 2019). While this reach is still nowhere near the numbers of youth involved in government-run workforce development systems in those same countries, USAID has had an outsized influence in consolidating certain research in the life skills domain, and has shaped practice through intentional learning coordination mechanisms,[1] through the assumptions set out within USAID requests for proposals, and through other means such as standardized indicators for measuring project achievements. Among other effects is USAID's adoption of the term "soft skills" for the social, emotional, cognitive, and employability skills that are the focus of the workforce development programming it funds. In contrast, USAID primarily uses the term "social-emotional learning" for basic education programs, and "life skills" for youth sexual and reproductive health-focused programs, despite significant overlap among the specific skills designated by these terms. Because this chapter is concerned with workforce development programming that has been influenced by USAID terminology, we use the term "soft skills" from this point forward (although we recognize these are broadly equivalent to "life skills" as conceived by other authors in this volume).

Some two dozen international organizations, both for-profit and non-profit, implement most of the large-scale workforce development programs funded by USAID, the US Department of Labor, and the US Department of State.[2] As the research and discourse around soft skills and employability has evolved over the past two decades in the fields of psychology, education, and economics, as well as within donor discourse, these organizations have increasingly converged in their language and practices even as they have deepened and clarified their approaches to soft skills programming. The three case studies featured in this chapter illustrate that convergence while also offering insight into the complexities of soft skills curriculum development and revision processes in very different contexts and with different target populations.[3]

Each organization included in this chapter first developed its own institutional approach to soft skills curriculum around 2009, beginning with projects in the core national contexts featured here. A brief timeline illustrates how these organizations, and their soft skills education programming and discourse, have been tied together within the larger community of practice described previously. EDC's soft skills

---

[1] In recent years, these include the Workforce Connections project and the YouthPower initiative.

[2] This dominance of large international organizations may be changing due to USAID's New Partnerships Initiative, focusing on making more funding accessible to a variety of institutions and organizations around the world.

[3] As co-authors of this chapter, we each had a particular role in one of the case studies described. Catherine Honeyman wrote the overall chapter framing and the World Learning Algeria case study, drawing on her experience as technical advisor for the project. Nancy Chervin wrote the EDC Rwanda Case study in collaboration with Melanie Sany, who managed the EDC projects in Rwanda. Laura Cordisco Tsai wrote the 10KW case study in collaboration with Janice Ubaldo, drawing on their involvement in the organization's curriculum development and research processes.

approach, first developed for Rwanda in 2009 and initially based on US and OECD curricular frameworks, became one of the sources consulted in a pivotal USAID-funded publication "Key 'soft skills' that foster youth workforce success: Toward a consensus across fields" (Lippman et al., 2015). Featuring an extensive international literature review, that publication aimed to determine the skills with greatest international research evidence of impact on four types of workforce outcomes—employment, promotion, income, and entrepreneurial success—as well as the skills with evidence of malleability during the youth years. The report ultimately recommended that programs focus on five soft skills: positive self-concept, self-control, social skills, communication, and higher-order thinking skills. Subsequently, USAID funded a literature review on effective pedagogical methods for soft skills development, which also drew on EDC approaches among a range of other models (Soares et al., 2017). USAID circulated these publications widely and referred to them in requests for proposals, ensuring that they became well-known among the organizations implementing workforce development programs internationally.

Meanwhile, World Learning and 10KW had also developed their own approaches to soft skills programming around 2009, drawing on a combination of US and international influences (Algeria and the Philippines, respectively). In 2017, after many years of program implementation, World Learning consulted the USAID publications above, as well as other research sources, to create guidance for its own soft skills curriculum revision process globally. World Learning also shared this guidance and a set of curriculum development tools externally in industry-specific conferences and other settings. It was in one such conference[4] that 10KW, EDC, and World Learning staff came together and began exchanging experiences around their soft skills curricula and programming, with 10KW subsequently using the World Learning tools for its own process of curricular revision.

Our conversations and experiences as technical advisors of organizations implementing soft skills programming for workforce development within this international community of practice have brought to the fore three major issues in developing our programs: contextualizing the focus of soft skills programming, determining and training for effective pedagogical approaches, and sustaining and scaling up these initiatives.

Contextualization

In the midst of a movement towards more uniform global recommendations for soft skills development, and despite a certain homogenizing influence from institutions such as USAID and the OECD as described previously, international development program implementers continue to recognize the key importance of having contextually relevant curricula that evolve based on experience with particular

---

[4] The Global Youth Economic Opportunities Summit, 2018.

populations. The cases in this chapter show how implementing organizations must both respond to the expectations of funders and report on standardized indicators, and also dialogue with and respond to important local actors, including government agencies, training institutions, and youth themselves.

Pedagogy

While the past decade has featured demonstrably greater consensus around the importance of teaching particular soft skills, *how* to do so effectively is another matter. The authors' experience with mainstream competency-based curriculum development processes around the world shows that education institutions often end up neglecting the non-academic skills and "attitudes" aspect of their curriculum development frameworks as they progress from initial outlines towards more detailed curricula, pedagogical recommendations, and learning materials (see Honeyman, 2016). In great part, this may be because the methods for developing soft skills are not well known or understood. The cases in this chapter therefore document our pedagogical approaches for developing these skills.

Sustainability and Scale

Another significant challenge that implementers of soft skills development programming face is the question of how to institutionalize effective curricula into a broader system capable of reaching much larger populations, or deepen it to achieve sustainable change for target populations over time. Research by the MasterCard Foundation (Ignatowski, 2017) examined three soft skills development programs in Sub-Saharan Africa that have achieved larger scale, identifying six key drivers: an enabling policy environment, evidence of impact on youth outcomes, strong political champions, wide stakeholder engagement, decentralization of authority, and flexible funding. This chapter's cases illustrate the importance of these factors and make clear that the dominant short-term project-based mode of the major funders of soft skills and workforce development programming poses a significant obstacle to sustaining and scaling up such programming, ultimately limiting the chances for many youth to develop these skills despite the significant resources invested for that purpose.

The case studies that follow focus on illustrating how the three aspects of soft skills curriculum development addressed above—contextualization, pedagogy, and sustainability and scale[5]—have played out in three very different contexts: Rwanda,

---

[5] A fourth question—how to measure these skills—is beyond the scope of what this chapter can cover in detail, particularly considering the burgeoning work in this area.

Algeria, and the Philippines. A concluding section following the case studies highlights common challenges with soft skills curriculum development processes, as well as discussing the new frontiers that are now emerging in the teaching of soft skills for labor market outcomes.

Rwanda: Work Ready Now (Education Development Center)[6]

Country Context

Since 2009, Education Development Center has been leading youth programs in Rwanda with funding from USAID and the MasterCard Foundation. EDC's local team and partners provide youth with the skills to continue their education, find employment, or start their own businesses. Rwanda is a youthful country: 50% of the population is below 20 years old. Despite impressive economic growth in the past decade, the national poverty rate is 39%; among youth, however, it is 70% (with 55% in extreme poverty). In 2018, 31% of youth were not engaged in education, employment or training, and 65% were underemployed (World Bank, 2020). Youth are disproportionately located in—and migrating to—urban areas, where youth unemployment is three times that of rural areas (YouthStart, 2016). Each year, 125,000 first-time job seekers enter the labor market, a number which the economy is unable to absorb, so only a handful gain access to the formal sector (YouthStart, 2016). As a result, most youth work in the informal sector.

Over the last decade, there has been a consistent, clear vision to propel Rwanda into middle-income status, which includes significant changes to the workforce development system. One of the main targets has been to create roughly 200,000 non-farming jobs per year, which has motivated action across national ministries. The government has also emphasized the role of TVET in reaching its economic goals, aiming to increase the number of lower secondary school students entering TVET from 21% in 2017 to 60% by 2024. Nonetheless, when EDC began our work in Rwanda in 2008 with the USAID Akazi Kanoze project focusing on out-of-school youth between the ages of 14 and 24, we found that there was:

- No curriculum informed by employer demand, nor localized labor market assessments
- No incorporation of soft skills into the secondary school curriculum
- Little to no use of hands-on, learner-centered pedagogical approaches.

In response to these gaps, we developed an approach that included work readiness training for youth. In close partnership with the Rwandan government, our

---

[6] Information provided for this case study was primarily collected in the form of practitioner reflections. It also includes reference to an experimental study with randomly assigned treatment and control groups, which was approved by EDC's ethics review board.

strategy grew organically as we adapted our work readiness curriculum to various youth populations. As the approach gained more interest from the government, demands to expand the program beyond out-of-school youth to those in the TVET and formal education systems increased, enabling us to work with the government and local organizations in adapting and incorporating our training into existing systems.

Contextualization

Our original program design, responding to USAID-required activities, proposed a model that networked out-of-school youth with business opportunities through local NGOs. As we grappled with the question of how these NGOs could better prepare youth for jobs, the idea of a work readiness curriculum emerged, focusing on building the soft skills and competencies youth need for their first entry-level jobs or to run their own small businesses. At the time, little detailed information existed in the international development space about curricula that met these requirements, so we began by developing a curriculum framework that defined the key content areas for a comprehensive skill development program with an emphasis on livelihoods and work. The curriculum framework initially drew from the Equipped for the Future standards, developed for adult learners in the United States, and which was externally evaluated in 2011 to ensure alignment with three internationally recognized work readiness frameworks: SCANS, P21, and ATC21S (Stites, 2011). In 2015, we also analyzed how the Big Five Personality Factors (see Murphy-Graham & Cohen, Chap. 2, this volume) were addressed because these categories of noncognitive skills are related to success in both school and the workplace. The Big Five are increasingly viewed as important for a variety of uses in workforce development: selection, training, outcomes assessment, professional development, and international comparisons (Roberts et al., 2015). In 2013, EDC and Professional Examination Services developed a learner assessment using situational judgement questions based on the Big Five Personality Factors and Work Ready Now (WRN) modules. It is important to note that the WRN framework was developed 5 years before USAID conducted its review of soft skills frameworks and skill areas, described in the previous section. Our framework was later included in, and seems to have significantly shaped, this research.

This framework served as a starting point for developing the curriculum in Rwanda, later becoming EDC's global Work Ready Now (WRN) curriculum. A curriculum framework, the scaffold upon which a full curriculum is built, defines the skills, knowledge, and behaviors that are to be taught and learned. EDC's WRN framework covers intrapersonal and interpersonal skills, including skills that are used in a variety of settings and not just work (such as goal-setting and communication), employability skills (such as workplace behaviors), and critical thinking skills (such as evaluation of appropriate strategies). Illustrative teaching and learning activities accompany each skill.

After a review of the framework in Rwanda, modules were drafted by a mix of Rwanda- and US-based technical advisors. Next, a series of curriculum development and revision workshops took place. A group of Rwandan NGO partners, facilitators, and business representatives as well as staff from the Rwandan Ministry of Public Service and Labour (MIFOTRA) and the Workforce Development Agency (WDA) reviewed the modules. They also provided feedback regarding the content, language, methodology, context, and cultural appropriateness. This process resulted in deleting, changing, and adding activities, particularly to align with Rwanda's skills development priorities in customer care and entrepreneurship.

The resulting Rwandan curriculum consisted of eight modules, with materials for 120 h of instruction, as depicted in Fig. 6.1.

These modules include personal development, communication, finding and keeping work, leadership, health and safety, workers' rights and responsibilities, financial fitness, and an introduction to entrepreneurship. Overall, the modules seek

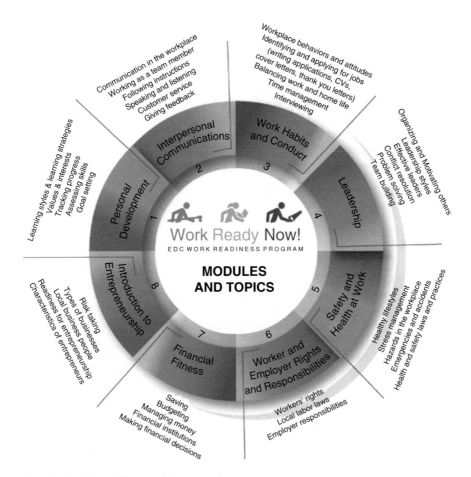

Fig. 6.1 Work Ready Now modules and topics

to develop a large number of specific soft skills, including: self-reflection, assessing, goal-setting, taking initiative, communication (listening and speaking in the workplace, giving presentations, giving and receiving instructions and feedback), social skills (cooperating, working in a team, providing good customer service), cognitive skills (finding and analyzing information, reading for information, decision-making, and problem-solving), behaving appropriately at work, planning skills (managing time, managing home and work life, tracking personal progress), and leadership, among others.

The original intention was that other countries could develop their own curriculum using the WRN framework. Though the curriculum development process proved to be time-intensive, taking almost a year in Rwanda, we found that the resulting curriculum and materials were easily adaptable for other contexts and that it would not be necessary for every country to start from scratch. We have been able to adapt versions of the Rwandan WRN curriculum to new countries according to youth levels of education and socioeconomic situations. Key players adapt WRN to the local cultural and economic context during a workshop, which brings together youth-serving organizations, government officials, instructors, and the private sector. A local adaptation will pinpoint issues such as needing to prepare youth for communicating with people from other cultures, identifying the specific finance service providers in a country, or localizing job seeking processes such as the use of virtual interviews and networking sites like LinkedIn which vary from country to country. Furthermore, the majority of scenarios, work-based situations, and role models come from examples from the country of adaptation. We developed a WRN implementation toolkit to formalize this adaptation process. This toolkit helped to maintain consistency and quality as we contextualized WRN for 26 countries in the last 10 years.

Pedagogy

The WRN curriculum developed first in Rwanda uses techniques such as group activities, role-plays, large- and small-group discussions, and personal reflection. Youth practice customer service interactions in role plays, simulate doing a complex office move to learn about cooperating as a team, and map out their goals as they create professional development plans. Like the World Learning and 10KW programs described below, youth also develop career portfolios comprised of items they will use for job seeking, and wraparound activities such as workplace exposure to complement the training outside of the classroom. Work exposure includes observations, informational interviews, and job shadowing assignments that require the youth to identify workplaces and build relationships with employees at local businesses. After completion of the WRN training, Rwandan youth enter an accompaniment phase of the program where they continue to do observations and conduct informational interviews as they seek employment or begin their own business.

Our experience in Rwanda demonstrated that for implementation to be successful, the content and pedagogy must be maintained, and sufficient teacher training provided. WRN's participatory learner-centered approach is intentionally outlined in very detailed steps. It is designed for use by both less experienced facilitators and instructors who may be accustomed to more traditional approaches. We found that, on the one hand, an NGO facilitator may be youthful and energetic and take naturally to the activities but have minimal prior facilitation experience. On the other hand, a Rwandan schoolteacher may have taught for 20 years, but mainly through lecture format. Both groups appreciate that the steps walk them through what they say and do all along the way.

The training of trainer's approach emphasizes mastering the content and pedagogy. Trainings are slowly paced, with a day spent on each module. The first training of trainers workshops in Rwanda averaged 10 days in total (split into two workshops, covering different modules, with the second workshop including reflection on their teaching so far). Each trainer gains a background in adult learning, experiences learner-centered instruction, and leads at least two teaching demonstrations. They receive structured feedback both during the training and while implementing the curriculum. Teachers tend to be enthusiastic adopters of the curriculum. While teachers in Rwanda had received professional development in learner-centered approaches as part of the formal school system, many have remarked that it was the WRN training that helped them finally grasp this approach. Practicing the delivery of activities during the training and using the methods in the curriculum with youth in their classrooms helped them to internalize learner-centered, participatory approaches. Class size needed to be considered carefully, however. The curriculum was originally designed for a trainer and assistant to lead a class of 25 youth. In the Rwandan school system, the ratio was often one teacher to up to 50 youth in a class. Activities were rethought so they could still be participatory within this constraint.

Sustainability and Scale

Today, these practices, particularly the pedagogy underlying the WRN approach and the use of the WRN curriculum itself, are widespread among a number of private and public service providers including public technical and vocational education and training (TVET) and formal education institutions. By including local stakeholders in the development process, they took ownership of the curriculum and promoted it in their institutions. For instance, following the first Rwandan curriculum revision workshop described above, the Ministry of Public Service and Labour requested that we provide training to several hundred youth. Ultimately, we trained and mentored over 200 trainers from private institutions, as well as over 700 school directors, master trainers, and teachers from public TVET and secondary schools. This learner-centered soft skills training reached over 200,000 in-school youth and 60,000 out-of-school youth.

While the soft skills program in Rwanda began with USAID-defined objectives and funding, it soon evolved beyond that frame towards institutionalization into permanent Rwandan structures and policies. Our work with out-of-school youth sparked interest from the Rwandan Ministry of Education, who in turn asked that we adapt WRN for the formal education system. This request took place in the midst of an education reform process that moved the system to a competency-based approach. Given WRN's standards-based framework, it was a good match. The in-school adaptation in Rwanda took place alongside national reforms in two types of schools: TVET and general secondary.

For TVET, there was an existing effort with the government's Workforce Development Agency to develop competency-based curricula in the national system. EDC plugged into that effort by mapping WRN content throughout the school year in each of the technical curricula. WRN aligned with the TVET qualification's required complementary competencies, which include employability and life skills that are applicable to all occupations. At the same time, the local EDC team advocated for work readiness skills to be taught through the entire TVET system. The life skills curriculum was then validated and mandated as Level 3 under the TVET qualification framework. EDC worked with the WDA to merge its eight modules into five courses that included dedicated time for our activities. Minor adjustments were made to the terminology of the WRN training manual so it aligned with their curriculum. For example, WRN's Personal Development module was integrated in their "Occupational and Learning Process" course.

For general secondary education, the government had started aligning the entire secondary curriculum to a competency-based approach, and it became clear that WRN could address some needs during this alignment. Through a comprehensive design process, we worked with the Ministry of Education (MOE) to embed WRN into their entrepreneurship instruction at all levels of lower and upper secondary. We participated in the competency-based curriculum reform process led by the Rwanda Education Board to help the entrepreneurship team integrate the curriculum. The team closely compared the existing materials with ours, developed a syllabus, and identified when WRN activities would be used by teachers in their units. Other than aligning terminologies, no major changes were required. The biggest challenge was deciding how to spread out the work readiness curriculum modules across the grade levels without losing continuity. We addressed this challenge by repeating essential topics within modules across the years. For example, goal setting and planning repeats itself over the years as learners' interests and skills develop and change.

Because the WRN soft skills content is embedded into a national curriculum, it is not something "extra" for the teachers to do, but rather helps by providing them with high quality content that addresses the skills they need to teach. A true collaboration with the MOE enables us not only to align the competencies and the skills prioritized by the government of Rwanda and WRN, but also to influence the broader curriculum reform through WRN pedagogy and approach. In this shift to a competency-based approach, teachers were going to be required to teach differently—in a more participatory and less didactic way. WRN provided a model of how to implement a competency-based curriculum.

While adapting the curriculum to an in-school program, several considerations had to be addressed. First, for both school systems, careful consideration was taken to align the WRN competencies with the government's own competency framework. In that process we helped the Rwandan Education Board integrate the content and methodology into entrepreneurship for secondary schools and we helped WDA integrate WRN into their core competencies in vocational schools.

Second, the flow and scaffolding of the competencies was considered carefully as the modules would be taught by different teachers at different levels. We needed to determine how the skills and activities in each module would be distributed across levels and subjects, ensuring that foundational knowledge and skills that feed into subsequent topics in the WRN curriculum were introduced before the more complicated topics. For instance, identifying one's values, interests, and skills feeds into the next step of goal setting and writing a professional development plan. In Rwanda, this instruction was taught across all 6 years of secondary school but within one subject (entrepreneurship). Experience has shown that it is better to integrate the curriculum into as few subjects and levels as feasible in order to keep the WRN training as intact and compact as possible, so as to encourage youth to build self-confidence and comfort with their group. Facilitators also become familiar with the strengths and areas for growth among the youth. When it is not possible to keep it intact, it is helpful to have a week, at the end of the school year, when the students all come together at a given time to review key lessons.

Third, we found that it is important to identify the teachers, their availability, and who will train them. These could be local implementing partners or the inspectors in the system responsible for teacher training. In Rwanda, the capacity of Rwanda Polytechnic officials is now being developed to be responsible for teacher training for the TVET level 2 programs.

Finally, there are considerations to be made beyond the content and methodologies when integrating into schools and institutionalizing training materials into a school system. Adjustments may need to be made to the activity lengths (to fit within classes of 40 or 45 min length instead of 1–2 h sessions), to the materials used so that they are affordable (for ministries who purchase classroom supplies and parents who purchase the school books), and to the assessments (to ensure that the soft skills assessment can be used nationwide across all schools and in a format that can be administered by teachers in a classroom).

To make this range of work possible over multiple years, EDC competed for additional funding under multiple projects and donors. Without piecing together resources over a longer period of time, this depth of institutionalization and influence on the Rwandan educational system would not have been possible within a single project's implementation timeframe.

Our research indicates that the route that we have taken – focusing on this particular content and pedagogy, while using a systems-strengthening approach – is meeting the needs of youth, employers, and educators. For out-of-school youth, 66% of program graduates have found employment or started an income-generating activity within 6 months of graduation. Ninety-seven percent met or exceeded employer expectations. In regard to in-school youth, youth in the program had larger gains in work readiness knowledge and key competencies than their peers. Participants were more likely to be employed after completing the program than those who did not participate (Alcid & Martin, 2017).

One of our key lessons learned was the extent of our curriculum's adaptability. Two primary factors stand out: firstly, that a detailed curriculum framework guided its development. Secondly, it was vetted locally at all stages, from the framework development to the original adaptation and all subsequent adaptations. In the 10 years since we first developed the curriculum, technology has quickly changed the nature of the workplace. Yet the curriculum stands the test of time. It emphasizes skills such as adaptability, willingness to be a lifelong learner, and diligence—all of which are cited as key skills by employers globally. In today's COVID-impacted world, we are exploring how to use technology for teacher training and delivery to youth without compromising quality and the value of face-to-face interaction.

Algeria: WorkLinks (World Learning)[7]

Country Context

World Learning has worked in Algeria since 2005, and we began workforce development-related programming in 2010 with support from the US State Department, later including private funders such as HSBC Bank and Anadarko Petroleum. In large part due to funder priorities, our focus in these projects has been quite different from EDC's initial emphasis on out-of-school youth, described in the previous case study. In Algeria, we work primarily with the country's large population of unemployed but educated youth with at least a high school diploma, and often a university or even post-graduate degree. Data on youth unemployment rates in Algeria varies widely. Even before the COVID-19 crisis, one study suggested that at least 39% of university graduates remain unemployed even three years after graduation (CREAD and ILO, 2017); official statistics—last reported in 2018 before a wave of protests that has continued to the present—documented overall youth unemployment at 29.1% (ONS, 2018). Algeria is considered an upper middle income country, but with a stalled economy that is nearly completely dependent on petroleum, accounting for over 94% of the country's export revenue and making the country extremely vulnerable to external oil price shocks.[8] In this context, our youth workforce development projects have focused primarily on improving youth integration into formal employment positions in a variety of industries, including petro-

---

[7] This case study is primarily based on practitioner reflections and routine analysis of project monitoring and evaluation data collected as part of an educational process. It also includes reference to qualitative research approved by World Learning's School for International Training IRB (IORG # 0004408).

[8] Observatory of Economic Complexity: Algeria Country Profile https://oec.world/en/profile/country/dza/

leum, plastics, construction materials, pharmaceuticals, IT, education and training, and more—across 12 Algerian governorates ranging from the highly-populated cities on the Mediterranean coast to desert regions in the south.

Contextualization

Since 2010, our approach to employability and soft skills training has evolved considerably, responding to local context, donor priorities, and implementation realities, as well as efforts to more deliberately incorporate research on effective soft skills instruction. World Learning's Algerian education specialists, specifically trained in experiential learning pedagogy (Kolb, 1984), began initially with a small set of core courses that we developed to meet the needs of a new career center at the University of Ouargla, following some informal employer outreach and observation of students' skills gaps in seeking employment. The modules, typically lasting 2 h each, included personal skills and interest assessments, writing customized CVs and cover letters, practicing interview skills, and learning about job search techniques. They did not overtly reference other soft skills, but they employed an experiential learning methodology used in all of World Learning's global programs, which formally or informally employs cycles of experience, reflection, conceptualization, and further experimentation, designed to foster the development of communication, social skills, and critical thinking. For subsequent projects starting in 2012 and 2015 with university and TVET career centers in other parts of the country, field staff reflected on a key obstacle young people faced in Algeria—the lack of work experience—and sought to encourage volunteering as a means for overcoming this barrier, as well as for encouraging broader civic engagement and fostering increased engagement of youth with disabilities and other barriers to workforce participation. This team revised the curriculum accordingly, introducing new modules on leadership, overcoming individual and collective obstacles, volunteering to gain work experience, and action planning. This revised version continued focusing on communication and social skills, and added a focus on additional soft skills such as goal-orientation, planning, problem-solving, and teaching the value of social inclusion.

In 2017, we decided to re-examine this soft skills curriculum again for two reasons. First, with the publication of the USAID-funded literature reviews described in the introduction, it was clear that the research base around soft skills had developed to the point that it could inform our curriculum development and implementation more clearly than before. And second, we had conducted an initial tracer study of 678 program participants, which did not show the clear correlation that we had expected between completion of the soft skills courses and improved employment outcomes. While the data showed that youth who took our soft skills courses were significantly less likely to be in the inactive NEET[9] (Not in Education, Employment, or Training) category than their peers who did not take our courses, that difference was largely due to furthering their studies rather than increased rates of employment. This data was non-experimental and so could not determine the direction of causality; additionally, the choice to pursue further studies could reflect one success of the soft skills courses in helping youth evaluate their own skills in relation to market opportunities, determining that they needed some further education/training to find employment. Nevertheless, these findings also suggested a need to re-examine the curriculum, to ensure that it was actually teaching the skills youth most needed in order to find employment in the Algerian context.

Anticipating that this question would affect not only our work in Algeria, but also around the world, we began first by cataloguing all the international research we could find regarding the range of soft skills we should consider to improve youth employment outcomes. We also convened World Learning staff implementing a variety of types of youth programs in different countries to discuss how they selected the soft skills to focus on in a particular context, how they developed curriculum frameworks, what they found to be the most effective pedagogical practices, and how they evaluated instructor pedagogy and student achievements. This process resulted in a set of practitioner-oriented curriculum development tools in a publication titled *Soft Skills Development: Guiding Notes for Project and Curriculum Design and Evaluation* (Honeyman, 2018). These tools included: an inventory of 44 soft skills terms and clusters found in the research we consulted, to aid curriculum designers in making more conscious and specific choices around which skills they intended to build; a checklist of pedagogical practices found to be effective in the research we consulted and in World Learning experience; an example pedagogical observation form for assessing current instructor practices; guidance on creating psychometric or observation-based soft skills assessments; an example observation rubric for assessing student skills; and curriculum framework planning guides for specific skills and for a cluster of skills, among other resources. This toolkit was intended to help World Learning staff design and implement a variety of youth programs around the world in an explicitly context-responsive way.

We next searched for context-specific information on the soft skills needs of youth in Algeria. However, we quickly found that the little information that was available struggled with vague terminology and a lack of clarity in skills definitions, making it difficult to know precisely which skills to teach. With support from the US Middle East Partnership Initiative (MEPI), we therefore designed and undertook qualitative research in Algeria to examine specific contextual needs for soft skills, as well as examine what the existing soft skills courses were achieving and where there may be gaps (Honeyman, 2019). This research included re-analyzing qualitative interview data with 140 employers and other stakeholders from nine local labor

---

[9] NEET statistics measure youth who are Not in Education, Employment, or Training—a complementary measure of youth inactivity beyond just the youth unemployment rate, which focuses only on those who are searching for work but have not been able to obtain it. Algeria's NEET rate in 2018 was 28.3% (21.3% for young men and 35.8% for young women) (ONS, 2018).

market assessments we had conducted (Farrand, 2019). It also involved new individual questionnaires and focus group discussions with stratified groups of 90 Algerian youth beneficiaries of our program—male and female, employed and unemployed—in six governorates. We asked youth to describe personal weaknesses that had hindered them in their job search, as well as contextual obstacles they faced, and they shared their own theories regarding the major differences between youth who had and had not succeeded in finding employment.

Not all the obstacles that youth face can be resolved with soft skills training. Youth spoke about several challenges that could only be significantly impacted through policy and institutional changes. For example, youth mentioned the few job openings in the fields emphasized by their university degrees (fields youth often felt they had not chosen for themselves), challenges with residency regulations and distance to jobs, delays due to public employment agency procedures, nepotism, low pay rates and indefinitely keeping youth in government subsidized "internship" positions, military service restrictions, and gender discrimination against both men and women in particular types of jobs.

Nevertheless, youth did also identify internal factors akin to soft skills that they felt hindered their job search even if the above issues were to be addressed. Employed and unemployed, male and female youth made comments like the following when trying to explain why some youth found jobs and others did not: "It depends on the level of motivation of the person. If you are a motivated person, you won't stop looking" (unemployed female), and "It all comes down to persistence—you have to be proactive during the search, you have to be aware of the job openings. Otherwise there is no way it is going to work" (employed male).

The youth also spoke about the importance of adaptability, and young women in particular cited this as an obstacle that they believed prevented many young men from accepting a job at a lower level than they had hoped for, or in a different field from their training. Finally, both young men and young women mentioned their need to develop skills for managing emotions, particularly stress—and young women particularly emphasized the relationship between stress management and learning planning and time management skills to balance their many daily tasks in their household, studies, and search for work. The research also re-confirmed the importance of teaching several functional job search skills: career planning, employing diverse job search strategies, building customized CVs and online profiles, and interviewing.

Overall, the research concluded that there were 12 essential soft skills for Algerian youth to obtain employment, which we divided into three domains, similar to the domains in the original definition of life skills by UNICEF (2012) (Honeyman, 2019):

- **Intrapersonal:** positive self-concept, self-motivation, perseverance, adaptability, managing emotions (particularly stress), goal-orientation, conscientiousness or being hardworking
- **Interpersonal:** social skills (combining building relationships with others and managing conflict), communication skills (combining oral, written, nonverbal, listening), and professionalism (as defined by Algerian employers, including self-presentation and etiquette)

- **Cognitive skills:** Thinking skills (learning from experience, seeking information, critical thinking, and problem-solving), and planning and time management

The team noted that while many of these skills overlapped with core USAID recommendations made in the publications mentioned earlier in this chapter—for example, youth spoke particularly passionately about the importance of the USAID-highlighted skills of positive self-concept and communication skills—some key skills were distinct. In particular, the skills of self-motivation, perseverance, adaptability, and managing emotions stood out as crucial in Algerian youth and employers' comments, although these were given less emphasis in the USAID literature review.

Based on these research findings, we revised our curriculum to be used in upcoming projects in Algeria, and included a set of procedures for adapting it to new contexts and projects, using baseline research with youth and employers. In total, the new courses—intended for youth aged 18–29 in contexts where both self-employment and formal employment are possibilities—offer up to 70 contact hours of experiential and learner-centered activities, with options for reducing the course length when necessary (see Fig. 6.2). The course modules focus

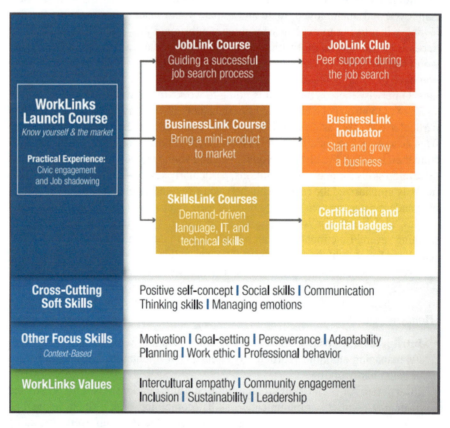

Fig. 6.2 World Learning's WorkLinks curriculum summary

on two areas: (1) career exploration (WorkLinks Launch: Know your purpose, Know yourself, Know the market, Know the workplace, and Know your next steps) and (2) the job search process (JobLink: Your job launch plan, Personal branding online and the CV, Professional writing, Professional communication and interviews, Workplace problem-solving, and Overcoming obstacles). Youth who demonstrate entrepreneurial aptitude and interest during the WorkLinks Launch course are directed to our separate business incubation process. Finally, youth who determine they need to further develop specific technical, vocational, or professional skills are directed to a range of other offerings, depending on program design.

We also chose to integrate World Learning's four core institutional values throughout the curriculum—intercultural empathy, community engagement and leadership, inclusion, and sustainability. In this way, the curriculum reflects both our global mission as an institution, and the particular contextual challenges we identified among youth in Algeria.

Pedagogy

The above qualitative research also reconfirmed that the existing experiential learning and student-centered pedagogy of World Learning's curriculum was already highly effective, according to youth themselves, at developing three specific soft skills: positive self-concept, communication, and social skills. Many participants also spontaneously described improvements in their self-motivation and goal-setting. One young man remarked, for example:

> Exchange with other students of the career center was amazing. People have taught me how to talk, when to talk, and that you don't have to talk all the time. The diversity of educational backgrounds was very enriching. Others added value from their own experiences. [...]. I developed my social skills and widened my network.

The instructional experiences that our Algerian youth beneficiaries highlighted as most useful to them were: experiential learning, group work, relationship-building and interaction with peers, group discussions, group presentations, and exposure to diversity and the concept that diverse talents and ways of being have value to the world. As a result of these research findings, we decided to retain much of our core pedagogical approach in the new curriculum.

We did, however, incorporate certain new pedagogical principles as well. First, we made a key pedagogical decision to fully integrate the 12 focal soft skills within modules focused on the more familiar processes of career exploration and the job search, rather than having separate soft skills modules each addressing, for example, communication, goal-setting, or adaptability. This decision arose out of World Learning's experience that most youth project participants are primarily interested in and motivated by learning the concrete functional skills they need to get a job (such as creating a CV or networking) and may not recognize initially the important role that soft skills play in the employment search process. Instead, we teach the importance of these skills gradually, beginning with our first module, which helps participants define a broader sense of purpose for themselves in participating in the course and prompts them to map out the linkages between achieving that purpose and developing certain soft skills. At the same time, World Learning decided that integration would also improve the effectiveness of the training experience, given that soft skills need to be learned and practiced in the context of achieving other tasks, rather than each in isolation. To ensure that the soft skills do not get lost in this integrated approach and to build the linguistic and cognitive structures that have an important—if not determinant—influence on behavior (Gumperz & Levinson, 1996), in the reflection phase of the experiential learning cycle, we guide youth to identify a soft skill they have just put into practice during a curriculum exercise, we provide a definition and foster discussion about the skill, and finally we encourage them to hang each skill term up on a Skill Wall where they can continue to see and refer to it when it is raised in a cyclical fashion in later course activities. For example, when we ask participants to analyze information about their own job market through a review of job board data and through informational interviews, they reflect on how they have used higher-order thinking skills through an independent search for information and critical examining what they have learned.

The new curriculum also adds more explicit emphasis on several other pedagogical principles highlighted in our soft skills curriculum development toolkit (See Table 6.1). For example, we develop a supportive environment by having a more organized "classroom constitution" process than previously, as well as by building in an emphasis on World Learning's core organizational values of intercultural understanding and empathy, and social inclusion and justice. Consistent

Table 6.1 Expanded list of pedagogical principles for effective soft skills development

Pedagogical principles for soft skills development
1. Develop a safe, caring, and supportive environment that allows participants to express themselves and take on challenges—including the risk of mistakes—without fear of ridicule.
2. Respect principles of adult learning: Participants have a lifetime of experience to draw on: they are not blank slates; and learning must be relevant to their lives to elicit full participation.
3. Build underlying skills of social awareness to help participants identify, evaluate, and—where appropriate—follow the norms and standards of particular social contexts.
4. Explicitly discuss what each soft skill is, why it is important, and what it looks like in practice. Define new concepts. Point out specific soft skills when they are enacted or observed in action.
5. Connect it all together into an overarching framework of principle and purpose that helps participants understand the larger picture of why developing these skills is important, and helps them apply principles to make decisions in new situations.
6. Promote skills development through experiential learning in cycles of concrete action, reflective analysis, relating the experience to abstract concepts, and planning for further action—including both prearranged exercises and demanding but achievable real-life experiences.
7. Draw on the arts, movement, and inspiring words to get participants thinking and acting in new ways. Options include theater, poetry and proverbs, painting murals, photography, digital storytelling, crafting, music, dance, sports, and more.

(continued)

Table 6.1 (continued)

Pedagogical principles for soft skills development
8. Provide consistent positive feedback when participants demonstrate core soft skills. Consider employing negative consequences when necessary.
9. Promote integration across the different learning contexts to which participants are exposed—family, community, education institution, workplace, etc—with clear and consistent standards.
10. Ensure that staff model in their own daily life the soft skills being promoted. Support staff in recognizing and addressing any personal areas for improvement.
11. Promote strong mentorship relationships among participants or between those who are more experience and less experienced (such as adults to youth), which are meaningful and caring, and in which participants are seen as valued contributors.
12. Allow for the development of soft skills over time and in a variety of situations, not just in single lessons. Employ multiple experiential learning cycles of action and reflection.

Adapted from: Honeyman (2018) and drawing on Soares et al. (2017)

constructive feedback to reinforce soft skills development is incorporated through regular classroom constitution and professionalism evaluations, involving both student self-assessment and an instructor pre/post assessment based on observation. Participants build a portfolio as the course progresses and maintain an evolving action plan, helping them see their own progress and gather useful materials. We build underlying skills of social awareness, particularly through a module focused on workplace problem-solving, so that participants gain a greater ability to identify for themselves certain soft skills they need to have in their repertoire for particular social situations. The extended course time of our new curriculum is intended to provide more opportunities for skills to be practiced multiple times in different contexts, strengthening their development. Finally, the instructor training materials emphasize the importance of instructors modeling these skills in their own lives and in their mentorship relationships with youth participants.

All these pedagogical elements are explicit within the curriculum's trainer guide, including step-by-step instructions to facilitate the many learner-centered activities. Nonetheless, World Learning recognizes that offering effective soft skills programming depends greatly on the quality of instructor training and finding ways to expand implementation over time. Advancing in this area has required nimble responses to institutional and funding constraints, as discussed in the following section.

Sustainability and Scale

Over time, we have sought a variety of means to institutionalize and scale up our soft skills programming in Algeria, ultimately reaching over 22,000 youth around the country. This scaling up process began with a recognition of the obstacles standing in the way to incorporation by the state-run education system, which was the focus of our first project. In addition to significant bureaucratic challenges, such as universities' inability to hire career advisors since no such title existed in the government-approved university staffing structure, Algerian public universities simply proved largely unwilling to grasp that students' employability skills were a part of their concern. "Stop asking me to care whether our graduates are employable," one university rector told World Learning staff, "We are a research and academic institution" (World Learning, 2016). While changing this perspective of Algerian universities could be helpful for youth employment outcomes, we determined that this would have to be a longer-term goal.

Consequently, World Learning shifted strategy towards scaling up through private TVET institutes around the country, and also developed and published a career center toolkit, including our original soft skills curriculum, making this publicly available on the internet and through large-scale Youth Employment Summit events. As a result of these initiatives, certain other private educational institutions, as well as youth-led clubs, have begun to use these materials on their own initiative. The directors of TVET institutes whose career centers we supported also decided to create a National Career Center Federation, Techghil, to further promote these skills and opportunities for youth around the country.

Our most recent large-scale tracer study of 3601 of our youth program participants, conducted in 2019 while we were still finalizing our new curriculum, showed that among youth who independently sought employment, nearly 80% succeeded— nine percentage points higher than the official national youth employment rate. While these findings and our efforts at diffusion are promising, the reality is that further employability and soft skills curriculum testing and refinement will continue to be influenced by funder priorities as well as by the complex Algerian political and economic context, as the country struggles to recover from public protests, oil price shocks, and now the COVID-19 induced economic crisis.

Philippines: Soft Skills Training and Empowerment Program (10ThousandWindows)[10]

Country Context

Since 2010, the nonprofit organization 10ThousandWindows (10KW) has been implementing soft skills programming for survivors of violence and exploitation in the Philippines. The Philippines is a newly industrialized economy with one of the fastest growing economies in the region. While the Filipino economy has made advances in recent years, concerns regarding income inequality, underemployment, and reliance upon remittances from workers outside the Philippines persist. The

---

[10] Data presented in this case study were gathered as a part of 10ThousandWindows' internal processes as a nonprofit, following the organization's own internal ethics guidelines for data collected in-house.

official national employment rate in the Philippines exceeds 90%, but includes unpaid family workers along with self-employed workers and wage/salaried workers. It is estimated that 18.7% of youth aged 15–24 in the Philippines are unemployed and/or not engaged in education or training (PSA, 2019). Primary employment sectors include manufacturing, agriculture, and services, with substantial growth in the service sector such as business process outsourcing (DOLE, 2019).

In contrast to EDC and World Learning, 10KW focuses on a very specific population that includes youth but also extends beyond them. We primarily serve survivors of human trafficking—Filipino women and men who were trafficked within the Philippines or internationally to work in a variety of industries, like sex work, domestic work, or construction. Additionally, we serve survivors of intimate partner violence (IPV), child labor, and other forms of sexual and physical violence. We assist these survivors in preparing for and obtaining safe, sustainable employment. Lack of access to safe employment is a ubiquitous, fundamental concern for survivors of human trafficking, and strengthening access to safe employment is an important component of reducing vulnerability (Cordisco Tsai, 2017; Lisborg, 2009; Richardson et al., 2009). While the educational levels and ages of our participants vary, the majority are young adults in their 20s who have not completed secondary school upon enrolling in our programs. Participants in our programs prepare for formal employment in a wide range of industries, and each participant's career path is individualized to his or her interests, competencies, and goals.

Our services for survivors include career counseling, soft skills training, formal and non-formal secondary school and college scholarships and academic support, employment counseling, employer engagement and network building, education regarding labor rights, work immersion opportunities, and crisis intervention. All survivors newly enrolled at 10KW participate in a foundational four-month training program called the Soft Skills Training and Empowerment Program (STEP), which will be discussed in this case study. STEP is only one component of our comprehensive array of services aimed at supporting survivors in achieving their own goals, including an initiative we have launched to educate employers about trauma and help employers create trauma-informed workplaces so that survivors' experiences of trauma are not perpetuated in the workplace.

Contextualization

Originally designed in 2009–2010, the initial version of STEP contained two components: career goal development and soft skills training relevant to school and workplace success. Upon completing this preliminary program, survivors proceeded to 10KW's other services. In 2018, we conducted a comprehensive program assessment. A key ensuing recommendation was to revise STEP to make it more suitable for survivors of human trafficking (Cordisco Tsai, 2018). From 2018 to 2019, we embarked on a systematic process for revising the STEP curriculum. Following completion of a literature review, we utilized World Learning's soft skills inventory tool (Honeyman, 2018) to formulate a survey to investigate how to prioritize soft skills. Survey respondents included 10KW staff and employers hiring for entry-level formal employment positions (n = 40). Using the inventory, respondents ranked soft skills in order of importance and identified the most important skills, with definitions provided to establish common understanding. Employment partners were asked to share observations regarding 10KW program participants' strengths and areas for growth. Finally, we conducted focus group discussions with 15 survivors who had completed STEP and obtained employment to discuss their strengths, workplace readiness, and challenges encountered in the workplace, and to identify soft skills they deemed most important (n = 15).

To solidify the final list of skills, we integrated feedback from survivors, staff, and employers, identifying skills prioritized by all groups. Significant consideration was given to the need to ensure the content was comprehensible and accessible in a four-month training program for a population who has experienced significant trauma. The four-month timeframe was deemed sufficient to cover the core components of the entire intervention at a foundational level without significantly delaying survivors' progress toward the next stages of our services. We decided to focus on intrapersonal, interpersonal, and cognitive/planning skills, encompassing the following specific skills: self-confidence, coping with stress, and self-discipline/control (intrapersonal); respecting others, teamwork, and resolving conflict (interpersonal); and managing time/tasks, responsibility, and decision making (cognitive/planning). Given survivors' histories of experiencing abuse, lessons on interpersonal skills such as respecting others and conflict resolution focused not only on adapting to another person, but also helping survivors prioritize their own safety and ensure their own needs were met.

Additionally, STEP was expanded beyond solely soft skills training to include a broader set of services deemed necessary to adapt the program for our target population. The revised version of the STEP curriculum entails five core components: expanded orientations and informed consent processes, career counseling and goal development, psychosocial education, soft skills training, and culminating activities (see Table 6.2). In the revised version, the career goal development component was broadened to include substantially more individualized sessions with counselors to further support survivors in developing individualized career goals over time. We added psychosocial education addressing key challenges for our participants, including understanding trauma, intimate partner and gender-based violence, substance use, suicidal ideation, and reproductive health. Given our target population, a foundational training focusing on soft skills only was deemed incomplete without enhancing individualized counseling services and education regarding systemic issues that deepen the vulnerability of our participants. A breadth of services follows the STEP program, as STEP alone is insufficient in ensuring survivors can access safe, sustainable employment.

Table 6.2 Overview of STEP curriculum

		Group session	Individual session
Month 1	Orientation and Informed Consent	General Orientation **Career Counseling Orientation** STEP Orientation	**CC1: Informed Consent** **CC2: Getting to know you**
Month 2	Goal Development and Career Counseling (CC)	Evaluate my strengths and motivations 1 **Evaluate my strengths and motivations 2** Explore career options 1 Explore career options 2 **Setting my vision 1** Setting my vision 2	**CC3: Exploring my track** **CC4: Strengthening my vision**
Month 3	Psychosocial Education	*Trauma* *Substance use* *Reproductive health* *IPV* *Human trafficking* *Suicide*	**CC5: Focusing on goals**
	Life Skills Training	Intrapersonal: 1: Self-confidence 2: Coping with stress 3: Self-discipline 4: Review/synthesis	**CC6: Action planning**
Month 4		Interpersonal: 1: Respecting others 2: Teamwork 3: Resolving conflict 4: Review/synthesis	**CC7: Determining readiness**
		Cognitive/planning: 1: Managing time/tasks 2: Responsibility 3: Decision making 4: Review/Synthesis	
	Culmination	Career Case Conference Culminating Activity	**CC8: Next steps**

Sessions facilitated by: Plain Text – STEP Training Manager; **Bold – Career Counselors**; *Italics – Social Worker*

Pedagogy

Several key pedagogical principles guide our implementation. First, a safe and supportive environment is essential. Traumatic events can destroy a person's sense of autonomy and fundamental assumptions about safety in the world (Herman, 1997). Survivors of human trafficking suffer from trauma symptoms, including anxiety, depression, terror, self-harm, attention difficulties, hostility, hypervigilance, difficulties identifying social cues, desperation to form relationships, emotional detachment, and helplessness (Clawson & Goldblatt, 2007; Kiss et al., 2015a, b; Moore et al., 2017). These trauma responses can interfere with the process of learning and embodying soft skills. Key principles of a trauma-informed approach to creating an environment conducive to working with survivors include emotional and physical safety, transparency and trustworthiness, choice/restoration of autonomy and control, collaboration, empowerment, and sensitivity to cultural, historical, and gender issues (Herman, 1997; SAMHSA, 2014).

Trauma-informed principles influenced the collaborative process that 10KW engaged in to identify the focal soft skills. Trauma-informed principles are integrated through the way in which the training is structured and facilitated—the informed consent process, wording of modules, session facilitation, activity design, setting group norms, mechanisms for providing feedback, and expectations for communication with survivors. For example, 1 month is dedicated to the informed consent process so that survivors can make an informed decision of whether or not they want to participate in STEP. Individualized career counseling sessions are included in the STEP curriculum so that survivors can partner with and receive support from staff in setting individualized goals for themselves and their participation in STEP. Soft skills are discussed in relation to survivors' own goals for themselves. Trauma-informed principles also influence session facilitation in numerous ways. For example, at the outset, 10KW staff facilitate a collaborative conversation with survivors regarding group norms that can guide all participants' interactions with each other to ensure that a safe and supportive environment is cultivated in the classroom. During group discussion and activities, survivors are invited to participate in group activities only to the extent that they feel comfortable and as they are ready. Affirmations are provided each time survivors share or participate. Staff ask permission before providing information to reinforce a sense of autonomy for survivors in the classroom, and to ensure they are comfortable with all activities.

Additionally, all of our services, including STEP, are designed to adhere to a culturally-adapted form of Motivational Interviewing (MI), an evidence-based, person-centered, and humanistic approach to communication designed to strengthen an individual's commitment to growth (Cordisco Tsai & Seballos-Llena, 2020; Miller & Rollnick, 2013). The MI spirit is based upon four components: partnership, acceptance, compassion, and evocation. The final principle reflects a commitment to evoke a person's own motivation and goals rather than imposing them from the outside. In addition to using a trauma-informed framework, the integration of MI skills into session design and facilitation reinforced a supportive and safe learning environment.

Our pedagogy is also consistent with other effective practices identified in Table 6.1, introduced earlier. Staff are intentional in providing consistent, positive feedback. People who have experienced trauma may misinterpret interactions as threatening or negative, undermining a sense of competency or safety (CODCHU, 2016). As survivors often struggle with shame and low self-worth, feedback is provided in a manner that will not amplify these feelings and affirmations are integrated in an MI-adherent manner (Gill & Cordisco Tsai, 2018). Staff are supervised to ensure that communication is warm, empathetic, and consistent (Ziegler, 2002).

10KW's staff development program includes MI training and monthly MI learning communities in which staff practice implementing MI skills.

We also ensured that the curriculum was connected to an overarching purpose. During STEP, survivors engaged in individualized goal development wherein they developed personalized visions and career plans with support from counselors. STEP sessions were linked to survivors' goals for their own lives, supporting self-determination. Additionally, we promoted skills development through experiential learning integrated with reflective analysis and planning for further action. Experiential learning activities include role playing, simulation exercises, team-building games, and solving real-life case studies. Group processing is facilitated after each activity. At the end of each soft skill session, survivors are given at-home application exercises that can be done in the next three days. The outputs of at-home exercises are processed during the review/synthesis session for each soft skill cluster.

The arts were incorporated into the learning process, with survivors expressing their thoughts and feelings through drawings, collages, poems, essays, and individualized learning portfolios. Other 10KW programs, such as career counseling and supported work immersion, provided ongoing opportunities to strengthen soft skills over time, while the employment engagement side of 10KW's operations focused on helping employers create trauma-informed workplace environments.

Sustainability and Scale

Given the distinctive experiences and needs of our target population, scaling the STEP intervention and integration with broader systems remains challenging. When serving a population that has experienced considerable trauma, substantial capacity building is required to prepare systems – including educational institutions, employers, and social welfare organizations – to successfully engage. Training, sensitization, and de-stigmatization surrounding mental health is needed, along with efforts to equip stakeholders in using trauma-informed methods. As referenced earlier, we launched a program to educate employers on how to create trauma-informed workplaces. While there has been heightened attention to mental health issues in the Philippines since the passage of the country's first mental health legislation in 2018, discussions about trauma and how trauma may impact employment-related soft skills are rare. The process of institutionalizing learning about mental health and trauma across a wide range of employers in diverse industries is a complex endeavor for a small nonprofit organization with limited funding.

Further, effective pedagogy requires significant investment of resources that are often not available. We previously used a train-the-trainer model for STEP, supporting other social welfare organizations in facilitating STEP. However, we deliberately transferred all facilitation of STEP in-house due to the need to ensure the training is implemented in a trauma-sensitive and MI-adherent manner, so that it is ultimately effective for survivors. Proper adherence to the program's guiding frameworks – a trauma-informed approach and MI – requires facilitators who have the knowledge, experience, and clinical skills required to implement trauma-informed and MI-adherent programming. These approaches are still nascent within broader systems, and require significant strengthening of the clinical skills of facilitators to ensure programming is implemented in a manner that adheres to these approaches. While training and mentoring can be provided on MI and trauma-informed care for other social welfare institutions, supportive organizational cultures and strong staff development systems are also required to ensure that facilitators have the training, clinical skills, and clinical supervision needed to successfully implement such approaches (Cordisco Tsai & Seballos-Llena, 2020).

When considering sustainability and scale, we are speaking from the perspective of practitioners implementing soft skills programming with a very specific population – survivors of violence and exploitation, and primarily survivors of human trafficking. Our experiences facilitating STEP with survivors are not necessarily transferable to soft skills programming more broadly. Ultimately, the decision to move facilitation internally was deemed necessary to improve training quality for our specific target population while we continue to work on broader community education and systems change efforts. However, this shift augmented the cost of services, raising concerns for donors unfamiliar with the on-the-ground realities of working with survivors of human trafficking, who also expect a lower cost-per-participant ratio than is realistic given the level of service specialization required. Questions remain about ensuring sustainability of this approach, as well as educating donors and other stakeholders in understanding the unique complexities of working with our target population. Despite challenges, we continue to prioritize strengthening our curriculum, ensuring suitability for survivors, enhancing evaluation methods, and embedding soft skills training within a comprehensive range of services to support survivors in achieving their own goals.

Discussion and Conclusion

These case studies, featuring soft skills curriculum for employability in three diverse contexts—Rwanda, Algeria, and the Philippines—raise important questions about such programming, including contextual decisions about what specific skills what specific skills to teach with particular populations and program goals, how to enact pedagogical principles, and how to ensure sustainability and scale both within formal education systems and outside them. Our work on each of these aspects, and likely the work of many other donor-supported soft skills programs, has also been influenced by the dynamics of the international community of practice we belong to, which is shaped by power and positionality—reflected in curricular frameworks first produced in wealthy developed countries, research promoted by influential institutions, and projects delimited by funder priorities and time horizons, as well as by organic connections and learning within and among implementing organizations. Acknowledging the existence of these dynamics gives a fuller picture of the influences and constraints shaping soft skills programming in the workforce development field.

While our professional community of practice has developed a shared understanding of soft skills that is influenced by donor priorities, these case studies also illustrate that implementing organizations can work effectively with local partners to contextualize their programs, moving through and beyond donor discourse. Many approaches to employability and soft skills curricula within our broader community of practice may have initially been developed either based on US-centered educational strategies, or on field staff insights into their own program contexts, but in either case with little context-specific research available for orientation. In the years since, programs have had to adjust their approaches to respond to both stronger funding agency guidance around specific skills to teach globally, as well as to a more nuanced understanding of local public and private sector priorities. In addition, as many organizations seek to offer their programming in multiple countries, they must face the challenges of maintaining a core curricular approach that is still contextually-responsive. The professional spaces that have shaped our broader community of practice in both intentional and organic ways—conferences, webinars, workshops, email listservs, and indeed the co-authoring of publications such as this one—continue to provide important contexts for learning about and adopting shared practices, as well as articulating and defending legitimate differences of approach and contextualization.

All three cases featured here have illustrated the resource constraints that affect the possibility of such contextual curriculum adaptation. Donor funding and project timeline expectations often do not prioritize curriculum revision, while a quality process can take many months of staff time from more than one person, including for desk reviews, field research, stakeholder engagement, and the detailed analysis and rewriting process, not to mention issues of translation and other details such as locally-adapted illustrations. Donor priorities may also shift significantly from one project to the next, while funding may be awarded to different organizations from project to project in the same context, risking the need for each new project to create a new curriculum from scratch. When powerful actors in the workforce development space overlook these issues, they contribute to maladapted programs that do not respond to the actual needs of participants. Further, they may perpetuate dynamics of cultural imperialism as a result, such as teaching workplace etiquette in a manner that reflects Western assumptions and patterns of behavior rather than a deep understanding the diverse norms that exist around the world with regard to issues such as negotiation, conflict management, authority, and politeness.

Another challenge that international workforce development programs face in creating effective employability and soft skills curricula is the issue of pedagogical fidelity in the enacted curriculum. Although there is increasingly greater clarity around the pedagogical practices and program designs that are more effective for developing specific targeted soft skills, it is often difficult to ensure these conditions are met. Projects must spend significant time and resources on training instructors in methodologies that are often not standard practices within the wider education and training systems of most countries of implementation. Furthermore, soft skills instruction requires much more than just mastery of some information and content. Instructors themselves must demonstrate these skills and attitudes in their own lives, and be able to mentor others through example as they develop them—often unevenly and organically—over time. Additionally, while cascade training models—in which an organization trains master trainers, who in turn teach other instructors—are often used because they are a more cost-effective means of reaching larger numbers of beneficiaries, sometimes this strategy must be abandoned in order to reach the desired quality of experience for project participants, as 10KW found. The degree of pedagogical reorientation required to effectively teach soft skills cannot always be feasibly accomplished without significant investments in instructor training, a point that holds significant time and resource implications for teaching soft skills in both informal systems and formal educational institutions.

Issues of pedagogical fidelity become even more challenging as one considers the effort to institutionalize and significantly scale up the offering of employability and soft skills curricula to large populations. EDC's experience shows the importance of thinking about the wider system and delivery model at the same time as making content adaptation choices. It often seems like an improvised dance, struggling to balance between the elements and constraints of a system on the one hand, and an organization's view of the ideal pedagogical methodology on the other, in order to design an approach that can be implemented in reality. Not only instructor training systems must be considered in the effort to scale up, but also realistic costing of staff time and materials. Identifying future budget sources for such needs, fitting within school timetables, integration within national frameworks and assessments, addressing institutional cultures that may lead to resistance to new approaches, and monitoring and support mechanisms to ensure quality delivery all pose significant challenges—often within institutions that do not have such mechanisms functioning strongly even for their core educational priorities.

Beyond simply adding a new course to an existing education or training system, our cases show that employability and soft skills development could be more fully integrated into the system as a cross-cutting focus of instruction, or even through a wholehearted overhaul of general teacher pedagogy. In our experience of implementing soft skills programs in multiple contexts, many soft skills are actually best built over a long period of time, and may be developed through year-after-year exposure to a more student-centered pedagogy that requires students to be involved in research, problem-solving, discussion, and group work. Short-term projects may influence these broader practices as unintended beneficial effects but most often, this requires significant intentionality and support for institutional change that may only be achieved through embeddedness in longer term reorientation of the general educational system—again a dynamic that requires a rare long-term continuity in funding and program purpose.

While continuing to grapple with issues of contextualization, pedagogy, and sustainability and scale, many organizations are also experimenting with alternate methodologies for soft skills development that respond to particular programming needs, constraints, and opportunities. World Learning, for example, is working with extended narratives—fictional stories focusing on characters and the challenges they confront over the course of several linked episodes or chapters—in conjunction with individual and group activities, to effectively model the skills participants can develop and to help participants visualize and practice, in an enduring way, the decisions they may make in their own lives (similar to the strategy of case studies described in Pacheco & Murphy-Graham, Chap. 10, this volume). Similarly, EDC partnered with Search for Common Ground in Rwanda to develop a radio series that used a soap opera style to emphasize many of the core skills found in the WRN curriculum. By following a character's story, participants share an "experience" external to themselves that serves as a touchpoint for skill-development exercises and discussion, enriching the learning experience in new ways.

Virtual reality, roleplay smartphone apps, and other online learning modalities also offer new prospects for scaling up soft skills development curricula, while still posing challenges for universal access and for approximating the rich social interactions that can more naturally occur in face to face programs (see, for example, Haley-Robbins et al., 2019). These contemporary approaches to soft skills development coexist with broader concerns about technological change and the future of work, offering the tantalizing prospect of building digital literacy and other contemporary technology skills at the same time as employability and soft skills. However, moving to these digital platforms requires careful thinking about how to preserve the learner-centered pedagogy and sense of community and confidence-building that comes from being a part of a learning group. As automation, artificial intelligence, increasingly ubiquitous broadband access, and post-COVID 19 changes to labor markets are accelerating shifts in skills demand within and across sectors, especially with respect to the application of digital skills, these new frontiers for soft skills development cannot be overlooked, even as they are by no means a panacea.

Regardless of the approach, there remains more to explore in the effort to understanding the on-the-ground challenges that soft skills initiatives face, as well as the best way forward as such programming navigates an international field of power and influence, works towards contextual grounding in local research, and seeks ways to achieve and sustain new pedagogical approaches with broader populations.

Acknowledgements   World Learning acknowledges the support of the U.S. Department of State and its Middle East Partnership Initiative (MEPI) in funding the projects and research described in our case study. The views expressed in this chapter are those of the author and do not represent the views of, and should not be attributed to, the U.S. Department of State or MEPI. World Learning Algeria field office staff who played a central role in the research and curriculum development processes described in the chapter include Andrew Farrand, Hamza Koudri, Mehdi Bentoumi, Zobida Tadj, Latifa Dehane, Abdallah Talhi, and Leah Bitat.

EDC acknowledges funding support from USAID and the MasterCard Foundation for the projects described in Rwanda, as well as contributions from Beth Miller Pittman, a technical advisor on the project, and Nora Nunn, a reviewer of the case study. The views expressed in this chapter are those of the author and do not represent the views of, and should not be attributed to, USAID or MasterCard Foundation.

10KW acknowledges the contributions of Jonna Eleccion (Director of 10KW Philippines) and Rosa Gabriela Benares (STEP Training Manager at 10KW). 10KW did not receive any specialized funding for the work relevant to the case study.

References

Alcid, A., & Martin, G. (2017). *Akazi Kanoze work readiness and employment outcomes: A randomized controlled trial of secondary school students in Rwanda.* Education Development Center.

Bourdieu, P. (1972). *Outline of a theory of practice.* Cambridge University Press.

Bourdieu, P. (1986). The forms of capital. In J. Richardson (Ed.), *Handbook of a theory of research for the sociology of education* (pp. 241–258). Greenwood Press.

Bourdieu, P. (1990). The social conditions of the international circulation of ideas. In R. Schusterman (Ed.), *Bourdieu: A critical reader* (pp. 220–228). Blackwell.

Clawson, H. J., & Goldblatt, G. L. (2007). Finding a path to recovery: Residential facilities for minor victims of domestic sex trafficking. *Human Trafficking Data and Documents, 10.* https://aspe.hhs.gov/system/files/pdf/75186/ib.pdf

CODCHU Center on the Developing Child at Harvard University. (2016). *Building core capabilities for life: The science behind the skills adults need to succeed in parenting and in the workplace.* http://www.developingchild.harvard.edu/

Cordisco Tsai, L. (2017). The process of managing family financial pressures upon community re-entry among survivors of sex trafficking in the Philippines: A grounded theory study. *Journal of Human Trafficking, 3*(3), 211–230.

Cordisco Tsai, L. (2018). *10ThousandWindows 2018 program assessment.* 10ThousandWindows.

Cordisco Tsai, L., & Seballos-Llena, I. F. (2020). Reflections on adapting motivational interviewing to the Filipino cultural context. *Practice: Social Work in Action, 32*(1), 43–57.

CREAD & ILO. (2017). Rapport principal de l'enquête algérienne sur la jeunesse. Unpublished Report.

DOLE Department of Labor and Employment. (2019). Labor Market Profile. *Issue, 1.* http://ble.dole.gov.ph/downloads/Publications/LMI-LMP-2018%20PH%20Labor%20Market-March%202019%20Issue.pdf

Farrand, A. (2019). *Algeria youth employment project: Labor market assessment.* World Learning.

Gill, M., & Cordisco Tsai, L. (2018). Building core skills among adult survivors of human trafficking in a workplace setting in the Philippines. *International Social Work, 63*(4), 538–544. https://doi.org/10.1177/0020872818819043

Gumperz, J. J., & Levinson, S. C. (1996). *Rethinking linguistic relativity.* Cambridge University Press.

Haley-Robbins, Z., Honeyman, C. A., & Murillo, K. (2019). *10 apps to build employability and soft skills.* World Learning.

Herman, J. (1997). *Trauma and recovery: The aftermath of violence – From domestic abuse to political terror.* Basic Books.

Honeyman, C. A. (2016). *The orderly entrepreneur: Youth, education, and governance in Rwanda.* Stanford University Press.

Honeyman, C. A. (2018). *Soft skills development: Guiding notes for project and curriculum design and evaluation.* World Learning.

Honeyman, C. A. (2019). *Soft skills for youth employment in Algeria: Qualitative research report.* World Learning.

Honeyman, C. A., & Fletcher, E. (2019). *Measuring skills for youth workforce development.* USAID.

Ignatowski, C. (2017). What works in soft skills development for youth employment? *A donor's perspective.* Youth Employment Funder's Group in partnership with the MasterCard Foundation.

Kautz, T., Heckman, J., Diris, R., ter Weel, B., & Borghans, L. (2014). *Fostering and measuring skills: Improving cognitive and non-cognitive skills to promote lifetime success.* OECD.

Kiss, L., Pocock, N. S., Naisanguansri, V., Suos, S., Dickson, B., Thuy, D., Koehler, J., Sirisup, K., Pongrungsee, N., Nguyen, V. A., Borland, R., Dhavan, P., & Zimmerman, C. (2015a). Health of men, women, and children in post-trafficking services in Cambodia, Thailand, and Vietnam: An observational cross-sectional study. *The Lancet Global Health, 3*(3), e154–e161.

Kiss, L., Yun, K., Pocock, N., & Zimmerman, C. (2015b). Exploitation, violence, and suicide risk among child and adolescent survivors of human trafficking in the Greater Mekong Subregion. *JAMA Pediatrics, 169*(9), e152278–e152278.

Kolb, D. (1984). *Experiential Learning: Experience as the source of learning and development.* Prentice Hall.

Lave, J., & Wenger, E. (1991). *Situated learning: Legitimate peripheral participation.* Cambridge University Press.

Lippman, L., Ryberg, R., Carney, R., & Moore, K. (2015). *Key "soft skills" that foster youth workforce success: Toward a consensus across fields.* WorkForce Connections. FHI 360/USAID.

Lisborg, A. (2009). *Re-thinking reintegration: What do returning victims really want and need?* Strategic Information Response Network United Nations Inter-Agency Project on Human Trafficking (UNIAP).

MasterCard Foundation. (2017). *Skills at scale: Transferable skills in secondary and vocational education in Africa.*

Miller, W. R., & Rollnick, S. (2013). *Motivational interviewing: Helping people change.* Guilford Press.

Moore, T., McArthur, M., Death, J., Tulbury, C., & Roche, S. (2017). Young people's views on safety and preventing abuse and harm in residential care: "It's got to be better than home.". *Children and Youth Services Review, 81,* 212–219.

ONS. (2018). *Activité, Emploi & Chômage en Septembre 2018.* Office National des Statistiques, Algeria. Accessed October 2018 from this website: http://www.ons.dz/IMG/emploiseptembre2018.pdf.

PSA Philippines Statistics Authority. (2019). *Youth population and labor participation.* http://www.psa.gov.ph/content/employment-rate-july-2019-estimated-946-percent

Richardson, D., Poudel, M., & Laurie, N. (2009). Sexual trafficking in Nepal: Constructing citizenship and livelihoods. *Gender, Place and Culture, 16*(3), 259–278.

Roberts, R., Martin, J., & Olaru, G. (2015). *A Rosetta stone for noncognitive skills: Understanding, assessing, and enhancing noncognitive skills in primary and secondary education.* Asia Society. http://asiasociety.org/files/A_Rosetta_Stone_for_Noncognitive_Skills.pdf?_sm_au_=iVVbvrLb7qLPqPMQ

SAMHSA Substance Abuse and Mental Health Services Administration. (2014). *SAMHSA's concept of trauma and guidance for a trauma-informed approach* (HHS publication no. (SMA) 14-4884). Substance Abuse and Mental Health Services Administration.

Soares, F., Babb, S., Diener, O., Gates, S., & Ignatowski, C. (2017). Guiding principles for building soft skills among adolescents and young adults. USAID YouthPower Implementation.

Stites, R. (2011). EDC international work readiness framework and assessment – Notes on the "state of the art" in 21st century work readiness standards and assessments. Unpublished internal report. Education Development Center.

UNICEF. (2012). *Global evaluation of life skills education programmes.* United Nations Children's Fund.

World Bank. (2019). *World development report: The changing nature of work.* World Bank.

World Bank. (2020). *World Bank data, share of youth not in education, employment or training, total (% of youth population).* Via International Labour Organization, ILOSTAT database. https://data.worldbank.org/indicator/sl.uem.neet.zs

World Economic Forum. (2018). *The future of jobs report.* https://www.weforum.org/reports/the-future-of-jobs-report-2018

World Learning. (2016). *Promoting Education, Altruism and Civic Engagement (PEACE) final performance report.* World Learning.

YouthStart. (2016). *Youth economic opportunity ecosystem analysis Rwanda via UNCDF.* https://www.un.org/youthenvoy/2016/01/youth-economic-opportunity-ecosystem-analysis-rwanda-via-uncdf/

Ziegler, D. (2002). *Traumatic experience and the brain: A handbook for understanding and treating those traumatized as children.* Acacia Publishing Inc.

Chapter 7
Life Skills Education for Urban Youth in Honduras and Guatemala: A Capability Analysis of the Sports-Based Job Training Program *A Ganar*

Erin Murphy-Graham

Abstract Drawing upon an extensive case study of a sports-based, life skills job training program for at-risk youth in Honduras and Guatemala, this chapter examines how program participants described the process of building skills, and how, if at all, this skill-building led to greater well-being. Second, it asks, to what extent are these experiences of program participants aligned with theories of education within the capability approach? These questions are addressed through a qualitative case study that was embedded within an experimental design (a randomized control trial) that took place over 5 years in urban areas of Honduras and Guatemala. The analysis suggests that the combination of exposure to new ideas and information in the three phases of the A Ganar program, coupled with concrete opportunities to test out such ideas, enabled youth to experience changes in their attitudes and behaviors around work, around themselves, and to develop new relationships and friendships. Based on these empirical results, the chapter identifies several elements that might better inform life skills education research and practice in s in the future. These include: (1) conceptualizing life skills as preconditions of capabilities (some of which might be better classified as values); (2) conceptualizing life skills as both ends and means of interventions, and (3) giving more consideration to the conversion factors, meaning the ability to convert resources into functionings, that limit the robustness of capabilities that life skills programs develop.

Keywords Education · Job-training · Sport · Skills · Capability approach · Central America · Qualitative research

E. Murphy-Graham (✉)
University of California, Berkeley, Berkeley, CA, USA
e-mail: emurphy@berkeley.edu

© The Author(s) 2022
J. DeJaeghere, E. Murphy-Graham (eds.), *Life Skills Education for Youth*, Young People and Learning Processes in School and Everyday Life 5,
https://doi.org/10.1007/978-3-030-85214-6_7

Introduction

If life skills are, broadly defined, the ability to live life well, a clear conception of well-being must inform programming with youth. As explained by DeJaeghere and Murphy-Graham (Chap. 1, this volume), the Capability Approach (CA) is a theoretical framework about wellbeing, freedom, freedom to achieve wellbeing, and the public values that can play a role in this process (Robeyns, 2017). For scholars and practitioners who wish to engage with life skills education from an approach that is "concerned with transformative change for persons and societies," (DeJaeghere & Walker, 2021, p. 775), what does the CA offer? Can a capability analysis of life skills education make a difference in practice by first examining "the unjust nature of social structures, economic institutions, or social norms" (Robeyns, 2017, p. 215) and crafting programs that are informed by such analysis?

This chapter examines these questions, and provides a capability analysis of a life skills education program. It presents findings from an in-depth qualitative case study of a sports-based, life skills job training program for at-risk youth in Honduras and Guatemala.[1] The program A Ganar, which means "to win" or "to earn" in Spanish, recruited youth in urban communities and provided nine months of life-skills, technical/vocational training, and an internship. This chapter does not examine the overall effects of the program (which can be found in Duthie et al., 2018). Here, I examine how A Ganar participants described the process of building "skills" and how this description is aligned with a notion of the purpose of education from a capabilities perspective. Based on this empirical analysis, the chapter suggests that there are several elements that might advance knowledge regarding life skills education research and practice. These include: (1) conceptualizing some life skills, particularly values, as preconditions of capabilities; (2) conceptualizing life skills as both ends and means of interventions; and (3) giving more consideration to the conversion factors, or the ability to convert resources into functionings, that limit the enactment of capabilities developed by life skills programs.

Theoretical Framework: Education
from a Capability Perspective

The Capability Approach provides an alternative to approaches to wellbeing that are focused on income or economic wealth. It asks the questions: what are people really able to do and what kind of people are they able to be? What they *can do* and be are referred to as their "capabilities," and what they are *actually achieving* is called their "functionings" (Robeyns, 2017). The overall approach can be thought of as an open and flexible multipurpose framework for thinking about issues related to wellbeing,

---

[1] Murphy-Graham was the lead qualitative researcher of a randomized control trial evaluation team (see Duthie et al., 2018).

freedom, and social justice. It also provides a broad framework within which individuals from different disciplines or fields can elaborate a capability theory for a specific use (Robeyns, 2017).

There is a growing number of educational studies that conceptualize education with regard to justice, accounting for both intrinsic and extrinsic roles of education, as well as what individuals value for their wellbeing (DeJaeghere, 2018; DeJaeghere & Lee, 2011; DeJaeghere & Walker, 2021; Peppin Vaughan, 2015; Peppin Vaughan & Walker, 2012; Saito, 2003; Tikly & Barrett, 2011; Walker, 2012). Scholars writing about education from a capability perspective have provided a rich set of ideas regarding the type of education we might aspire to, and have critiqued education commonly found around the world, including life skills education (DeJaeghere et al., 2016; Saito, 2003; Tikly & Barrett, 2011; Peppin Vaughan, 2015; Peppin Vaughan & Walker, 2012; Walker, 2012). As Walker and Unterhalter (2007, p. 15) explain, to count as education, processes and outcomes must enhance well-being by making one's life "richer with opportunity of reflective choice" and by enhancing the ability of people to help themselves and influence the world. Rather than a "bag of virtues" approach to education that lacks a clear theoretical rationale for defining objectives that can withstand philosophical criticism and that are at odds with research findings (Kohlberg & Mayer, 1972), the capability approach allows education to expand students' capabilities to form goals and values rooted in social justice (Peppin Vaughan & Walker, 2012, p. 497). The capabilities gained through educational interventions, including life skills and job training programs, should not be understood only in terms of specific skills and academic outcomes (which are indeed important), but also in terms of the *values* that are cultivated through the educational process.

Skills, or the ability, coming from one's knowledge, practice, and aptitude to do something well, might be considered the necessary elements of a capability, or a precondition for a capability. This implies that life skills, or the skills that help a person through everyday tasks and to be active and productive members of a community, must be coupled with favorable external conditions and circumstances. Stated more simply with a domain-specific example: one might have job skills, but to convert these skills into a functioning (paid work), the environment must have employment opportunities. Thus, the skills alone are not enough: they must be paired with real opportunities for individuals to *do something* with these skills.

This idea (conversion of skills into practice) is important for the capability approach, also called "conversion factors," which refer to the "different abilities that individuals have to convert resources into functionings" (Robeyns, 2017, p. 45). There are three types of conversion factors: (a) personal factors, such as sex, intelligence, physical condition, disabilities, etc., (b) social factors, such as social norms, societal hierarchies, power relations, etc., and (c) environmental factors, such as the environment in which a person lives, infrastructure, resources available, etc. When conceptualizing how a "skill" begets a capability (what a person can do) and a functioning (what they actually do), a key insight is that people have different abilities to convert resources into functionings (Robeyns, 2017). A capability approach, and its application to life skills education, acknowledges the structural constraints that exert a great deal of influence on individuals' conversion factors and capability sets (particularly when examining labor market and health outcomes).

The recognition of structural constraints may also help explain why interventions for youth are often deemed ineffective or have mixed results, as explained in Murphy-Graham and Cohen (Chap. 2, this volume), in the empirical review of studies focusing on labor market outcomes (see also Heckman & Kautz, 2013). However, this raises one final point, which is that the *measures* used to determine effectiveness of life skills interventions might require additional refinement. This is related to the distinction of "means and ends:" Are life skills valuable because they are means to being employed, or might certain elements of life skills be important ends in themselves? As Robeyns points out, "there are some very important ends that do not depend very much on material means…For example, self-respect, supportive relationships in school or in the workplace, or friendship are all very important ends that people may want" (2017, p. 49). I explore these questions further through an empirical case study of youth in Honduras and Guatemala.

Research Context: A Ganar in Guatemala and Honduras

Young people in Honduras and Guatemala face a number of challenges, particularly if they are among the 59–66%[2] of the population that lives in poverty. Education, unfortunately, offers little hope for poor youth to escape poverty because there is limited coverage at the secondary level, low quality resulting in weak student learning, and low transition and graduation rates (Adelman & Székely, 2016). Only a small percentage of poor youth gain the educational experiences they need to enter the formal labor market, and youth unemployment is twice as high as the total unemployment rate (International Labor Organization, 2021).

Implemented by Partners of the Americas (POA), a non-governmental organization based in Washington, D.C., the A Ganar program aims to address the serious problem of youth unemployment in Latin America and the Caribbean by utilizing soccer and other team sports to help at risk youth find positive ways to engage in their communities. A Ganar is a 7–9 month, three-phase job training program that combines sports-based field and classroom activities, vocational training, internships/apprenticeships, and various follow-on activities to help participants (1) find jobs, (2) start or expand their business, or (3) re-enter the formal education system. POA works with youth aged 17–24, and defines "at risk" as youth who have one or more of the following characteristics:

- Come from socially or economically-disadvantaged households or communities;
- Are school dropouts or are one or more years behind in school; or,
- Belong to communities plagued by high levels of drug use and/or trafficking, youth violence, and/or youth gangs.

The program aims to help youth develop "life and employability skills" through sport-based activities, classroom training, and on-the-job experiences. Through this progression of activities, the program attempts to increase self-confidence and build trust between the youth and instructors, allowing for the reinforcement of key competencies. The specific life-skills that the A Ganar curriculum focuses on include: communication, teamwork, results, continual self-improvement, and discipline.[2] As Kwauk (Chap. 5, this volume) finds, sports-for-development interventions often emphasize the idea that important life skills can be transferred from the playing field to day-to-day realities – and like many of the programs she reviewed, A Ganar leans heavily toward a prosocial, self-improvement paradigm, particularly emphasizing teamwork and cooperative behavior.

The United States Agency for International Development (USAID) commissioned an impact evaluation (a randomized control trial) of A Ganar in Honduras and Guatemala. Key quantitative findings were:

- The program did not have any significant impact on employment rates, number of jobs, or hours worked in either country.
- A slight increase in job "quality" – particularly in wages, benefits, and job satisfaction – was detected in both countries. A Ganar youth in Honduras had significantly higher wages (2 more lempiras or ~$0.10 per hour, on average), marginally higher prevalence of benefits, and greater job satisfaction. A Ganar youth in Guatemala had 15% higher hourly wages and were 89% more likely to have a work contract.
- The program had a positive impact on some socio-emotional outcomes in both countries, including sense of positive identity, social competencies, commitment to learning, constructive use of time, and empowerment (see Duthie et al., 2018).

Here, I focus on findings from the qualitative case study that was embedded within the randomized control trial study.

Methodology: Qualitative Case Study

This qualitative case study was embedded within an experimental design (randomized control trial) of the A Ganar program.[3] The entire study sample included approximately 3,000 youth who participated in A Ganar (we conducted interviews with a smaller qualitative subsample, described below). The study took place over 5 years, from 2012 to 2017, with cohorts of youth beginning and ending their

---

[2] These areas of emphasis are consistent with the social and emotional competencies area described in Murphy-Graham and Cohen (this volume). A Ganar also emphasizes the acquisition of information/knowledge through the technical training and internship phase – but the program does not have an emphasis on building critical thinking skills *per se*.

[3] The study was approved by Social Impact's Institutional Review Board (IRB) and consent was given by research participants at every stage of the process.

participation in A Ganar at different times in each country (see Duthie et al., 2018 for a full description of the staggered nature of A Ganar implementation and research design and findings).

The qualitative study included data from a sub-sample of selected youth. I worked together with three Guatemalan and five Honduran research assistants to conduct a total of 362 in-depth qualitative interviews in Honduras and Guatemala. All interviews were conducted in Spanish. Our data collection involved two different types of interviews: (1) 24 "rich case studies" with youth at baseline, endline (after the program completed), and 18 months later; and (2) a larger sample of youth whom we interviewed at the program "exit" and "long term follow-up" – 18 months later. Rich case study interviews involved a purposive selection (see Maxwell, 2013) of 12 youth in each country (we wanted an equal representation of male and female youth, a range of age, and a range of educational backgrounds) that participated in the pilot phase of A Ganar implementation in each country. For each "rich case study", we also conducted interviews with a family member, a program facilitator, an internship supervisor, and if applicable, an employer. The purpose of these interviews was to gain a deep understanding of the overall context in which youth lived, their experiences in the A Ganar program, as well as the perspectives of those who came into contact with them throughout their participation in the program. Our early experiences with the rich case study interviews informed our decision to interview a greater number of participants when they completed the program, as well as during the long term-follow up; a larger sample would help us explain our quantitative findings and give us a greater sense of the range of experiences in the program.

For our larger sample, we interviewed a total of 208 youth (115 in Guatemala and 93 in Honduras) when they finished the program, and a total of 130 youth (86 in Guatemala and 44 in Honduras) 18 months after they finished the program. Both exit and long-term follow-up interviews prompted participants to reflect on their experiences in the A Ganar program, to name specific activities that they remembered from the various stages of the program (sports-based life skills training, technical training, internship), and to recount what had stayed with them from these activities. Every effort was made to not ask leading questions. All interviews were conducted in a private space (often a small office at a local youth organization) and recorded using digital recorders. All names used in this paper are pseudonyms.

Data Analysis

Digital recordings of interviews were transcribed and the transcripts were analyzed using Dedoose, a qualitative data analysis software analysis program. As a first stage of analysis, we drafted profiles of the rich case study youth. In these profiles, we drew upon interviews with the youth, their family members, their A Ganar facilitators, and internship supervisors. The rich case studies allowed us to identify salient themes to include in our subsequent interviews with the larger sample of youth.

All interview coding was conducted by the author and a research assistant, using both inductive and deductive coding (Miles et al., 2014). A preliminary code list was developed from intended outcomes of the *A Ganar* program as well as from our insights from an initial read of interview transcripts. This code list was further refined as we coded the interviews and new themes emerged. The final code list had roughly 30 codes. Ten of these focused on context and background of youth's lives (for example, the difficulty of using public transportation due to frequent robberies), not program outcomes. One of the most frequently applied codes was "Impact of A Ganar" – this code also had seven different sub-codes that provided more specificity, including: academic benefits/school re-entry, employment, gender perceptions/attitudes, life skills/employability features, self-esteem/confidence, social relations, and values.

After initial coding was completed, greater attention was given to the codes that were both most frequent and related to predefined program impacts. This attention allowed us to create a second-round coding system (Miles et al., 2014). Table 7.1 below lists our first and second round coding categories that focus on the impact of A Ganar:

Table 7.1 Codes and frequencies related to the impact of A Ganar used in qualitative analysis

Code first round (frequency)	Code second round
Impact of A Ganar (parent code relating to any mention of program impact)	
Academic benefits, school re-entry (31)	Re-enrollment in formal schooling Enrollment in certificate or specified training courses
Employment (76)	Paid employment
Altered gender perceptions/attitudes (16)	Challenging gender norms Difficult for women to work outside of home Men must be breadwinners
Employability (471)	Work ethic: Discipline Respect
Self-esteem/confidence (425)	Feeling more confident generally Feeling more confident about particular skills (i.e. writing a cv, being interviewed) Confidence provides enhanced sense of agency, of being "unstuck"
Social relations (754)	Feeling less shy Importance of play to foster relationships Group as a team New friends through the program Getting along with others
Values (271)	Mentioning respect, discipline or punctuality as a *value*

Findings

The analysis of the interview data at all three stages of the study suggests that the combination of exposure to new ideas and information in three stages of the A Ganar program, coupled with concrete opportunities to test out such ideas, enabled youth to experience changes in their attitudes and behaviors around work, around themselves, and to develop new relationships and friendships. Figure 7.1 below summarizes the findings that have emerged from the data analysis and illustrates how what A Ganar calls "theory and practice" combined during each phase of the A Ganar program. The combination of theory, written lessons in the A Ganar workbook that introduce core ideas such as the importance of teamwork, and practice, when youth participate in the games/activities that are part of these lessons, allowed youth to change their attitudes, behaviors, and socialization patterns. We group these into three categories: preconditions of capabilities, capabilities, and functionings.

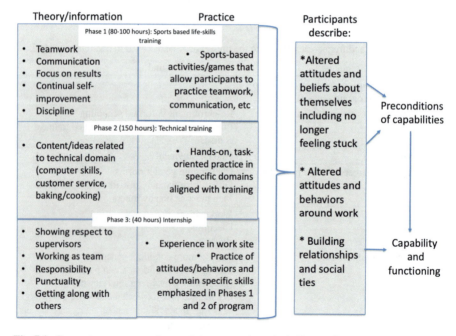

Fig. 7.1 Concept map representing participant experience in A Ganar. (Created by Author)

Preconditions of Capabilities: Altered Attitudes and Beliefs Including Not Feeling Stuck, Improved Self-Confidence, and Altered Work Ethic

Youth described a number of preconditions that might allow them to accomplish the goals of A Ganar, and in particular, becoming employed or furthering their education. Exposure to the concepts regarding life skills and the practical experience that A Ganar offered allowed some youth to no longer feel "*estancado/a*" which translates to feeling stagnant, stuck, or bogged down. Youth explained that prior to their participation in the program they felt bogged down, that they did not have a future. As one program facilitator explained: "Emotionally, the youth come from a negative environment, with violence and without many opportunities. So being in the program, they see a light of, of hope one could say, knowing that, yes, one can have other things."

Excerpts from of our interviews with the participants Jimena and Madina capture how youth describe the ways in which A Ganar allowed them to feel differently about what each could accomplish:

Madina: It [the program] guided me a lot, it guided me so that I don't remain stagnant in only one place, in order to move forward, to give of myself, my hard work, and to give to other people because I'm not the person that they imagined.

And with Jimena:

Interviewer: You told me that your plan was to study and work, right, do you believe that the program had any influence on this plan or not?

Jimena: Yes it had a lot to do with it, because first I said, "why would I study, for what reason would I study, I'm going to waste my time! But thanks to them now I have a different mentality. I want to study if only to set an example for my daughter that I can graduate and she can continue and do so.

Interviewer: And in what way do you think the program influenced you?

Jimena: In many things because they supported us, they told us and taught us to have our own goals, to have our own goals and to try to achieve them, to finish them.

Keiley, another youth we interviewed, used strikingly similar language in describing what she learned from her experience in A Ganar. She remarked, "they taught me to not be *estancada* [bogged down] and to move ahead." Likewise, a student named Rachel described a similar sentiment:

Well, that we have to continue moving forward no, not falter, and that the goals that we have in front of us we always have to achieve. To not remain stagnant…To persist, to persist because many times young people, sometimes because they don't have work, sometimes they don't have economic support, family support. So youth come to make decisions, it [A Ganar] helps them to take a different path.

Here, Rachel hinted at negative decisions that youth can make, and that A Ganar provides an alternative. In addition to feeling an increased capacity to act in ways that would help youth *seguir adelante,* or get ahead in life, youth also mentioned trying to help others. In the case of Dugan, A Ganar helped him to stop hanging around with friends in a gang, and he said he became a "changed person."

> One's mentality is not like, how should I say it... my mentality before, let's say that my mentality had been not to continue studying because I hung out with those gangs. Today my mentality is distinct and my mentality says I lost so much time with those gangs that I could have graduated...Now that I have entered the project I am now, how shall I say, a changed person. And I have the mentality to help others and involve them in the project in the new phase of A Ganar.

Youth frequently mentioned feeling more motivated to look for work or re-enroll in school due to their participation in the program. For many youth who we interviewed, low self-confidence was an underlying issue that prevented them from socializing with others and looking for work. However, their experience in A Ganar made them more confident. For example, Ramona explained:

Interviewer: What was important about what you learned?
Ramona: Important, I believe that it was the confidence in myself, something that I didn't have.

Improving self-confidence allowed youth to improve their ability to communicate with others. An anecdote that a youth named Jordana shared during her interview illustrates the interconnection of self-confidence and the ability to communicate. Jordana explained that she was very shy before entering the program. When asked to share something specific she learned in the program, she spoke without hesitation regarding a recent experience that illustrated her newfound confidence. Jordana completed her internship at Grupo Intur (a fast food conglomerate). Unlike many of her classmates who worked in the kitchens, she was placed in an office, doing human resources work. She enjoyed it very much, and felt that she had done a good job. When the internship ended, she had high hopes that she would be called back to continue working at Grupo Intur. At around the same time, Jordana became ill with a kidney infection. During her illness she indeed did get a call back from Grupo Intur, but she was unable to go to their offices because she was so sick. However, as soon as she felt better, she went to the office and explained what happened. She did not want them to think that she was irresponsible, and ultimately, she was rehired. She said that prior to her participation in A Ganar, she would not have known how to handle this situation. Jordana explained:

Jordana: So, how can I say it? Everything got complicated, so I couldn't go to work and as a result I had to leave my job. So that they did not see me as irresponsible I went to talk to them and they told me that when I was better and felt better that the doors were open. I think that this is also what I liked, I mean what I learned, I learned so so much from the project that this helped me to get the job.
Interviewer: uh huh, why exactly, why?

Jordana: As I was saying I think because of the communication, because I was so timid, and to resolve this myself helped me earn the respect and affection of so many people at the company, which I now have.

Another youth, Gloria, said that before her participation in A Ganar her self-confidence was so low that it physically hurt, "as far as, I don't know, it went as far as feeling pain in my body that my self-confidence was low, my self-confidence was so low." Now, she says that she feels much better about herself: "I am what I am!"

The emphasis on teamwork and communication in the first phase of the program, coupled with the practical activities that forced youth to practice these concepts, allowed youth to feel less shy and more self-confidence. For example, Yaron links his ability to no longer feel shy/ashamed with the new friendships that he has made in the program:

> Well the experience that I have is that before I never spoke in public and… before I didn't get along with very many people because I felt ashamed to speak. I felt ashamed to speak in public. And now no, now I have a lot of friends and they taught me what respect is and why it is important.

Here we see how certain preconditions of capabilities, such as feeling more confident, can enable valued functionings, in this case having friends. Several participants, at all stages of the data collection, mentioned learning self-respect and respect for others as the foundation for being able to socialize with others and make new friends, described below.

In addition to describing improved self-confidence, participants in A Ganar described changed attitudes and behaviors around work, consistent with the themes presented in the curriculum and including the development of a more responsible and respectful work ethic, and increased discipline. Karina, for example, links many of these, and ultimately explains that they are important in the work environment as well as in the social sphere:

Karina: To work in a disciplined way, with respect, responsibility, we learned a lot because sometimes, how can I say it, sometimes we do things hastily. So now I speak in a more disciplined way. I learned how to be more responsible and to work more as a team, and more than that I learned control with other people

Interviewer: In what ways do you think that the program has helped you most in your life?

Karina: Well, discipline, I learned a lot. As I was saying before I used to do many things hastily and I learned that things shouldn't be done like that. They should be done in a way that is disciplined, with patience and to be responsible with things as well, not to do them in a way that is rushed.

Table 7.2 provides additional examples of how youth described altered attitudes and behaviors that they developed through A Ganar. These fall into the general categories of discipline, persistence, and responsibility. Together these might be considered the "work ethic" that A Ganar fostered among youth.

Table 7.2 Examples of data regarding changed attitudes and behaviors in workplace

Work ethic category:	Examples from interview excerpts:
Discipline (arriving to work on time, behaving and dressing well)	Interviewer: What of the aspects that you learned in the program helped you the most when you completed your internship? Elena: To pay attention and follow instructions. Interviewer: Of the activities that you mentioned, which were your favorite? Caleb: Discipline Interviewer: Why? Caleb: Before I wasn't very disciplined.
Persistence	Edelio: Well on the court they taught us that one falls, if one falls one can get up Interviewer: What does that mean to you, that that you yourself can get up? Edelio: Look, there are people that want to see others fall. And thanks to this course it taught me many things… that for every time that one falls, one has to get up. Candi: First of all I learned that a person has to keep moving forward in life.
Responsibility	Sinty: In terms of my life it changed my life, it taught me to be more responsible…it helped me a lot in terms of responsibility and being punctual and it helped me to plan my time… Interviewer: And what did you learn from the internship? What did the internship teach you? Ria: Well, well I learned to have much more responsibility.

Another component of the work ethic was to get along with co-workers even if they had difficult personalities. For example, Jimena mentioned that she learned how to get along with people with "different personalities."

Interviewer:	Now if we talk a bit about other aspects that you learned in the program, which of these aspects that you learned during the program helped you most when you completed your internship? Of everything that you learned, what were you able to put into practice in your internship?
Jimena:	Well the stuff about personality (*carácter*), that one is always going to work with people that have different personalities.
Interviewer:	Okay.
Jimena:	Perhaps one looked at them as friendly in the beginning and everything right?
Interviewer:	Yes.
Jimena:	But then later one has to see what their personalities are like, to not butt up against them…So to mold my personality with those of others…So more than anything this is what most helped me more than anything in the internship to interact with people, to socialize and all of that with the social part.

Mateo's remarks reveal that the work ethic he developed through A Ganar's focus on teamwork, communication, and discipline, coupled with the technical skills he learned in the second phase, were all assets he brought to the work environment:

Mateo: It helped me a lot in terms of discipline, self-development. Because one looks to develop oneself… and the teamwork is fundamental, communication, respect, right, are things that the focus produces results. Which was the focus that I wanted to have in the internship. All of this helped me to concentrate on myself and to have a good attitude when carrying out my work. From there the technical part was very easy for me, because I as I was saying I had the necessary pillars to succeed, so what I learned here didn't produce a single problem. What's more it gave me a way of knowing how to develop myself even more.

This describes how certain preconditions, including discipline, self-development, and a "good attitude" enabled a valued functioning, being employed. For Mateo, these preconditions allow him to *be* something different – in his words to "develop" himself even more. This is very consistent with the notion of life skills as something that can allow people to improve their lives – to live life well.

Capabilities and Functionings Through A Ganar Participation: Building Relationships and Social Ties

One of the most consistent phrases uttered by participants in the in-depth interviews was teamwork (*trabajo en equipo*). Working as a team was one of the skills that youth described learning through sports activities, and this skill was linked closely with developing communication skills and learning to trust their peers. For example, Ileanna described learning to work as a team as one of the things she learned in the program:

Ileanna: The teamwork, because we played together, but we didn't communicate well. And there, values became important, communication. So in the moment of playing we made an agreement: "look let's play like this, you like this," this is how communication works in soccer.

When an A Ganar group starts, most of the youth do not already know each other. The games/activities are intended to "break the ice" and to allow the youth to socialize and to communicate. As Yolanda explained, during the first phase of the program, they "taught us to work in a team." She elaborated "thanks to sports and the instructors we were able to really connect with each other."

Yolanda: As I said in Phase 1 we did a lot of activities that required working in groups they taught us how to work in a team because when we first arrived we didn't know each other very much and there were tensions. But thanks to the sports and to the instructors we were able to connect with each other. We learned respect. We learned how to get along through the activities that we did. They put us together to play ball, we did some activities, we did some group games and it taught us how to work as a team. Because we had to listen, to listen to just one person and the others had to pay attention.

There are at least three reasons why making new friends is an important outcome for youth in the Honduran and Guatemalan context. First, many of these youth are socially isolated, particularly those that are no longer attending school. They lack a social group, and often they do not have contact with friends they used to go to school with. Second, they live in an environment characterized by violence and fear, and so making a new friend, particularly one that is not from their neighborhood, could have important implications in terms of improving social connections in these communities. Finally, for some youth, making new friends allows them to leave behind friends who engaged in risk behaviors (e.g. drinking, drug use, gang activity).

Making new friends was a consistent finding across the youth we interviewed (both male and female). Table 7.3 below summarizes a few of the youths' commentaries regarding their new friendships. One youth, Julian, even likened his new friends to an extended family. This extended social network is both a capability (to be able to have friends) and a functioning (being in a supportive social network). Therefore, in this outcome, we might think of A Ganar directly supporting the cultivation of the capability and functioning of what Nussbaum (2011) calls "affiliation", or "having the bases of self-respect and non-humiliation, to live with and towards others and show concern for other human beings…" (p. 34). This also echoes DeJaeghere's (Chap. 4, this volume) arguments about the importance of framing life skills from a relational approach – toward caring for others or reciprocity.

Table 7.3 Youth describe making new friends through A Ganar

Alec	And who knows with whom one is going to meet up, with bad company and all… But it is helpful, because here [A Ganar] one learns what type of relationship to have.
Ovidio	Ovidio: Well finish my course and meet new people, make new friends. Interviewer: Why? Ovidio: Because in part it is good for me to meet new people, have new friends… We cook, we play sports like soccer, we learned different games and we had good relations between us as classmates.
Katia	With regards to sociability with others, with the other people I believe that it made me a bit stronger in this aspect. In other words, to learn to make new friends, to learn to be more sociable I think. I liked that a lot.
Juan	Meeting many friends, more than anything. Also it helped me get along better with my classmates.
Gaby	Well because I got along with many, I made many friends and I got along with my friends.
Julian	Well some specific things were living together, like with my classmates. Because there were classmates from many different places from here in Tegucigalpa. And, over time, we became a big family.
Jorge	There was motivation, I mean with everything, concerning friendships that we made, with the whole team, so there was motivation.
Lara	Well it involved learning a bit how to interact with classmates, to have friendships.

In summary, A Ganar youth frequently and consistently mentioned a variety of inter-related attitudes and behaviors that allowed them to learn to work as a team. The activities that were conducted during the first stage of the program served to allow them to establish close relationships with their peers, to overcome shyness, and to become more conscientious. They made new friends. Some who started the program quite shy, were able to learn how to communicate and treat their peers with respect. These skills allowed them to learn to work well with others and to get along with their peers and potentially their future co-workers. Jordana's remarks capture how all of these outcomes are related and mutually-supporting, with sports playing an important role:

> What I liked most is that we learned respect, discipline, a lot of qualities like team work. We also went to the soccer field we also got over our shame. We made friends and after that we respected each other. And those of us who were ashamed to speak in public, I was one of them, are no longer. It no longer makes me embarrassed to get up in public and speak. This is how I have developed. The project taught me so much, and it is very beautiful!

Structural Constraints of the Honduran and Guatemalan Contexts

While participants expressed positive sentiments about their participation in A Ganar, many expressed frustration regarding the lack of formal work opportunities in Honduras and Guatemala. Again, the quantitative findings suggest that there was no impact of the program on employment. This points to the challenges of the labor market in their communities. As Cedric, one participant explained, "I think that here, opportunities are what we need more than anything. I think that there are a lot of people here like me, that have potential, but they get lost." Nancy also cited the national context as an impediment to finding work, although she also realized that part of the possibility of finding work is seeking out opportunities. She stated:

> there are no opportunities, the ones that there are one has to give oneself, look for by one-self ...there are people that say I don't have any jobs, but jobs there are, to become some-body in a company one has to start from zero, and there are people who give with just one opportunity... I have learned that everything is one step at a time.

Again, while Nancy shows persistence in looking for work, she does so while acknowledging that there are few opportunities. Kyle, another youth interviewed, attributes his inability to find work to the problems in Honduras: "I believe that the situation is a bit complicated in this country."

In addition to the lack of formal employment opportunities, participants named a number of other issues that made things "complicated" in their countries. Crime and violence were consistently mentioned when youth discussed their neighborhoods. Cell phone theft was common on public buses, and youth discussed not wanting to work at night because of the danger of returning home in the dark. Some had papers stolen – for example Katherine had her work permit stolen when her home was robbed, and she was not able to replace it for many months. The everyday challenges of high crime and violence were a common theme in the lives of youth.

The participants acknowledge the many difficulties they faced when seeking employment, including stigma and gender discrimination. Youth mentioned, for example, that if they had a tattoo, employers assumed they were members of a gang. When employers heard where the youth lived, again they faced stigma because the neighborhoods are *"rojo,"* or violent. Sex discrimination was also reported. For example, Evelyn, wanted to work in a kitchen, a space that in some restaurants is considered not appropriate for a woman:

> I have tried in a few places, my sister-in-law works in Pollo Campero [a fried chicken fast food franchise], but she told me that they don't accept women in the kitchen, and my sister works at Lai Lai and they don't accept women there either.

Gender norms also made it difficult for women to work, as they were expected to care for young children. In Evelyn's case, even though A Ganar has influenced what she wanted to do and while she said she had not "lost faith in finding work" she acknowledged that "now with my daughter it is difficult."

The structural constraints of the Honduran context, including the availability of jobs, the high levels of crime and violence, stigma facing youth who live in certain neighborhoods, and gender discrimination, make their capabilities lack robustness. By "robust" I follow Robeyns who introduces robustness to refer to the probability of a capability being realized (2017, p. 98). Youth in Guatemala and Honduras have *some* opportunity to succeed in getting jobs, but their opportunities are less robust than other youth in Honduras who may be from less "complicated" (to use the words of one youth interviewed) communities.

Discussion

In our interviews with youth, they used language to describe program benefits that echoed terminology in the program curriculum, particularly the "life skills" of communication, teamwork, and discipline. As Fig. 7.1 illustrates, the combination of exposure to new information was combined with opportunities to practice, in games and activities, the ideas presented. The technical training and internship provided additional spaces for youth to practice concepts and behaviors that the program attempted to foster. These findings echo those of Honeyman et al. (Chap. 6, this volume) who also find that effective pedagogies for the development of what they term "soft skills" include those that are student-centered and that require active participation, problem-solving, and group work.

Applying a capability analysis to these findings, we consider the altered attitudes and beliefs participants described to be *preconditions* of capabilities. The stronger social ties that the program fostered are both capabilities and functionings because youth explained that they had both *the real opportunity* to be in friendships and they *developed a stronger social network* through their participation in the program. In other words, their attitudes were the precondition to being able to do and to be something – to socialize and live a life with close social ties. They *are able to have* more friends (a capability) because of their attitudes and values (the preconditions), and they actually do have friends who they socialize with (a functioning). These insights from the descriptive analysis of A Ganar, viewed through the lens of the capability approach, provide several important ideas for future programmatic and empirical work on life skills training programs, particularly for those who want to understand why, from a capabilities perspective, fostering educational opportunities for youth that help them develop life skills improves their well-being.

What Counts as Success: Means and Ends of Life Skills Education

Among all the youth we interviewed in Honduras and Guatemala, there was not a single account of an individual believing that the program was a negative experience. In fact, the interviewees described an overwhelmingly positive experience in the program. While some were frustrated that they still were not able to get jobs at the end of the program, they all believed it had a positive impact on their lives. The quantitative results support this qualitative finding, as the few statistically significant impacts of the program were in the overall social and emotional outcomes, including personal strength and positive identity (Duthie et al., 2018). However, for A Ganar and many other life skills programs, these are considered "secondary" outcomes – not of primary interest for donors and researchers.

A capability analysis can broaden the criteria by which program effectiveness is determined (see DeJaeghere et al., 2019, who make a similar argument in their analysis of a life skills program for youth in East Africa). Again, Robeyns argues that, "there are some very important ends that do not depend very much on material means...For example, self-respect, supportive relationships in school or in the workplace, or friendship are all very important ends that people may want" (2017, p. 49). DeJaeghere and Walker (2021) explain that from a capabilities approach, education has the potential to foster individual wellbeing through the formation of many aspects to their life quality – and our data suggest that the social ties were something that youth want, and view as a positive outcome of their participation. In Honduras and Guatemala violence and political instability have stagnated economic growth. It is unrealistic to expect that job-training programs will improve employment outcomes without accompanying macroeconomic shifts that create more employment opportunities for youth. Likewise, the violence that is prevalent in neighborhoods of Tegucigalpa, San Pedro Sula, and Guatemala City has made many youth afraid of leaving their homes, of socializing with new people, and of simply being in public spaces (Adams, 2012). Given the challenges of the context, programs that can improve youth wellbeing by fostering outcomes that youth value and want, given the challenges of their context, should be expanded – these may be more feasible goals than improving employment outcomes, particularly in the short term. While they are not tied to improved material status, they are an important component of youth well-being. These are important ultimate ends for life skills programming.

Values in Life Skills Programming

In addition to fostering the capability to be in supportive social networks, A Ganar participants described changes in beliefs that included a sense that they were no longer "stuck," higher self-confidence, and attitudes that could be categorized as an improved work ethic. Again, these changed attitudes and beliefs can be thought of as "preconditions" of capabilities, or "internal characteristics" (Robeyns, 2017, p. 93). This finding highlights the importance of making explicit that *values* are part of the social and emotional competencies that life skills programs often attempt to foster. As Brush et al. (Chap. 3, this volume) explain, social and emotional learning is a process through which individuals learn and apply a set of related "non-academic" skills – attitudes, behaviors, and values – to help direct their thoughts, feelings, and actions in ways that enable them to succeed in school, work, and life. For example, "discipline" and "responsibility" were common themes in our interviews with A Ganar participants, who considered these attitudes and values a key reason for their improved sense of wellbeing; they enabled actions that helped them in their personal and work lives.

One of the reasons why scholarship and programming in the field of "life skills" is so muddled (as mentioned Murphy-Graham & Cohen, Chap. 2, this volume) is that skill is often used to describe both learned behaviors and values. We can develop greater habits of discipline and we also *value* being disciplined. Likewise, we can develop respect for others and we *value* this practice. Life skills programs, such as A Ganar, are attempting to cultivate a set of values around work: being disciplined, working hard, etc. Scholars writing from a capability perspective have made very helpful contributions regarding how to regard values and how these connect to life skills, namely, that certain values enable one to live life well. For example, Peppin Vaughn and Walker (2012) write that values are significant in shaping and influencing behavior and actions (in this sense we might consider them preconditions to capabilities). These values can be promoted "through meaningful educational activities; and that the educational opportunities provided in schools and colleges ought to foster behaviors and values which advance human development and well-being for individuals and society" (Peppin Vaughn & Walker, 2012, p. 497).

As such, it might be clearer to be explicit that life skills programs are teaching **values** that have been deemed important for individual and social well-being that are related to individual identity and work ethic. At the same time, several authors (including Brush et al., Chap. 3, this volume; Peppin Vaughn & Walker, 2012; Yitbarek et al., Chap. 11, this volume) have raised the question of *whose values* are present in life skills frameworks, and how do we ensure that these values do not reflect Western, Eurocentric frameworks? How do we ascertain that values reflect a commitment to equity and justice and an intolerance for discrimination and inequality, or in other words, that education is justice-enhancing (DeJaeghere & Walker, 2021)? The Harvard Taxonomy Project classifies values as one of six domains of social and emotional learning, to "include understanding, caring about, and acting upon core ethical values; the desire to perform to one's highest potential; and the habits required to live and work together with others as a friend, family member, and citizen" (Brush et al., Chap. 3, this volume). A deeper engagement with the "core ethical values" and attitudes that life skills frameworks are informed by will be necessary to advance programming – particularly given Honeyman et al.'s finding that the non-academic skills and the "attitudes" aspect of curriculum development frameworks often end up neglected (Honeyman et al., Chap. 6, this volume).

A capabilities approach to life skills education suggests that values should not be imposed or transferred. They should not be taught through indoctrination, but rather, education should enable an individual to "learn, realize and clarify what is valuable to them; to form their own significant values" (Peppin Vaughn & Walker, 2012, p. 508). This can happen through a kind of curriculum and pedagogy that creates spaces for values to be formed through activities, experiences, and exposure to knowledge. In the case of A Ganar, participants discussed learning these values through play, through the metaphor and practice of games and sports. They were exposed to the ideas, such as the importance of communication, in the A Ganar classes. In short, A Ganar seems to be an example of how education can expose – while not indoctrinating – individuals to values, allowing them to be formed through activities and experiences.

Conversion Factors Limit the Robustness of Capabilities

While it is important to acknowledge that there is a set of explicit and implicit values that are often at the core of life skills programming, it is also important to recognize the ways in which the context may thwart putting these values into practice. This has been a major critique of "character education" programs in the United States. By shifting the focus onto "character" or "life" skills, these programs often fail to capture the context in which youth live. Programs emphasizing "character" or values often ignore the larger forces in society, such as the economic and social terrain, where these characteristics play out (Rose, 2014). As DeJaeghere and Walker (2021) explain, there is a mistaken belief that skills development and education will somehow solve defective labor markets.

A capability approach can take the structural constraints into consideration by engaging the concepts of conversion factors at individual, social, and environmental levels. For A Ganar youth, these included sex and gender-based norms and discrimination, the lack of safety, complications with transportation, and the larger economic context that made employment opportunities scarce. Without recognizing the conversion factors that may make individuals' capability sets less robust, life skills programming runs the risk of attempting a "quick fix" for a complicated problem. Boler and Aggleton (2004) argue that "if contexts are not taken seriously, educators risk speaking to a fictional world. In the hands of poorly prepared and hard-pressed teachers, life skills education appears to offer an instant one size fits all panacea, but complex problems require complex solutions" (p. 7). A more comprehensive model of how skills are mediated by conversion factors to ultimately lead to life-cycle outcomes is needed – hopefully future work will give greater attention to structural constraints.

Conclusion

This case study of A Ganar provides a capability analysis of life skills programs for youth. It clarifies a few points for scholars and practitioners that hope to better understand how skills might be conceptualized as part of programming for youth informed by a capabilities approach. Broadening our understanding of the outcomes that matter, as well as using concepts including preconditions, capabilities, and functionings, may prove useful when trying to understand the benefits and goals of life skills programming from a capabilities perspective. Finally, a careful analysis of conversion factors will provide a more realistic account of how life skills might lead to valued functionings for youth who live in such challenging contexts as urban Honduras and Guatemala.

References

Adams, T. M. (2012, August 6). *Chronic violence and its reproduction: Perverse trends in social relations, citizenship, and democracy in Latin America*. Wilson Center. https://www.wilsoncenter.org/publication/chronic-violence-and-its-reproduction-perverse-trends-social-relations-citizenship-and

Adelman, M., & Székely, M. (2016). *School dropout in Central America: An overview of trends, causes, consequences, and promising interventions*. World Bank. http://documents.worldbank.org/curated/en/308171468198232128/pdf/WPS7561.pdf

Boler, T., & Aggleton, P. (2004). *Life skills based education for HIV prevention: A critical analysis*. Paper prepared for the working group on HIV/AIDS. 17 May, 2004. Available at https://healtheducationresources.unesco.org/sites/default/files/resources/life_skills_new_small_version.pdf

DeJaeghere, J. (2016). Girls' educational aspirations and agency: The critical role of imagining alternative futures through schooling in a low-resourced Tanzanian community. *Critical Studies in Education*. https://doi.org/10.1080/17508487.2016.1188835

DeJaeghere, J. (2018) A capability approach to entrepreneurship skills: Social inclusion, community care and a moral economy. In McGrath, S & Powell, L (Eds) *The International Handbook of Education for the Changing World of Work*. Springer Press.

DeJaeghere, J., & Lee, S. K. (2011). What matters for marginalized girls and boys in Bangladesh: A capabilities approach for understanding educational well-being and empowerment. *Research in Comparative and International Education, 6*(1), 27–42.

DeJaeghere, J., & Walker, M. (2021). The capabilities approach in comparative and international education: A justice-enhancing framework. In Jules T.D., Shields, R. & Thomas, M. A (Eds) *The Bloomsbury Handbook of Theory in Comparative and International Education*. Bloomsbury Press.

DeJaeghere, J., Wiger, N. P., & Willemsen, L. W. (2016). Broadening educational outcomes: Social relations, skills development, and employability for youth. *Comparative Education Review, 60*(3), 457–479.

Duthie, M., Pucilowski, M., Anzoategui, L., Agpoon, B., & Murphy-Graham, E. (2018). *A Ganar alliance impact evaluation synthesis report Guatemala and Honduras.* Social Impact. https://pdf.usaid.gov/pdf_docs/PA00T78T.pdf

Heckman, J., & Kautz, T. (2013). *Fostering and measuring skills: Interventions that improve character and cognition* (Working Paper 19656). National Bureau of Economic Research (NBER).

International Labor Organization. (2021). ILOSTAT Database. https://ilostat.ilo.org/data/

Kohlberg, L., & Mayer, R. (1972). Development as the aim of education. *Harvard Educational Review, 42*(4), 449–496. https://doi.org/10.17763/haer.42.4.kj6q8743r3j00j60

Maxwell, J. A. (2013). *Qualitative research design.* Sage.

Miles, M. B., Huberman, A. M., & Saldaña, J. (2014). *Qualitative data analysis: A methods sourcebook.* Sage.

Nussbaum, M. C. (2011). *Creating capabilities: The human development approach.* Harvard University Press.

Peppin Vaughan, R. (2015). Education, social justice, and school diversity: Insights from the capability approach. *Journal of Human Development and Capabilities, 17*(2), 206–224. https://doi.org/10.1080/19452829.2015.1076775

Peppin Vaughan, R., & Walker, M. (2012). Capabilities, values and education policy. *Journal of Human Development and Capabilities, 13*(3), 495–512. https://doi.org/10.1080/19452829.2012.679648

Robeyns, I. (2017). *Wellbeing, freedom and social justice: The capability approach re-examined.* Open Book Publishing.

Rose, M. (2014, October 22). *Character education: A cautionary note.* Brookings Institution. https://www.brookings.edu/research/character-education-a-cautionary-note/

Saito, M. (2003). Amartya Sen's capability approach to education: A critical exploration. *Journal of Philosophy of Education, 37*(1), 17–33. https://doi.org/10.1111/1467-9752.3701002

Tikly, L. & Barrett, A. (2011). Social justice capabilities and quality of education in low income countries. *International Journal of Educational Development, 31*(1), 3–14.

Walker, M. (2012). A capital or capabilities education narrative in a world of staggering inequalities? *International Journal of Educational Development, 32*(3), 384–393.

Walker, M., & Unterhalter, E. (2007). *Amartya Sen's capability approach and social justice in education.* Palgrave MacMillan.

Chapter 8
Career Life Skills for 10th Grade Boys in Delhi, India: Mapping Information Literacies for Sustainable Development

Aditi Arur and Mansi Sharma

Abstract The pressure is high on career educators to develop information literacies as a life skill for themselves as well as for youth, particularly those from disadvantaged communities, and to document and process career information in a rapidly changing world of work that is relevant to their sociocultural and environmental contexts. We employ a critical or transformative approach to information literacies to explore young people's socially situated practices of collecting, validating, and processing career information as well as how they might "democratically transform structures of authority over information exchanges, and then maintain scrutiny over this authority" (Whitworth A, Radical information literacy: reclaiming the political heart of the IL movement. Elsevier, 2014, p. 2). We draw from qualitative interviews with ten boys studying in 10th grade at a government school in Delhi, India, and videos produced by them to map their career information landscapes. Using an education for sustainable development lens, "bumps" were made visible in their information landscapes, that is, the tensions that emerge between multiple informational actors for reimagining sustainable futures. We suggest that these tensions can serve as cultural resources that students can democratically engage with in developing crucial career and life skills for their futures.

Keywords Information literacy · Careers education · Sustainable development goals (SDGs) · Critical literacy · Career guidance · Education for sustainable development · India

A. Arur (✉)
Christ (Deemed to be) University, Bengaluru, Karnataka, India

M. Sharma
KU Leuven, Leuven, Belgium

© The Author(s) 2022
J. DeJaeghere, E. Murphy-Graham (eds.), *Life Skills Education for Youth*, Young People and Learning Processes in School and Everyday Life 5, https://doi.org/10.1007/978-3-030-85214-6_8

Acronyms

ESD   Education for Sustainable Development
ICT   Information and Communication Technologies
SC   Scheduled Castes
SD   Sustainable Development
SDG   Sustainable Development Goals
ST   Scheduled Tribes
TI   Teach India

Introduction

Providing relevant career information to youth, such as a range of available occupations, qualifications required, working conditions, remuneration and other benefits,
labor market trends and so on, is a central task of career educators and counselors
(Hooley, 2012; Kumar & Arulmani, 2014). In India, much career guidance serves
middle-class and elite students. In this research, we wanted to understand what it
would mean to employ an Education for Sustainable Development (ESD) perspective[1]
in career guidance for first-generation learners studying in government (public)
schools in India, specifically in Delhi. In particular, we wanted to better understand
how one ESD competency, namely the "acquiring and processing of information"—
or the capacity of the learner to "acquire information on topics of globalization and
development and process it topic-relatedly"—could inform career guidance and planning for young people (Schreiber & Seige, 2016, p. 95).

Career information literacy is considered to be a core competency for career
educators, defined as the ability to find, access, evaluate, and produce information
pertinent to education, training, and, employment opportunities, and enable students to utilize this information effectively (Hooley, 2012; Kumar & Arulmani,
2014). The rise in information communications technologies (ICT), particularly the
internet and online technologies, have changed the context of career guidance and
education significantly and raised several challenges for youth, and career educators, and counselors (Hooley, 2012). Youth often face information overload. That is,
the production of career information as well as access to such information has
expanded due to the rise in information and communication technologies (ICT).
Selecting, validating, and organizing relevant information so that it can be easily
retrieved when needed is a challenge and an important life skill in itself. Further,
while youth often have access to such information, they need guidance in processing the information meaningfully. Career educators need to also develop their

---

[1] We deployed the Education for Sustainable Development (ESD) competency framework developed by members of the ESD Expert Network in this project (see Schreiber & Seige, 2016, for a
description of this framework).

interpretive skills to process such information so that they can be responsive to the specific contexts of the youth they serve (Kumar & Arulmani, 2014).

At the same time as youth are overloaded with information, there is also a lack of information available, particularly in geographies away from urban centers, and for students from socioeconomically disadvantaged backgrounds. In addition, the information available for students from middle-class and upper-class backgrounds, and/or for urban geographies, has limited relevance for disadvantaged youth. For instance, youth from scheduled castes (SC) and scheduled tribes (ST)[2] religious minorities, women, gender and sexual minorities, and persons with disabilities need specific information regarding government programs, scholarships, bank loans, hostel and travel facilities, among other information (Kumar & Arulmani, 2014). Sourcing relevant labor market information for these students is a major challenge.

Information literacy skills are not merely technical skills, but they are also sociopolitical in that they involve making choices regarding the kind of information to look for, for whom, and from whose perspective to interpret such information (Andersen, 2006; Whitworth, 2014). Making sense of youth's values and needs, as well as labor market information, is invariably shaped by one's cultural and political orientations. For instance, educators have to make choices around guiding students from disadvantaged backgrounds to adjust their aspirations to what is "realistically" possible within their labor market horizons, and/or work towards raising their aspirations and employability skills beyond these horizons (Watts, 1996). While the first choice entails being complicit with the status quo of the labor market, the second choice would mean that students would individualize their struggles and failures in challenging this status quo. A radical approach to career guidance would require transforming the labor market to be more equitable and sustainable, by teaching young people to make consistent collective demands on powerful authorities for better work conditions, raising pay structure, and/or better work/life balance (Watts, 1996). The risk involved is that employers are likely to read employees or potential employees, and particularly youth, who make such demands as disobedient and troublemakers, and not hire them.

In this chapter, we explore the information literacy practices of young boys for the purpose of career planning from a sustainable development perspective, to have a better understanding of how students: (a) make sense of the environmental and social implications of their career aspirations within their specific contexts, (b) consider how they might "green" particular careers, that is, think through how they could work towards environmental and social justice through their careers of interest, (c) reflect on how social, economic, cultural, and environmental inequalities

---

[2] Scheduled castes (SC) refers to those groups historically deemed to be outside of the caste system in the Brahmanical order, and who suffer from extreme social, educational and economic backwardness arising out of the historical practice of untouchability as specified in Clause 1 of Article 341 of the Constitution of India (also referred to as *Dalit* meaning oppressed). Scheduled tribes (ST) refers to indigenous tribes as specified in Article 342 of the Constitution of India (also referred to as *Adivasi* meaning earliest inhabitants). Both groups are entitled to reservations in education and employment.

shape their career aspirations and choices, and/or (d) make career-related decisions based on the sustainable development issues that they are most interested in addressing (Plant, 2014). While the information literacy skills needed for career planning and competencies for learning about sustainable development may seem different and unrelated, we argue that they are deeply connected as exploring the issues that are most relevant to students' lives allow for more situated understandings of students' career aspirations and motivations.

Education for Sustainable Development and Career Guidance

In response to the challenges faced by the world due to globalization, the sustainable development (SD) agenda emerged initially during the Decade of Education for Sustainable Development. Later in 2016, the Sustainable Development Goals (SDG) were released as a set of goals that the world needed to collectively address certain global issues by 2030 (McKeown & Hopkins, 2007; Sustainable Development Goals, 2015).

Career guidance and education scholars have mostly engaged with SDG 8 (Promote sustained, inclusive and sustainable economic growth, full and productive employment and decent work for all) and SDG 4 (Ensure inclusive and equitable quality education). These scholars and practitioners have acknowledged the tensions between economic growth and decent work, and the precarious links between education, employability skills, and employment (DeJaeghere, 2018; Di Fabio & Maree, 2016; Pouyaud & Guichard, 2017; Sustainable Development Goals, 2015). This work has elaborated how neoliberal economic policies create unsustainable ways of living by disrupting the balance between work and other aspects of life for individuals (Pouyaud & Guichard, 2017), and how career and entrepreneurship education programs in neoliberal contexts have contributed to the production of social inequalities globally (DeJaeghere, 2018). For instance, globalization has led to the precarization of work for the world's poor, increased migrations from rural to urban areas in search of decent work, and poor working and living conditions for laborers (Kumar & Arulmani, 2014). Even for middle-class youth, job security has shifted to employability security, meaning they are expected to secure employability through the development of life skills such as learning to learn and adapting to changing work contexts, and they can no longer expect to secure their jobs by staying in one organization (Hooley et al., 2017).

Scholars writing about the changing world of work for youth have often not made explicit connections between social and environmental inequalities, particularly in non-Western contexts. Arulmani (2011) has also made the connections between social and environmental inequalities explicit in his cultural preparedness model for career guidance in India. He has argued that although globalization and neoliberal economic development have changed the world significantly in India, career guidance models developed in the "west" designed for particular cultural orientations towards life and work are not relevant for diverse communities in India.

Modernist orientations of work are based on notions of economic growth that value the over-consumption of resources for certain individuals, communities, and nations, which is necessarily dependent on the overexploitation of natural resources and the impoverishment of other individuals, communities, and nations (Arulmani, 2011; Plant, 2014). This has resulted in the marginalization of traditional occupations and livelihoods that are perceived as irrelevant in the knowledge economy, such as for example, engaging in sustainable agricultural production (Arulmani, 2011; Ratnam, 2014). Arulmani (2011) argues, therefore, for a cultural preparedness model of career guidance as an alternative to dominant notions of career development. In this model, youth are culturally prepared by their communities to develop particular kinds of attitudes and beliefs regarding work and occupation that may be inconsistent with those of modernist notions of appropriate career choices. For instance, a small business owner who provides services to a local community and is more or less self-sufficient may be pressured to expand their business, and to participate in a wider network in order to earn more money and/or to gain more visibility over a larger geography. Such a growth model may involve investing further in infrastructure and human resources and extracting these resources as much as possible to maximize the returns from the investment.

Plant (2014) offers a more collective and environmentally oriented form of career guidance in contrast to the contemporary western models of career guidance with its individualistic focus, and free-market thinking, that, in turn, can result in social and environmental destruction. He terms this approach "green guidance." Green guidance involves the documentation of information on green careers (such as environmental law or sustainable agricultural practices), that is, work and career opportunities include environmental aspects and also minimize environmental harm. Further, it takes an educational role in creating awareness among students and youth about the importance of green careers, and the potential to "green" careers of interest. It also engages with educational institutions and employers to consider their impact on sustainability issues and to integrate these issues within their curricula and training. For instance, the Sustainable Development Goals is part of the 10th grade curriculum in civics and environmental science. Green guidance invites young people to reflect on what counts as decent work for themselves, for marginalized others in the present time as well as for future generations, and how they could find balance between work and other aspects of life to lead a sustainable way of life (Plant, 2014; Pouyaud & Guichard, 2017).

Attention to culture and social inequalities in relation to environmental concerns, however, need to be developed further in this "green guidance" approach. For instance, Arulmani (2011) reinterprets concepts such as *dharma* (i.e., code of duty or of "right living") and *ashrama* (i.e., life stages with clearly defined duties at each stage) in Brahmanical epistemologies to explore what a culturally resonant and environmentally friendly career guidance might look like in the Indian context. Yet, these concepts effectively define Indian culture in Brahmanical terms. For instance, women and oppressed caste groups need to enact their *dharma,* that is, prescribed codes for work and living, in order to maintain and reproduce Brahmanical supremacy. This framework also tends to equate indigeneity with Brahmanism in constructing a romanticized and harmonious relationship between indigenous communities in India and nature through work, an artifact of colonial as well as Brahmanical knowledge production in anthropology (Bhukya, 2008). Postcolonial, feminist, and Dalitbahujan epistemologies in the South Asian context argue for understanding culture as contested and negotiated (Arur & DeJaeghere, 2019; Paik, 2016; Rege, 2006; Waghmore, 2007). For instance, the neoliberal ideology of the Indian state is closely tied with political Brahmanism in promoting anti-environmental projects in different localities in India, which are often contested by SC and ST communities whose livelihoods are affected through such projects (Kumar & Puthumattathil, 2018). In the next section, therefore, we explain the sociocultural and critical approaches we used to conceptualize information literacies as a set of life skills needed in career guidance and planning for these contested contexts in which educating for sustainable development takes place.

Critically Analyzing Information Literacies

Information literacy, an important life skill, is often defined as the "careful retrieval and selection of information" to inform decision-making and emphasizes procedural knowledge as well as critical and meta-cognitive thinking to evaluate the "quality, authenticity, and credibility" of the information (Koltay, 2011, p. 215). Information literacy in practice, however, is applied to many different forms of information and contexts; thus, it is usually referred to as multiliteracies or as a metaliteracy (Mackey & Jacobson, 2011; Whitworth, 2014).

In this project, we examined multiliteracy skills, such as media literacy, digital literacy, and information literacy, and their applications in a specific communicative context or information landscapes. By using a multiliteracy approach, we assume that young people have an increasing need to engage with diverse communicative modes and media through which information travels (Boche, 2014; Whitworth, 2014).

Youth are embedded in different information landscapes — spaces "in which information is created and shared and eventually sediments as knowledge…. characterized by signs, symbols, artefacts, sayings and doings that define these spaces to its members and identify the boundaries of the environment to outsiders" (Lloyd, 2010, p. 9). Media, understood as artefacts, are actors that produce particular kinds of meanings. For instance, Facebook and LinkedIn afford and constrain access to different kinds of information, people, and identities that reflect the specific contexts from which they emerged.

One way of understanding multiliteracies in these different landscapes is through a sociocultural approach. This approach regards literacy as a socially situated practice, embedded within specific communities and shifting "according to context, purpose, and social relations" (Hamilton, 2016, p. 5; Lave & Wenger, 1991). Using this approach, we assume that youth have skills to navigate their landscapes; and we can map their literacy practices, or their "funds of knowledge" related to specific careers of interest and/or sustainable development issues (González et al., 2006). To this perspective, we added a transformative analysis to mapping their information literacies. That is, we explore how unequal power relations shape the dominance and circulation of certain literacy practices over other forms such that they come to be seen as universal and standard (Janks, 2012; Lupton & Bruce, 2010). For instance, dominant information literacy practices may be about collecting career information from dominant caste networks, or from websites or magazines that rank the "best" colleges or "best" courses at national and international levels on the basis of criteria. Thus, a transformative approach to information literacy is about (re)distributing cognitive authority that is concentrated in particular dominant information sources, such as paid career information services and dominant caste social networks (Whitworth, 2014).

For this project, we conducted workshops that enabled youth to document their collective knowledge of career information embedded within their communities, and we engaged in a collective dialogue to scrutinize the credibility of this information. The aim was to help youth widen the distribution of authority they assign to career counsellors and educators to include community funds of knowledge that dominant information systems ignore. Using these frameworks, analyzing multiliteracy skills and usage can be "critical, consciousness-raising, subjective, political, empowering, and liberating" for young people (Lupton & Bruce, 2010, p. 5).

The Research Project

This research project emerged out of Sharma's participation in a global think tank, the Education for Sustainable Development (ESD) Expert Network, and her leadership role at a career guidance for-profit company in India[3] that served largely middle-class to elite students.

Given our interest in better understanding what it would mean to employ a sustainable development perspective in career guidance with non-elite Indian students, we conducted a single-sited exploratory qualitative research study at a government school for boys in Delhi, India with 10 boys studying in 10th grade who were first-generation learners living in unsafe and economically insecure neighborhoods. They were selected based on three different academic levels (identified in consultation with their class teacher) in order to explore how their career aspirations might be shaped by their academic performance. The site selection was informed by the experiences shared by a mentee of the ESD expert network, a young Muslim man who was raised in this neighborhood, and whose brother was studying in the same government school. He was already working in his neighborhood to encourage young boys to focus on their skill development and to not get drawn into groups that participated in violence. We hoped that the documentation and analyses from this

---

[3] One Step Up Education Services Pvt. Ltd. is a for-profit start-up that provides career information and life skills education to mostly private English-medium schools in India (https://onestepup.in/).

study might help inform his and others' work on career guidance for young men living in unsafe neighborhoods.

It is important to note that the government school was not typical in that the secondary school did not employ government schoolteachers but rather fellows from a non-governmental organization (NGO), Teach India (TI) (pseudonym), who taught in the school for two years on a rotational basis. Our goal was to understand career guidance in this specific context, and not to generalize to other similar urban or government school environments. Our theoretical framework and methodology reflect this interest.

Data Collection Methods

The data collection process, following a sociocultural and transformational literacies framework to map and transform boys' multiliteracies landscapes, included multiple methods and were conducted sequentially in phases, with each subsequent phase being informed by the experiences and analysis of the previous phase. Data were collected in the following order: participation observation, individual interviews, an interactive session, student-created videos, and a second round of interviews with selected boys who had created videos. Students and parents were informed that participation was voluntary at every stage, and consent was given by students and their parents at every stage of the process.

Participant observations were conducted by Sharma, who volunteered at the school for a period of 3 months from November 2018 to January 2019 with the goal of understanding the school context from an emic perspective. Her voluntary work included largely teaching classes for 9th grade students. She interacted with the TI fellows and with boys in her class. These interactions enabled the authors to better situate the meanings of boys' articulations in relation to school life. This phase occurred before and along with the other data collection processes discussed below.

We conducted semi-structured qualitative interviews in a mix of Hindi and English, which ranged from 45 min to an hour. Most interviews were conducted by both authors in order to ensure consistency in questions, probes, and meaning-making across participants. We transcribed and translated the interviews into English, and then coded the data using Dedoose software.

After the semi-structured interviews, Sharma facilitated a career information workshop for the entire 10th grade class of 35 boys for 6 hours spread over two days. Data sources included a questionnaire to collect students' career interests and field notes. The workshop covered three themes: information literacy, career information, and networking. The workshop involved familiarizing students with authoritative sources of information used by careers educators that did not come up in earlier interviews, discussing differences between sources in terms of their credibility and relevance, sharing career-related information collated from authoritative sources of information specific to interest areas identified by students in a questionnaire, an open session inviting students' specific questions, and lastly, activities related to collating students' information sources embedded within their specific social networks related to careers discussed in the previous session.

From the semi-structured interviews, we learned that most students had access to a phone camera, either directly (owning) or indirectly (borrowing from the family members), and a few students had already used phone cameras to make videos on themes relating to the SDGs for leisure. Hence, we explored further how the students' use of the visual medium acted as a mode for both mapping and redefining their information landscape within the context of career planning and/or the SDGs. For this purpose, we invited the entire class of 35 students to, over the course of a week, observe and document on video any SDG issues they would like addressed in their immediate environment. They were invited to experiment with the format of this video. Six students among the 35 students shot videos. The themes included poverty, gender discrimination, and natural resource management. We conducted detailed follow-up interviews with three students who submitted videos. These interviews were conducted with the aim to understand the connections that students made between their respective careers of interest, local sustainable development issues, and how these related to the Sustainable Development Goals.

Data Analysis

We coded interview data initially using the ESD competency framework. We then focused on the data that were coded in relation to information literacy skills specifically and conducted a second round of coding using the critical information literacies framework. We then selected excerpts from the data that illustrate these themes for further contextual analysis in the paper. In the next section, we map the career information landscapes that emerged from boys' information literacy practices.

Boys' Information Literacy Practices and Career Information Landscapes

In this section, we document boys' information literacy practices and the career information landscapes that emerged in our findings. We also illustrate the use of specific SDGs such as SDG 3 (Gender Equality) and SDG 10 (Reduced Inequalities), and the SDG framework as a whole to orient boys' information literacy practices, and render particular aspects of their career information landscapes more visible. Our analysis includes (a) a mapping of boys' information sources and their processes of assigning cognitive authority to these sources; (b) a mapping of the asymmetrical topographies of their career information landscapes, first in terms of how these were gendered, and second, how they were differentiated by caste, ethnicity and class; (c) examining boys' media production activities as they mapped local SD issues; and (d) exploring the connections made between these different information landscapes.

Mapping Boys' Information Sources and Processes of Assigning Cognitive Authority

Broadly, the boys sourced their career information from the internet and from individuals with relevant experience. They assigned more cognitive authority to individuals with experience to discern the credibility of the information that they acquired from the internet. Individuals with relevant experiences often were the Teach India (TI) fellows who were currently teaching them or had previously taught them in school; parents, siblings or other influential family members; tuition teachers or individuals from other non-governmental organizations that they were associated with; and certain influencers within their neighborhood. We discuss boys' engagement with each of these different sources in the following paragraphs.

All students mentioned relying on the internet to search for career-related information. They mentioned searching on Google and Youtube the most frequently, and none of them named specific primary or secondary online sources of career information. The boys' access to information and communications technologies (ICT) was varied. Most of them said they accessed the internet through mobile phones, usually those of their parents, and did not have access to a laptop or computer at home. Hence, the boys often had to negotiate with their parents to use mobile phones for short periods of time. For example, Gautam's ICT use was often incumbent on whether his parents were in a "good mood":

> 9 o' clock for half an hour or 1 hour, I study what's done in school or whatever I feel like. After that, I have dinner. Then, I ask my parents, if their mood is good, they give me their phone when I ask them. Then I check the phone. I log on to Facebook, chat, check any messages, reply. Then, I sleep.

Thus, their information literacies were mediated not only by parents' material access to technology, such as a smartphone and a laptop or computer, but also students' social access to these tools, meaning their ability to negotiate with parents to interact with the technology, learn it, and navigate it.

The boys spoke about using platforms such as Google and YouTube to search for general information, as well as for career-related information, with familiarity. For example, Deepak describes how he used Google to source career-related information:

Deepak: First of all, I'll search on Google. After Google, I'll ask the [TI] fellows.

Interviewer: Any specific website?

Deepak: Not a specific website, I'll put it straight in Google. Then I'll confirm with the [TI] fellows. I'll ask them and ask them if it's true or not. I'll share the link with them to make sure it's not fraud. Then they verify and tell me whether this is right or wrong. Otherwise I'll ask previous fellows. They know a lot about these things. I'll ask them.

Thus, Deepak, like many of the other boys, did not trust the cognitive authority of information accessed through the net, and assigned cognitive authority to individuals with experience within his physical network from school to validate the information. Most boys had mastered the generic skills of searching and categorizing information. They had also used their sociocultural knowledge to assess the relevance of the information they had collected, and to determine its credibility.

Boys also depended significantly on trusted individuals with experience within their own families or neighborhoods for information. Most boys mentioned that they sought guidance from TI fellows, especially the men who had taught them earlier but were no longer associated with the school. The boys still actively maintained contact with these fellows through phone or social media like Facebook. For instance, Kabir said that the idea of doing law came from his conversations with one of the TI fellows: "A lot of *bhaiyas* [brother referring to TI fellows] had come to teach in school… So, I got a lot of inspiration from them… Like Jeet *bhaiya*, he was a lawyer. He used to teach us very well." Similarly, Karan too referred to these TI fellows as inspirations to study law, "There was Jeet and Abhay *bhaiya* – they spoke a lot about law and then I got interested and inspired." Whereas several boys' interests in particular careers were inspired by TI fellows' educational profiles, Prem spoke about getting advice from a TI fellow about pursuing a career in sports based on his understanding of its labor market potential:

> So Sudhanshu *bhaiya* had counselled me that you have to pick up one thing and then dedicate yourself to it. If you are joining the [sports] academy, then do that night and day. But try and not leave your studies right now. There are *lakhs* (hundreds of thousand) of students who are playing and they still don't get selected. If you are not able to make it, and you have also left your studies, you will be completely stranded. So I now go for inter-zone or school level matches.

Apart from TI fellows, boys also sought information and guidance from tuition teachers, people within their neighborhoods, and older siblings. Parents, too, were sources of information for particular careers. For example, Kabir's father wanted him to get into the police services, which prompted him to do some research related to this career. He was preparing himself for this career in terms of building his fitness by doing exercise frequently, as physical training is an important component of the training program in the police services. He also revealed to us later that he harbored a desire to pursue performing arts like acting and singing. He had learned from a peer that the National Institute of Drama was an institute where he could pursue this career. His participation in a community-based theater education activity also appeared to have influenced his desire to pursue this career. In addition, he was also considering studying law inspired by TI fellows who were lawyers. Although Kabir remained undecided regarding his career goals, his information landscape revealed a richness dotted by multiple influential actors with different kinds of experiences.

Other sources of information included people within their familial networks or neighborhoods who have had experience pursuing particular careers. For instance, Prashant's sister's friend gave the exam for the National Defense Academy, while Gautam's neighbor was undergoing training to become a flight attendant, and from whom he had gathered credible information. Indeed, almost all participants assigned more cognitive authority to people who had experience in a particular career over information collected online or in textbooks. Students' networks influenced their career aspirations, the information they searched for, as well as their evaluations of the credibility of information they acquired on the net. These sources provided a form of local, culturally-specific knowledge about careers that framed the horizons of possibility for them in their environments.

Students demonstrated resourcefulness in learning digital skills with limited access to resources. For instance, Gaurav had independently learned photography, Vfx (visual effects), and photo editing skills by observing others in the same field, and helped others who needed his skills. Rahul, who didn't have access to a laptop, had learned how to create Powerpoint presentations on the phone. He had even created a presentation on careers in humanities for his class.

In sum, these young boys developed technical and digital skills through their participation in local networks and made use of local knowledge that was culturally relevant within their networks to make decisions related to their career aspirations.

Mapping the Asymmetrical Topographies or "Bumps": Gendering the Labor Market Information Landscape

Boys sourced information from the human and non-human, i.e., internet, actors in their network, and validated the credibility of information by assigning cognitive authority to particular sources more than others. Using a critical information literacy perspective, we wanted to understand how the asymmetrical topographical features, or "bumps", of their otherwise flat information landscape were shaped by unequal power relations, including their understanding of gender- and caste-segregated labor markets.

Almost all the boys recognized gender differences in work opportunities. Karan, who we noted earlier wanted to study law based on his interactions with male TI fellows, shared his observations around how educational opportunities were gendered:

> Mostly around me, in my society, girls don't study much. Mostly, their choice is to take up Arts. They may want to do business. They feel they have more options in Arts. But, I feel, to a large extent, their parents don't let them study too much. Maximum, in my society, 5-10 families only allow their girls to study. There's quite a lot of discrimination.... Mostly boys also take up Arts. Nobody thinks about Science or Commerce. They think that commerce and science require more hard work. All of them [take up Arts], 100%.

In Karan's information landscape, Arts was perceived as having more options with relatively less effort as compared to Science and Commerce for both boys and girls. He also revealed the gendered topography of his information landscape in noting the differentiated opportunities that girls had with respect to studying further. While Gaurav reiterated Karan's observations regarding differentiated opportunities for girls, he described the complex relationship that boys have to education and work in his community as well:

Gaurav: Girls, only some girls study more. But, most leave studies at some point. Some fail. In my tuitions, there was this topper girl, she studied science. Everyone else gets married after 12th. Very few study. Most leave. Those who study do so through the open system [correspondence or distance education]… What I've seen is that some of the boys around me did exceedingly well. Whereas, there are few more people who, even with the education, didn't do much – they are only at home. There is one *bhaiya* who did LLB (Bachelor of Law) but somehow didn't do anything after that. He has been at home for the last 1-2 years… They themselves don't want to work. Their parents are earning so they don't want to … They just want to be at home and go to the gym. The environment is such. Everyone I know is just 'gymming.'

Interviewer: The ones who do well- what kind of work do they do?

Gaurav: They go to the office, sit on the computer and do data analysis.

Within Gaurav's information landscape, as in other boys', certain jobs signified success, such as working in an office or with a computer. But he also pointed to a curious phenomenon around young men being inclined towards "gymming," which hints at the circulation of particular constructs of masculinity within this landscape. These constructs would need to be explored further, particularly, if as Gaurav suggested, they also shaped a resistance towards finding conventional work.

Prem, who expressed his desire to be a sportsman, wasn't particularly interested in studies. He talked about his conversations with a TI fellow and others about the risks of pursuing a career in the sports at the cost of leaving studies. His strategy was to just do well enough in studies to be able to enter the Army so that he could continue to play. His older sister, on the other hand, was planning to become a Chartered Accountant and had support from his parents in this endeavor. He commented that:

It's upside down these days, girls are supported more… Because of this, boys are getting spoilt. There's not much attention paid to them. There's this fixed thinking from before about boys that people have. Boys are like this only, they won't do anything. They'll keep roaming around. Girls are sincere, and study properly – let's educate them and do more for them.

Although Prem believed that he had gotten attention from within his family, he was concerned that gender perceptions were shifting more favorably towards girls as compared to boys regarding educational opportunities in his neighborhood.

In sum, exploring how gender differentiated work opportunities offered texture to the information landscapes of young boys. Moreover, these conversations can be a useful starting point for discussing gendered desires, masculinity, and changing gender norms that are the focus of SDG 4 (Gender Equality).

Caste, Ethnicity, and Socioeconomic Differentiation of the Career Information Landscape

Most of the boys in this study were first-generation learners from lower middle-class socio-economic backgrounds. They did not have to work to support their families, and their fathers were security guards or small grocery shop-owners. Many were also migrants from elsewhere such as the states of Bihar, Uttarakhand, Uttar Pradesh, as well as Nepal. While most of the boys were quite attuned to the gender differentiation of the world of work, the caste-based organization of the labor market was less visible to many of them. Instead, most of them tended to see work opportunities as being shaped by the power acquired through an accumulation of economic capital. For instance, Prashant, who belonged to the Brahmin caste (dominant caste group), noted:

> There is [a difference in opportunity between rich and poor]. If there is conflict in our localities, then people who are rich intimidate and threaten by paying off cops. There is a difference. Even in getting jobs. Some people cannot afford the college fees that are high.

Here, Prashant articulated his understanding of how money has been used to secure power as well as opportunities for education and work through observations in his locality. Only a few, such as Prem, highlighted the historical relationships between particular caste identities and the work that they do. Prem belongs to the Garhwali community and the Rajput (dominant caste group) caste.

Prem: Many Garhwali people head to the army or go to the kitchen line or as tourist drivers. I have seen this mostly….

Interviewer: How does caste or religion affect work opportunities? Like you said Garhwalis are more suited for certain jobs?

Prem: You can't exactly say that they are suited or not for certain jobs but they themselves take more interest in this. It may seem a bit odd to the ear. But they have been in the profession for long, and even the ancestors have been working in the same area. For example, Valmikis [Dalits, that is, an oppressed caste group]. I have a lot of friends and know a lot of people. The ladies of the families are sweepers in MCD (Municipal Corporation of Delhi). So, mainly the ladies do a lot of the cleaning work…. Pandits [Brahmin Hindu priests] I have seen. Those who sit in the temple. They are told by their fathers to not eat meat but they anyway go and do it.

Prem's career information came from the historical knowledge embedded within his specific caste and regional community. Indeed, the Garhwali Rifles is an infantry regiment in the Indian Army that is predominantly made up of Rajput and Brahmin castes from the Garhwali community (Sharma, 1990). Prem knew several people in his Garhwali community who had entered the army, and thus, was culturally prepared for a career in the army (Arulmani, 2011). He aspired to enter the army also so that he could continue to pursue his passion for sports. Importantly, Prem clarified that people from particular identities do not tend to work in particular fields because they are "suited" for it, thus problematizing a casteist understanding of a naturalized relationship between caste and occupation. Yet, he pointed out that even though people of particular identities appeared to take an interest in particular fields, this did not imply choice, but rather it is a historically constituted predisposition towards particular kinds of work. He gave examples from his observations around caste and gender differentiated occupations, such as women from the Valmiki community working as public sweepers and cleaners, and Brahmin men working as priests in temples. But he also recognized that "interests" and "suitability" or "choices" are shaped historically through caste-based differentiation of people and labor.

Although boys appeared to be relatively unfamiliar with the caste-based organization of work, possibly because many of them belonged to upper caste groups themselves (in part because we did not stratify our sample using caste as a criterion), examples such as those above form a rich information base from which to explore the issue in greater depth as a group in a careers education classroom. The dialogue that ensues from the collection of such information could allow for a dialogical understanding of the labor market, how it impacts them and members of their class differentially, and what it means to address SDG 10 (Reduced inequalities) within their local context.

Producing Videos to Reveal Local Inequalities

In today's information society, attention is a valuable resource. The process of acquiring multiliteracy skills requires that students' attention is drawn towards certain aspects, such as particular technologies of communication (Norris & Jones, 2005). The media production activity oriented towards mapping local sustainable development issues thus offered an opportunity for students to focus their attention towards certain patterned interactions between human and non-human actors in their information landscapes, and heighten their and our awareness towards these aspects.

Six students shot videos on their phones capturing issues of homelessness, natural resource management, sanitation, gender inequity, and hooliganism. In some of the videos, students engaged their families and friends in making the videos. In one video, Jeet involved his mother and sister in reconstructing a fictional scene of the lived experiences of everyday discrimination where his mother stops his sister from studying, thus rendering visible to us this tension around girls' education that constitutes a bump or a conflict within his information landscape. Other students ventured out to focus their attention towards familiar spaces within their environment to articulate their concern for SDGs, such as a nearby barren park or homeless people sleeping on the streets. Ravi shot a video of his daily morning routine to fill buckets of fresh water owing to the lack of running water facilities in his community. In making the video, Ravi recognized the community water tap as an important actor in his information landscape, rendering it visible for us with its situated meanings. Specifically, he used this tap to highlight water wastage as people do not turn it off. He connected the documentation of this tap to his aspiration of becoming a journalist, and of how he could report on stories from the margins and cover issues of environment and development:

Ravi: There is a lot of water scarcity.. water gets wasted.. we don't get water for many days. We have to get water from very far. Cleanliness is also a big issue. There is a big pile of garbage.. there is a very bad smell.. also diseases. [...]

Interviewer: What do you understand by sustainability?

Ravi: Development for all, I feel this means, development for all people. Poor rich, middle class... or development without any harm. For everyone there should be development, he or she is for poor, rich, any economic background, and they feel that they are improving. Their needs are getting fulfilled. Then we can use media for bringing development for them, make awareness videos, like we use our channel vines for making awareness videos. Maybe if we do that, then there is development for not just my own self but for others also.

Illustrating the concept of "green careers", Ravi was able to make the connections between persisting environmental issues and how they intersect with class inequities, with his career aspiration of becoming a journalist that might expose these injustices. He believed that the media underrepresents issues of the poor. However, to his admission, he was mainly informed by popular depictions of journalists in mainstream media.

> I don't watch that much news. I watch a lot of movies in which journalists run after famous people to get important news. It's a bit weird but I guess it is important. I guess they have been told to do this by their bosses. [...] It's not important to only ask famous people. Maybe if we talk to the poor people they will have much more information to give. They may talk about how their need is not getting fulfilled. We don't need to ask only rich people about development. Maybe we will get to know more about this from poor people, whose needs are not fulfilled. So, we can do something.

Ravi, along with his classmates, had been creating videos to raise awareness of social issues they found relevant. One of Ravi's classmates, Kabir, shared with us details on videos they had produced before the start of our research project:

Interviewer: On what themes do you make vine videos?

Kabir: On social issues. Like we did one on dengue. In Dengue, we made like, you must wear full-sleeved clothes. Like we had a friend. He'd always wear t-shirts. We used to tell him, why are you wearing t-shirts, nowadays mosquitoes are biting a lot. So, he says a dialogue. Then he says a dialogue that he won't wear [t-shirts]. Then we're on a playground. He suddenly gets dizzy and he can't

	see anything. He asks how many balls are these? 1 or 2. Then we ask, say how many fingers are these. He says 3. We tell him it's only one finger. Then he faints. Then we take him to the hospital. He has dengue. Then the doctor talks.
Interviewer;	What made you think of making a video on this?
Kabir:	Little funny type, so that people get information and enjoy it also [I wanted to make a funny video that is informative but also one that people will enjoy]

Above, Kabir described the plot of a short story they created around a social issue. As mentioned earlier, Kabir had told us that he was interested in singing and acting and wanted to apply to the National School of Drama. When asked about how he could green a singing career, he suggested that music could include rap about social issues.

In summary, boys used phone cameras to document sustainable development issues within their neighborhoods, and further, to explore how they could green their career aspirations by connecting them with issues pertinent to their everyday lives. The use of this media to document local realities opened up the possibility for the development of their critical/transformative information literacy skills; they acquired some cognitive authority through the production of their own knowledge, rather than consuming other people's knowledge. They also circulated their own knowledge, and conducted a dialogue around specific local issues that matter to them.

Transforming Career Information Landscapes Through Collective Sharing

In the career information workshop held over two days, we utilized a transformative approach to expanding boys' information literacy skills through a collective mapping of the students' and our career information landscapes. Engaging with students' situated knowledge about specific labor markets in a collective manner in the workshop served to redistribute cognitive authority from the career guidance practitioner to the students themselves, as well as from the students' caste-specific networks to one that is potentially shared by the class as a whole.

Students engaged with the career educator's toolkits to collect career information which included primary sources of information like university websites, secondary sources like websites offering a collated and filtered layer of career information, and stories of career successes drawn from personal or online social networks. In contrast to a deficit perspective where one would simply pour in additional information assuming students' lack of access to authentic information sources, we employed a transformative information literacy framework by inviting students to critically evaluate these different sources for their credibility and authenticity, and compare these sources with their own, thus facilitating a redistribution of cognitive authority from the career educator to themselves. For example, students shared how they often sought videos of people offering information on their professional journeys on social media. Amar, one of the boys in the classroom, spoke about how he had gathered information on the centralized civil services exam by watching a video of someone who had excelled in the examination on Youtube. This allowed Amar to redistribute cognitive authority from individuals with professional experience within his physical contexts to actors in his virtual network, affording him the possibility of leveraging these virtual actors as critical sources of knowledge and cognitive authority in negotiating his career choice with his family members.

In another session, students shared the various careers that they were interested in. In addition to the career educator sharing information on entrance procedures related to various careers, students also discussed linkages between these careers. For instance, the question of how one can become a Youtube influencer was linked to skills of media production, and potentially to careers in film-making or journalism. Further, students evaluated the credibility and authenticity of the information on entrance procedures provided by the career educator, concluding that this knowledge was secondary and needed to be validated using other sources.

Most importantly, students discussed various ways of building their social networks. Together, they reflected on and analyzed current and anticipated hurdles that might limit their ability to reach out and build a professional network. The solutions too were discussed collaboratively. The session created a space for the boys to name and discuss shared inhibitions of reaching out to professionals, and to devise creative solutions to handle them together. For instance, each of them listed the number of professionals they knew from the list of selected careers. When seen collectively, they found that they had access to a wider and richer network than as individuals.

In this collective discussion, they became aware that they had named careers that were aspirational but within reach—these were careers they would aspire to it only if they knew someone in that profession. The cognitive authority of individuals with experience was reaffirmed in this session, as they offered the students not just credible career information but also shaped their ambitions for particular career choices. Role models are not new in their presence as cognitive authorities for youth making career choices; however, in this case, interestingly, this authority was also in part shared by influencers, or those not personally known to the boys, in social media networks. We observed this trend as students expressed a desire to work in several media related careers, such as Youtube influencers, fitness models, actors, and singers.

In sum, our findings suggest that the career information workshop was not about passing down information from the career educator to the students, nor was it about teaching students technical information literacy skills. Informed by a transformative information literacy approach, it went beyond engaging with students' sociocultural information literacies towards a collective mapping of their information landscapes with the goal of facilitating a dialogue among them.

Discussion

One of the biggest challenges for career counselors and educators is to constantly document, update, and validate career information that is both continuously increasing and changing for certain demographics, and sparse for other demographics (Hooley, 2012; Kumar & Arulmani, 2014). At the same time, they have to also empower students to develop information literacy skills that include not only technological skills to search, select, and organize information but also to analyze, validate, and process it to inform decision-making. Career educators working with youth from socio-economic backgrounds that are different from their own, and particularly with those from disadvantaged backgrounds, are likely to make assumptions about their information literacy skills from a deficit perspective. Using sociocultural theories of literacy practices, we learned that the boys had already developed technical skills to use information and communications technologies (ICT), such as social media platforms like Whatsapp and Facebook, in varied and creative ways. For instance, they used ICT to expand and stay connected with their networks, to consume popular culture in Hindi and English on YouTube, to create vine videos on social and environmental issues of interest, to learn Vfx (visual effects) photo editing skills, and to make presentations. Importantly, they demonstrated negotiation skills to acquire social access to smartphones, which were shared resources in their families as only a few boys had access to a computer.

We mapped students' information sources— both online and offline—that shaped their interests and motivations in non-deterministic ways. Evaluating the credibility of information from various sources is an important aspect of information literacy. The boys often assigned cognitive authority to individuals with experience in particular fields or careers to validate their information, and they did not depend necessarily or entirely on information received from online sources whose cognitive authority could be dubious. Thus, boys distributed cognitive authority across their social networks within their neighborhoods, schools, and online spaces, bringing these sources in interaction with each other. Hence, their career interests were re-shaped by a polyphonic career information landscape.

Situating the information literacy skills of both career educators and youth within a sustainable development perspective, and specifically the SDGs that attend to reducing inequalities, orients them in critical ways to make informed decisions around what information to look for, how to validate it, and process it towards whose ends. Using data from how youth think about issues related to sustainable development and their futures, we were able to explore the bumps in an otherwise flattened career information landscape. For instance, the SDG 4 (gender equality) and SDG 8 (reduced inequalities) framed our explorations to find that most boys, except for a few, had a limited information literacy skills regarding the caste-based differentiation of the labor market, whereas most boys' information landscapes regarding how gender and socioeconomic differences unequally shaped opportunities for education and work represented a more complex and textured, or what we termed "bumpy", landscape of the interaction and conflict among multiple actors.

For instance, many boys felt that girls had fewer opportunities to study further, while a few felt that gendered perceptions were shifting in favor of girls and particular negative perceptions related to boys were harming them. These kinds of conflicts or bumps could potentially be crucial entry points for deeper conversations and dialogues on the meanings of masculinity in relation to particular kinds of education and work.

Similarly, the media production activities created an opportunity for establishing a "slightly different awareness" and "sensitivity" towards their local realities with the goal of highlighting particular sustainable development issues relevant to them (Decuypere et al., 2019, p. 12). For instance, students noted a range of issues such as the wastage of water, gender inequalities, and health-related issues. Further, students made connections between their local realities and their careers of interest such that they illustrated what "greening" careers meant to them in specific, culturally relevant ways. These student-created media products empowered students to mobilize their funds of knowledge. They also afforded opportunities for career educators to facilitate dialogues with and among students about what these issues meant to them personally and as members of communities, and what actions would be needed as individuals and more importantly, as a collective, to reconfigure their realities.

The transformative approach to information literacy affords the possibility for careers educators to map young people's rich information landscapes. These information landscapes can become the basis for co-designing with youth a culturally relevant, dynamic, and collectively validated information system. The career information workshop constituted a site of engagement, that is, a specific moment in time and space in which the boys' and our (or career counselors) social histories converged and mediated particular actions related to career aspirations (Norris & Jones, 2005). In co-mapping the various informational actors regarding specific careers, the boys were able to (re)distribute cognitive authority from the career counselor as an expert to include their own funds of knowledge. Further, students mapped individuals with experience within their social networks regarding the careers discussed in class as a collective. In doing so, students widened the distribution of the cognitive authority beyond their individual networks, and such individuals could now serve as potential resources for the entire collective.

Conclusion

In this chapter, we have illustrated how the SDGs can be deployed in the context of career guidance to help students develop relevant life skills toward a meaningful career path. Elsewhere, career guidance scholars and practitioners have deployed the SDGs to help students find personal meaning in their lives (Rochat & Masdonati, 2019). There is, however, a danger in using this approach in a deterministic manner in a world that is unknowable and rapidly changing. Sustainability education can also promote anxiety in part due to a loss of meaning produced by the unknowable and unpredictable quality of our futures, and of the geographical spaces that we live in due to neoliberal practices and globalization (Ojala, 2016). The coronavirus pandemic is a glaring instance of how our relationship to space (staying at home) and time (disruption of routines) has been reconfigured in different ways for different groups of people within a span of a few weeks, and whose impact will be felt for much longer, particularly for youth. The pandemic, shaped by globalization, has triggered a global economic crisis and has significantly affected job markets, producing much anxiety for young people. Hence, we suggest that the SDGs can serve as a compass to orient practitioners' and youths' information literacy practices as they navigate the tensions, contradictions, and existential anxieties that emerge in their career information landscapes (Decuypere et al., 2019; Ojala, 2016). The role of career counselors and educators, thus, would involve empowering youth to collect and process information, and their emotional responses to it, in order to prepare youth to negotiate existential anxieties for an uncertain future.

To conclude, this study contributes to an understanding of career information literacy skills from a sociocultural and transformative approach. Such an approach is different from technical approaches to information literacy skills, which positions career educators as cognitive authorities that provide students and youth who are lacking these skills with valid and legitimate career information. This unequal relationship is disempowering for career educators and students alike. While career educators are put under stress to constantly update their knowledge base in a rapidly changing world, students' cultural knowledge remains unacknowledged, even though such knowledge crucially shapes their career aspirations and choices. A transformative approach builds on the culturally preparedness model of career guidance (Arulmani, 2011) as it aims to recognize students' socially situated career information literacy skills. Importantly, it facilitates students' critical reflections on how their career information landscapes are shaped by unequal power relations, and how they might collectively transform these landscapes. For instance, a young boy may reflect on how his career aspiration is shaped by his caste network and his gendered relationship to particular kinds of work. He may further engage with the career information landscapes beyond his immediate familial and caste networks to consider alternative opportunities for work, and in turn share his cultural resources with his peers. Our engagement with young boys has also suggested that particular constructs of masculinity might be influencing how they (dis)engage with studies, and how they align themselves towards particular kinds of work. It would be crucial for career educators to understand in further depth how boys make sense of and negotiate shifting gender norms as they make particular choices for work.

Future research and practice should engage students to reflect on how caste and gender have unequally shaped their career aspirations and opportunities with each other. This study further encourages a dialogue about what students can do individually and collectively to transform these unequal opportunity structures. Transformative information literacy skills are crucial life skills that career guidance practitioners and youth need to develop in dialogue with and among each other in order to design a culturally relevant, dynamic, collectively validated information system, and help young people consider meaningful and sustainable futures.

Acknowledgments This research was funded by Engagement Globale through the ESD Expert Net mentorship programme, Germany. We thank our collaborators, Saransh Sugandh of In Vaarta Communications, the Teach for India fellows of the school, the boys who participated in this study, Sachin Kumar, the peer reviewers, and the editors, Joan DeJaeghere and Erin Murphy-Graham for their rich and critical contributions to our thinking on this paper.

References

Andersen, J. (2006). The public sphere and discursive activities: Information literacy as sociopolitical skills. *Journal of Documentation, 62*(2), 213–228.

Arulmani, G. (2011). Striking the right note: The cultural preparedness approach to developing resonant career guidance programmes. *International Journal for Educational and Vocational Guidance, 11*(2), 79–93.

Arur, A., & DeJaeghere, J. (2019). Decolonizing life skills education for girls in Brahmanical India: A Dalitbahujan perspective. *Gender and Education, 31*(4), 490–507.

Bhukya, B. (2008). The mapping of the Adivasi social: Colonial anthropology and Adivasis. *Economic and Political Weekly, 43*(39), 103–109.

Boche, B. (2014). Multiliteracies in the classroom: Emerging conceptions of first-year teachers. *Journal of Language and Literacy Education, 10*(1), 114–135.

Decuypere, M., Hoet, H., & Vandenabeele, J. (2019). Learning to navigate (in) the Anthropocene. *Sustainability, 11*(2), 547–562.

DeJaeghere, J. (2018). A capability approach to entrepreneurship education: Fostering recognition and community care to address inequalities for marginalized youth. In S. McGrath, M. Mulder, J. Papier, & R. Suart (Eds.), *Handbook of vocational education and training: Developments in the changing world of work* (pp. 1–19). Springer.

Di Fabio, A., & Maree, J. G. (2016). Using a transdisciplinary interpretive lens to broaden reflections on alleviating poverty and promoting decent work. *Frontiers in Psychology, 7*, 503.

González, N., Moll, L. C., & Amanti, C. (Eds.). (2006). *Funds of knowledge: Theorizing practices in households, communities, and classrooms*. Lawrence Erlbaum.

Hamilton, M. (2016). Imagining literacy: A sociomaterial approach. In K. Yasukawa & S. Black (Eds.), *Beyond economic interests: Critical perspectives on adult literacy and numeracy in a globalised world* (pp. 1–17). Sense Publishers.

Hooley, T. (2012). How the internet changed career: Framing the relationship between career development and online technologies. *Journal of the National Institute for Career Education and Counselling, 29*(1), 3–12.

Hooley, T., Sultana, R. G., & Thomsen, R. (2017). The neoliberal challenge to career guidance: Mobilising research, policy and practice around social justice. In T. Hooley, R. G. Sultana, & R. Thomsen (Eds.), *In career guidance for social justice: Contesting neoliberalism* (pp. i–27). Routledge.

Janks, H. (2012). The importance of critical literacy. *English Teaching: Practice and Critique, 11*(1), 150–163.

Koltay, T. (2011). The media and the literacies: Media literacy, information literacy, digital literacy. *Media, Culture & Society, 33*(2), 211–221.

Kumar, S., & Arulmani, G. (2014). Understanding the labor market: Implications for career counseling. In G. Arulmani, A. Bakshi, F. Leong, & A. Watts (Eds.), *Handbook of career development. International and cultural psychology* (pp. 225–239). Springer.

Kumar, D., & Puthumattathil, A. (2018). A critique of development in India's predominantly Adivasi Regions with Special Reference to the Hos of India's Jharkhand. *Contemporary Voice of Dalit, 10*(1), 10–27.

Lave, J., & Wenger, E. (1991). *Situated learning: Legitimate peripheral participation*. Cambridge University Press.

Lloyd, A. (2010). *Information literacy landscapes: Information literacy in education, workplace and everyday contexts*. Elsevier.

Lupton, M., & Bruce, C. (2010). Windows on information literacy worlds: Generic, situated and transformative perspectives. In A. Lloyd & S. Talja (Eds.), *Practising information literacy: Bringing theories of learning, practice and information literacy together* (pp. 3–27). Centre for Information Studies at Charles Stuart University.

Mackey, T. P., & Jacobson, T. E. (2011). Reframing information literacy as a metaliteracy. *College & research libraries, 72*(1), 62–78.

McKeown, R., & Hopkins, C. (2007). Moving beyond the EE and ESD disciplinary debate in formal education. *Journal of Education for Sustainable Development, 1*(1), 17–26.

Norris, S., & Jones, R. H. (Eds.). (2005). *Discourse in action: Introducing mediated discourse analysis.* Taylor & Francis.

Ojala, M. (2016). Facing anxiety in climate change education: From therapeutic practice to hopeful transgressive learning. *Canadian Journal of Environmental Education, 21*, 41–56.

Paik, S. (2016). Forging a new Dalit womanhood in colonial Western India: Discourse on modernity, rights, education, and emancipation. *Journal of Women's History, 28*(4), 14–40.

Plant, P. (2014). Green guidance. In G. Arulmani, A. Bakshi, F. Leong, & A. Watts (Eds.), *Handbook of career development. International and cultural psychology* (pp. 309–316). Springer.

Pouyaud, J., & Guichard, J. (2017). A twenty-first century challenge: How to lead an active life whilst contributing to sustainable and equitable development. In T. Hooley, R. G. Sultana, & R. Thomsen (Eds.), *In career guidance for social justice: Contesting neoliberalism (pp. 31–45).* Routledge.

Ratnam, A. (2014). Traditional occupations in a modern world: Career guidance, livelihood planning, and crafts in the context of globalization. In G. Arulmani, A. Bakshi, F. Leong, & A. Watts (Eds.), *Handbook of career development. International and cultural psychology* (pp. 397–410). Springer.

Rege, S. (2006). Writing caste, writing gender: Reading Dalit women's Testimonios. Zubaan.

Rochat, S., & Masdonati, J. (2019). Sustainable career cards Sort (SCCS): Linking career choices to the world needs. In J. G. Maree (Ed.), *Handbook of innovative career counselling* (pp. 505–520). Springer.

Schreiber, J., & Seige, H. (2016). *Curriculum framework: Education for sustainable development.* Engagement Global.

Sharma, G. (1990). *Valour and sacrifice: Famous regiments of the Indian Army.* Allied Publishers.

Sustainable Development Goals. (2015). *17 Goals to transform our world.* http://www.un.org/sustainabledevelopment/development-agenda/

Waghmore, S. (2007). Exploring the unexplored: Dalit workview in development discourse. *Indian Journal of Social Work, 68*(1), 7.

Watts, A. G. (1996). Socio-political ideologies in guidance. In A. G. Watts, B. Law, J. Killeen, J. M. Kidd, & R. Hawthorn (Eds.), *Rethinking careers education and guidance: Theory, policy and practice* (pp. 351–366). Routledge.

Whitworth, A. (2014). *Radical information literacy: Reclaiming the political heart of the IL movement.* Elsevier.

Chapter 9
A Life Knowledge Approach to Life Skills: Empowering Boys with New Conceptions of Masculinity

Urvashi Sahni

Abstract This chapter argues for a structural, human rights and social justice-based approach to life skills, contextualized in an urban setting in the state of Uttar Pradesh, India. This approach takes a more socially and politically embedded view of life skills than most other life skills approaches, which take a more individualized, decontextualized, and apolitical approach. I argue that since our lives are framed and structured by the socio-political contexts in which they are lived, a deeper conceptual understanding of these contexts is essential in order to navigate this terrain skillfully and successfully. This chapter provides a descriptive analysis of a school program for girls and boys from marginalized backgrounds, which educates them to become active democratic citizens with gender-just perceptions and behaviors. The school, Prerna, was established and is run by Study Hall Educational Foundation (SHEF). Prerna focuses on life outcomes and learning outcomes, with the educational goal of educating its students to develop egalitarian and gender-just habits, and the intellectual, emotional, and behavioral skills that will enable them to live as equal persons, including respecting others' (girls') right to equality. This chapter focuses particularly on the school's program for boys, where they are empowered to develop an egalitarian conception of masculinity and of themselves in relationship to girls.

Keywords Life skills · Empowerment · Gender · Transformation · Masculinity · Critical feminist pedagogy · India

Introduction

I want to have a family where I earn enough and my wife works alongside, too, if she wants to, and I want an environment at home where no one is getting oppressed, or beaten and abused, everyone is equal and happy. (Rahul, student of Prerna Boys School)

U. Sahni (✉)
Study Hall Education Foundation, Lucknow, Uttar Pradesh, India

J. DeJaeghere, E. Murphy-Graham (eds.), *Life Skills Education for Youth*, Young People and Learning Processes in School and Everyday Life 5, https://doi.org/10.1007/978-3-030-85214-6_9

Rahul is a typical student of the Prerna Boys School. [1] A 16-year-old boy, he lives with his single mother and two sisters in his uncle's house. His parents are separated. His mother was pulled out of school after completing grade 5, because she was needed at home to take care of her younger siblings. She was married off at 15, and has been a victim of severe and repeated domestic violence. It was only after she was almost beaten to death by her drunk husband that her parents reacted and sent her brother to bring her back to their home. Rahul witnessed this abuse his entire life. His mother now works as a cleaning woman in a school. Rahul supplements their family income working at his uncle's shop. He joined Prerna in 2016 when he was 12. Initially a frightened little boy, he's now a confident lad with high aspirations for his life. He wants to become a successful businessman and make sure his mother has a good life when he grows up, and he wants everyone to be "equal and happy."

India is home to one-third of the world's 15 million child brides (more appropriately called girl slaves), like Rahul's mother (UNICEF, 2014). For most girls the world over, child marriage means the end of education and the beginning of child bearing, increased vulnerability to physical, emotional and sexual abuse, and an abrupt end to options for a future of their choice (Girls Not Brides, 2019). India also ranks 112th on the global gender gap index (World Economic Forum, 2020), and recently, the Thompson Reuters Foundation (2018) declared India the most dangerous country in the world for girls and women. [2]

It is not difficult to see why. High rates of female feticide, (i.e. sex selective abortions of female fetuses) render them unsafe in the womb, while high rates of violence and rape render them unsafe on the streets. More than 32,500 cases of rape were registered with the police in 2017, about 90 a day, according to the most recent government data (Reuters, 2019).They are not safe at home, where they're at risk for child marriage, and are subject to both physical and emotional abuse by their husbands, fathers, and brothers. Why? Because they are girls, seen as burdens and objects, to be valued and used only for their reproductive, sexual, and domestic labor, with very little autonomy or agency in their lives. The unfair power structures that render girls so vulnerable are supported beliefs and practices sanctioned by deeply embedded patriarchal mindsets and social norms. Patriarchy has lethal consequences for girls and women. It also places an unfair burden on boys and men to be sole providers and decision makers for the family, which while giving them more power, also leaves them with enormous stress, often leading to violent behavior. While Rahul's mother bore the brunt of the violence at the hands of her drunken husband, it was her brother who had to take on the responsibility of taking care of

---

[1] Prerna is run by the Study Hall Educational Foundation (SHEF), which was founded by the author in 1994. SHEF runs a network of 7 schools in and around Lucknow. Our schools reach out to all representative population groups, and all ages. We also have 4 outreach initiatives, which share our best practices across the state, the country and globally. These include teacher trainings, community-based education centres, campaigns, and online video lessons. Through all our initiatives, we have touched more than 7,000,000 lives.

[2] Incidentally, the U.S was ranked 10th.

her when she left her husband. Even now, he takes care of her and Rahul's family. One of Rahul's biggest goals is to be able to provide for his family, and to take care of his mother and sisters.

There is urgent need for change – change in belief, and change in practice. Schools can either reinforce the status quo, or play a critical role in changing toxic mindsets to make the world a safer, freer, more welcoming, and enabling place for girls and boys. Education is a very powerful personal and social transformative force, *provided it is transformed*. Societal and political power structures construct conceptual structures, which reinforce and maintain societal power structures. Education can play an important role in deconstructing conceptual structures, thereby disrupting unfair and discriminatory patriarchal systems and norms.

In this chapter, I describe the history and pedagogical approach of the Prerna School, and in particular how it works to promote critical life skills among its male students. I first explain the theoretical framework that underpins our work and how this framework is present in our curricular and pedagogical approach. This work includes the employment of critical dialogues, which I describe in detail as they are a key element of our work. I then explain how our work has made an impact on the boys and teachers with whom we work, through the analysis of focus group interviews conducted as part of a preliminary evaluation of our efforts. The key impacts that emerged from these focus groups included: improving boys' confidence and self-expression; increasing their gender awareness/sensitization; influencing their family dynamic and becoming advocates for their sisters; allowing them to develop non-dominant perceptions of masculinity and manhood; and making them more aware of other social inequalities.

In Order to Be Transformative, Education Must Be Transformed: The Prerna School

Believing in all girls' intrinsic right to an education, I established Prerna Girls School in 2003 with the goal of providing high-quality education to girls from low-income families. Most of the students belong to historically marginalized communities, and live in extreme poverty. Because of this, many girls work in the morning and the school runs in the afternoon. Also, most of the girls are first-generation learners who have either never been sent to school or have been pulled out to help at home, either to help care for their siblings or due to the illness or death of their mothers. Looking at the lives of our students, I quickly realized that a traditional, academic-focused education was not enough.

Like Boleslavsky (1949), I believe that the goal of education is not just to know, but to live. As we educated our students, we had to consider what kind of knowledge and education would help them navigate the difficult terrain of their lives. If you are at risk of being married at the age of 13, then learning addition, subtraction, or geography isn't necessarily the knowledge you need most. At SHEF, we believe that education must enable you to answer the question, "Who am I and what is my relationship with the universe and others in it?" To do this, education must be relevant to your life. It must help you locate yourself in the universe, particularly the social and political universe, to know where in the power structure you stand. This knowledge enables you to understand your life and the power structures that enable or limit them. It is this structural understanding that enables students to challenge the structures that define their lives and to work towards changing them.

SHEF's Life Knowledge Approach to Life Skills

SHEF's approach to life skills is structural, holistic, and embedded in students' social and political reality. We belong to the discourse community that identifies skills as an essential component of "quality education" (Murphy-Graham & Cohen, Chap. 2, this volume). We like to think more in terms of life "knowledge" rather than life "skills." We treat life skills as emerging from one's knowledge, and as such they are not given special focus as a separate agenda – they are integrated into our curriculum. Nonetheless, they are a central part of our officially-stated goal to help children learn who they are and how they are related, and should/can relate, to the universe and others in it. Our concept of quality education and its goals as implemented through the official curriculum includes knowledge that is relevant to life and enables students to *live life well* (Murphy-Graham & Cohen, Chap. 2, this volume). This knowledge is co-constructed by teachers and students through critical dialogue, which then facilitates development of the appropriate skills. The belief that education's goal is not just to know, but to live, is reflected in our attitude and approach toward life skills as well. If life skills are those skills that allow us to effectively navigate our lives, or "to live life better" (Murphy-Graham, 2008) they are essentially woven into and embedded in our curriculum in the name of life knowledge. While our aim is to empower our students personally, and to help them become confident, articulate, and self-assured young persons, our focus is also to empower them socially and politically.

Inspired by Amartya Sen and Martha Nussbaum, we adopt a capability approach in order to enable our children to achieve well-being, not only in economic terms, but also in their ability to take control of their lives and live a fully human life (Nussbaum, 2011; Sahni, 2017; Sen, 2000). We ask the important question: How can education enable our students to be who they want to be and to do what they want to do, while at the same time develop their capacities to aspire for more than they have come to expect for their lives?

At SHEF we promote "life knowledge" through a school and a curriculum. We focus on implementing elements of feminist curricular theory, designing interactive, engaging activities, and we work on teacher professional development. Since our work with boys has its origins in and emerged from our work with girls, I first briefly describe our work with girls before detailing the work with boys, showing also how we empower both our boys and girls—albeit differently because of the social and political context of gender inequalities.

Prerna Girls' School: Classrooms as 'Radical Spaces of Possibility'

Our goals in Prerna are to help girls learn that they are equal persons who deserve respect and have the right to a life of their own choosing, and to equip them with the appropriate knowledge and skills to live a fully human life – respected, free, and equal! We structured Prerna's school culture, organizational structure, curriculum, and pedagogy around the goal of achieving not only empowering learning outcomes, but also, and more importantly, empowering life outcomes.

We came to define our overall *educational* goal as the following:

> To empower our students, i.e.to raise their feminist consciousness, to help them emerge as emancipated women with a perception of themselves as equal persons having the right to equal participation in society, and to equip them with the appropriate social, emotional, conceptual, and academic knowledge and skills to live a life of their own choosing (Sahni, 2017).

In practical terms, the school must teach girls to recognize themselves as equal and autonomous persons. Many women in strong patriarchal societies like India do not believe that they are equal to men, causing them to accept discrimination as a given, natural part of life. Thus, we teach our girls to question discrimination, and help them gain a critical understanding of the social and political structures that frame their lives. Additionally, they develop a capacity to aspire, and gain the confidence and skills necessary to realize their aspirations. They develop a sense of voice and agency in their lives. Lastly, they successfully complete the government-mandated syllabus up to grade 12. To reiterate, these are our *educational* goals—not our extracurricular or after-school program goals—taught along with the government-mandated curriculum by their regular teachers, who are trained to teach lessons of equality along with lessons of math, science, and language.[3]

Along with bell hooks (1994), we believe that classrooms are radical spaces of possibility. In exploring and leveraging this possibility, I developed a critical feminist pedagogy, based on Freire's critical pedagogy. Freire (1970) said that we must read our world before we read our words. To help our girls do this, teachers conduct weekly critical dialogue classes to develop their feminist consciousness, i.e., so that they understand that what is happening to them is wrong. Girls become critically aware of their social and political reality and gain a structural understanding of patriarchy and how it shapes their lives. They learn that patriarchy is a social construct, not a natural one, which means that it can be changed. Finally, they learn to collectively imagine a new reality for themselves and collectively find a way to

---

[3] For greater detail of how we do this, see my book (Sahni, 2017).

make space for it despite the restrictive social norms. Parents are included in this "collective" as they are also engaged in regular dialogues both by the teachers and the students.

The learning and life outcomes at Prerna Girls School have been extremely encouraging. Our retention rate is substantially higher than the national average, and 97.5% of the girls have transitioned to higher education. Additionally, the threat of child marriage for our students has become almost nonexistent. So, what has this education enabled our students to be and to do? Today, many of our students have earned master's degrees, have successful careers, including law, teaching, business executives, entrepreneurs, earning a respectable middle-class salary. They say they are respected and valued more at home, with a voice in family decisions. Most importantly, our students are recognizing, resisting, and fighting sexist oppression at home and outside. They are making every effort to steer the course of their lives, exercising choice and agency.

What About Our Boys? Classrooms as Spaces of Radical Possibility and Care

With time, we started receiving increasing numbers of requests from parents to open a school for their sons, who meanwhile were out of school, roaming the streets, and getting involved in gangs, drugs, and street violence. Many of these boys had dropped out of school because of the violent behavior of teachers, or because they found the education there of poor quality and irrelevant to their lives. Poor and lower caste, they saw very few possibilities for their lives, and had no faith in the education that they had received in schools . While engaging with the community we also realized that if we want a better world for our girls, then their fathers, brothers, and future husbands need to be part of the solution. We were motivated by the belief that, in order to achieve a gender-just society, boys and girls both must receive an empowering education that teaches them to critically examine the construction of gender in patriarchal societies. Like their female colleagues, boys, too, must learn to fight, resist, and end sexist oppression. They must be enabled to deconstruct a patriarchal conception of masculinity and reconstruct an egalitarian one in its place.

With these motivations, Prerna Boys School was founded in 2009 to provide boys with a quality education, an essential component of which is *the development of a strong critical feminist perspective*. We defined boys' desired life-outcome as becoming autonomous persons who can take care of themselves and their families, beyond simply providing for them. They should come to perceive themselves not just as financial providers, but also as nurturers and caregivers of their families.

As of 2019, Prerna Boys School had 150 students (90 primary level and 60 senior level), ages 4–19, cared for by nine teachers (three male and six female). Of these students, 39% are brothers of Prerna girls. All are poor, with an average monthly family income of approximately Rs.9000 ($135) and an average family size of 5.6

members. A full two-thirds (67%) belong to the most marginalized castes in India, officially classified as "Scheduled Castes" and "Other Backward Classes," and 26% either work or have worked before. Forty-one percent of fathers and 62.8% of mothers are illiterate and have never attended school, and 12.3% of boys either live in a single-parent household or are orphans.

The school follows the same ethic of care that characterizes all SHEF schools, and is governed by the same holistic, locally contextualized pedagogy and philosophy as Prerna Girls School. It focuses on boys' lives in a caring, responsive, and respectful environment, with the goal of achieving better life and learning outcomes. We aim for boys to gain academic knowledge and skills, and, more importantly, *to gain the knowledge and skills needed to live empowered lives as empathetic and egalitarian-minded persons.*

Consistent with the goals established for our girls, we adopted the following set of educational goals for Prerna Boys School.[4] Our boys must:

- Develop a sense of agency and control over their lives, aspirations for a future, and the confidence and skills to realize it.
- Learn to recognize girls as equal persons with boys.
- Develop a critical understanding of patriarchal social and political structures that frame their lives and minds.
- Develop a critical feminist consciousness.
- Learn to read, write, and successfully complete the government-mandated syllabus up to class 12.

Developing a Critical Feminist Consciousness in Boys: Our Approach

Prerna Boys School also practices the critical feminist pedagogy developed through our work with girls. At the beginning of 2016, a year after opening the secondary school, teachers began engaging students in weekly critical dialogues on issues that impact their lives, their families, and others in their neighborhood. Our approach aimed to help boys understand that, though patriarchy is not their fault, it is extremely cruel to their mothers and sisters. It also grants them unfair power and privilege, along with an unfair share of the burden of providing for the family. Critical dialogues are part of the official Prerna Boys School curriculum, and are both taught separately once a week and also often embedded in language, math and science classes.

While dialogues are mostly conducted in parallel to those at Prerna Girls School, they are occasionally conducted together as well. The boys' school is housed separately from the girls' school in response to the parent community's concern for their daughters' safety. As many of our girls come from families who do not support their

---

[4] See Epilogue, Sahni (2017).

education, a co-ed space would act as a barrier to SHEF's commitment toward girls' education and empowerment. However, boys and girls meet regularly for critical dialogues, sports, drama, music, and other activities. This mixed-sex interaction is encouraged with the motive of helping boys and girls gain a better understanding of each other, become friends, and learn to negotiate relationships across gender in a safe, mediated setting.

In hierarchical, patriarchal societies like India, it is difficult to understand and conceptualize the idea of equality. It is particularly hard for boys, as they are raised with a sense of entitlement, superiority, and privilege. Regardless of their class, caste, or religion, boys enjoy preferred status over their female counterparts. Changing these conceptual frameworks involves a paradigm shift, almost Copernican in nature. Working with girls, and the oppressed in general, is in many ways easier, as they have everything to gain by resisting. Working with powerholders, on the other hand, becomes trickier as they often feel they have something to lose in granting equal status to others. Thus, as we worked with our boys, we sought to understand the best way to engage with boys and men on topics of gender inequality, help them develop an empathetic understanding of girls' lives, and enable them to envision how to be different kinds of boys and men.

With these questions in mind, we built a curriculum (Sahni et al., 2018) together with the boys. The curriculum emerged from our dialogues with the boys. Its goal was to develop an understanding of gender equality and reframe their notions of masculinity, manhood, and boyhood. Because the boys themselves are the experts on their lives, involving them in the process was critical in enabling our fuller understanding of their realities and thereby designing an effective curriculum. The final curriculum is based on our interactive sessions, and was built by incorporating their voices and their experiences. It also includes our observations of what was most effective and fruitful in developing an understanding and acceptance of gender equality in boys. All the boys are poor and lower caste, so we built on their existing perception of themselves as unequal and their desire for equality, in terms of caste and class

The curriculum includes critical dialogues on a wide range of topics, including facilitating boys' greater self- and socio-emotional awareness, topics of masculinity, violence against women at home and on the street, gender, and marriage. Alongside discussion and dialogue, poetry, art, and drama in particular are used extensively, guided by the belief that the arts provide a powerful medium for developing the expression and education of feelings. Encouraging boys to share their feelings and experiences is an essential part of dialogues, especially since, in most settings, boys constantly receive the contrary message. Educating feelings and developing self-awareness and empathy is critical in provoking a change, and is also more effective and impactful than solely rational dialogue.

We have sought to empower our boys and girls differently: while both boys and girls learn to recognize the unfair structure of patriarchy, and both learn to resist and fight sexist oppression, we focus more on developing voice and agency in girls because they face sexist oppression more directly. With boys our focus is on developing empathy for girls' lives and how to support girls in their struggle by struggling alongside, while also learning that the world is unsafe and unfair to girls precisely *because* boys are raised to be dominating and violent, due to the differential norms of sexual behavior for boys and girls. Girls must ideally be meek, submissive, subservient, and chaste, while boys are expected to be strong, powerful, in control, aggressive, and assertive, and sexually free to express themselves as they desire. Our goal is to deconstruct these gendered perspectives and norms and to move both girls and boys towards an egalitarian perspective of femininity and masculinity. Understandably, working with boys has proven to be much harder than it has been with girls, because they feel they are losing power and privilege.

Given below are two sample lesson plans with excerpts of critical dialogues[5] conducted with the boys:

Critical Dialogue 1: Girls' Lives

In this dialogue, the boys discuss their mothers' and sisters' responses to a short interview about their daily routine, their likes and dislikes, and their fears. As boys share these responses, the teacher continues to ask scaffolding questions, especially pointed at bringing out discriminatory differences.

S: *My sister is older than me. She also goes to school. She gets up at 6 am, gets dressed, makes breakfast for me and herself. After coming back from school, she has lunch, then does housework, like cleaning the house, doing dishes, etc. Then she studies for a while. Then she cooks food, studies for a while, has dinner, and goes to sleep. She likes listening to music, dancing, travelling, reading comic books, and spending time with her friends.*

T: *When does she play? It's not in the routine you have described.*

S: *She plays sometimes at home.*

T: *Doesn't she go out to play like you do? You said you go out to play cricket after school every day.*

S: *No, at home only.*

T: *Why can't she go out to play?*

S: *She has to study and do the housework.*

T: *And when does she spend time with her friends?*

S: *In school and when she walks back with them after school.*

T: *What about hanging out with them later, after school, in the evening?*

S: *No, parents don't let them go out in the evening. And they have to cook and all.*

T: *So, she doesn't get to go out a lot, but she likes to, right? Hm...So, I heard the daily routines of your sisters, your aunt, etc., and I'm thinking of your own routines, which you had shared earlier. What differences do you see?*

S11:   *We get to play, they don't.*

S7:   *They don't get to go out.*

S5:   *They can't go out without permission, we can.*

S11:   *They have to cook.*

---

[5] All dialogues were conducted in Hindi and translated to English for the purpose of this chapter.

T1:   *Yes, they get up so early. Your sister gets up at 5am. What time do you get up?*

S11:   *8 or 8:30am.*

T1:   *Exactly! So, they have to cook food. What other difference is there? Some of you also work outside, they also work outside but they come back and do household chores also; they have to study also in that time. So, neither do they get time to play, nor are they allowed to. Why aren't they allowed to play?*

S11:   *Now they've grown up, parents say they have to work at home, and it's not an age to play.*

T1:   *Why not? Let's think about it. Why do they say that it's not appropriate to play at this age?*

S11:   *If they go out to play, then who will do the work at home?*

T1:   *You all. Think about it. Just like you, they also like playing but they can't because they have to work at home. Is this fair? We never even thought about it. When I was little, my three brothers used to go out in the evening to play cricket. I was very rarely allowed to go because I had to work at home and take care of my younger cousins. I had to iron all the clothes at home. I didn't like that. Do you think they like it? No, right? They are also just like you…But their life is very different from yours. We haven't talked about their fears yet, we will. We need to think about it. We should think what must be going on in their heads. They get up before you, cook for everyone, serve food, then have it themselves, then get ready and go to school. Many of them work outside also. They come back and work at home also. How many of you are 16 years old? There isn't much difference between your ages. He is also 16 and she is also 16. So why can't she play at that age?*

As illustrated in Critical Dialogue #1, the teachers work to help boys see how different girls' lives are—more circumscribed, less free, and with more work, less leisure—and that their fears, too, are different. They're related to marriage, in-laws, and leaving their parents' home. By illustrating that girls are not so different from them, she/he encourages the boys to see the differential treatment of boys and girls at home in a personal way, empathize with girls, and question the fairness of this discriminatory treatment.

Importantly, teachers make a special effort to do so without making the boys feel guilty, explicitly stating that it is not their fault. They emphasize the fact that society is a socio-historical construct, which is not fixed but is constantly changing. It can and does change when social action is taken. They give examples from history, including how child marriage was a commonly accepted practice and legal, and now is not; how Sati (the custom of burning wives alive on their dead husband's *pyre*) was legal but was outlawed and now does not exist; how women had no share in parental property, but are now entitled by law to an equal share. And that these changes happened because of social action by both women and men. Thus, social gender norms can be changed if everyone – boys and girls – takes action.

This dialogue is often supported by a short drama activity, in which boys act out their lives, showing what they learned about their sisters'/girls' lives. The teacher helps boys understand that household tasks are not "women's work" as a result of any natural difference between men and women.

To help develop empathy, the teacher asks boys to prepare a short role reversal skit in which they imagine they are in a world where the conventional standards are reversed. Boys must now conform to the roles that girls are traditionally given: they cook, cannot go out, must take care of babies, must obey men at home, must be submissive, etc. Their plays should show a day in a boy's life in this new universe. After all the groups perform, the teacher does a reflective exercise with the boys to help them process the experience, asking questions such as:

- How did they feel? What were their lives like? Did they like their lives? Why not? Are these standards fair to girls?
- If differences aren't natural, then society need not have these standards. Aren't they a way of keeping men in power and perpetuating inequality?
- How might we work towards more equal standards?

The teacher also assigns homework, asking the boys to discuss at home what they learned about the differential treatment of boys and girls, and whether they think it is fair to girls, thus including families in the dialogues too. Additionally, she/he can subsequently discuss all the themes regarding working towards equality mentioned over three to four sessions with the students.

In another example critical dialogue, the teacher focuses on promoting non-dominant understandings of masculinity. The teacher illustrates how crying is seen as acceptable only for girls. She also discusses the "ego" issue raised by students, pointing out that there seems to be an implicit hierarchy in behaving like a girl or a boy, in which a boy acting like a girl is an inferior thing to do. She helps them question and challenge this proposition.

Critical Dialogue 2: Denaturalizing Conceptions of Boyhood and Manhood

S1:   *If we fall and get hurt, a girl will cry, a boy won't.*

T: *But I've seen boys cry.*

S1:   *Little boys cry, not big ones.*

S2:   *Boys are told not to cry like a girl from childhood, so they learn to control it.*

T: *So, it isn't natural, right? But tell me, what's the harm in crying when you're in pain?*

S1:   *People will make fun of you if you do that.*

S2:   *Boy's ego will get hurt if people say you're crying like a girl.*

T: *Why is that? It's quite normal to cry when you are in pain. And why does our ego get hurt when someone says we're doing something like a girl? Does a girl's ego get hurt when she's told she's behaving like a boy?*

S1:   *No, not her ego, but she will feel it is not a compliment. It means she's not normal but strange.*

T: *Yes, but if both boys and girls sometimes behave like each other, then there's no "natural" way of behaving, right? It's all taught to us. Actually, tell me, don't you feel like crying sometimes? I do. Let's see - when do we feel like crying, but don't because someone will laugh at us? Everyone share one such incident. I'll share mine first...*

Throughout the critical dialogues, teachers try to emphasize how boys' own lives will improve as well through dismantling patriarchy, and they use examples of egalitarian men who cook, clean, are nurturing fathers, cry when they feel like it, and do not feel like they are inferior or weak men. Boys may laugh and feel uncomfortable at first. They should be allowed to find their comfort level with the teachers' help. The teacher should drive home the message that boys and men doing these things is not unnatural, demeaning, or unmanly; it can be fun and rewarding.

The School Culture: An Ethic of Responsive Care/Pedagogy of Care

At SHEF we believe that school culture forms an integral part of children's education. It teaches as much as the official curriculum; it is the "hidden" curriculum. In our schools, we aim to create a safe, caring, and nurturing learning environment for our students.

In our work with the Prerna girls, we have learned that care itself is empowering, and the key ways in which care manifests itself are trust, respect, and attentiveness. Teachers must pay attention to the realities of boys' lives, earn their trust, listen to them, and respond respectfully. Teachers must also ensure that the boys believe that they care deeply about them, and that they will do everything they can to help the boys build better lives. This is grounded in my belief that it is only when we are cared for that we learn to care. Boys must experience a different way of being treated and perceived as boys if they are to learn to change their own perceptions of what it means to be a boy.

The school is based on an ethic of care so that boys develop caring, nurturing dispositions, and the pedagogy is contextualized in boys' lives. Teachers adopt a sympathetic, responsive listening stance, so that boys feel heard and understood. The teachers let the boys see that they understand the realities and compulsions of their lives, the ways in which they feel oppressed and burdened by poverty and the resulting child labor. Boys are given curricular space to discuss their fears, anxieties, dreams, and hopes. At the same time, they see that as hard as their lives are, their sisters' lives are still harder. Boys are encouraged to care about others in their world, develop an empathetic understanding of girls' and women's lives, and challenge the social structure and traditional gendered social norms and mindsets. While experiencing care, they also learn to care.

While boys cared immensely about their mothers' and sisters' well-being, their initial concept of care was limited to earning more, providing more goods, and protecting their mothers and sisters, which manifested itself in restricting their mobility and other protective limitations. Boys as young as 14 expressed concerns about future marriage expenses for their younger sister(s). For most, these were perceived as the singular ways in which a man can care for his family – as a distant patriarchal head of the family, exercising full control over their lives and executing the duty of providing for and "protecting" the family.

In order to illustrate a less gendered way /a non-sexist and non-patriarchal definition of caring, we helped them understand that fighting for their younger sister's education would allow her to become an independent person capable of making her own decisions about her life and marriage. We discussed how sharing the responsibility of domestic chores allowed her to go out and play, which is another way of caring for her.

Schools as Safe Spaces and Sanctuaries

Boys are frequently witnesses, victims, and perpetrators of violence from a very young age. Many of our boys had abusive fathers and saw their mothers verbally and physically abused by them. They narrated incidents of being brutally beaten in their previous schools, both by teachers and peers. Violence quickly becomes a way of life—in homes, in schools, on the streets—and boys learn to see violence as a way to gain respect and power.

In *The Will to Change: Men, Masculinity and Love*, bell hooks (2004, p. 35) points toward a deeply rooted problem in patriarchy, that "boys are not seen as lovable." Patriarchy values boys for their ability to earn and provide. Very early, boys learn that they will be respected only if they conform to hegemonic masculine norms. Soon after establishing Prerna Boys School, we realized that our boys needed to know that they are indeed lovable.

It was also important that we not replicate patriarchal school cultures, which hooks (2004) warns can harm boys by enforcing rigid sex roles. Thus, we recruited as many male teachers as possible, all of whom were gentle and caring, to show our boys that alternate forms of masculinity are possible. Additionally, we worked to help boys make a critical connection to their emotions.

Echoing our own understanding, hooks (2004, p. 54) says that,

> to truly protect and honor the emotional lives of boys, we must challenge patriarchal culture…until that culture changes, we must create the subcultures, the sanctuaries where boys can learn to be who they are uniquely, without being forced to conform to patriarchal masculine visions.

Schools can be these subcultures and sanctuaries, provided teachers and the school culture support boys in perceiving themselves as lovable. In addition to being safe and caring spaces, schools must help boys become emotionally self-aware, autonomous human beings who consider themselves worthy of love and respect, and define their self-worth as boys and men independently from their ability to dominate or to provide financially. This will help them imagine alternate conceptions of masculinity and ways of inhabiting the world as boys and men. It is only in such an environment that boys can be educated for gender justice (Sahni et al., 2018).

Training Teachers

To create this culture, teachers also learn to change their own gendered perceptions of themselves and of boys. Our teachers receive intensive workshops and participate in regular critical dialogues. As a result, the teachers have reported many changes in their own lives. Female teachers have learned to recognize the gendered nature of their own lives, as well as their right to equality. Male teachers shared that they have become more empathetic with the women in their lives and have gained a deeper understanding of gender issues. Like the boys, they too now help with household chores. Pratima, the principal, speaks of her own raised awareness:

> When I came here, I did not question most things, like why women get food at the end…I'd accepted that after marriage only I had to wash my husband's clothes...Nobody cared if I had eaten or not, if I had a headache, if it was my birthday. I had no value as a person, especially as a daughter-in-law. And all of this didn't matter to me also…After 15 years of marriage I realized that I didn't really have to do that.

Alok, her male colleague, reports something similar, saying that "My understanding of these issues was very narrow. I knew these problems existed but I didn't know they were so deep. Through critical dialogues I understood their depth and width. The problems are much bigger than I thought." Alok and Ankur, both male teachers at Prerna, report that they have changed how they behave at home with their wives, and have begun to share household chores.

What Can Boys Do and Who Can They Be? Action Research About How Boys Develop Critical Life Knowledge and Skills at Prerna School

Methodology: Action Research for Organizational Improvement

To understand whether our approach was working, we employed an action research methodology (Coghlan, 2001), in which action research was

> …defined as an emergent inquiry process in which applied behavioural science knowledge is integrated with existing organizational knowledge and applied to solve real organizational problems. It is simultaneously concerned with bringing about change in organizations, in developing self-help competencies in organizational members and adding to scientific knowledge. Finally, it is an evolving process that is undertaken in a spirit of collaboration and co-inquiry. (Shani & Pasmore, 1985, p. 439)

To assess the impact of critical dialogues on boys in terms of their thinking and behavior, we held focus group discussions with students, parents, and teachers.[6] We

---

[6] Students and parents were informed that participation was voluntary at every stage, and consent was given by students and their parents at every stage of the process.

chose six focal students and their parents. The boys were part of the school program for at least 3 years. The boys ranged in ages 13–17 years old. We had engaged with these boys in critical dialogues in the course of developing the curriculum and so knew them from the inception of the program. We also included the teachers who had conducted critical dialogues and other classes with the boys, and were well acquainted with their behavior over three years. We asked all three focus groups the same questions (interview protocol in appendix), and all of the focus group discussions were audio-taped and transcribed. We then triangulated the boys' self-reports with teacher and parent reports. This analysis is part of an ongoing cycle of inquiry that we use to improve our practice at SHEF.

Findings

From the analysis of the transcripts of the focus groups, we found that the boys have experienced and displayed change in the following areas: (1) confidence and self-expression, (2) gender sensitization including more equitable perceptions of girls, (3) influence in their families in trying to advocate for their sisters, (4) development of non-dominant perceptions of masculinity and manhood, and trying to influence their peers in this regard, (5) increased awareness about other social inequalities, (6) development of new skills and abilities previously seen as "feminine."

Confidence and Self-Expression

When asked how they had changed as a result of participating in critical dialogues, boys stated that their confidence had increased, their personality had developed, and that they now feel better able to articulate themselves. They no longer feel as shy about expressing themselves, nor are they afraid to speak out against behaviors they consider wrong. They also report that they now know how to talk differently to different people, and how to persuade them and negotiate with them. This was corroborated by their teachers. Ankur, a male teacher at Prerna Boys School said,

> They have started sharing more; they speak their mind now. Before they were introverts. After learning about these issues through the dialogues and speaking in class, their confidence increased a lot; the manner in which they talk has changed. They have started expressing themselves confidently…And because of this their personality has developed a lot.

Aakansha, his female colleague further added,

> They express themselves much more. Initially they never used to cry, they used to shout and try to solve every problem by fighting. Now they cry if they feel bad and try to solve problems through discussion, rather than violent fighting.

Increased Gender Sensitization

When asked to reflect on any changes in their attitudes and perceptions towards girls, the boys shared that they have learned to empathize with their sisters, to see them as persons with feelings, desires, and fears, and to recognize discrimination (change of perception). They now recognize that girls carry an unfair burden of household work and have begun to help them at home (behavior change resulting from changed perceptions). They also recognize the unfairness of girls' restricted mobility, and have begun advocating for their sisters. Lastly, they have begun advocating for their changed perception of masculinity with their peers and their parents outside school.

For example, Rahul shared, "We also understand girls now, that even they have feelings, they also want to go out, they also want to play." Beyond the critical thinking skills that boys developed in relation to how they think about gender and other social inequalities, they also explained a number of practical ways their actions and behaviors have changed, and the skills that they have learned. For example, when asked what new skills they believed they had acquired, boys stated that they had learned to cook, do many household chores, understand others' feelings, respect others, and behave appropriately with others. They also stated that it had given them the opportunity to get to know themselves and facilitated a greater sense of self-awareness. All of these are critical life skills (see Brush et al., Chap. 3, this volume).

Tarun explains that,

> Initially we didn't know what was happening in our own homes. Sister and mother used to work all day outside and at home. We used to order them to make this and that for lunch, dinner, etc. Through critical dialogues I realized how much they work and the level of pressure my sister is under. We just roam around all day. Then I understood that we should also work at home, so now I cook and clean.

Rahul further expressed his understanding of his own role

> I've understood my responsibilities. If the streets aren't safe then I should accompany my sister when she wants to go out. Before I felt that if she's cooking then that's good, because eventually, she will get married and cook at her in-laws' place. Now I feel that if girls don't progress then society won't either. They can become something after having an education.

Aakansha, their teacher, corroborates this

> Initially the boys took it for granted that these are girls' duties and the boys have nothing to do with them…So we asked them to do a role reversal at home, just for one day. Slowly, the boys started helping at home and then they realized how physically and mentally draining it was for their sisters to study and cook and clean and do everything at home. Now, they share the housework, complete it quickly and go together to play outside. They even study together with their sisters. They even share their problems with their sisters and listen to their problems.

Pratima, the principal, explained that boys had begun to see that gender equality is not just a girls' issue, but theirs too:

> Initially the boys used to get defensive and feel accused. They felt like we only talked about girls…But now they understand that these issues aren't only girls' issues but society's and

boys' also. This is a huge realization. All the boys who've been with us for two or three years, their minds have opened up.

Shivpoojan's sister (also his guardian since their mother's death) spoke of the change she has seen in her brother:

> I've seen a lot of change in him since he joined Prerna Boys. Before he used to sit idle, and my sister…if they both were having dinner, he used to ask her for water. She would stop eating and get him water. Now…if she's doing something, then he does his work on his own. Now he understands her feelings…He helps us in the household work a lot. I have a three-year-old son and he cares for him and helps him to study. He tells me, "The environment we keep at home, this baby will become like that, so we should cooperate with each other and talk politely. The way we treat each other, he will treat others the same way."

Both Ambrendra's mother and Tarun's father commented on the change in their sons, adding that their sons often take their critical dialogues home:

> [Ambrendra] has changed a lot, his behavior towards his sister and me also. He helps us with all the chores. I had an operation recently, so he and his sister do all the housework together. He talks a lot about gender issues.

Tarun's father added that,

> Tarun's behavior is good, he's good at studies, and also talks about the dialogues that happen here. And he takes the lead in all the housework. In the morning, he makes tea for everyone. He tells his mother, "It's so cold, you don't get up, I'll make the tea"…He buys all the groceries and also helps make dinner.

During the discussion, we also asked boys how they thought other boys' perceptions of girls should change. They mentioned that their perceptions are now very different from those of friends who attend other schools, which they attribute to critical dialogues. For example, Ambrendra said, "[Boys] should realize that a girl is not an object to satisfy their physical needs." Rahul added, "She's a human being with feelings."

Their teacher, Aakansha, noted that, "Prerna boys used to see the Prerna girls as objects, like 'Wow, she's so hot! She's so beautiful!' But that, too, has changed. Now, they see them as people, just like the boys themselves." The comments of boys and their teachers during the focus groups indicate that they have become more sensitized to gender inequality, and now see girls as human beings, not as sexual objects.

Influencing Their Families and Advocating for Their Sisters

Boys also described how their parents' attitudes and treatment towards them and their sisters had changed. For example, Rahul reported that,

> Before, when I used to ask my mother for food, she would tell my sisters to serve me. Now, if they're resting, then my mother tells me, "Take it yourself, you also have hands. Let them rest. And after eating take your dishes outside and wash them."

Another student, Ambrendra, said with some pride, "My sister wasn't allowed to play more than an hour outside. Now she can play for two or three hours. If she washes dishes in the morning then it's my turn in the evening." Likewise, Shubham added, "Initially, when we were given homework in critical dialogues to interview our family members, mine used to say, 'What kind of questions are you asking!' Now they understand that I'm becoming more mature so they answer properly."

Boys' influence in their homes was corroborated by parents, who reported that their sons are trying to educate their mothers and have influenced their views on dowry and the treatment of their daughters. Pooja said, "Shivpoojan says, 'Only after my sister is twenty plus and has become independent, you should think of her marriage, and only if she wants to. And if they ask for dowry, you should refuse immediately.'" Meena said that her son advocates against dowry and child marriage at home, too. "Ambrendra also says that we shouldn't take or give dowry…that his sister is too small, that we shouldn't marry her too soon."

Change in their Perceptions of Manhood

Prior to the dialogues, the boys' concept of manhood was defined by shouting, drinking, smoking, bullying, and refusing to cry or express pain. When asked whether they felt less masculine since the change in their behavior, they denied it vehemently. Rahul said, "Now we think we've become a real human being," and Shubham echoed, "Now we've become real men." Ambrendra went a step further, saying, "I think we're better than [others'] version of a man."

They also stated that while their friends might make fun of them or consider them sissies, it no longer bothers them. Ankur, their teacher, corroborated this by saying,

> They used to take that burden of manhood upon themselves, imitating their fathers and uncles; they tried to show they're "men"…to be dominating…in our critical dialogues they understood that because of this dominating nature, women are hurt, get left behind, and our society is losing a lot because of that. They understand that they must be different as men.

In addition to advocating for girls within their families, some boys reported trying to influence the way their peers thought about gender and what it meant to be "manly." Ambrendra explained a harmful practice associated with being a "tough" man—cigarette smoking. He spoke of his own experience:

> I have a friend who was addicted to cigarettes, he had to have at least one a day, no matter what. I slowly made him come down to one cigarette a week and now he smokes just one a month. Slowly, I'll make him quit completely.

Cigarette smoking is taboo for girls, while seen as a manly thing to do for boys. Shubham also explained,

> My friends used to abuse a lot verbally. Initially, I didn't say anything…but after coming here I felt this was wrong. I told them these abuses are ultimately aimed at someone's

mother or sister, who didn't do anything to them, and that they should stop saying all this. Now, whenever I'm with them, they don't use any bad words.

Arun, another student, explained that he has also successfully motivated two boys from his neighborhood who had dropped out of school to reenroll.

Understanding Social Inequalities More Comprehensively

Boys also described their greater understanding and changed attitudes toward other forms of inequality, including religious inequalities and caste-based discrimination. For example, Rahul explained, "When I first came here, I wouldn't talk much with lower caste boys or eat anything from their home. Now, we're all very friendly, talk to everyone, and share lunch with everyone." Shivpoojan made a similar remark:

My parents used to shout at me whenever I went to my friend's house because he's Muslim. Then, my sister also came to study here and started doing critical dialogues. Initially, I was the only one telling them that it was wrong to discriminate like this. But then my sister also started saying the same thing. Now, if there's a function at my house, like a birthday party, then everyone comes, and my parents also allow it.

Shubham added on to his classmate's comment, explaining:

My grandmother never liked us to mingle with people from lower castes. She told us never to drink water from their house. On my birthday, I would invite all my friends so she didn't like that. I used to talk to her about this, now she has changed somewhat.

Seeing these religious and caste-based inequalities are a key element in developing the critical thinking skills of the Prerna students.

Conclusion

As evidenced by the descriptive analysis of our work with boys (and girls) in Prerna, we think of education as educating for life, rendering our approach as more of a "life knowledge" approach than a life skills approach. We believe in a structural and ideological approach, grounded and contextualized in social and political reality, and undergirded by an ideology of democratic values. Our curricula and pedagogy are rooted in helping children gain a greater sense of self-awareness, recognizing themselves and others as equal persons, developing agency and voice, and critically examining societal norms and oppressive social structures.

Using a life skills approach as an addendum or an after-school program, though useful, implies that the traditional curriculum does not need changing, and is contrary to all the current thinking in education, which advocates for a more broad-based definition of school learning (Learning Metrics Task Force, 2014; United Nations, 2012). Similarly, teaching life skills in a social and politically decontextualized way implies that social structures need no changing, and that it is possible to live successfully in an inequitably structured society and polity. We therefore integrate life skills throughout the curriculum, placing special emphasis on learning to think critically about gender and social inequalities so that students can work toward social transformation.

Our students do not live in a social and political vacuum, so taking an individualized, decontextualized view of knowledge or life skills is less effective and also, in my opinion, inadequate. Pedagogy and school culture are very important; these cannot be at odds with the content and are as instrumental in the development of knowledge, and the skills thereof, required to empower girls and boys to live life well. The knowledge that enables children to live a life of their own choosing must be incorporated into the formal curriculum, and the content of the classroom must be relevant to children's lives and the challenges they face. Teachers and schools must acknowledge children's realities, and be caring and responsive to their needs and context. For example, teaching girls to be confident and assertive without also teaching them that they have a right to be so, contrary to what they have been taught by tradition and social norms to believe, might leave them not only confused but also less convinced and in some cases more vulnerable. Similarly, teaching boys to distinguish between being assertive and dominating, to develop a new egalitarian conception of being a "strong man" involves enabling them to critically examine and disrupt their current socially learned definitions. Such education is not only personally empowering but also socially transformative.

Our critical pedagogy focuses on democratic values of gender, caste, and class equality, enabling our children to critically examine gender- and class-related power structures in their society and to locate and reposition themselves within these. We aim for our students to (1) develop a social and political consciousness in order to see all inequality (especially gender inequality) as undemocratic, discriminatory, and unjust, (2) to understand the underlying causes of such inequality, and (3) to collectively envision an egalitarian and democratic future. In other words, our goal is to empower them to disrupt and deconstruct unjust conceptual frameworks, which they have been socialized into by tradition, social norms, and patriarchal power structures, and help them reconstruct an egalitarian conceptual framework. We perceive this as a cognitive act and important life knowledge. Our critical pedagogy includes critical dialogues, drama, critical literacy, art, and dance, all of which help children develop the life skills necessary to live a life of their own choosing, present themselves as equal persons worthy of dignity and respect, and therefore act accordingly. Furthermore, they learn to view and respect others as equal persons, and to redefine gender roles and gender relations in more egalitarian terms. Taking a life knowledge approach to life skills, and making this an integral part of the official curriculum, with specially allocated time and curricular space for lessons in equality along with lessons of math, science, and language, has the additional, important effect of redefining the scope of education, deepening and widening it to make it more relevant to the lives of its students and the societies that they live in and can change in the future.

References

Boleslavsky, R. (1949). *Acting: The first six lessons*. Taylor & Francis.

Coghlan, D. (2001). *Doing action research in your own organization*. Sage.

Freire, P. (1970). *Pedagogy of the oppressed*. Bloomsbury Publishing.

Girls Not Brides. (2019). *Child marriage: A form of violence against women*. Policy Brief. https://www.girlsnotbrides.org/resource-centre/child-marriage-a-form-of-violence-against-children/

hooks, b. (1994). *Teaching to transgress: Education as the practice of freedom*. Routledge.

hooks, b. (2004). *The will to change: Men, masculinity, and love*. Beyond Words/Atria Books.

Learning Metrics Task Force. (2014). *Developing metrics for a post-2015 Equitable learning agenda*. Center for Universal Education at Brookings. https://www.brookings.edu/product/learning-metrics-task-force/

Murphy-Graham, E. (2008). Opening the black box: Women's empowerment and innovative secondary education in Honduras. *Gender and Education, 20*(1), 31–50.

Nussbaum, M. (2011). *Creating capabilities: The human development approach*. Belknap Press.

Reuters staff. (2019). *Statistics on rape in India and some well-known cases*. https://www.reuters.com/article/us-india-rape-factbox/statistics-on-rape-in-india-and-some-well-known-cases-idUSKBN1YA0UV

Sahni, U. (2017). *Reaching for the sky: Empowering girls through education*. Brookings Institution Press.

Sahni, U., Jain, A., & Chitravanshi, A. (2018). *What about our boys: Curriculum to educate boys for gender justice*. Unpublished manuscript. Study Hall Educational Foundation. http://www.studyhallfoundation.org/downloads/What-about-our-boys-FINAL.pdf

Sen, A. (2000). *Development as freedom*. Anchor Books.

Shani, A. B., & Pasmore, W. A. (1985). Organization inquiry: Towards a new model of the action research process. In D. D. Warrick (Ed.), *Contemporary organization development: Current thinking and applications* (pp. 438–448). Scott Foresman and Company.

Thompson Reuters Foundation. (2018). *The world's most dangerous countries for women*. https://poll2018.trust.org

UNESCO. (2012). *Global education first initiative*. http://www.unesco.org/new/en/gefi/about/

UNICEF. (2014). *United Nations Children's Fund, ending child marriage: Progress and prospects*. https://www.unicef.org/media/files/Child_Marriage_Report_7_17_LR..pdf

World Economic Forum. (2020). *Global Gender Gap Report 2020*. http://www3.weforum.org/docs/WEF_GGGR_2020.pdf

Chapter 10
Fostering Critical Thinking as a Life Skill to Prevent Child Marriage in Honduras: The Case of Holistic Education for Youth (HEY!)

Diana Pacheco-Montoya and Erin Murphy-Graham

Abstract This chapter presents findings from a design-based research project between the University of California, Berkeley and a Honduran non-governmental organization, Bayan Association called Holistic Education for Youth (HEY!). We explain why critical thinking is a crucial life skill to prevent child marriage in rural areas of Honduras and illustrate how critical thinking (specifically around gender inequality and marriage) was incorporated into a secondary school curriculum. We describe the pedagogies used to develop this curriculum and offer insights about its implementation. Finally, using classrooms observation and interview data, we discuss how students developed critical thinking and decision-making skills related to the gender inequality in society that has perpetuated the practice of child marriage.

Keywords Child marriage · Gender equality · Critical thinking · Secondary education · Honduras · Design-based research

Acronyms

HEY!	Holistic Education for Youth
DHS	Demographic Health Surveys
DBR	Design-based research
SAT	*Sistema de Aprendizaje Tutorial* (Tutorial Learning System)
SRH	Sexual and reproductive health

D. Pacheco-Montoya (✉) · E. Murphy-Graham
University of California, Berkeley, Berkeley, CA, USA
e-mail: dianapacheco@berkeley.edu; emurphy@berkeley.edu

© The Author(s) 2022
J. DeJaeghere, E. Murphy-Graham (eds.), *Life Skills Education for Youth*, Young People and Learning Processes in School and Everyday Life 5,
https://doi.org/10.1007/978-3-030-85214-6_10

Introduction

More than one-third of girls in developing countries are married before the age of 18 and one in nine are married before their fifteenth birthday. If current trends continue, 150 million girls will marry before the age of 18 over the next decade (ICRW, 2015). Preventing early, child, and forced marriage is a major goal of the international community, evidenced by target 5.3 of the Sustainable Development Goals.[1] Child marriage is a global problem, as it is found in every region of the world, but it has different characteristics that are contextually-specific (Girls Not Brides, 2020). Education has been identified as an important strategy to delay marriage; trends from Demographic Health Surveys (DHS) indicate that as girls' participation in secondary education increases, rates of child marriage decrease (Bongaarts et al., 2017).

Latin America, however, has not experienced a significant reduction in child marriage as education levels have increased, making it a global outlier in this regard. An analysis of trends in education and reproductive outcomes in DHS data from 43 countries (since 1986) found that in all world regions *other than* Latin America, with increases in educational attainment, age of first sexual intercourse, first marriage, and first birth increased correspondingly (Bongaarts et al., 2017). But in Latin America, the age of first sexual intercourse decreased by almost a year, age at marriage increased by less than a year, and the age at first birth remained constant *despite increased levels of education*. As a result, although Latin America does not have the highest rate of child marriage globally, it is the only region in the world where it is not decreasing. If these trends continue and no tangible efforts and investments take place for prevention, the region is projected to have the second highest child marriage rate in the world by 2030 (UN Women et al., 2018). This troubling scenario raises urgent questions about the connections between the quality of education and the prevention of child marriage in Latin America. Often what students study in secondary school is disconnected from their context and does not cultivate the life skills that they need to "do life well" (Murphy-Graham and Cohen, Chap. 2, this volume). Particularly, schooling may not foster critical thinking – a key life skills domain valued across different life skills frameworks and discourse communities (Murphy-Graham and Cohen, Chap. 2, this volume).

In this chapter we turn to the question of how a curriculum can foster critical thinking among youth, particularly in the context of their thinking and decision-making regarding gender inequality and marriage. We present findings from a design-based research project that builds upon a 20-year research-practice partnership between the University of California, Berkeley and a Honduran non-governmental organization, Bayan Association. Our collaboration began with a shared goal of examining the underlying causes of child marriage in Honduras, and

---

[1] Child Marriage is defined as "a marriage of a girl or boy before the age of 18 and refers to both formal marriages and informal unions in which children under the age of 18 live with a partner as if married" (UNICEF, 2017, p.1).

resulted in the design of an educational intervention, a program called Holistic Education for Youth (HEY!). The aim of HEY! is to prevent child marriage through an interactive curriculum that supplements the existing curriculum for grades 7–11 and that focuses on fostering the life skills of critical thinking and decision-making so that youth can make informed choices about their futures. Here, we share findings from our study that explain *why critical thinking is a key life skill* to prevent child marriage in rural areas of Honduras. We illustrate how additional materials emphasizing critical thinking (specifically around gender inequality and child marriage) were incorporated into a secondary school curriculum and highlight the pedagogies that can support critical thinking and decision-making. We then examine how critical thinking can foster cognitive processes that inform adolescents' decision-making.

Research Context and Background

Almost half (48.3%) of the population of Honduras lives in poverty, and high levels of crime and violence have stymied economic growth (World Bank, 2020). Honduras has one of the highest rates of child marriage in the Western Hemisphere, with the fourth highest prevalence of child marriage (34%) in Latin America after Brazil (36%), Dominican Republic (41%), and Nicaragua (41%) (UNICEF, 2016). Poor, rural Honduran girls are the most vulnerable to child marriage, and approximately 8% of girls are married by the age of 15 (Honduran Secretary of Health et al., 2013). While child marriage is technically illegal, the vast majority of unions are informal: in Honduras, only 10% of unions formed by adolescents are legal (Remez et al., 2009). Therefore, legislation alone is insufficient to reduce child marriage. Despite the lack of ritualization and legalization, consensual unions are socially perceived as formal marriages. That is, once a couple lives together, they are considered husband and wife (Murphy-Graham & Leal, 2015).

Murphy-Graham and Leal (2015) found that, in rural areas of Honduras, girls exercised agency in their decisions to marry. Girls' agency, or their "socioculturally mediated capacity to act" (Ahearn, 2001, p. 112) was characterized as simultaneously "thin, opportunistic, accommodating, and oppositional" (p. 25). Their agency was "thin" because they were driven to marriage by the limitations of their context, and "opportunistic" because young girls saw marriage as an opportunity to gain freedom and/or improve their financial well-being. Girls in the study reported experiencing limitations on their mobility and ability to socialize with their peers given the control their parents or grandparents exerted over them due to fear that girls would engage in romantic relationships or run away with their partners. The agency exercised by these girls was also described as "accommodating" since girls adapted to the traditional gender roles that were prevalent in their communities. Given the few alternative options for girls besides being wives and mothers, girls adjusted to these roles and saw them as worthwhile. Finally, their agency was "oppositional" because girls married against their parents' or other adults' advice. Murphy-Graham and Leal's (2015) results suggest that girls are not forced or coerced into to marry by their parents, community members, or their partners. Rather, in most cases, girls *chose* to begin cohabitating with their partners (often running away from home after a hasty decision). Their research and other studies suggest that girls' decision to marry is influenced by poverty, the lack of alternative life options available other than becoming a mother and housewife, and social norms around early marriage (Murphy-Graham & Leal, 2015; Taylor et al., 2015, 2019; UNICEF, 2017). The implications of this research informed the design of HEY!, as we identified a need to work with girls (and boys) to improve their critical thinking and decision-making skills and to challenge the social norms that contributed to child marriage. Secondary schools are an ideal site to work with youth on critical thinking and decision-making, as the Honduran government is currently attempting to universalize schooling through grade 9.

Secondary Education in Honduras

For the past two decades the Honduran government, with multilateral and bilateral partners, has attempted to expand secondary education coverage. There is still a great deal of progress to be made: UNICEF data indicates just under half of adolescents are enrolled in lower secondary school and approximately 30% of adolescents are enrolled in upper secondary school (UNICEF, 2019) – signalling the serious challenge Honduras faces to achieve universal participation in lower and upper secondary school. Recently the government has attempted to promote alternative modalities for secondary school completion, particularly in rural areas. One such model, *Sistema de Aprendizaje Tutorial* (Tutorial Learning System, or SAT), is implemented as a partnership between the Honduran government and Bayan Association. SAT is an alternative secondary education program for rural areas of Honduras whose populations are not served by the traditional public-school system. Although SAT is administered by Bayan, SAT is fully funded by the Honduran government and SAT students receive the same academic credentials as those from traditional schools (i.e. they receive the same high school diploma). SAT has its own curriculum but complies with the core subjects as established by the national curriculum. SAT encompasses lower (7th–9th grades) and upper (10th–12th grades) secondary education levels.

SAT is a rare example of a cost-effective system of teaching and learning, particularly for rural areas. Results from a quasi-experimental impact evaluation found that students in SAT had 45% higher rates of learning than their counterparts in traditional rural secondary schools in Honduras (McEwan et al., 2015). SAT has operated in rural areas of Colombia, Honduras, Nicaragua, and Ecuador for over three decades, serving youth in remote rural areas, in a public-private partnership between the government and local NGOs. Despite these positive characteristics, our previous research and interviews in SAT communities revealed high rates of child marriage (see Murphy-Graham et al., 2020; Murphy-Graham & Leal, 2015). Our research team, together with staff from Bayan, were in agreement that SAT could do *more* to confront this social problem. We worked together to launch HEY! in January 2016.

While we recognized the opportunity to create a school-based intervention with Bayan that addressed the causes of child marriage, we also were aware that there are structural causes of child marriage, such as poverty, state fragility, and lack of economic and educational opportunities, that are beyond the scope of what schools can be expected to change. What was feasible for our research-practice partnership was to enhance the SAT curriculum with materials that more explicitly examine social norms, family relationships, knowledge about child marriage, and decision-making processes. With these ideas in mind, we created HEY! with the goal of helping students think critically and make informed decisions about marriage in a setting where they have a constrained choice set, given the sociopolitical and economic context.

Methodology

Design-based research (DBR) is a fairly new methodology "designed with and for educators that seeks to increase the impact, transfer, and translation of education research into improved practice" (Anderson & Shattuck, 2012, p.16). DBR attempts to close the gap between the problems and issues of everyday practice and research by designing and developing interventions that aim to create solutions to complex educational problems, thereby generating usable knowledge (Design Based Research Collective, 2003). As such, its purpose is not limited to creating programs or interventions; DBR advances knowledge about the characteristics of design strategies and processes, with the intention of developing interventions and generating and/or validating theory (Plomp, 2010). There are six stages in a DBR intervention (Mintrop, 2016). Table 10.1 describes each stage, how it was addressed in HEY!, and the dates of each stage:

From March to June 2016, we conducted the first three stages of this DBR study.[2] In order to understand the problem and generate ideas for changing child marriage practices, we conducted a needs assessment of the SAT schools and communities were HEY! would be tested. This assessment included focus groups with teachers (N = 1), SAT coordinators (N = 1), and students, parents, and community leaders (N = 3). We also interviewed stakeholders (activists and government representatives) (N = 5) and former SAT students (N = 2). We hosted and developed a design workshop, where key stakeholders – including staff at Bayan, teachers, parents, Secretary of Education representatives, and students – came together for a three-day interactive session where we jointly agreed on the conditions that cause child marriage and the potential ways that we could address those problems in SAT. This

---

[2] This study was approved by the ethics review board of the University of California, Berkeley, and it followed ethical guidelines for research with young people in Honduras.

Table 10.1 Stages of a DBR study, how they were addressed in HEY!

Stage	Description	Date
1. Defining and framing problem of practice	Researchers and educational leaders defined and framed child marriage as a problem of practice because educational expansion did not lead to child marriage reduction.	March–June 2016
2. Making intuitive theories of action explicit	Practitioners and researchers engaged in developing possible avenues to address the problem based on their personal experiences, observations and intuition.	
3. Understanding the problem and change process	Researchers conducted a needs assessment. Before and after conducting the needs assessment, researchers lead the consultation of the knowledge base to give theoretical explanations about the patterns identified in the framing of the problem and the needs assessment. The purpose was to develop an understanding of the problem that is both practice-oriented and theory-based, in order to provide high-inference explanations of the problem of practice that was being addressed. The next step in this third stage was to understand the change process to comprehend the environment in which the ACMHE would take place and the activities and resources needed to promote change. With this information in place, researchers and practitioners developed a "theory of action" (Mintrop, 2016) – a plan that seeks to address a specific problem of practice and promote changes to improve educational practices.	
4. Designing a research based intervention	Once researchers and practitioners had developed a theory of action, they designed and developed the curriculum. Before implementing the fully designed intervention we conducted quick trials or mini experiments in order to test the curricular products and improve them before the first full implementation.	June 2016–March 2018
5. Implementing the intervention and collecting data	Once the design was ready, and several iterations of the curriculum had taken place, we implemented the intervention. We collected process data during this stage.	July–November 2018
6. Evaluating the intervention and deriving design principles	Finally, we conducted an evaluation of the implementation and from the lessons learned and outcomes documented, we (Pacheco and Murphy-Graham) developed design principles to guide similar interventions in other contexts.	November 2018

work stemmed from previous in-depth qualitative research in rural Honduras that investigated the circumstances and processes that led to child marriage (see Murphy-Graham & Leal, 2015).

From June 2016 to March 2018, we developed several versions of the curricular products, which consisted of three workbooks (two for students and one for parents). After piloting these workbooks (which involved a continuous collaboration with Bayan staff, teachers, students, and parents), we began our prototypical implementation, which refers to the stage of testing and adjusting the intervention while in practice (Mintrop, 2016). The first prototypical implementation took place in 21 schools in the Department of Atlántida on the North Coast of Honduras from June to November 2018, and reached a total of 1200 students from 7th to 11th grade. During this prototypical implementation of the curriculum, from June to August 2018, we collected the **process data** that included 21 h of class observations in five schools.

In November 2018 (at the end of the school year, when students finished studying the curriculum), the UC Berkeley team conducted an evaluation to examine if the curriculum elicited the desired learning outcomes. During this assessment phase, data were collected via post-intervention interviews with 58 students from 7th, 9th, and 11th grades (36 female students and 22 male students), 20 teachers from 7th, 9th, and 11th grades (13 male teachers and 7 female teachers), and 18 parents (3 fathers and 15 mothers) in all 21 participating schools. Table 10.2 describes the gender and number of students per grade that participated in the interviews.

The instrument developed for the student interviews consisted of scenarios that were relevant to child marriage and intended to examine key concepts studied through the curriculum. These concepts were guided by, and aimed to address, the problems identified during the first three phases of this study. Each scenario was followed by a set of questions that was designed to examine if and how students used the knowledge and skills that they ideally acquired by studying the workbooks. The scenarios were crafted to reflect situations that students experience or witness in their lives and communities. The questions were developed in a way that students had opportunities to provide a rationale for their answers. The full results are described in Pacheco Montoya (2019). In this chapter, we focus on the analysis of the process data (observations) and the interviews related to learning outcomes (with students and teachers) described above.

Data Analysis

All observations were audio-recorded and field notes were also taken during these observations by researchers. The focus of these observations was to capture interactions between students that could provide evidence of the desired dialogues/discussions (e.g., discussions around social norms, evidence of cognitive dissonance, etc.) intended to be fostered by the curriculum. During the data analysis "codes" (Miles et al., 2014, p. 72) were used to categorize, organize, and find patterns in the data.

Table 10.2 Gender and grade of students interviewed

Grade	Number of female participants	Number of male participants	Total
7th	12	9	21
9th	11	5	16
11th	13	8	21
Total	36	22	58

To create the codes, both deductive and inductive coding were used (Miles et al., 2014). The codes captured emotion (students' experiences, reactions, and sentiments) and values (participants' tenets, attitudes, and beliefs). Additionally, analytic memos were written about key class observations.

All interviews were audio-recorded and later transcribed. Categorical codes related to key ideas, such as gender equality, were created for each scenario. For instance, one scenario depicts two siblings who are treated in different ways. In this scenario, depending on the answers provided by participants, the answers were coded as "able to identify gender inequality" or "unable to identify gender inequality". A code that emerged (i.e., an inductive code) was "justifies as protection" and was added to the coding system. These responses were then tallied to generate numerical results for each question of each scenario.

Understanding Child Marriage in Rural Areas of Honduras Through the Identification of Problems That Cause Child Marriage

As a result of the needs assessment conducted during the third stage of this DBR study, we identified eight main issues that needed to be addressed in order to develop a curriculum aimed at preventing child marriage in rural areas of Honduras[3]:

1. The prevalence of gender inequality in families and society at large.
2. Lack of awareness about the biological, psychosocial, and cognitive changes that occur during adolescence.
3. Adolescents are not aware of the consequences of child marriage and hold false beliefs about child marriage.
4. Adolescents engage in impulsive decision-making processes regarding romantic relationships.
5. The prevalence of unhealthy romantic relationships among teenagers.
6. Community members, parents, and students are not aware of the legislation that protects bodily integrity, particularly of minors.
7. There is limited knowledge and access to sexual reproductive health (SRH) resources.
8. Conflict at home and/or poor communication between parents and children are common.

In this chapter we focus on how the curriculum addressed problems 1 and 4, or issues related to gender inequality and adolescents' impulsive decision-making

---

[3] Again, we focused on the problems that can be addressed in a school-based setting. We acknowledge that there are structural causes such as poverty that cannot be adequately addressed in an educational context.

Table 10.3 Causes of child marriage in rural areas of Honduras and HEY's related goals for prevention

Problem	Brief description	Goal of HEY!
The prevalence of gender inequality in families and society at large.	Girls are not treated equally to their male counterparts in their families and communities, especially in terms of mobility and socialization opportunities. Girls have limited economic and academic opportunities. Girls see marriage and motherhood as their most worthwhile role.	Change attitudes, beliefs, and behaviors about unequal gender norms. Change attitudes beliefs, and behaviors about what girls and boys can do and be. Inform students' decision-making processes regarding child marriage.
Impulsive decision-making processes regarding romantic relationships.	Girls exercise agency in their decision to marry. That is, they are not being forced to do so. Girls elope with their partners without being able to explain their reasoning behind their decision. These impulsive decision-making processes are influenced by the cognitive changes that individuals experience during adolescence. Girls are not happy about their decision to elope with their partners years later. Girls elope with their partners without knowing them well (short courtship). Girls see marriage as the only way to engage in a romantic relationship freely.	Improving students' capacity to think critically about gender (in) equality. Improving students' capacity to think critically about their future/ romantic relationships. Expanding students' values, beliefs, and experiences to make informed decisions about child marriage.

processes regarding romantic relationships.[4] Table 10.3 describes problems 1 and 4 and the related goals of HEY!, which, broadly speaking, intended to improve the key life skills of critical thinking and decision-making.

Brief Description of HEY!'s Curriculum Implementation Design

HEY!'s curriculum consists of three workbooks: *Living my youth with purpose* (for students), *Youth with equality* (for students), and *How to guide our young children* (for parents), which were designed and developed collaboratively through several iterations (the workbooks are also discussed extensively in Pacheco-Montoya, 2019). These workbooks were written to respond to the eight problems identified in

---

[4]For a discussion of how the rest of these problems were addressed in HEY! see Pacheco Montoya (2019).

the third phase of this intervention, as well as a theoretical framework developed to understand how these could be addressed. We followed a cascade approach for training SAT staff and students. The researcher/author[5] coached SAT's district supervisors, who in turn trained tutors (the equivalent of teachers), who then trained 11th graders. Eleventh graders implemented the curricular materials with 7th and 9th graders. The purpose of implementing in three different grades was to reach students during two stages of adolescent development: early (10–13) and middle (14–17) adolescence (Steinberg, 2011). The goal was to address students before they reach critical ages (12–14 for 7th graders) as well as during those critical ages where adolescents are at greater risks of entering unions in rural areas of Honduras (15–18 for 9th and 11th graders; see Murphy-Graham et al., 2020).[6] Students studied this curriculum in homogenous groups (classmates with similar ages and backgrounds, with the classmates that correspond to their grade) through a peer education system, using a pedagogical approach based on critical and feminist pedagogies (English and Irving, 2015; Freire, 2000; Shrewsbury, 1993). As a result of their study and interactive learning, adolescents will ideally be able to enhance their critical thinking and decision-making processes to make informed decisions about child marriage and will be empowered to overcome the constraints imposed by their socio-economic reality and limited choice set.

Previous studies have identified that peer education programs have difficulty sustaining positive outcomes over time (Agha & Van Rossem, 2004). Other criticisms about peer-led programs include unequal power dynamics between peer educators and participants (e.g. gender dynamics) (Campbell & MacPhail, 2002), lack of experience and knowledge compared to professional educators (Sriranganthan et al., 2012), and inadequate training (Walker & Avis, 1999). This intervention addressed the lack of long-term behavioral change, inadequate training, and lack of experience and/or knowledge by using a longitudinal implementation approach. That is, students are exposed to the curriculum during a five-year period, and not during a single session/training. Students study the materials for the first time in 7th grade and then again in 9th grade. When these same students are in 11th grade, they will be trained as peer educators in the use of the materials they already studied in 7th and 9th grades. This means that over time, students are exposed to the curriculum three times. There are distinct advantages afforded by this implementation/training design, including: (a) students are exposed to content relevant to the stage of adolescence they are in; (b) students will be exposed to this curriculum

---

[5] The workbooks *Living my youth with purpose* and *How to guide our young children* were written by Juanita Hernández, an author with decades of experience designing interactive texts for youth. The book *Youth with equality* was written by the co-author of this chapter, Diana Pacheco-Montoya. All books were written in collaboration with Bayan staff members, teachers, students, and parents. Each author conducted the training of the workbook(s) she wrote.

[6] Murphy-Graham et al. (2020) conducted a longitudinal study of adolescents in rural areas of Honduras and followed their life trajectories during adolescence. These authors found that by age 20, 46% had entered a union at some point. Most of the growth in entrance into first union occurred from age 15 through age 18.

before and during the time they reach critical ages, when they are most vulnerable to child marriage and unhealthy relationships, and (c) it ensures that once students become peer educators, they will already be familiar with the content they facilitate. In this sense, through time, students become both recipients and implementers of the curriculum. Additionally, students are accompanied and supervised by teachers, who also undergo a training process. If students lack knowledge or need support, they can rely on the teacher to provide it.

Understanding the Change Process: The Roles of *Critical Thinking and Cognitive Dissonance*

In addition to understanding these causes of child marriage, we also needed to hypothesize how to create a learning environment and scaffold activities and resources to promote change. We developed a theoretical framework for fostering critical thinking related to gender inequalities and norms, drawing upon existing theory and research that helped clarify the key concepts and goals of the project. For example, we incorporated Brookfield's (1997, 2012, 2017) work on critical thinking to develop HEY's curriculum. Assumptions play a central role in Brookfield's conceptualization of critical thinking. Assumptions are taken-for-granted beliefs which might seem commonsense until we think critically about them. Brookfield (2012) proposed three kinds of assumptions: causal, prescriptive, and paradigmatic.

Causal assumptions are explanatory and predictive. They explain cause and effect linkages. For example, someone might think that if they marry, they might have more freedom than what they have at home. Prescriptive assumptions refer to desirable ways of thinking and acting. For instance, individuals might hold assumptions that girls should be modest and submissive. Paradigmatic assumptions frame the way we understand and look at the world that surrounds us. These assumptions are grounded in dominant ideologies, or sets of practices and beliefs that organize the world and influence how we think and act, which are accepted by the majority as commonsense. Patriarchy, the system of society in which men hold the power and are thought of as superior to women, is an example of a dominant ideology. An example of a paradigmatic assumption linked with patriarchy is that boys are inherently better leaders than girls.

We reflect upon and make hundreds of decisions daily. However, most of these reflections and decisions are not critical; they are merely technical. We start thinking critically about our assumptions and our actions when we consider the social or political context, or when we reflect about power and hegemony (Brookfield, 2017). According to Gramsci (1971), hegemony refers to the process in which a dominant class establishes ideas, beliefs, and structures that benefits them. These set of values and beliefs are then viewed as natural and preordained by the majority of people and are thought to be good for everyone (as cited in Brookfield, 2017). For instance, one such belief is that men are more capable or smarter than women, and that is the reason why there are more men in positions of power. People come to internalize this oppression and becomes normalized: it comes to be "deeply embedded, part of the cultural air we breathe" (Brookfield, 2017, p. 16). As such, critical thinking has two main purposes: (a) understanding power relationships in our lives and redirecting the flow of these relationships, and (b) uncovering hegemonic assumptions, which are "typically paradigmatic" (Brookfield, 2017, p. 40). That is, assumptions one might consider to be in her best interest but actually harm her (Brookfield, 1997, 2017). According to Brookfield (2012), critical thinking encompasses: (a) identifying assumptions; (b) checking the accuracy and reliability of these assumptions; (c) listening to others' perspectives and opinions; and (d) and taking informed action. Because our intervention took place in a school-based setting, it is important to consider the social nature of critical thinking. Critical thinking is a social process where peers and teachers become "critical mirrors" through dialogue (Brookfield, 1997, p. 19). Being critical mirrors means that through dialogue, students have opportunities to reflect together upon assumptions that were taken for granted before. Having critical mirrors facilitates being exposed to new perspectives. Ideally, these new perspectives or ideas, removes them from their comfort zone and help them examine parts of their thinking that would otherwise remain vague, unclear, or obscure. Critical thinking is continuously emphasized as a goal of the SAT curriculum.

In HEY!, we wanted to support critical thinking specifically with regards to gender inequality and child marriage. The lessons created followed a similar pedagogical approach to the SAT curriculum, often starting and ending with questions and activities that encouraged discussion (for a more detailed description of the SAT curriculum, see Murphy-Graham, 2012). In addition to questions and discussions aimed at hunting for and checking assumptions, the curriculum includes the introduction of new concepts and ideas to aid in the critical thinking process, including "multiplicity of perceptions" and exposing students to alternative ideas and ways of thinking (Brookfield, 1997, p.19).

However, critical thinking in itself is not enough to change child marriage practices. Students can participate in a discussion that promotes critical thinking, study lessons that provide a multiplicity of perceptions, and still not experience a change of attitude or behavior. In an ideal scenario, critical thinking should also lead to **cognitive dissonance** (Festinger, 1962).

By cognition, Festinger refers to "any knowledge, opinion, or belief about the environment, about oneself, or about one's behavior" (1962, p. 3). Dissonance, on the other hand, refers to the unpleasant state that occurs when an individual is exposed to "two or more elements of knowledge that are relevant to each other but inconsistent with one another" (Harmon-Jones & Harmon-Jones, 2012, p. 72). Festinger theorized that when an individual is confronted with this unpleasant state, this will motivate the person to engage in psychological work to reduce inconsistencies between cognitions. Cognitive dissonance is "an antecedent condition which leads to activity oriented toward dissonance reduction just as hunger leads to activity oriented toward hunger reduction" (Festinger, 1962, p. 3). Cognitive dissonance is measured through attitude change. As such, one of the main objectives of HEY!

is to change attitudes and beliefs of students about child marriage and its causes, which can ultimately inform their decision-making processes. For critical thinking and ultimately cognitive dissonance around gender equality and child marriage to happen in the classroom, students need an environment where they are allowed to examine, question, and reconsider their assumptions about these issues. Students need a space where critical thinking is championed. To create this learning environment, we drew insights from critical and feminist pedagogies.

Pedagogies to Support the Incorporation of Critical Thinking and Cognitive Dissonance in the Classroom

We followed Giroux's (2004) definition of pedagogy, which emphasizes the need to address power relations and representations of the self and the social environment in the learning process. To develop curricular materials that addressed issues of power, inequality, and social change, this intervention drew upon critical (English & Irving, 2015; Freire, 2000) and feminist (Shrewsbury, 1993) pedagogies to design, develop, implement, and evaluate HEY!. Critical pedagogy establishes that education should be used to promote emancipation from oppression through the emergence of a critical consciousness. To achieve critical consciousness, or *conscientização*, a deep awareness of one's reality, the learning process should be guided by dialogue and critical thinking. In order to achieve radical changes in society through education, it is necessary to "develop forms of critical pedagogy capable of appropriating from a variety of radical theories" like feminism (Giroux, 2004, p. 32). Because the focus of HEY! is to address the causal factors of child marriage by challenging the social norms that perpetuate gender inequality, critical pedagogy is paired with feminist pedagogy. According to Shrewsbury (1993), "at its simplest level, feminist pedagogy is concerned with gender justice and overcoming oppressions. It recognizes the genderedness of all social relations and consequently of all societal institutions and structures" (p. 9). Feminist pedagogy, consistent with the conceptual framework of SAT, views the classroom as a mutualistic environment where students become a community of learners who engage in a reflective process to promote social change. These key ideas, shared between the team at UC Berkeley and Bayan, informed the design, implementation, and evaluation of HEY!. Following these two pedagogies, the workbooks include the discussion of important concepts and case studies that promote an awareness around issues of power and inequality associated with gender relations. They also include questions at the beginning, middle, and end of each lesson aimed at promoting group discussions and reflections that invite students to analyze their personal and social realities and their role in promoting social change.

Examining Critical Thinking and Cognitive Dissonance During and After the Implementation of HEY!

After students studied the HEY! materials, we examined if and how critical thinking and cognitive dissonance occurred during and as a result of the implementation of HEY!'s curriculum through classroom observation and in-depth interviews (see Stage 6 in Table 10.1). We also explored if and how critical and feminist pedagogies supported critical thinking during the implementation of the curriculum. The following tenets informed our assessment of critical thinking for these purposes: (a) it should be locally crafted and context specific; (b) peers can participate in assessment as they act as critical mirrors; and (c) assessment should allow learners to demonstrate and justify their engagement in critical thinking (Brookfield, 1997).

Dialogue, Critical Mirrors, and Re-examining Assumptions

During the interviews, we asked teachers (who accompanied 11th graders during implementation) if they thought the workbooks were successful in eliciting discussions that promoted critical thinking and social analysis. Most of the teachers thought this was the case, particularly around discussions of gender equality. They provided concrete examples, including:

Interviewer: What themes generated rich conversations among students?
Teacher (Male): It was the lesson about gender equality. As I mentioned to you before, some say that girls can't play soccer, because we see that only boys get to play soccer, no girls at all. We saw that boys had a *machista* attitude and it is clear that it comes from dynamics at home that promote it. For example, men work in agriculture and do not help to clean, wash dishes, or mop the floor, and they have more freedom and girls have no freedom. So, the girls in some way stood up for themselves, they said that they also worked and deserved the same rights.

When another teacher was asked whether he believed these texts were useful to students, he shared that students not only changed their attitudes and beliefs but their behaviors as well:

Interviewer: Can you give me an example of something you have observed/ listened from students or parents that makes you think this intervention is helping prevent child marriage or change behaviors?
Tutor (Male):   Mostly with things related to equality. I have a student that always said that "girls have to do this, and boys have to do that." He had this marked division girl/boy, boy/girl. But now he has understood. For instance, before he would not help with cleaning the

classrooms. He would take the trash out, but he wouldn't touch a broom or a mop. He thought that was something for women. He would rather do chores that required strength. But now it's different. We are all astounded. Now he is the first one grabbing the mop... I feel that he understood what the norms to live in society are.

As noted by these teachers, the workbooks provided an opportunity for students to recognize their positionality and how they were affected by gender inequality and/ or how restrictive notions about gender norms affected their behaviors. Students had the opportunity to engage in a series of discussions that allowed them to uncover power dynamics and hegemonic assumptions around gender norms. This process of uncovering assumptions about the role of gender norms required a social context (in this case the SAT classroom) where individuals could be exposed to different viewpoints, a context where individuals' assumptions were mirrored through others. For instance, lesson 6 of the workbook *Youth with Equality*, "Our lives during and after puberty," describes how the biological changes that adolescents experience during puberty intersect with youth's emotions and the expectations society has for them. The lesson contains a table where students are expected to describe two biological changes that take place during puberty, two emotions or feelings they experience during puberty, and two ways in which societal expectations during puberty are different for boys and girls. During this exercise, two female 11th graders, Melissa and Victoria,[7] discussed how the beliefs around condoms reflected unfair expectations for girls and boys. During this discussion, a male 9th grader, Juan, intervened and his comments reflected commonly-held beliefs that girls had no business carrying condoms:

Melissa (11th): Nowadays, if a person sees that a boy is carrying a condom, they tell him "buy more," "you're the man!" But if they see a girl carrying a condom...

Victoria (11th): They start judging her.

Melissa (11th): They start saying "who knows how many more she has bought before, how many more she has used before." But they do not say that about a boy.

Then Juan, implying that girls should not carry condoms, asked:

Juan (9th): Then, why is she carrying them? [The condoms]

Melissa then tried to challenge his comments by asking why would he carry a condom (pointing out that condoms are for sex, whether you are a boy or a girl). He evades this question with a joke:

Melissa (11th): Let's see, if you carry a condom, what do you carry it for?

Juan (9th): Just to carry it around.

(students laugh)

---

[7] All names used are pseudonyms.

Melissa (11th): Well, a woman can carry a condom just for the sake of carrying it as well.

(silence followed by laughter)

Teacher (F): This is where the machismo becomes apparent.

Melissa (11th): Yeah, that is gender inequality! Because they treat the boy as if he were a champion if they date many girls. And sometimes if a girl has several admirers, they call her a …

Victoria (11th): Boys can have many female friends but girls can't have male friends.

Juan (9th): No

In this exchange, Juan's interjections reflect the belief that girls have no business carrying condoms, and he does not seem to indicate that his belief is subject to change. However, what is important in this exchange is how dialogue around the differential treatment of girls and boys took place in the classroom. Juan's peers and teacher responded and reflected on the views that he accepts as normal or acceptable (i.e., the hegemonic assumption, grounded in patriarchy, that only men should carry condoms). This kind of exchange is crucial in uncovering how one's assumptions about a subject might be questionable: a further examination about the assumption can help lead to a broader understanding of the subject. In this exchange, dialogue played a central role as it allowed peers to become critical mirrors of Juan's assumptions (and everyone participating in this discussion). This exercise is an example of how the workbooks, guided by elements from critical and feminist pedagogies, generate activities and discussions. These provided students like Juan with the opportunity to engage in a collective reflective process that enabled them to become aware of their own assumptions and develop a greater awareness of the society in which they live.

Another example of dialogue that allowed assumptions to be uncovered occurred during a training of 11th graders. A male student, Mario, expressed the common notion in these communities that labels girls "*locas*," meaning that they are acting "crazy," "easy," and/or too "flirty." The HEY! workbook generated a discussion about the role that puberty plays in behavioral changes of adolescents and why terms like these should not be used to describe girls' behaviors. This exchange shows how the text "Puberty, teen pregnancy, and child marriage", from *Youth with Equality*, provided a new framework to understand these behaviors:

Mario (11th): Teacher, there is an interesting relationship between puberty, pregnancy, and marriage. Well, thanks to puberty, that girl is around acting like a "*loca*."

Teacher 1 (F): Do you think it is appropriate to say that a girl is acting like a "*loca*."

Julio (11th): 2: No. She's acting crazy.

Teacher 1 (F): Why do you think she behaves like that? Because she is in that phase, because we like to judge others and say that girls are acting like *locas* but it is not that they want to act inappropriately.

Mario (11th): It's thanks to puberty.

Teacher 1 (F): She is simply going through changes that you have already studied. You need to know how to approach this with the younger students. You can't make them uncomfortable saying "these girls are acting like *locas*.". We know what is behind all of this, girls go through changes…and maybe because of lack of knowledge people interpret it in a wrong way like your classmate here. That is not the right way, girls and boys have behavioral changes because they are going through biological changes…we should not say inappropriate things like she's acting like a *loca*…We should help them, help them understand what is happening with their bodies.

At the end of the discussion of this lesson, the two teachers who were training the 11th grade students explained that they should not use these pejorative terms and that they should instead help younger students understand why these behavioral changes happen. The conversation continued:

Teacher 2 (M): So, what are you going to say if your see a girl that is starting to like boys and she is only 14 years?

Mariana (11th): That she is going through puberty.

Pedro (11th): That it is a normal thing in adolescents like her.

Teacher 2: Correct. It is a result of a process she is going through.

Carla (11th): That her hormones are going crazy.

Teacher 1 (F): Exactly. It is a process.

Teacher 2 (M): In that moment she feels attraction towards boys, and hormones are the cause of that attraction. Do you think sexual appetite is greater or less?

11th grade students (collective response): Greater.

Mario inadvertently repeated a common notion that stigmatizes girls' behaviors. It was a prescriptive and hegemonic assumption (i.e. that girls should behave in a certain way and any deviation is unacceptable) that reflects not only gender inequality, but also a deep misunderstanding of the changes that youth experience during adolescence. Mario was able to reassess his assumption after his teachers and other peers elaborated an alternative way of understanding those behaviors.

In addition to recognizing and challenging assumptions around gender inequality, the workbook also invites students to imagine alternatives to the reality that they experience. The following exchange was captured during a peer implementation between 11th graders and 9th graders of lesson 3 of the workbook *Youth with Equality*, "Gender (in)equality." The following exchanges are excerpts that took place throughout the one-hour class discussion of this lesson:

David (11th): Can somebody tell me what gender inequality is?

Jessica (9th): When men and women do not enjoy the same rights.

David (11th): Can someone give me an example of gender inequality?

Francisco (9th): An example can be when either a boy/girl has a preference to go to school over a girl/boy.

The conversation continued:

David (11th):   Some examples of gender norms are "men can't cry because they are men...or can't sweep because he is a man, can't do laundry because he is a man." Those are gender norms. Where are these gender norms applied?

Rosa (9th):   In the family, at home, in society.

The peer tutor then invited 9th graders to reflect about where gender inequality can be practiced:

David (11th):   Where should we practice gender equality?

9th grade students (collective response):   In our families, our homes, in society.

David (11th):   Where else?

Rosa (9th):   Everywhere!

David (11th):   Wherever we go, it is important that we practice gender equality. At work, in our families.

Martha (9th):   At school.

David (11th):   Do you think this [gender inequality] happens amongst friends?

9th grade students (collective response):   Yes.

The peer tutor continues to read the reflection questions included in the lesson:

David (11th):   *(Reading from the workbook)* How can boys contribute to gender equality?

Dennis (9th):   Sweeping, helping out at home.

Tania (9th):   Practicing gender equality.

David (11th):   What else?

Pablo (9th):   Not being *machistas*!

David (11th):   Men can contribute by setting a good example.

The discussion ended with a reflection about the impact that gender equality could have on society:

David (11th):   If gender equality changes are achieved, who will they affect?

Paola (9th):   Our kids, future generations.

Bessy: (9th):   Society.

   The classroom dialogue captured here illustrates how, through the use of strategic questioning, the curriculum pushes students to recognize and challenge inequality. It also provides students with an opportunity to reimagine and propose alternative ways in which they can promote and achieve gender equality. Importantly, following a feminist pedagogy, the workbook pushes this analysis beyond the walls of a classroom and invites students to analyze how gender equality might not only improve their lives, but society overall, and how they can become agents of change.

Assessing Critical Thinking Through Scenarios

We developed a scenario-based interview instrument to assess students' ability to use key concepts and knowledge learned through the curriculum, as well as their ability to think critically (in this section we discuss the scenarios related to gender inequality only, and there were other scenarios in the instrument discussed in Pacheco Montoya, 2019). These scenarios were based on stories or experiences that we have documented over a decade of research in these communities. As such, they reflected the context that students experience in their daily lives. The first scenario described two siblings, María and Juan:

> María and Juan are siblings. María is 16 years old and Juan is 15 years old. Their parents treat them very differently. Juan is allowed to go out freely to play and spend time with his friends. María can rarely leave the house and have fun. Juan has a girlfriend and the whole town knows about it and approves. Last year, María had a boyfriend without her parents knowing. Her neighbors found out, and started calling her "slutty." The neighbors are always criticizing María for the way she dresses, or if she hangs out with boys. She feels surveilled. Juan doesn't worry if others approve of his behavior or not.
>
> (a) Why do you think that these differences exist in how men and women are treated?
> (b) Do you agree that they should be treated differently? Why/why not?

In the interviews, 73% of the 58 participating students identified gender inequality as the reason why María and Juan were treated differently, 20% were not able to explain conceptually why these differences existed, and only 7% explained that they justified this scenario given that girls needed to be more protected (a well-established belief in these communities). Eighty-nine percent of the students disagreed with this differential treatment while 11% did not find a problem with it. Below are some sample responses:

Fernanda (7th): Well, maybe because the father thinks that only women do incorrect things, so they treat her with gender inequality. The father thinks that the boy only goes out to play with classmates and friends, men have vices as well, they can learn and do wrong things... The father doesn't let the girl go out because he thinks that she will be with a man or something like that when in fact, some girls actually get married because they don't let them go out.

José (9th): There's no gender equality, it should be equal. If the boy goes out, the girl should go out too, and both have to have fun, not just the boy while the girl is at home like a slave. I think there shouldn't be inequality, both of them should have fun.

Fernanda's response suggests that she was able to uncover the assumption of the father in the scenario (note she says "father" although the scenario mentions "parents"). Fernanda's response reflects a common causal assumption in these communities: if you are a girl, you need to be protected and your mobility limited, because if not, you will wind up pregnant or harmed. She is able to dismantle the assumption that girls are the only ones that need to be protected, and points out that boys can also encounter danger outside the home – an argument that is not discussed in the workbooks, and therefore we can assume is a result of her own analysis or a result of something she learned during class discussions. She then continues to make a connection between the lack of freedom and girls' decisions to elope. That is, she is making a direct association between gender inequality and child marriage. It is important to note that she is not necessarily legitimizing this decision, but rather explaining how treating girls unfairly can inform girls' decision or contribute to their desire to leave their home, pointing out negative consequences of gender inequality.

José, a ninth grader, also revealed an important behavior in his response: he rejected gender inequality even when his position as a male allowed him to benefit from this differential treatment. He energetically condemned girls' lack of opportunity to have fun, and he connected this situation to the burden of housework that falls upon girls (describing it as slavery). He advocated for equal treatment. Importantly, both responses used the concept of gender inequality to explain their reasoning and demonstrated a deep understanding of this concept. However, they did not simply regurgitate "gender equality" in their response. Instead, they offered critical insights regarding why this happens and why it is wrong, demonstrating their capacity to use a concept and apply it in a practical and meaningful way. Over four lessons, the curriculum provided students with facts and information about gender inequality that influenced their reasoning. As shown in these responses, this information was coupled with their ability to critically analyze these scenarios.

The second scenario described tensions in a family due to the fact that family members do not think that men should do housework that is thought to be a woman's job:

> Lourdes has a husband named Alexis. Alexis has a small cornfield in which he works in the mornings. Lourdes is a SAT teacher and works in the afternoon. When Lourdes goes to work in the afternoon, Alexis takes care of their children, helps cleaning the house and makes dinner. Alexis' mom and brothers don't like that he does "women's stuff" and they are bothered that Lourdes is not taking care of the things that Alexis has to do, because they think that taking care of the home and children is not a man's job.

Ninety-eight percent of the 58 students that were interviewed said they disagreed with this scenario. Fifty percent of students were able to explain this scenario through the concept of gender norms. Thirty-four percent of students explained this scenario using the concept of gender inequality, which is also a fine response but not as specific as gender norms. Fifteen percent of students were unable to provide an explanation for why they disagreed with it. Many students explained how socialization played a role in these beliefs. For example, Carlos, a 7th grade male student explained that these beliefs form due to gender inequality during socialization:

Carlos (7th):   That happens because they don't teach them when they are young what gender equality is. That's why they think men can do certain things and women can't, and it's not like that. Both have the capacity to do the same things.

Finally, almost 90% of students reported they would challenge Alexis' family members' resistance to his behavior. Gabriela, a 7th grade female student stated that she would tell Alexis' family that "if women can take care of the home, men can too."

As shown by the responses above, students were able to use key concepts to explain and justify their responses. They were able to (a) identify their assumptions; (b) check their assumptions through dialogue with their peers and teachers; (c) be exposed to different perspectives using their peers as critical mirrors; and (d) imagine alternatives to the reality that sustains hegemonic views. One noteworthy accomplishment is that HEY!'s curriculum has provided a context in which boys were able to develop a greater awareness of the importance of gender equality and develop attitudes that are conducive to more equitable relationships (see also Sahni, Chap. 9, this volume). This is a salient result given that many interventions do not include boys or examine boys' attitudes towards issues such as gender inequality or child marriage (CEFM and Sexuality Programs Working Group, 2019).

Experiencing Discomfort and Hope: How Critical Thinking Can Lead to Cognitive Dissonance

During interviews, several students stated that gender inequality was one of the most relevant topics for their lives and reported changing the ways they viewed themselves and what they were capable of doing. For instance, Javier, a male student, described how HEY! made him confront his previous beliefs about gender inequality:

Javier (11th): Of course, gender equality as well because women are valuable too. I was taught to have a *machista* attitude.

Interviewer: Who taught you to be *machista?*

Javier (11th): My dad

Interviewer: What would he say?

Javier (11th): Well, my dad used to say that women are here to serve and that a man's obligation is to be the head of the home and only men's ideas are valid. Women should not have a voice or dictate what should happen. As I was learning, I understood that I should not have those attitudes.

Interviewer: So, the content in the text collided with what you believed?

Javier (11th): Yes, it collided a lot. It became a controversy.

Interviewer: During the class or for yourself?

Javier (11th): For me.

Interviewer: What was the controversy?

Javier (11th): Why should I serve a woman?

Interviewer: That was your dad's voice.

Javier (11th): Yes, my dad's voice was there but that started to fade away and I was able to see that it was good to be equitable.

The unpleasant state that Javier experienced when he was exposed to new information that challenged previous knowledge is an example of "dissonance" (Harmon

Jones & Harmon Jones, 2012). As Javier explained, he engaged in a psychological work (an internal "controversy") to reduce the inconsistencies of these two views. In the end, he was able to clarify his new standpoint on gender equality. Javier was able to identify the unfairness in the power dynamics between men and women into which he was socialized.

Other students reported changing their views about themselves and who they could become. For example, a 7th grade student, Mercedes, reported that learning about gender equality helped her believe that she could do anything because she has the same capabilities as boys:

Mercedes (7th): I used to think that we women had fewer rights than men.
Interviewer: Why did you think that?
Mercedes (7th): I thought we were weaker…
Interviewer: Can you give me an example?
Mercedes (7th): When I used to see my cousins play soccer, I would see them and think I could not do what they were doing, I felt underestimated because they could play, and I couldn't.
Interviewer: Why? Because they were given permission to play or because they were stronger?
Mercedes (7th): Because they were stronger…
Interviewer: And now that you read these things, what do you think?
Mercedes (7th): That when I see someone doing something, I feel that I can also do it because we are equal, and we have the same capabilities.

Mercedes was able to challenge her own hegemonic assumptions – of her inferiority because she was a girl, and she was naturally weaker than boys – and reimagine what she was capable of. Her response shows that Mercedes now has a framework to understand, explain, and reject gender inequality, and to recognize her inherent worth, a key component of empowerment (Murphy-Graham, 2012). Mercedes' account suggests that she experienced cognitive dissonance as a result of the lessons, and that she was exposed to a new set of beliefs that were different to those she held before participating in HEY!.

Vignettes, based on real-life, contextually relevant scenarios, that were included in the curriculum were instrumental in helping students expand their knowledge about gender. In one of our interviews, an 11th grade student, Michelle, made reference to vignettes included in lesson 2 in the text *Youth with Equality*. One vignette tells the story of "Freddy," a young man who is a chef, which challenges the cultural norm of men staying out of the kitchen. The second vignette is about "Dunia," a girl who always wanted to become a soldier. Despite her family and friends telling her that only men can be soldiers, she was able to make her dream come true. From Michelle's response, we see evidence that the vignettes helped to informed her analysis and interpretation of what men and women can do:

Michelle (11th): I really liked the lesson about gender. It explains that women and men should have the same rights…It also teaches us that just because someone is a woman, it does not mean that she can't do things that men do and vice versa... For example, a man can cook, not just women. There are men who are cooks that are (professional) chefs. A woman can be a soldier, a president, things that are supposed to be restricted to men. Women can also do those things.

Interviewer: So before reading these lessons, you thought that those things were restricted to men or did you know that you could be a soldier, for example?

Michelle (11th): No.

Interviewer: You did not imagine this could happen? What did you think of these stories?

Michelle (11th): I like them because they taught me that one can achieve things if one desires.

Michelle's response suggests that she had accepted as normal and commonsense that there were certain professions and leadership roles that were exclusive to men. The vignettes helped her challenge these views and reconsider what women are capable of doing. Vignettes that attempted to provide positive and negative social images about gender inequality and child marriage were always accompanied with a discussion that promoted dialogue and critical thinking, as well as activities to further the analysis of important concepts such as gender norms. For example, the vignettes described above are followed by the questions:

(a) What lessons do Freddy and Dunia teach us?
(b) What role did family members play in helping Dunia and Freddy challenge traditional gender norms so that they could reach their dreams?
(c) After studying this lesson, what would your reaction be if someone tells you that you cannot do something because you are a boy or a girl?

The curriculum helped Mercedes and Michelle realize that they are capable of doing things regardless of their gender such as playing soccer or becoming a president.

The responses of students in these three examples suggest that a curriculum can provide students with opportunities to recognize hegemonic assumptions, understand the context and dynamic of power relationships, create opportunities to reconsider their beliefs, and provide hope that things can be different and that they have capability to become who they desire. These three examples also offer an opportunity to examine the different ways in which girls and boys experience cognitive dissonance. Javier, the student who reported experiencing cognitive dissonance, struggled in letting go of the comfort that male privilege provided him. The discomfort stemmed from accepting that he needed to let go of being waited on by women and being the only one who made decisions. Ultimately, he concluded that giving up the comfort that inequality provided him was the fair thing to do. On the other hand, girls' experiences (like Mercedes and Michelle) were less uncomfortable and more enlightening. For girls, studying HEY! provided them with reassurance and a newfound sense of possibilities. As Brookfield (2017) mentions, it is common for individuals to experience initial resistance to examining hegemonic assumptions critically, "but when they are challenged and changed, the consequences for our lives are explosive" (p.18).

From Class to Life: How Can Studying HEY!'s Curriculum Influence Students' Decisions and Actions?

Our interviews did not examine behaviors or change of behaviors. We did not directly ask about the decisions that students have made since being exposed to the curriculum. However, during our interviews, some students reported instances where their experience with the curriculum informed their decisions and behaviors. The following examples do not intend to show or claim an impact of this intervention. Instead, what follows provides evidence that the curriculum *can* inform adolescents' decision-making processes and actions regarding gender inequality and child marriage, and we give examples of students' desired outcomes.

The first case is that of Martha, an 11th grade female student. She shared that after being exposed to HEY!, she was able to realize her worth and her right to be treated equally to men. As a result, she confronted her parents and encouraged them to treat her and brothers with equality:

Martha (11th):   We are six sisters and two brothers. My parents always used to say that I better study because they would only leave me the house as my inheritance. They used to say that the land was for my brothers because they were able to work, because they were capable of working the land, and we girls could not do that. So, I read to them the content of the workbook where it said that girls and boys have the same rights because we are capable of doing any kind of work. As a result, they changed their attitude towards me. I believe they love all of us equally now. I have also told some of my friends that they should respect their girlfriends. If their girlfriends turn around, they are already flirting with other girls. I tell them that that is not respect, it is not love. I have learned all these things through the workbooks.

Another example is that of Xiomara, an 11th grade female student. During her interview she shared that she changed her mind about eloping with her boyfriend after studying the workbooks. She explained that the social images she was exposed to during this intervention informed her decision:

Interviewer: Can you tell me about something specific that you might say changed after studying these workbooks?

Xiomara (11th):   I changed my decision to marry. I was thinking about getting married and after studying these workbooks I retracted [from getting married].

Interviewer: Tell me about this process, what things made you change your mind?

Xiomara (11th): So many things, the workbooks included some dramas, some case studies including one of a girl who decided to marry and she did not like it and that is not worth it.

Interviewer: So, you got scared?

Xiomara (11th): Yes, I do not want anyone telling me I cannot go out. I like my freedom.

Interviewer: Do you think you did the right thing?

Xiomara (11th): Yes. I did the right thing. In my house I have everything I need.

Interviewer: Do you think you would have eloped if you had not studied these workbooks?

Xiomara (11th): I would probably have; I am not sure.

Finally, a teacher reported that one of his students, Rosa, was thinking about getting married, but after being exposed to HEY!'s curriculum, she changed her mind:

Teacher (M):   One of my students told me that she had plans to drop out. When I asked her why, she said "I have too many problems at home. They are not helping me economically to pay for my education expenses so I think I will marry or I will leave to San Pedro Sula to work." So I told her "you should think about it because I do not think that what you are planning to do will make your situation better. In fact, it might make it worse." After the workbooks came [to our school], she was one of the students that was involved the most in this project. Afterwards, she told me, "I will not drop out, I will see how I can get a part time job in the area so I can buy the books for school, I will keep studying." The day we finished implementing the workbooks she posted on Facebook things she had learned and how what she learned had changed her.

The stories shared by Martha, Xiomara, and Rosa's teacher suggest that adolescents are using this knowledge to think critically about issues of power in gender relations and to consider other alternatives to child marriage. Xiomara, for example, reported not wanting to experience the consequences of child marriage as depicted in the vignettes. Martha decided to act against the inequality she was experiencing, based on the knowledge and information she learned through the workbooks. Furthermore, Rosa's case suggests that HEY!'s curriculum might be helping to address false beliefs about child marriage as an option when things at home are tense or when the economic circumstances are difficult. In short, our results suggest that participants' decision-making processes are being influenced and informed both by the knowledge they have gained through HEY!'s curriculum and their newly cultivated capacity to think critically.

Conclusion

Adolescents around the world are often forced to make difficult life choices. It is crucial that educational systems equip them with the necessary life skills to make well-reasoned decisions, especially in contexts with limited choice sets, such as rural Honduras. A crucial life skill and component of decision-making is the ability to think critically. Being able to make decisions and take actions that are based on the ability to understand and analyze critically the world that surrounds us is of utmost importance. The point of critical thinking is to "take informed action…We think critically not just to survive, but also to live and love well" (Brookfield, 2012 p.13). Thinking critically can help adolescents live more satisfactory lives, lives in which decisions and actions are not arbitrary, but well-reasoned.

Promoting social norms that reflect gender equality and disrupt child marriage in an educational context is a challenging endeavor. In this chapter, we provided an empirical example of *how* a school-based intervention addressed these issues. This study provides important insights into how critical thinking, as a life skill, can be incorporated into curriculum and pedagogy to address gender inequality and prevent child marriage.

Addressing gender inequality and child marriage requires a careful incorporation of pedagogies that foster social analysis, assess and change power relations, promote critical thinking, and challenge oppression. As described in this chapter, critical and feminist pedagogies provide a pedagogical framework to incorporate these components in the classroom. The implementation of a curriculum should also follow principles of critical thinking, which include the examination of hegemonic assumptions and the opportunity to imagine alternatives ways of thinking and acting. To achieve this, the classroom should create a community of learners who act as critical mirrors, guided through and by dialogue. It is crucial that boys *and* girls participate in this process. Ideally, an educational context that allows and teaches students to think critically will lead students to experience cognitive dissonance and also support them in making sense of these inconsistencies (Harmon-Jones & Harmon-Jones, 2012). In the case of HEY!, students experienced cognitive dissonance about beliefs they were socialized into, like gender inequality, and made sense of their feelings by learning through the curriculum.

The results of this study suggest that gaining critical thinking skills is an achievable and powerful process that encourages boys to recognize and challenge gender inequality. At the same time, the learning process provides girls with opportunities to reimagine their roles and worth. While our initial results are quite positive, we do not yet have the ability to conduct a rigorous study on the impact of HEY! on rates of child marriage and teen pregnancy. We hope to be able to eventually document the processes and impact of HEY! on a variety of outcomes, including behavioral outcomes. In the meantime, the case of HEY! can inform the design and implementation of like-minded programs to foster critical thinking as a life skill for youth in other contexts.

References

Agha, S., & Van Rossem, R. (2004). Impact of a school-based peer sexual health intervention on normative beliefs, risk perceptions, and sexual behavior of Zambian adolescents. *Journal of Adolescent Health, 34*(5), 441–452.

Ahearn, L. M. (2001). Language and agency. *Annual Review of Anthropology, 30*(1), 109–137. https://doi.org/10.1146/annurev.anthro.30.1.109

Anderson, T., & Shattuck, J. (2012). Design-based research: A decade of progress in education research? *Educational Researcher, 41*(1), 16–25.

Bongaarts, J., Mensch, B. S., & Blanc, A. K. (2017). Trends in the age at reproductive transitions in the developing world: The role of education. *Population Studies, 71*(2), 139–154. https://doi.org/10.1080/00324728.2017.1291986

Brookfield, S. D. (1997). Assessing critical thinking. *New Directions for Adult and Continuing Education, 1997*(75), 17–29. https://doi.org/10.1002/ace.7502

Brookfield, S. D. (2012). *Teaching for critical thinking: Tools and techniques to help students question their assumptions.* Jossey-Bass Publishers.

Brookfield, S. D. (2017). *Becoming a critically reflective teacher* (2nd ed.). Jossey-Bass Publishers.

Campbell, C., & MacPhail, C. (2002). Peer education, gender and the development of critical consciousness: Participatory HIV prevention by South African youth. *Social Science & Medicine, 55*(2), 331–345. https://doi.org/10.1016/S0277-9536(01)00289-1

CEFM and Sexuality Programs Working Group. (2019, June 1). *Tackling the Taboo: Sexuality and Gender Transformative Programmes to End Child, Early and Forced Marriage and Unions.* Girls Not Brides. https://www.girlsnotbrides.org/resource-centre/tackling-the-taboo-sexuality-and-gender-transformative-programmes-to-end-child-early-and-forced-marriage-and-unions/

Design-Based Research Collective. (2003). Design-based research: An emerging paradigm for educational inquiry. *Educational Researcher, 32*(1), 5–8. https://doi.org/10.3102/0013189X032001005

English, L. M., & Irving, C. J. (2015). Critical feminist pedagogy. In L. M. English & C. J. Irving (Eds.), *Feminism in community: Adult education for transformation* (pp. 103–113). Sense Publishers.

Festinger, L. (1962). *A theory of cognitive dissonance.* Stanford University Press.

Freire, P. (2000). *Pedagogy of the oppressed.* Bloomsbury Publishing.

Girls Not Brides. (2020). *Child marriage around the world.* https://www.girlsnotbrides.org/where-does-it-happen/

Giroux, H. A. (2004). Critical pedagogy and the postmodern/modern divide: Towards a pedagogy of democratization. *Teacher Education Quarterly, 31*(1), 31–47.

Gramsci, A. (1971). *Selections from the Prison Notebooks* (Q. Hoare and GN Smith, Trans.). Lawrence and Hishart.

Harmon-Jones, E., & Harmon-Jones, C. (2012). Cognitive dissonance theory: An update with a focus on the action-based model. In J. Y. Shah & W. L. Gardner (Eds.), *Handbook of motivation science* (pp. 71–83). The Guilford Press.

Honduran Secretary of Health, National Institute of Statistics, & ICF International. (2013). *Encuesta Nacional de Salud y Demografía 2011–2012* [National Survey of Health and Demography 2011–2012]. National Institute of Statistics. http://dhsprogram.com/publications/publication-FR274-DHS-Final-Reports.cfm#sthash.ohl3qWVJ.dpuf

International Center for Research on Women (ICRW). (2015). *Child marriage facts and figures.* http://www.icrw.org/child-marriage-facts-and-figures

McEwan, P. J., Murphy-Graham, E., Torres Irribarra, D., Aguilar, C., & Rápalo, R. (2015). Improving middle school quality in poor countries: Evidence from the Honduran Sistema de Aprendizaje tutorial. *Educational Evaluation and Policy Analysis, 37*(1), 113–137. https://doi.org/10.3102/0162373714527786

Miles, M. B., Huberman, A. M., & Saldaña, J. (2014). *Qualitative data analysis: A methods sourcebook.* Sage.

Mintrop, R. (2016). *Design-based school improvement: A practical guide for education leaders.* Harvard Education Press.

Murphy-Graham, E. (2012). *Opening minds, improving lives: Education and women's empowerment in Honduras.* Vanderbilt University Press.

Murphy-Graham, E., & Leal, G. (2015). Child marriage, agency, and schooling in rural Honduras. *Comparative Education Review, 59*(1), 24–49. https://doi.org/10.1086/679013

Murphy-Graham, E., Cohen, A. K., & Pacheco-Montoya, D. (2020). School dropout, child marriage, and early pregnancy among adolescent girls in rural honduras. *Comparative Education Review, 64*(4), 703–724.

Pacheco Montoya, D. P. (2019). *Developing a curriculum for a formal education setting to prevent child marriage in rural areas of Honduras: A design-based research study* (Publication No. 27736539). Doctoral dissertation, University of California, Berkeley. ProQuest Dissertations Publishing.   https://search.proquest.com/openview/7732120ccbf0ad264973ed2f3e42762f/1?pq-origsite=gscholar&cbl=18750&diss=y

Plomp, T. (2010). Educational design research: An introduction. In T. Plomp & N. Nieveen (Eds.), *An introduction to educational design research* (pp. 9–36). SLO Netherlands Institute for Curriculum Development.

Remez, L., Singh, S., & Prada, E. (2009). Trends in adolescent unions and childbearing in four Central American countries. *Población y salud en Mesoamérica, 7*(1), 1–20.

Shrewsbury, C. (1993). What is feminist pedagogy? *Women's Studies Quarterly, 21*(3/4), 8–16. http://www.jstor.org/stable/40022001

Sriranganathan, G., Jaworsky, D., Larkin, J., Flicker, S., Campbell, L., Flynn, S., & Erlich, L. (2012). Peer sexual health education: Interventions for effective programme evaluation. *Health Education Journal, 71*(1), 62–71. https://doi.org/10.1177/0017896910386266

Steinberg, L. (2011). *Adolescence* (9th ed.). McGraw-Hill.

Taylor, A., Lauro, G., Segundo, M., & Greene, M. (2015). *She goes with me in my boat' child and adolescent marriage in Brazil: Results from mixed-methods research.* Instituto Promundo & Promundo-US.

Taylor, A. Y., Murphy-Graham, E., Van Horn, J., Vaitla, B., Del Valle, Á., & Cislaghi, B. (2019). Child marriages and unions in Latin America: Understanding the roles of agency and social norms. *Journal of Adolescent Health, 64*(4), S45–S51.

UNICEF. (2016). *State of the world's children 2016: A chance for every child.* https://www.unicef.org/publications/index_91711.html

UNICEF. (2019). *Secondary education.* https://data.unicef.org/topic/education/secondary-education/

United Nations International Children's Emergency Fund (UNICEF). (2017). *Child marriage: South Asia.* https://www.unicef.org/rosa/what-we-do/child-protection/child-marriage

United Nations Women (UN Women), United Nations International Children's Emergency Fund (UNICEF) & United Nations Fund for Population Activities (UNFPA). (2018). *A commitment to end child marriage and early unions.* https://www.unicef.org/lac/en/reports/commitment-end-child-marriage-and-early-unions

Walker, S. A., & Avis, M. (1999). Common reasons why peer education fails. *Journal of Adolescence, 22*(4), 573–577.

World Bank. (2020). *Honduras: Country overview.* https://www.worldbank.org/en/country/honduras. Last accessed 23 June 2020.

Chapter 11
Life Skills Education in Ethiopia: Afar Pastoralists' Perspectives

Sileshi Yitbarek, Yohannes Wogasso, Margaret Meagher, and Lucy Strickland

Abstract Pastoralists constitute a large proportion of the population of Ethiopia, representing an estimated 14–18% of the population (MoE, A standard and manual for upgrading Alternative Basic Education (ABE) Centers, Level 1–4 to Level 1–6. Addis Ababa, Ethiopia, 2018a). The provision of formal education through a school-based delivery model has failed to deliver the desired outcomes for Afar children and youth in terms of inclusion and participation, and quality of and relevance of education in support of building pastoralists' skills for life and thriving. Formal education for pastoralists should be concerned with curricular relevance as experienced from the perspective of the pastoralists' daily reality and extant knowledge that is well-adapted to environmental conditions and emphasizes collective community wellbeing (Krätli & Dyer, Mobile pastoralists and education: strategic options. International Institute for Environment and Development, 2009). This chapter explores the ways in which the current curriculum in the Afar region addresses Krätli and Dyer's (Mobile pastoralists and education: strategic options. International Institute for Environment and Development, 2009) four dimensions of curricula necessary for pastoralist education to be considered relevant. It also explores key stakeholders' perspectives about which life skills matter most to the Afar pastoralist community and the extent to which the current curriculum reflects and incorporates these skills. This chapter offers a new perspective on how to reconceptualize and teach these skills through the education system, highlighting recommended adaptations to the curriculum aligned with national and international development goals and notions of quality and relevance. These adaptations respond

S. Yitbarek
Kotebe Metropolitan University (KMU), Addis Ababa, Ethiopia

Y. Wogasso
Ministry of Education, School Improvement Directorate, Addis Ababa, Ethiopia

M. Meagher (✉)
Be the Change Inc, Duluth, MN, USA

L. Strickland
Refugee Education Consultant, Canberra, Australia

to the knowledge, attitudes, values, skills, mobility patterns, and calendars grounded in pastoralist populations' values to maintain a complex and sustainable equilibrium among pastures, livestock, and people.

Keywords Life skills · Education · Pastoralists · Relevance · Curriculum · Afar · Indigenous knowledge

Acronyms

ABE	Alternative Basic Education
EFA	Education for All
ESDP	Education Sector Development Plan
FDRE	Federal Democratic Republic of Ethiopia
GECFDD	General Education Curriculum Framework Development Department
MDGs	Millennium Development Goals
MoE	Ministry of Education
NER	Net Enrolment Rate
NPES	National Pastoralist Education Strategy
PTA	Parent Teacher Association
QESSP	Quality Education Strategic Support Program
REB	Regional Education Bureau
SDG	Sustainable Development Goals
UNICEF	United Nations Children's Fund
WEO	Woreda Education Office

Introduction

Formal approaches to education and life skills[1] for pastoralist communities grounded in human capital and human rights approaches have failed to achieve the social change objectives of resilience and sustainable development. Life skills informed by indigenous pastoralist perspectives regarding what skills matter most, for what purposes, and how they are (or can be) taught to children and young people may offer a new perspective on how to conceptualize and teach these skills through the education system. As Murphy-Graham and Cohen's and DeJaeghere's chapters (Chaps. 2 and 4, both in this volume) discuss, educators and policymakers need to consider the broader ecology and systems within which young people develop and enact these skills, how these skills could be more meaningfully articulated and

---

[1] This chapter utilizes the definition of 'life skills' noted in Chap. 1, as 'skills that help you through everyday tasks and to be active and productive members of a community (*to be able to do life well*)'.

incorporated into the education system, and pedagogical practices that have the potential to create transformation toward more equitable life outcomes.

Pastoralists constitute a large proportion of the population of Ethiopia, representing an estimated 14–18% of the population (MoE, 2018a). The two predominantly pastoralist areas of the country are the Somali region and Afar region (C4ED, 2017). Afar refers to both a geographic area within Ethiopia as well as to a cultural group indigenous to this region, with the Afar Regional State situated in northeastern Ethiopia. Despite an overall enabling policy environment and significant improvement in access to education at the national level in Ethiopia since 1994, enrollment, retention, and learning attainment remain low in the pastoralist areas, especially for girls (MoE, 2017b). For instance, the net enrollment rates (NER) in 2018 for primary education (grades 1–8) in the Somali region and Afar region, at 66.4% and 45.9% respectively, are far below the national average of 94.7%. The primary education dropout rates are also higher in these regions, at 22% in the Somali region and 19.3% in the Afar, compared to the national average of 17.5% (MoE, 2019b). There is a level of consensus that, in spite of national education reforms and specific strategies and policies designed to serve the education needs of pastoralist communities and to enhance access to and the quality of school-based education in pastoral areas, the national education system has not succeeded in providing a relevant education through a contextually-appropriate modality for the children and young people in these communities. The modality and curricula will require more than a simple contextualization and "copy and adapt" set of approaches designed for sendentarized communities (Ziyn & Wogasso, 2017).

Conceptualizing and teaching life skills grounded in a relational approach present an opportunity to leverage indigenous pastoral social relations as collective protective assets (DeJaeghere, Chap. 4, this volume). These assets can be aligned with national and international development goals and notions of quality education. This chapter offers a new perspective on how to reconceptualize and teach these life skills through the education system, highlighting recommended adaptations to the nationally-framed, regionally-adapted curriculum in the Afar region, its delivery modalities, and pedagogical approaches. Such adaptations respond to the knowledge, attitudes, values, skills, mobility patterns, and calendars grounded in pastoralist populations' values to maintain a complex and sustainable equilibrium among pastures, livestock, and people. This chapter draws on interviews with a small but diverse representation from the Afar community including male and female youth, community elders and leaders, and regional and district education officials, in order to shed light on their perspectives regarding which life skills matter most and are most relevant to this context and its way of life, as well as how these skills are traditionally taught and learned. Building on the rich foundation of perspectives and insights that stakeholders offered, an analysis of the current primary-level curriculum in the Afar region is made using Krätli and Dyer's (2009) four dimensions of curricula framework, keeping the pastoralist perspective firmly at its center.[2]

---

[2] For this analysis, only three of the four dimensions of the Krätli & Dyer (2009) framework will be employed, that of subject content, socialization and localization. Status will be elaborated on later in the chapter but is not a considered dimension of the analysis itself.

Through this framework, this chapter explores the extent to which foundational life skills (per the national curricular framework) are represented as intended in the current curriculum in the Afar region; as well as the extent to which the life skills and corresponding traditional pedagogies and approaches that matter most to Afar pastoralists are reflected therein.

This chapter concludes with suggestions related to bridging the divide between the current curriculum in the Afar region and the life skills that "matter most" to the Afar community and to counterbalance the "trade off" between school-based education and pastoral livelihoods. This work contributes new perspectives to support the development of culturally and contextually relevant education that can enable the children of pastoralist communities to fully participate in and benefit from foundational skills gained through a formal education experience, while simultaneously retaining and fortifying life skills grounded in traditional pastoral production, livelihoods, and collective wellbeing.

Pastoralist Education Context in Ethiopia

The Federal Democratic Republic of Ethiopia (FDRE) established education as a constitutional right for all Ethiopians through the Education and Training Policy in 1994, and over the last two decades, the country has experienced an almost revolutionary movement in the education sector through a series of sector reforms, policies, and strategies. Pastoral education as a priority was mainstreamed in the third Education Sector Development Plan (ESDP) (2005/2006—2010/2011) across all sub-sectors of the educational system. To guide this sector focus, a national strategy to promote pastoral education was developed in 2008 to outline the specific challenges and opportunities pastoral communities face and to identify strategies to promote access to and strengthen the quality of primary and post-primary education (MoE, 2008). With a changing environment for pastoral communities and seven years of experience in implementing the strategy, the MoE revised the pastoral strategy in the form of the National Pastoralist Education Strategy (NPES) in the 2015/2016 academic year with support from UNICEF and the Quality Education Strategic Support Program (QESSP).

Prior to the NPES, studies revealed a centralized approach and national "solution" in its response to a local situation, ironically rendering the pastoralist community, toward whom such approaches and policies were geared, invisible in their development and implementation process. This was further compounded by under-capacitated regional and district-level authorities to lead this "pastoralists first" approach. There was a strong need to shift from "tactics" to articulate a new and responsive national strategy for pastoralist education that went beyond just extending the current system (Krätli & Dyer, 2009). The current iteration of the NPES attempts to do this and offers targeted support towards the education and development of pastoralist children and communities (MoE, 2017a).

The revised strategy strongly emphasized a decentralized implementation model meant to ensure stakeholder ownership and commitment, and localization for each of the pastoralist areas, with one of its six guiding principles to "ensure the curriculum is relevant to pastoralist livelihoods and indigenous knowledge, context and developmental needs, and is delivered in an appropriate language of instruction" (MoE, 2017a). The recent Ethiopia Education and Training Roadmap (N.D., in progress) also reaffirms the need to have an education strategy that guides the provision of education and training using appropriate curriculum and flexible delivery modalities suitable to pastoralist and semi-pastoralist populations (MoE, 2018b).

Formal Education and Curriculum: A Concern for Relevance

The 2017 NPES aspired to integrate pastoralist livelihoods into the regional curriculum content and impart foundational skills per the national curriculum framework in partnership with Regional Education Bureaus (REB). The resulting curricular content and corresponding textbooks form the basis of the current curriculum in the Afar region, which is used in both school-based and Alternative Basic Education (ABE)[3] delivery modalities. Current curricular materials were initially developed at a national level in Amharic, subsequently abridged and condensed by non-Afar subject experts, and finally translated into Afar language by native Afar educators (Ahmed, 2017). The Afar REB was responsible for contextualizing and translating the curriculum and for developing teaching and learning materials, though with very little consultation of pastoralist communities for whom the materials were designed (C4ED, 2017). Although the current curriculum in the Afar region may have been "complete enough" to meet national standards in terms of foundational skills and corresponding subject content, the process of its development meant it remained incomplete, and was lacking relevance in terms of localization of content and collaborative engagement with pastoralists in its development (Krätli & Dyer, 2009).

Although the same curriculum is used for school-based and ABE delivery modalities, it was found that many community members and the implementers at the *woreda*/district level[4] in the Afar region construed ABE as a substandard mode of delivery (Ahmed, 2017), referring to the curriculum as an inferior education that only included textbook knowledge (Anwar, 2010). A key factor underpinning issues associated with ABE is that it is delivered by community-based, para-professional "facilitators" rather than formally-trained teachers used in formal schools (MoE, 2019a, b). The Centre for Evaluation and Development's 2017 Impact Evaluation of the ABE program in Ethiopia identified that although the ABE program documents

---

[3] Alternative Basic Education (ABE) is an alternative to the formal primary school delivery modality that condenses teaching of the first four years of primary school into three years.

[4] A woreda is a local unit of governance.

specifically identified the learning needs of pastoral children and youth, the lack of endorsement of a clear and binding pastoralist education strategy with ABE as the cornerstone prevented efforts from fully meeting the learning needs of pastoralist children (C4ED, 2017). ABE as a delivery modality therefore has subsequently remained a temporary solution to extend access to education in the Afar region without sufficient resourcing and supervision at the district level to provide quality education, and it lacks buy-in at the regional level to drive, support, and oversee its adoption, adaptation and implementation.

In order to examine the relevance of the current curricula in the Afar region, Krätli and Dyer (2009) propose a framework for nomadic populations that considers four separate but inter-related dimensions that include, yet go beyond, subject content to consider status (the acquisition of formal recognition of learning); socialization (the acquisition of essential social skills necessary to live in a national society); and localization (the acquisition of skills and information rooted in a specific section of society and help to define people's identity) (Krätli & Dyer, 2009). While research suggests the status of the ABE program modality and corresponding curriculum in the Afar region is low from the perspective of community members and implementers as noted above, this study further analyzes the relevance of the current curricula in the Afar region through the Krätli and Dyer (2009) framework to identify the types of life skills that matter most from the perspectives of the Afar pastoralist communities, in order to offer new perspectives on how to reconceptualize and teach these skills through the education system.

Methodology

This study employed both a desk review and primary data collection using focus group discussions and key informant interviews. The desk review surveyed MoE policy documents and sector plans, MoE National Pastoralist Education Strategies (2008, 2017a, b), Afar Bureau of Culture and Tourism documents, the MoE curriculum framework, Afar regional-level textbooks and teacher guides, and other related reports, research studies, and evaluations on pastoralist and nomadic education.

The secondary data were complemented by focus group discussions and interviews with a purposefully-selected set of Afar participants, with the aim of including a small number of respondents representing key voices across each of several stakeholder categories. A sample of twenty-one stakeholders participated in the study and included male and female youth from the Afar community, community elders and Parent Teacher Association (PTA) members, representatives from the Afar Regional Education Bureau (REB), and an Afar cultural expert.[5]

---

[5]This study was approved by the MOE Institutional Review Committee of the FDRE, and they followed ethical guidelines for research with young people in these specific contexts.

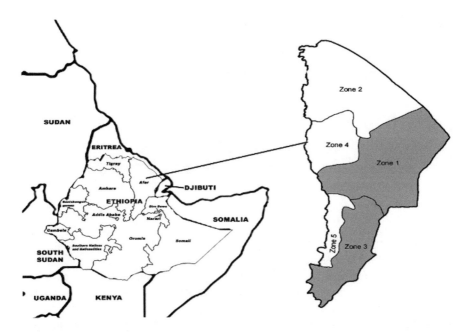

Fig. 11.1 Map of Afar Region and Zones

The primary data were collected in two of the five zones of the Afar region, Zones 1 and 3 (Fig. 11.1). Although with some difference in terms of cultural customs, these areas are culturally and politically very similar. The *woredas* included were Amibara and Awash–Fentale in the southern part of the Afar region in Gebi Resu or Zone 3, and Afambo, Aysaita and Chifera in the lower Awash area or Zone 1. These two zones were purposefully selected to represent the diverse lifestyles yet shared understanding and approach to life skills of the Afar pastoralists. Given limitations of the small sample size and limited geographic representation, findings cannot be generalized to the whole Afar pastoralist population.

Data collection was carried out across two phases. The first phase included tools development and testing, which included a pastoralist communities survey and interview protocols for the focus groups and interviews; collection and analysis of secondary data, including MoE policies and strategy documents; and the facilitation of focus groups with pastoralist youth and the subsequent data analysis. The second phase included interviews and focus groups with community elders, PTA members, scholars, and experts on life skills and customs. Interviews were also conducted with Afar regional and *woreda*-level education experts. Finally, an analysis of curriculum materials was conducted using the Krätli and Dyer (2009) four dimensions of curricula framework, taking into consideration three of the four dimensions: subject content, socialization and localization[6]. Conclusions related to analyzing the curriculum content as presented herein were derived through consensus between one of the authors and two Afar curriculum experts.

---

[6] The dimension of 'status' was addressed through secondary literature as presented in the section above.

Table 11.1 Dimensions of relevance & grades/subjects analyzed

Krätli & Dyer's dimension of curriculum relevance	Grades/subjects analyzed	
Subject content	Mathematics	Grades 1–4
	Languages	Grades 1–4
	Environmental science	Grades 1–4
Socialization	Environmental science	Grades 1–4
	Civics and ethics	Grades 5–8
	Social sciences	Grades 5–6
Localization	Environmental science	Grades 1–4
	Social studies	Grades 5–6
	Integrated sciences	Grades 5–6

Focus groups with youth participants explored themes relating to hopes and dreams, life skills that matter most, why and/ or for what purposes; where and how these skills are learned; and role models and caring/cooperation practices. Focus groups and interviews with adult participants explored similar themes, as well as perspectives on the formal education curriculum and delivery modalities; perceptions related to drivers of low education participation and high dropout; and gendered attitudes and perceptions related to the education of children.

Content analysis of curricular materials was conducted utilizing the national curriculum framework and syllabi, and current Afar regional level student textbooks. Following Krätli and Dyer's (2009) framework, skill domains were identified based on the national curriculum framework and interviews for each of the three dimensions explored. The dimensions of curriculum relevance and the subjects by grade analyzed are reflected in Table 11.1.

Afar Perspectives on Life Skills

This section of the chapter captures a rich cross-section of voices from and closely connected to the Afar pastoralist community to understand the different perspectives of and insights into Afar pastoralist cultural practices, preservation, and life skills. It also identifies the foundational life skills that are included in the national curriculum framework, and where additions, revisions or enhancements could or should be made. A set of recurring themes emerged across the different stakeholders, despite generational and geographic differences, including: the notion of relevance of the curriculum in the Afar region from a pastoralist perspective; that education matters and is valued by pastoralist communities; and the content children learn during their educational experience matters. The majority of stakeholders agreed that formal education is prioritized by their community and it is not incompatible with the pastoralist way of life and culture. Afar youth specifically expressed the priority that their community places on education and the sacrifices the community makes, such as "selling cattle to educate us", to ensure an education is attainable for their generation. Stakeholders' perspectives contrast, however, with the current conceptual understanding of school-based education, its delivery modality, and the whole notion of a "national" curriculum.

Stakeholder interviews with regional and district level education representatives particularly noted the need to rethink pastoralist education (education for pastoralists) whereby the system itself and the curriculum:

> [should] reflect the livelihood, it should be relevant and take into account the rich knowledge and skill of the community. There should be a thorough study and reflection to include the content and methodology of pastoralists in the education system. It's not enough to have policies, strategies and guidelines and then only ask for an adapted translation. What is required is to first of all listen to the people (i.e. those from pastoralist communities) and work on creating enabling conditions.

One education expert used an example of mother-tongue based education and suggested that, should the MoE work through a mobile school model, it's upon them to first ensure there are teachers proficient in mother-tongue, and who are willing to work in these environments and to adapt to the mobility patterns and calendars of the people. Stakeholders suggested that Afar youth are a critical cohort that the MoE could be training and encouraging to assume education leadership roles in the future as a "local approaches" strategy toward bridging the divide. There should be no expectation of a compromise made between a child enjoying the benefits of a formal (school-based) experience and that which is community-based and rooted in his or her immediate social context (Krätli & Dyer, 2009). The matter, quality, and extent of formal and traditional education can be greatly amplified if they are genuinely mutually-reinforcing, complementary, and viewed as equally valid.

Stakeholders emphasized the importance of the pedagogies and methodologies found in the Afar community practices of inter-generational transfer of knowledge, skills, and practice, and one Afar REB representative suggested the "modern education system" presents an "excellent opportunity to deploy such techniques, practices and institutional arrangement embedded in our community". The idea to integrate Afar knowledge and pedagogy into the formal system was welcomed by another REB representative who observed that, while teachers in the formal system are relatively well-trained with college or university education, their skills level and knowledge base are still very limited, noting:

> Either one or both teacher education system and the school service delivery mechanism should be harmonized with the methodology of the pastoralist community, which transfer knowledge and skills from one generation to the next through … authentic techniques (i.e. observation, experiential learning, assisting, coaching) and institutional arrangements, such as the indigenous conflict resolution system, *Med-a*.

In sum, our findings illustrate the need for the formal education system to become more relevant by infusing it with traditional Afar life skills and knowledge systems, including Afar pedagogies and methodologies.

Afar Perspectives: Shared Voices About What Matters Most

Although stakeholder discussions revealed some slight divergence of perspective, which for the most part was generational, there was a consistent and tightly-knit cross-generational convergence regarding the types of life skills that mattered most, such as reciprocal caring and sharing, reinforced by a commonly-held high value placed upon clan, community, and on traditional ways of knowing and doing, as well as teaching and learning. Stakeholders provided explicit examples of skills that should be included in the curricula in areas such as animal husbandry and livestock health and management, traditional building and construction practices (*Afar AREE*), environmental preservation, indigenous approaches to conflict resolution and social cohesion (*Med-a*), and communication techniques (*Dagu*). They also offered pedagogical processes and approaches for acquiring these skills, including experiential learning, observation and listening, mentorship and apprenticeship, and learning by making mistakes. They felt these approaches could be reflected or adapted and elaborated upon within formal education to ensure a more accurate, holistic, culturally-relevant, and successful education experience for all children, from pastoralist and non-pastoralist communities alike.

Livestock management and animal husbandry are life skills central to the Afar way of life. But in a context of rapid socio-economic change, elders and parents from the pastoralist community expressed concern that Afar children and youth also need to learn skills and have experience for the changing economy and conditions. They felt that the school system and the curriculum could take responsibility for teaching animal production for a livestock economy, income generation, and financial literacy. Historically, animal production was a measure of household wealth and status in the Afar community, and used for household consumption, not for economic wellbeing. "Culturally, the community has no experience in selling cattle for income generation and saving for future life. The community, however, shares and the clan will support those in need", one elder noted. Another elder also spoke about modernity, urban sprawl, and the diminishing pasture land, all of which have threatened the pastoralist way of life and highlighted the need for Afaris to adapt to the changing conditions, such to engage in a livestock economy and to manage savings. One parent observed that, although there is still a relatively low level of awareness in the community of the importance of "modern" education (in contrast to traditional learning), parents do recognize the changing circumstances, including widespread logging and pervasive drought, that are putting their livelihood assets and subsequent legacy to be left to their children at risk. Educating their children through formal (school-based) education is commonly seen as a means of helping to mitigate such shocks and to better prepare them for a changing future. Treatment of diseases in livestock was also considered an important skill set to be learned alongside the corresponding prayer ceremonies; however, the prayer ceremony was not tied to the curriculum, but rather was the responsibility of the community to ensure indigenous knowledge and local belief systems in diagnosis and treatment were passed on.

Stakeholders highlighted the unique set of life skills required to construct an indigenous Afar home, known as Afar AREE, which is conferred onto young people (specifically girls) by way of observation, apprenticeship, and learning by doing. Stakeholders believed engineers and those from non-pastoralist communities should be invited to understand the unique Afar structure and design, which uses local materials uniquely suited to the region's hot and dry climate, making it more resistant to wind and floods. Stakeholders noted that although the social studies curriculum makes some references to the Afar traditional house, it is extremely limited in the description and does not include the corresponding science and engineering skills involved in its construction. Elders emphasized that this skill should be reflected in the curriculum, and highlighted the idea that there may then be a level of adaptation of construction materials used due to technological advances. They felt that not only do Afar youth need to learn this knowledge, but so do others so they understand these locally relevant and environmentally useful techniques, which also build life skills of collective wellbeing through caring for the environment.

Learning about this system of home building is also tied to another life skill of Afar peoples, namely, that of equity in enacting collective wellbeing. All members of the community, including children, are expected to build life skills in order to contribute to the collective wellbeing of the community. Division of labor is gendered in the Afar community to ensure equity and sharing of the work more so than "what men do" or "what women do". It is the role of women to lead the work of engineering and home construction, and young girls learn from their mothers by way of observation, assisting, and coaching. It is the role of men to lead the work of child rearing and, as young girls shadow women in learning skills for engineering and home construction, young boys learn life skills underpinning animal medicine, husbandry, grazing, and herd mobility, etc. from men.

Related to the skills of building and their environmental relevance, Afar youth consider the preservation, protection, and honoring of the environment as central to their way of life as pastoralists. The felling of trees "without reason" is prohibited in Afar culture and is penalized "through social isolation or giving cattle or another means of livelihood as compensation. Trees are only allowed to be cut in a time of severe drought subject to the consent of the clan leader of the community". Thus, life skills regarding traditional environmental practices within the Afar community are important to teach in school.

Med-a, a cultural governance and conflict resolution system with its own customary administrative process, frequently came up as an important indigenous practice that needs to be protected and preserved at a community level, but its practices and approaches to social justice, cohesion, and associated life skills of reciprocal caring and conflict resolution should also be reflected in and taught in the education curriculum. Proficiency in *Med-a* is seen as a critically important life skill in that "it helps with peace, justice and social cohesion" and "helps us to learn how we should communicate with other non-Afar communities". *Med-a* allows "us to continue as Afar", meaning it is central to who they are as a people. Male youth also stated they wanted to "modernize the *Med-a* system that binds our communities as one. It is the source of peace and justice". The system helps to manage and resolve intra- and

inter-ethnic, clan, and personal conflicts, and while it was not clear what modernization in this case implied, Afar pastoralists see the value in promoting the life skills
that underpin this traditional governance and conflict resolution system.

The practice of *Med-a* should be, as one district-level education representative
stated, "included as a major life skill in the curriculum as it touches every aspect of
the pastoralist community". Additionally, stakeholders mentioned that curriculum
writers should "study and read the Afar history first. The history of the Afar joining
to fight the Italians in defense of Ethiopia's sovereignty is scarcely mentioned in the
grade eight history subject matter textbook". Therefore, making the content relevant
to the livelihoods and history of Afar requires understanding these practices within
their historical context and use, and from the perspective of Afar pastoralists.

Alongside *Med-a* is *Dagu*, also learned in the community and not in schools, and
also often cited by all stakeholders as being of value, needing to be retained, and
central to "being Afar". *Dagu*, meaning "information, news and knowledge", is a
word-of-mouth communication technique and skill set used throughout Afar culture
whereby, "even in the absence of ICT [Information and Communications
Technology], we are able to share important information," a male youth shared.
Afar people have a well-developed oral culture whereby word of-mouth plays the
most important role in connecting, informing, and educating, especially about
accounts of current events (Mohammed, 2016). Afar people painstakingly swap and
meticulously fact-check news and share knowledge through *Dagu*. The enthusiasm
they have to obtain news and information together with the reciprocal accountability attached to *Dagu*, i.e. accountability for what one reports or relays, and universal
and reciprocal responsibility to share news and knowledge, makes *Dagu* a highly
interactive traditional communications network (Mohammed, 2016; Morrell, 2005).
All stakeholders expressed the importance of preserving the life skills—listening,
speaking, fact-checking information, and sharing knowledge—related to *Dagu*.

The fabric of Afar culture, including its way of life and its maintenance, is under-
pinned by a sense of a shared life and belongings and corresponding life skills of
collective asset management and stewardship. As one representative from the district education bureau said:

> Helping each other is the most respected value of the Afar people. The culture of sedentary
> people is of that of individuality (living for oneself) however, in our case, if someone who
> has money or information or skills from the clan, the money and so on doesn't belong to
> him or her or his or her household. It belongs to the clan and automatically for all.

Another respondent spoke to the survival of its culture over the centuries and "if
someone in the community has a problem, everybody (clan) will help". With the
changes of urbanization, the loss of viable of pasture land and "modernization",
these traditional practices of sharing may be at risk but they are no less valued.
Although Afar youth respondents spoke of individualized aspirations for their
futures and desires for increased access to technology, their ideas, beliefs, and attitudes were not individually learned or enacted. Rather, the Afar youths' ideas,
beliefs, and attitudes are influenced and enacted in relation to others and their environment; they are tied to the collective, imbued with ideas of mutual support and

care, and keep community, clan, and collective aspirations at the heart. Youth attributed notions of value, self-value, and self-esteem to the community and to "being Afar": "As you know our community is clan-based and the clan-based relationship is a highly valued connection. If I encounter a serious problem, the first responsible body is my clan. The clan protects and supports."

With regard to aspirations for "modern skills" and employment prospects, Afar youth did not see any contradiction between the need to expand their livelihood opportunities and to retain their Afar values and practices. They recognized a need to diversify livelihoods and income generating options, and emphasized the value of "modern skills" to advance education to the tertiary level, referring to higher education aspirations toward becoming a doctor, social scientist, engineer, teacher, or business person. Teaching was identified by one male youth as a profession to aspire to, while his peers referred to "going to university and becoming a doctor (and living in the city)". Female youth referred to becoming engineers who could "dig wells and free their communities of water scarcity and introduce environmentally friendly agriculture" while also acknowledging the value of education and schooling for the future wellbeing of their families and their communities. Male youth did not explicitly link economic wellbeing nor aspirations (in terms of professions/dreams for the future) to their pastoralist experience around livestock or animal production, and they mentioned technology as something of value and important for their future.

In summary, a number of skills were universally identified by stakeholders as the most important life skills for this community. All stakeholders regarded the life skills of reciprocal caring and sharing, and of collective asset management and stewardship as central to "being Afar". Afar youth also associated the collective wellbeing of the community with their surroundings, their environment, and its protection. Life skills in animal husbandry, livestock management, and animal (and human) disease prevention were considered extremely important for all community members, with Afar elders and parents expressly concerned that Afar children and youth develop financial literacy skills in the context of the livestock economy and "a changing world". All stakeholders said that life skills in traditional building and construction were highly valued and with new technologies and materials on the market, Afar elders encouraged the idea of adapting techniques and approaches to incorporate such "advances". All stakeholders said life skills associated with being proficient in *Med-a* and *Dagu* were extremely important indigenous life skills that needed to be protected and preserved. At the same time, they represent skills that hold many benefits for others and should be shared with non-pastoralist communities.

Formal Schooling and Traditional Learning

Based upon this small yet representative selection of stakeholder voices, there were no apparent cross-generational tensions nor disconnects. All voices were unanimous in their belief that formal education is highly prized and of value to their community, and that there are specific life skills that the community prioritizes, values, and believes would enhance the education curriculum if meaningfully infused and not "grafted on" as means of checking off "inclusion". Additionally, there are foundational life skills that are not currently learned at the community level, but which should be reflected in the formal system to ensure that Afar children and youth are even better equipped to navigate a rapidly changing and increasingly complex world. There was a genuine desire to see some traditional Afar life skills taught through the formal system, and a belief that incorporating into the formal system some of the traditional pedagogies and methodologies for teaching and learning used in the Afar community could strengthen formal education as well.

What mattered most to all stakeholders was that the formal system should reflect the values and necessary life skills of the Afar pastoralist community, from a pedagogical as well as a content perspective. The level of sophistication in teaching and learning strategies used by the Afar community to transfer knowledge and skills, using experiential learning pedagogies and methodologies and encouraging listening and observation, could easily overwhelm an average teacher in the formal education system who may be less comfortable or trained in these kinds of pedagogical approaches. Heath (1982) and Harris (1984) propose that "good" teaching in any culture should include traditional learning techniques and that a teacher in a cross-cultural setting will try to make learning as context-specific and real to life as possible. To achieve this, formal schooling for Afar students must include learning by observation and imitation, learning by trial and error, learning through real-life activities, and learning in context-specific settings. The culture of formal schooling can often create a significant barrier to learning for many students, and the goal of the teacher is to create a learning context that is familiar to students, yet stretches them beyond their previous experiences (Lingenfelter & Lingenfelter, 2003). Thus, for schooling and the curriculum to be relevant to Afar students, a teacher needs to lead students to understand the place and purpose of both traditional and formal learning, and utilize the pedagogical and methodological approaches found in indigenous Afar pastoralist culture.

Curriculum Content Analysis

After identifying the skills and related pedagogies and methodologies that matter the most to pastoralist stakeholders, a curriculum content analysis was conducted using three of the four dimensions of the Krätli and Dyer framework (2009)—namely, subject content, socialization and localization—to examine the extent to which these prized life skills are reflected in the curriculum, and relatedly, to determine the curriculum's relevance. Through the lens of Krätli and Dyer's (2009) subject content and socialization dimensions of relevance, the first level analyzed the extent to which foundational skills, as intended per the national curriculum framework and its syllabi, are reflected in current Afar regional-level textbooks and teacher guides. The second level focused on the extent to which the life skills valued by Afar pastoralists are represented in the curriculum through the lens of Krätli and Dyer's (2009) socialization and localization dimensions of relevance.

Foundational Life Skills Intended Under the National Framework: Curriculum Analysis

This analysis considered the extent to which foundational life skills, as intended per the national curricular framework, are represented in the current Afar region subject content of primary grades (1–4) student textbooks, teachers' guides, and the syllabi for mathematics, Afar-Af language, and environmental science[7]. These three subjects were selected as they offer a good representation of the coverage of foundational skills intended under the national framework. Each life skill was assessed as either not meeting, somewhat or partially meeting, or fully meeting expectations per Krätli and Dyer's (2009) dimensions of relevance, in terms of the corresponding skill domains.

Foundational skill domains of literacy, numeracy and communication skills were found to meet a level of expectation in terms of representation in the curriculum across the three subjects. Numeracy is addressed in these materials through teaching number relationships, measurement, shapes, solids, and basic data handling. Financial literacy, a critical life skill prioritized by Afar adult stakeholders, is not addressed. Moreover, the curriculum is extremely limited in its approach to problem solving in relation to the challenges faced in Afar pastoralists' day-to-day lives as specified in the curriculum framework (MoE, 2009, p. 15). Literacy skills are acceptable at the expected standard per the curriculum framework and syllabus, that is, they attend to how students gain information and experience, exchange views, ideas, and different cultural and social values. As Afar stakeholders pointed out, however, there are many examples from traditional teaching and learning pedagogies and practices that could be infused into the curriculum to reflect and build relevant life skills in problem solving that are related to everyday challenges in Afar communities, such as in the construction of traditional homes, or in the management and stewardship of collective community assets like animals and the environment. Moreover, the set of communication skills undergirding *Dagu* represent a rich opportunity to strengthen the relevance of the curriculum and fortify the corresponding development of life skills critical for pastoralist communities through the formal education system.

Foundational skill domains of history and geography as per the national framework were found to only somewhat meet expectations of curricular relevance. The textbooks demonstrate a concerted effort to contextualize the subject content with the inclusion of references to the landscape and geography of the Afar Regional

---

[7]Environmental Science is an integrated subject in grades 1–4 comprising strands of natural sciences, health, agriculture, social sciences, home science and civics education (MoE, 2009).

State, wild and domestic animals indigenous to the region, commonly found diseases in livestock, key rivers in Afar, Afar names, cultural clothing, and commonly produced crops. However, content specific to history, geography, and corresponding foundational understanding from Afar perspectives is broadly lacking.

The foundational skill domain of critical and analytical thinking was not represented in the analyzed curricular materials. Skills such as hypothesizing, predicting, analyzing, and making generalizations, as specified in the syllabus, were not identified in the curriculum subject content. Moreover, as outlined in the curriculum framework, skills and competencies such as information technology (IT) literacy, being able to adapt to a changing world, higher-order skills, participation and contribution, independence, and adapting to change, are not systematically and consciously treated throughout the textbooks (MoE, 2009). These skills are highly valued by Afar stakeholders, who see these skills as necessary in order for their children and broader community to adapt to rapidly-changing socioeconomic and environmental conditions.

In terms of Krätli and Dyer's (2009) socialization dimension of curricular relevance, which relates to the essential social skills necessary to live in a national society, student texts from the following grades and subjects were analyzed: primary school grades 1–4 environmental science; grades 5–8 social sciences, and grades 5–8 civics and ethics. The domains of life skills examined under this dimension of relevance included: democratic systems and the rule of law, respect for cultural differences, and respect for state laws as derived from the national curriculum framework and syllabi. Curricular relevance in terms of life skill domains related to respect for state laws and democratic systems (i.e. rule of law, equality, justice, patriotism, responsibility, industriousness, self-reliance, saving, active community participation, and the pursuit of wisdom) were determined to be adequate in the materials reviewed. Respect for cultural differences (multiculturalism) as per the national framework only somewhat met expectations of relevance in the analyzed curricular materials.

In sum, using Krätli and Dyer's (2009) framework for life skill domains to analyze the current Afar regional curriculum and its relevance, we find that there is significant room for improvement especially for, but not limited to, critical and analytical skills. Afar stakeholders offered numerous examples of indigenous pastoralist content, such as Afar AREE, relevant Afar pedagogies and methodologies such as learning by doing, and even traditional games such as *Gebeta* (Mancala), that could be incorporated into the current curriculum, thereby strengthening its relevance while building foundational skills for pastoralist youth through the formal education system.

Life Skills That Matter Most to Pastoralists: Curriculum Analysis

Using the lens of Krätli and Dyer's (2009) socialization and localization dimensions of relevance, this section presents an analysis of the extent to which life skills most valued by pastoralists (determined through stakeholder consultations) are represented in the current Afar regional curriculum. In terms of socialization, which relates to the essential social skills necessary to live in a national society, the analysis drew upon the same grades and subjects as in the preceding section, this time highlighting the particular life skills most valued by pastoralists: traditional conflict resolution, law enforcement, moral/ethical values, and reciprocal caring/cooperation. Krätli and Dyer's (2009) curricular dimension of localization, which centers on the acquisition of skills and information rooted in pastoralist society, context, and identity, was applied through analysis of the following curricular materials: primary grades 1–4 environmental science, grades 5–6 integrated science[8], and social studies.

As noted above, the life skills of reciprocal caring and sharing are of paramount importance to Afar pastoralists. Regarding caring and cooperation, the curriculum was determined to be somewhat relevant with respect to social skills necessary to live in a national (Ethiopian) society. However, when analyzed using Krätli and Dyer's (2009) dimension of localization, the extent to which the curriculum included content and information related to life skills of reciprocal caring, mutual dependence, and solidarity rooted in Afar traditions, customs, and practices, was found to be entirely lacking. Life skill domains relating to traditional pastoralist conflict resolution skills, proficiency in aforementioned *Med-a* governance enforcement skills/ mechanisms, and cultural moral/ethical values, all of which matter greatly to pastoralists, are also absent from the curriculum. Such a void is critical, as a male youth described:

> If there is a conflict, we don't need the police. How does the *Med-a* system then enforce the decision? It is through social pressure and the penalty is not for the individual only, but all clan members to contribute to and settle the penalty.

While *Med-a* is mentioned in social science and civics materials, there is no elaboration or explanation in terms of procedures, nor explanation of how it is used for conflict resolution or to enforce expectations of equitable use and protection of collective community assets, including the environment. Equally absent is elaboration of *Dagu* and the corresponding set of life skills (i.e. listening, speaking, fact-checking information, and sharing knowledge) it represents for pastoralist society.

---

[8] The integrated science: for grades 5 and 6 is structured by a thematic approach and adopts six themes studied at both grades; Air, Water, Plants, Animals, Our Body and Earth. Issues such as HIV and AIDS, harmful traditional practices, rural development, health, agriculture and environment are addressed through these thematic areas. A 'learn (science) by doing' methodology is used, enabling students to develop scientific knowledge and skills through practical application, as well as develop the attitudes and values needed for effective citizenry.

Traditional life skills that matter greatly to pastoralists related to environmental protection and stewardship are intertwined with pastoralist life skills related to traditional science and engineering—especially skills related to house construction, rearing and care of animals (grazing, in particular), mobility patterns, and the use of local materials for animal (and human) medicine. Notably, none of these life skill domains are sufficiently represented in the curriculum, and there is an absence of representation of the related body of pastoralist knowledge in the materials reviewed. Afar communities have a rich body of related knowledge about many aspects of life acquired over generations and handed down as local knowledge traditions, which includes managing livestock, the environment, economic use of water, house making, and traditional medication and healing. For instance, with regard to Afar house construction and the environment, as one community member noted, "only the picture [of the house] is drawn in the environmental science textbooks, without discussing the details of its construction ... Instead of presenting its shape, I recommend engineers should study how these houses are resistant to wind and flood." It is striking that traditional pastoralist knowledge about animal husbandry and indigenous animal medicine is not found in the curriculum, given the central importance of these life skills to this community. As one male youth noted:

> For the treatment of certain diseases with our livestock, we use a leaf called *Agdagto*. We soak it in water and administer it through the nose or mouth for two days and they will be cured. For a male camel with a high desire for sex, put coffee through its nose and in its mouth. For the treatment of donkeys, we use a leaf called *More*.

There are many examples of illustrations in the texts that are irrelevant for the local Afar context, such as fruits, vegetables, and animals not found in the region, which could be substituted for relevant localized examples such as the leaves and plants used to treat various ailments for animals and people.

In summary, none of the life skills that matter most to pastoralists, and that are associated with Krätli and Dyer's (2009) localization dimension of curricular relevance, were found to be sufficiently represented in the current Afar regional curriculum through this analysis, and only some skills associated with the socialization dimension of curricular relevance were found to be partially represented. Nonetheless, stakeholders offered a host of examples of traditional pastoralist practices and approaches that could further strengthen the education curriculum as noted above and in the previous section, such as those related to Afar collective sharing of assets, equitable division of labor, and using traditional governance systems (*Med-a*) and peer pressure to enforce expectations of cooperation and appropriate use of shared resources, including the environment. The central theme that resonates throughout this section is both the need and the opportunity for the curriculum to be made more relevant to Afar pastoralists by infusing it with important traditional life skills, and localized content and knowledge systems.

Discussion and Conclusion

This chapter has attempted to explore which life skills matter most from the perspectives of Afar pastoralists themselves, in the context of the low rates of education inclusion, participation, and retention of pastoralist communities in Ethiopia. Using Krätli and Dyer's (2009) framework to analyze the current curriculum, this study reveals that only a limited representation of those life skills that matter most to pastoralists are depicted. The exclusion or only partial inclusion of indigenous knowledge could be attributed to the fact that the syllabus was not developed from the pastoralist perspective, but rather it was an "add on" to its original design for a sedentary or urban learner. While the sample of Afar pastoralist perspectives represented herein is limited and further research is needed to validate and generalize findings regarding which life skills matter most to this indigenous population, the study highlights a host of opportunities to strengthen the curriculum quality in terms of relevance. Correspondingly, it also highlights ways to improve outcomes for Afar children and youth, both in terms of educational inclusion and participation, while building pastoralists' skills for life and thriving.

This study sheds light on the central importance and opportunities represented in the relational values and corresponding life skills that shape how Afar people live: how they govern themselves, address conflict, and at once protect and hold all members of the community reciprocally accountable for sharing, caring, and stewarding collective assets, including the environment. These are not life skills used to dominate, but rather they are used in the service of promoting the wellbeing of all. Reconceptualizing and teaching life skills grounded in a relational approach through the formal education system presents an opportunity to leverage indigenous pastoral social relations as collective protective assets. This study has also shed light on foundational skills that are not currently learned at the community level—such as financial and computer literacy—and which should be included in the formal educational system, to ensure Afar children and youth are even better equipped to navigate a rapidly changing world.

In sum, there is a substantive disconnect between the current regional curriculum and the teaching of life skills that matter most to and are most needed by indigenous Afar pastoralists. A focus on these life skills– inculcating and fostering life skills around mutuality of caring and solidarity, social cohesion and collective social security, shared caring and responsibility that can transcend traditional pastoral livelihoods—holds promise for improving Afar wellbeing even in the context of a changing climate and economy. Despite the disconnect between the current curriculum and the life skills that matter most for them, Afar pastoralists all expressed the belief that formal education matters, that it is prioritized by the community, and that it is not incompatible with the pastoralist way of life and culture, and in fact, Afar culture has much to offer the formal system. Relatedly, traditional pastoralist education utilizes pedagogies and methodologies that are integral to teaching and learning in the Afar context, which have undergirded their ability to maintain a complex and sustainable equilibrium among pastures, livestock, and people for centuries, and that, if adopted in the formal education system, could fundamentally change how we learn in relation to our community and our environment.

Acknowledgements We wish to acknowledge and thank the Ministry of Education of Ethiopia, Afar Regional Education Bureau, Afar Language Development Institute, and the Afar Bureau of Culture and Tourism for their close collaboration; and the Amibara, Awash-Fentale, Afambo, Aysaita, and Chifra District community members of the Afar region for sharing their voices.

References

Ahmed, E. (2017). *An assessment on the viability of the modalities for provision of primary education to the children of pastoralists in the Afar Region of Ethiopia*. Unpublished doctoral dissertation. Addis Ababa University.

Anwar, A. (2010). *An assessment of the contributions of alternative basic education to primary education (Grade 1–8) in the Afar region*. Unpublished master's thesis. Addis Ababa University.

Center for Evaluation and Development (C4ED). (2017). *An impact evaluation of alternative basic education in Ethiopia: The case of the Regions Afar, Oromia, and Somali. Final evaluation report*. https://www.unicef.org/evaldatabase/files/Ethiopia_ABE_Final_Report_22.09.pdf

Harris, S. (1984). *Culture and learning*. Institute for Aboriginal Studies.

Heath, S. B. (1982). Questioning at home and school: A comparative study. In G. Spindler (Ed.), *Doing the ethnography of schooling* (pp. 102–131). Holt, Rinehart & Winston.

Krätli, S., & Dyer, C. (2009). *Mobile pastoralists and education: Strategic options*. International Institute for Environment and Development.

Lingenfelter, J. E., & Lingenfelter, S. G. (2003). *Teaching cross-culturally: An incarnational model for learning and teaching*. Baker Academic.

Ministry of Education (MoE). (2008). *Strategies for promoting primary and secondary education in Pastoralist areas*. Addis Ababa, Ethiopia.

Ministry of Education (MoE). (2009). *National Curriculum framework, grade 1-4, environmental science*. Addis Ababa, Ethiopia.

Ministry of Education (MoE). (2017a). *National Pastoralist education strategy*. Addis Ababa, Ethiopia.

Ministry of Education (MoE). (2017b). *Pastoralist community mobility patterns with the virtue of promoting quality education for all. The case of the Essa Clan in Somali and the Hable Haysemele Clan in Afar*. Addis Ababa, Ethiopia.

Ministry of Education (MoE). (2018a). *A standard and manual for upgrading Alternative Basic Education (ABE) Centers, Level 1-4 to Level 1-6*. Addis Ababa, Ethiopia.

Ministry of Education (MoE). (2018b). *Mobile schooling implementation manual*. Addis Ababa, Ethiopia.

Ministry of Education (MoE). (2019a). *Alternative Basic education standard for Pastoralist and Semi-Pastoralist Areas*. Addis Ababa, Ethiopia.

Ministry of Education (MoE). (2019b). *Education Statistics annual abstract (2018/2019)*. Addis Ababa, Ethiopia.

Mohammed, J. (2016). Dagu: Its nature, attributes and reporting Praxis. *Ethiopian Journal of Language, Culture and Communication, 1*(1), 24–50.

Morrell, V. (2005). *Africa's Danakil Desert: Cruelest place on Earth*. National Geographic Magazine. http://ngm.nationalgeographic.com/ngm/0510/feature2/

Ziyn, E., & Wogasso, Y. (2017). *Pastoralist community mobility patterns with the virtue of promoting quality education for all*. The Case of the Essa Clan in Somali and the Hable Haysemele Clan in Afar. Addis Ababa, Ethiopia.

Chapter 12
Concluding Thoughts on Life Skills Education for Youth

Dana Schmidt

Abstract This chapter summarizes the answer to the motivating question for this book: "Which life skills are important, for whom, and how can they be taught?" Drawing on research reflected in the preceding chapters, I highlight three broad themes. First, that teaching life skills helps marginalized adolescents in particular – but should not put the onus of overcoming marginalization squarely on their shoulders. Second, that consensus seems to be emerging that a cluster of social and emotional skills and cognitive abilities like critical thinking are particularly important for success. Third, that the way in which life skills are taught matters as much as which skills are taught. I also reflect on three big barriers that we need to address if we really want to advance the agenda of life skills. First, governments may not embrace the transformative change we want to see. Second, life skills programs are complex to implement and to measure. Lastly, we cannot ignore the risk of unintended consequences on the path to developing life skills. I suggest that each of these challenges is worth contending with to give youth of today a fighting chance to deal with the expected and as-yet unimagined challenges of tomorrow.

Keywords Life skills · Low and middle-income countries · Capabilities approach · Wellbeing

Introduction: Which Life Skills? It Depends

The key question posed by this volume of work is: "Which life skills are important, for whom, and how can they be taught?" If we look at life skills as the skills "to be able to do life well," which is the simple definition offered by Murphy-Graham and

D. Schmidt (✉)
Echidna Giving, San Francisco, CA, USA
e-mail: dana@echidnagiving.org

J. DeJaeghere, E. Murphy-Graham (eds.), *Life Skills Education for Youth*, Young People and Learning Processes in School and Everyday Life 5,
https://doi.org/10.1007/978-3-030-85214-6_12

Cohen (Chap. 2, this volume), the answer to the motivating question of the volume is "it depends."

It depends on *objective* factors, like which individual, at what point in time, and in what place. Skills to do life well will not look exactly the same for a 13-year-old boy living with a pastoralist community in Ethiopia today as they do for an 18-year-old girl with two young children in Honduras, let alone for the same 13-year-old boy in Ethiopia 20 years hence, or, for that matter, for his sister today. Their lives look different so the skills they need will be different, too.

It also depends on *subjective* factors, like how any of these given individuals define what it means to do life well. Is doing life well about having economic stability? Becoming wealthy? Succeeding in school? Staying healthy? Securing strong relationships? Achieving happiness? Some combination thereof?

Time and again contributors to this volume point out the ways in which life skills education looks different across various contexts and schools of thoughts. For example, Murphy-Graham and Cohen (Chap. 2, this volume) show us in Chap. 2 how different discourse communities have defined different goals for life skills, and therefore emphasized different skill sets. Economists have stressed labor market outcomes and landed on teamwork, communication, problem solving, and the Big 5 personality traits as key skills to foster. For those focused on public health prevention and protection, decision-making, self-knowledge, and resisting peer pressure are paramount. In Chap. 3, Brush et al. (this volume) describe a diversity of frameworks—40 of which they have coded—each of which have been developed with particular contexts and viewpoints in mind, and which therefore each feature distinct combinations of skills. This set of diversity should not surprise us. As Honeyman et al. (Chap. 6, this volume) stress in Chap. 6, program designers need to undertake a contextualization process that examines which skills to teach in combination with the context in which they will be taught. In the case of youth in Algeria, perseverance and self-motivation stood out as critical skills required for finding a job.

That said, "it depends" is not a very actionable answer to the question posed by this volume. Nor is it all that we can say on the basis of the research presented here. So although it does, indeed, "depend," the research presented in this book points to three broad themes that provide more interesting answers to the question "Which life skills are important, for whom, and how can they be taught?"

1. Life skills are especially important for marginalized adolescents, but should not be used as an excuse to put the onus of creating a life well lived entirely on the individual, particularly not on an individual already marginalized by his or her community. Societal transformation requires more than this.

2. Whether you care most about health outcomes, economic prosperity, or broader empowerment, there are some common denominators with respect to which skills are important. In particular, clusters of social and emotional skills and cognitive abilities like critical thinking stand out as important for success. More specifically, critical thinking skills related to who holds power in society and why emerges as one key to the types of transformational changes that are drawn

out under the first theme. These common denominators are a good starting point for at least some of the life skills that are likely to matter most.

3. How life skills are taught may be as important, if not more important, than prescribing a very specific set of skills to teach. Given this, the ways in which teachers are prepared to teach life skills and the skills they themselves embody are important pieces of the puzzle.

The remainder of this conclusion unpacks each of these themes in more detail. Drawing from the chapters that precede this one, I highlight some critical takeaways for actors trying to improve the lives of adolescents and identify key unanswered questions for the research community to tackle as well.

Theme 1: Teaching Life Skills Helps Marginalized Adolescents, But Not in Isolation

The very fact that different discourse communities have articulated the importance of life skills (as highlighted in Chap. 2), multiple frameworks have been developed around life skills (as highlighted in Chap. 3), and countless programs have been designed to teach life skills (as highlighted in Chaps. 5, 6, 7, 8, 9, and 10, to name but a few), lends credence to the idea that adolescents need more than academic skills to "do life well." Brush et al. (Chap. 3, this volume) describe how social and emotional learning programs tend to have a disproportionately large effect on students who are most at risk. This suggests that marginalized adolescents may stand to benefit the most from life skills programs.

At the same time, chapter authors have emphasized the risk that providing life skills programs to marginalized adolescents will put the onus of creating change on the very people who face the greatest disadvantage. One key implication here is that skills alone are not enough. In Chap. 4, DeJaeghere (this volume) points out that the dominant approach to life skills tends to be oriented towards changing the behavior of individuals and placing the responsibility on youth for addressing societal problems that cannot be overcome by individuals. As Murphy-Graham (this volume) articulates in Chap. 7, skills need to be paired with real opportunities for individuals to do something with them, but individuals often face structural constraints to converting their skills into action. These come in the form of personal constraints (sex, intelligence, disability, etc.), social constraints (norms, hierarchies, power relations, etc.), and environmental constraints (infrastructure, resources, etc.). For example, the life skills job training program that Murphy-Graham studied failed to generate employment opportunities for youth because there simply are not many formal work opportunities in Honduras and Guatemala. Furthermore, program participants faced social stigma, sex discrimination, and practical constraints due to the crime and violence in their neighborhoods that limited the success of their job searches.

The second key implication is that the types of life skills that are taught and the way in which they are taught can either uphold the status quo of marginalization or be transformative. Unfortunately, most life skills programs are not designed to be transformative. By way of concrete example, in Chap. 4 DeJaeghere (this volume) describes how "considerable literature on girls' education and gender inequalities have raised the concern that educating girls alone cannot create transformative change, yet the renewed focus on life skills for girls is another iteration of seeking education solutions to do so." Underscoring this point, in Chap. 5 Kwauk (this volume) finds that "the dominant normative approach of 'fix the girl, not the system,' is quite pervasive" in sports for development programs. Only 4% of targeted skills in these programs were constructed in an intentionally transformative way.

All of this suggests the need to change the larger context even as we give people skills and agency to deal with the current system. It also suggests the need to incorporate skills that help youth navigate towards more transformative change, as described in the theme which follows.

Theme 2: Convergence Around Certain Life Skills Domains, with an Emphasis on Critical Thinking

Researchers and practitioners arrive at the importance of life skills education from multiple perspectives, but regardless of whether they bring a lens of health and wellness, economic prosperity, or broader empowerment, the skills they prioritize include several common denominators. In Chap. 2, Murphy-Graham and Cohen (this volume) consolidate areas of overlap across different discourse communities into the themes of mastery of knowledge, social and emotional competencies, and critical thinking. In Chap. 3, Brush et al. (this volume) cluster skills into cognitive, emotional, social, values, perspectives, and identity domains. They find that social and emotional learning frameworks place the greatest emphasis on the cognitive domain (which includes critical thinking, planning skills, attention control), and the social domain (which includes, e.g. social problem solving, cooperative behavior). Many life skills frameworks also emphasize the values domain (consisting of ethical, intellectual, performance, and civic values) and, to a smaller extent, the emotion domain.

To summarize this in the simplest of terms, there is agreement that youth need to understand and regulate themselves, be capable of relating to others, and know how to interpret the world around them. These capabilities are central to being able to live life well.

If there is one single skill area that the volume draws out as particularly important, it is critical thinking. Youth need higher order thinking skills, including the capacity to be critical of the world and its injustices. They also need to develop problem solving skills that enable them to tackle these injustices. Across several chapters, we see arguments that this type of critical thinking is the key to ensuring that programs are transformative and not merely helping youth better deal with their marginalization. For example, in Chap. 5, Kwauk (this volume) argues that youth must have the opportunity to understand the broader structures of power and privilege in which they are embedded. They must learn to decode dominant culture with the aim to transform not only their own experiences in the world, but also the world itself.

This is not just about being better able to understand power structures, but also about getting youth to challenge these structures, including by changing their own perspectives. One example of this comes in Chap. 9, where Sahni (this volume) describes how the Prerna school in India equips students to both understand and change their realities. Sahni's school is about "helping children gain a greater sense of self-awareness, recognize themselves as equal persons, develop agency and voice, and critically examine societal norms and oppressive social structures." Importantly, the schools work not only with the marginalized, but also with power-holders. For example, when it comes to supporting greater gender equality, the school works with boys to shift their "toxic mindsets." Although this is more difficult because boys have something to lose when it comes to relinquishing their power, the example shared in this chapter shows that change can be fostered carefully, respectfully, and effectively.

We see a second example of this in Chap. 8, in which Arur and Sharma (this volume) describe how adolescent boys of lower castes in India are taught critical literacies that help shape their career aspirations. As these boys engaged in documenting their lived realities by video, they were able to critically understand local issues (particularly around sustainable development) and analyze what mattered to them in ways that helped to uncover potential career choices.

A third example comes from Chap. 10, where Pacheco and Murphy-Graham (this volume) describe the ACHME program in Honduras, which aimed to help students make informed decisions about marriage despite the fact that their economic and sociopolitical context constrained the choices available to them and presented them with ideas and values that encouraged early marriage. The program developed critical thinking in students, helping them to understand power relationships, to redirect the flow of these relationships, and to uncover mainstream norms that they assume to be in their best interest even if they are actually harmful. By getting students to think critically, the program sought to increase cognitive dissonance and lead them to shift their thinking in order to reduce inconsistencies in it. This seems to have played out in practice. For example, students developed the capacity to uncover assumptions about gender roles—like the idea that housework is a woman's job that men should not engage in—and began to articulate their dissatisfaction with the status quo.

Even when life skills frameworks and programs include critical thinking, they often leave out some of these important components. In Chap. 5, Kwauk (this volume) argues that the way we conceptualize critical thinking could be expanded so that it captures skills like understanding and recognizing unequal power relations and picking up on unspoken cues. She argues that a "transformative approach would attend to the metacognitive elements of equipping girls with the tools to read, decode, and act upon the opportunity structures around her, as well as the sociological elements of building collective resistance against conditions of inequality."

This concept of building collective resistance points to the other shortcoming in the way that many life skills frameworks are framed, which is that they focus on developing individual skills that youth can independently enact. The hyper-focus on individuals is arguably a very "WEIRD" view of schooling, applied in Western, Educated, Industrialized, Rich, and Democratic countries. The concept of WEIRD societies was developed by anthropologist Joseph Heinrich and psychologists Steven Hein and Ara Norenzayan. In a 2010 study, they argue that behavioral scientists frequently publish findings that claim to unearth universal truths about human psychology, but these studies draw on research done only with subjects from WEIRD societies, who are in fact frequently outliers when it comes to many dimensions of psychology, motivation, and behavior. Research done on subjects from WEIRD societies is therefore not representative, nor generalizable to the entire human race. One of the differences they point to is the fact that Westerners tend to view themselves as independent, autonomous agents, whereas non-Westerners tend to have a more interdependent view and think of themselves in terms of roles and relationships with others. From this research we can infer that educational interventions designed for students in WEIRD societies are not equally applicable in non-WEIRD societies. In WEIRD societies, an emphasis on individual skills independently enacted might be well-suited to context, but that might not be as helpful to youth in non-WEIRD societies, where there is a greater emphasis on the collective. Yitbarek et al. (this volume) describe this disconnect in Chap. 11 when they demonstrate how the skills that matter most for Afar wellbeing, which include an emphasis on collective and community wellbeing, are not the same as the skills that are covered in the general education curriculum.

In Chap. 4, DeJaeghere (this volume) argues that youth need to develop relational skills. There is a disconnect between teaching life skills to youth as individuals and expecting them to act on these skills independently, and the need to change larger social outcomes like gender inequality, which are societal and not individual in nature. DeJaeghere argues that "The ideas, beliefs, and attitudes that young people practice to live a good life are not individually learned or enacted; they are influenced and enacted in relation to others and their environment." She further argues that a relational approach would rethink both *which* skills are taught, as well as *how* they are used. For example, teaching self-confidence does not change the barriers youth face or allow them to be confident in settings that continue to reject them and deny their dignity. I would argue that it's not only how skills are used that matters, but also the way in which they are taught, an idea we turn to in the third theme, which follows.

Theme 3: How Life Skills Are Taught Matters as Much as Which Skills Are Taught

In the previous section, we examined which life skills appear to be most critical for youth. As much as this book helps point to areas of consensus in this regard, it also suggests that how life skills are taught matters as much as which skills are taught.

The first insight in this regard is that life skills do not always need to be directly taught. Instead, they can be learned through modeling and through shifts in the way teachers engage their students. As DeJaeghere (this volume) reminds us in Chap. 4, "humans live and learn always in relation to others and their environment." For this reason, students pick up on skills simply by imbibing what they see around them. This is absorbed as much from community members as it is from teachers. Indeed, in Chap. 8 Arur and Sharma (this volume) demonstrate that it was students' personal networks that influenced their career aspirations more than anything they read online or in textbooks.

Honeyman et al. (this volume) argue in Chap. 6 that the best way to teach many life skills is through "student-centered pedagogy that requires students to be involved in research, problem-solving, discussion, and group work." A good example of this type of pedagogy is documented by Arur and Sharma, who describe how adolescent boys in India created videos as a way to better understand the nature of their home environments and how their skills could be harnessed for work within that context.

Some of these shifts in teaching practice that are critical for unlocking life skills could happen without ever stressing what life skills they are building. This is useful because teachers and students might not always be motivated to teach and learn life skills. In the context of Algeria, for example, most youth were more interested in "learning the functional skills they need to get a job and may not recognize initially the important role that soft skills play in this process" (Honeyman et al., Chap. 6, this volume). In Ethiopia, youth picked up on skills for living in a sustainable way in their community through observation and modeling, not explicit instruction where these skills were named for them (Yitbarek et al., Chap. 11, this volume).

The second insight is that helping to develop teachers' life skills is an important path to imparting life skills in youth. As Honeyman et al. (Chap. 6, this volume) point out, "instructors themselves must demonstrate these skills and attitudes in their own lives" in order to model and teach them to students. Although this may involve training teachers in approaches that are far from common within the wider education system, the good news is that teachers themselves stand to gain from learning life skills. As Sahni (this volume) discovers and describes in Chap. 9, the critical conversations about gender and power facilitated at the Prerna school in India were as transformational for instructors as for the students. Similarly, I have seen in my own work how teachers are highly motivated to teach the resilience curriculum developed by the NGO CorStone because the skills they teach are skills they learn and find relevant to their lives. Likewise, Dream a Dream has found in their work in India that one of the most transformative ways to teach life skills is to transform how teachers see themselves and their students, which transforms how they engage with students and what they teach.

The third insight is that promoting stronger relationships could be a means to teaching life skills but also an important end in and of itself. This comes out in Chap. 7, where Murphy-Graham (this volume) describes how the relationships built by youth in the A Ganar program in Honduras was both a capability and a functioning. The supportive network that students developed helped them to overcome structural constraints. Similarly, Honeyman et al. (Chap. 6, this volume) highlight "promoting strong relationships between adults and youth and among youth themselves" as one of the best practices for developing life skills. In the Prerna school that Sahni describes in Chap. 9, individual change is only possible through supportive relations. Much as our relationships teach us skills, relationships themselves are an external asset that should themselves be a goal, not simply a by-product.

Final Thoughts for the Way Forward

This book suggests that life skills should be taught to youth, but they should not be viewed as a panacea for helping youth overcome their marginalization. Youth need to understand and regulate themselves and be capable of relating to others. They especially need to be able to critically analyze the world around them and act in concert with others to achieve social change. We can help youth build the skills that they need by cultivating these same skills in their teachers and providing opportunities to build strong relationships with others.

The implication for school systems and other practitioners serving youth is that we should push for life skills to be integrated within formal primary and secondary education curriculum, just as other skills like literacy and numeracy are. Furthermore, we should do this through a more radical approach than has traditionally been adopted. We should teach critical thinking and relational skills in a way that provokes transformative change.

If we really want to advance this agenda, there are three big barriers that have been hinted at in this volume but deserve to be more fully unpacked by future research and discourse. First, governments may not actually want education to be transformative. Second, it is complex to implement life skills programs well, and to measure whether and how they work. Third, there are ethical dilemmas and risks of unintended consequences with which we must wrestle.

Governments May Not Want It

The problem with transformative change is that it seeks to upend traditional power structures. We see this come up in various chapters of the book with relation to challenging students in the classroom to give up power (see, for example, Chaps. 9 and 10). Scaling up work of this nature would pose a challenge to all those who hold privilege within society—including the very elite within government who help to define the curriculum that is taught in schools. As DeJaeghere (Chap. 4, this volume) points out, there is a "conflict between reproducing and changing norms"—and the types of changes proposed under this theme may be the toughest changes to enact in school systems that seek to protect the status quo as much as they profess to change it. This may be the very reason that, as Murphy-Graham and Cohen (this volume) point out in Chap. 2, the terminology of "life skills" has crowded out the more threatening discourse around empowering education for girls.

What, then, is the way forward? Gentler reforms that are palatable to government may not promote the type of transformation that is encouraged by authors in this volume. On the other hand, implementation of more radical approaches outside of the government system—which is all that is feasible without government funding—may not promote change at a scale that can truly be transformational. Perhaps the best we can settle for is incremental changes in this generation that can snowball for future generations.

Life Skills Programs Are Complex to Implement and Measure

To teach the skills that are called for in this volume requires skilled facilitators who understand these issues themselves and who are willing to confront power and engage with their students in difficult subjects that have no defined answers. Fortunately, in this book there are a number of examples of programs that have been able to do just this (see, for example, Chaps. 7 and 10). We also see, however, that more often than not programs do *not* contend with the more transformational elements of life skills (e.g., in Chap. 5), and this could in part be because it is so complex to do so.

A second challenge is that life skills are difficult to measure. This is made all the more complex because contextual factors matter both for how individuals develop and display life skills. As argued in both Chaps. 2 and 4, we need to measure these contextual factors as well: "Without examining features of the setting that may be contributing to or hindering children's social-emotional development, we risk merely capturing children's responses to characteristics of the environment rather than anything meaningful about their skills or capacities" (Brush et al., Chap. 3, this volume). Until we crack the question of measurement, we cannot look at life skills as an outcome of interest in and of themselves.

We Must Contend with the Risk of Unintended Consequences

The process of transformation is far from smooth. Teaching life skills in ways that enable transformative change may, at times, sit in conflict with the simple definition of life skills as the ability to do life well. To take one example, opening up a critical dialogue about gender inequality may open up girls' minds to the ways in which they are oppressed, ultimately rendering them less happy and satisfied, not more so. Getting youth to dream bigger about what they can do in life may widen the gap between their aspirations and reality, again hampering their sense of wellbeing. Trying to change norms may make it *harder* to succeed in a particular context, not easier. Examples like the Afar in Chap. 11 hint at ethical questions like whether it is better to prepare youth to live life well where they are currently situated, or to prepare them to transition and be successful in new contexts. All of these examples point to the possibility for large unintended consequences. Future research should both grapple with these ethical questions as well as seek ways to define and measure the potential for unintended consequences.

All of these challenges are well worth engaging. Youth of today are part of a generation that will grapple with rising levels of inequality, the economic and health fallout of a global pandemic, the near and present danger of climate change, and more challenges that we cannot yet imagine. They need and deserve these skills to have a fighting chance of living life well. We owe it to them to continue working to define and teach these skills, and to do it at scale.